Shadows and Light

A Journey of
Healing and Empowerment

Susan Yerburgh

Vertue Press

Cover image: Susan Yerburgh, September 1947
All photos are from the author's personal collection.

Some names have been changed to protect the privacy of those individuals.

copyright ©2019 Susan Yerburgh

All rights reserved. No part of this book may be used or reproduced in any manner whatsoever without the written permission, except in the case of brief quotations.

Shadows and Light

A Journey of
Healing and Empowerment

Dedication

To my great-great grandmother, Ann Mathilda Vertue,
who could not tell her story.

Ann Mathilda Vertue
1829–1904

Acknowledgements

To my loving partner, Don: thank you for all your love, support, and countless hours of listening to me over the past three years it has taken to write this book. I feel blessed every day to have you in my life.

To my dear sons, Tim and Peter: from day one, I have never stopped loving you. Many thanks for supporting me over the years in my many ventures. I am deeply grateful to have you, your wives and your children for the family you have surrounded me with. All of you bring me endless joy, love, and hope for future generations.

To Maggie: Accepting me into your life and thank you for allowing me to tell our story. It has brought me joy and peace, at last.

To those in the afterlife/spirit world: my eternal gratitude. Mattie, my grandfather (the Bishop), my parents, my spirit guides, Wei Chi, and others who contributed to my journey with their words of wisdom, guidance and healing. Thank you.

To my soul sisters, Katie, Kim, Linette, and Rita: thank you for your love, support and acceptance of me. You have all played a role in my healing.

To the folks at The Memoir Network: my heart-felt thanks. Denis Ledoux's coaching, editing, and endless patience over the past three years made this book possible. You understood me which was very important to me and, for this, I will always be grateful. Sally Lunt did the excellent job with the cover, the layout, and the photos. Francis King provided her expertise in proofreading.

Last but not least, my thanks to all other family members, friends and acquaintances—you know who you are—whose interest in my book has motivated me to keep writing.

Contents

Preface 15

Chapter 1 Harder Than Hard 19

Chapter 2 My Wrong Decision 35

Chapter 3 Settling into Paris 51

Chapter 4 More Changes.. 67

Chapter 5 Having a Baby in Brussels 81

Chapter 6 Unraveling and Putting Myself Back
    Together Again 93

Chapter 7 Remembering Trauma and Looking
    for Maggie 105

Chapter 8 My Marriage Goes Its Inevitable Way.. 115

Chapter 9 Living a Single Life Amid Recovered
    Memories 129

Chapter 10 Surviving a Crisis and
    Deciding to Date 149

Chapter 11 Reaching Out for a Life Companion .. 161

Chapter 12 A Surprise Ending 177

Chapter 13 A New Era Begins 191

Chapter 14 Expanding After Johnnie 203

Chapter 15 Putting Many Things Together 213

Chapter 16 Expanding My Horizons 227

Chapter 17 Maggie and Settling Issues
With Work 243

Chapter 18 Some Things Change But Not
My Marriage 257

Chapter 19 Making a New Friend and
Meeting Maggie at Last 275

Chapter 20 Realizations and Mattie Enters
My Life 291

Chapter 21 Progress with Kevin as My
Marriage to Stuart Wobbles 313

Chapter 22 The Pressure Cooker 333

Chapter 23 Stuart Fails to Rise to the Occasion .. 349

Chapter 24 Shop Plans and Ruby's Decline 365

Chapter 25 Misunderstanding with Maggie,
 and Ruby Dies 373

Chapter 26 Some Dark Days 387

Chapter 27 More Healing and Integration 401

Chapter 28 The End of My Second Marriage...... 415

Chapter 29 Moving On.. 431

Chapter 30 Making a Choice – A Right Choice .. 451

Chapter 31 Final Healing 467

Chapter 32 Making the Commitment 483

Afterword 491

"A genuine odyssey is not about piling up experiences. It is a deeply felt, risky, unpredictable tour of the soul."
— Thomas Moore

"The shadow is the greatest teacher for how to come to the light."
— Ram Dass

"There is no sun without shadow and it is essential to know the night."
— Albert Camus

Preface

There are many reasons a person writes a memoir. Certainly, people write to celebrate something important, but for me the impetus was not only to bear witness to the life I had lived but my driving force was even more to heal a life that had been difficult in too many ways.

It's not so much that I wanted to set the record straight — although that may have played a part. No, what I really wanted was to have a good look at my life and forgive and put aside so much that had been painful. As I started to write, I realized I had to do more than tell my family — my sons, their wives and their children—all that had happened to me. I needed to break the code of silence present in my family for generations and reach others — hoping they might garner a piece of wisdom to see their lives in a new light.

I believe I came into my life with an agenda of experiences I needed to have in order to grow as a soul. My experiences were challenging. At times, it seems that I have lived two lives. The first is my tangible, physical life on earth with all the experiences that go with it. That life began in 1944. The second is my psychic, spiritual life which helped me heal and make sense of my childhood and my earthly life. My second life started to come to my awareness in the year 2000 after my parents and my brother had died.

In this book I write about both of my lives which are, of course, intertwined.

In June of 2007, I was still in the discovery stage of my healing, but after years of searching, I was finally in contact with some healers who could help me — although I had not yet met the healer who would have the greatest impact on me.

That month, my fifth grandchild, Ben, was born. On a visit to the hospital to see him, as I was sitting and chatting with my two sons and their wives — my five grandchildren, ranging in age from newborn to three years old, were in the room — I was suddenly overcome with emotion.

There seemed to be so much love in the room that, unexpectedly, I began to cry. My childhood had been filled with abandonment and isolation. There was so little love. I had felt emotionally starved all the years of my growing up, and what is more, I endured some very real abuse. Now, in my sixties, I was surrounded with the love of family.

My five grandchildren at Ben's birth
June 2007

Seeing my dear sons and their thoughtful, loving wives and being surrounded by their healthy, joyful children made me understand that the sadness and the difficulties that had characterized both my life and that of generations of my family were finally over!

After all these years, I was now in a loving family.

Tears of joy and relief flowed down my cheeks.

Shadows and Light

"Grammy, why are you crying?" Sam, aged three, asked when he saw my tears. He came right over to me. I could see the concern in his eyes. I wasn't sure how to answer him.

Then I said, "I am crying because I am happy."

He was puzzled. I explained that people cry for many reasons and today I was crying because I was happy. I was happy to be in this moment surrounded by my family: a newborn, infants, toddlers, my sons and their wives.

That day, contrary to how I had too often felt, I had hope for the future and I had a deep connection to the past.

I was now the oldest in my extended family and there was a new generation below me. I hoped each of these little children would have a happier childhood than I had had, and deep in my heart, I knew they would. I had changed some negative family patterns in my own life, and this would affect who I would be with them and with their parents.

I was starting to heal and finally I had an identity. I was about to learn more about myself as I entered the final stage of healing my childhood.

When I thought about writing a memoir, I had a vision of a red rose which I connected to these words I had written a few years earlier.

"A rose of great beauty succumbed to her thorns; she withered and died. Only a gradual picking out of these thorns will restore her wounded self."

The wounded rose is me, and this book is about the process I went through.

Shadows and Light

Chapter 1
Harder Than Hard

In February of 1967, when I was seven months out of college and had some extra income as a staff nurse on the evening shift at Massachusetts General Hospital, I went skiing with a friend for a weekend in New Hampshire. There we met some guys. One man took an interest in me. He was a great looking man and a lot of fun to be with. Together, we partied and drank. Need I say more?

In the weeks and months that followed, I noticed I was gaining weight. Feeling fat, I started to exercise to lose what I thought was unwanted weight. At some point, my worried — and perhaps more perceptive — roommates convinced me to see a doctor for a pregnancy test. One of them, Kathy, even gave me a referral. To my shock and horror, I learned

Susan's Boston College graduation, 1966

that I was already more than three months pregnant. It should not have been a total surprise. However, my denial mechanism was well entrenched. I was not, as you will read in this memoir, my parents' daughter for nothing.

I found an obstetrician who was very sympathetic and kind. When talking about options, Dr. Murphy articulated several. First, I could get an abortion. Second, I could have the baby and give it up for adoption. (He never counseled me to consider whether I might be able to raise the baby myself.) Third, exhibiting what I thought was an odd option, he suggested I could kill myself.

Well, I didn't particularly want to kill myself so I decided to pursue the other two options.

I sought advice on getting an abortion from an M.D. who did them on the side. He was deeply lacking "bedside manner." It was obvious from his facial expression that he thought, How could she possibly get herself into this mess! It was only after he had indulged in a certain amount of putdown that he told me I was too far along for an abortion. Since I had already decided I did not want to die, that third option — suicide — was already out. (During the next year, suicide would appear as a viable option to my problems, but it did not at this time.) So, I was left with going through with the pregnancy and giving up the baby.

Going through with the pregnancy was clearly not the option I preferred; I simply wanted to be not pregnant. While I had a job to support myself during the pregnancy, a nurse's salary was meager in those days compared to today's salaries. I wondered how I could afford to raise a baby who would become a toddler, a child, and then a teenager.

There was much angst in my head. How could I give my baby away, but then how could I not? The unattractiveness of what I was about to do appalled me. In my debased self-worth, I kept thinking, How had I let this happen? Was the M.D. who had looked at me with such disdain been correct?

When I asked my friends for advice, they concurred that giving the baby up for adoption was for the best (especially given the state of society in 1967). Eventually, what I had to do became clear to me. Since being not pregnant was not an option, I accepted I had to have and then give the baby up. Once I had made the decision, I knew in my heart it was best for my child. This is not to say the decision was easy. I was an emotional basket case and I knew I would have no nurturing support from my parents in whom I had decided not to confide.

How could I appreciate how hard the following year would be as a result of this decision!

In the beginning of the summer of 1967, I quit my job at Massachusetts General, and with three friends in whom I had confided my condition, I rented a cottage in Eastham on Cape Cod. Two of us got positions at the hospital in Hyannis working the evening shift. For my colleagues there, I wore a wedding band and made up a story that my husband was doing a tour in Vietnam. This allowed me to work without revealing my personal problems, which would soon enough become evident, and to enjoy the summer on the Cape with my friends. The days passed pleasantly. Every day, weather permitting, we lounged on the sandy beach and swam in the Atlantic. Then, we worked the evening shift at the hospital. I kept my pregnancy hidden for as long as possible. (Thank goodness for the era of girdles holding everything in.) When the time came that I could no longer hide my pregnancy, I told my coworkers who were under the assumption that I had a husband in the service. I was affectionately called a pregnant Twiggy!

The days passed. I still had no plans to tell my parents — Robert and Elizabeth Yerburgh (Bob and Beth) — but at the insistence of Dr. Murphy, I finally agreed to. Keeping to the Yerburgh tradition of avoiding personal contact, I wrote a letter to share the news and invited them to come visit me on the Cape. My mother came down — as usual my father was "otherwise occupied" — and as we sat outside my rental cottage, I told her my plan to give my baby up for adoption.

I suppose I should be grateful she came to visit me but I had wanted more than a perfunctory visit. I wanted to have her to throw her arms around me and declare, "My dear girl, how can your father and I support you through this time?" I would have to have been another person with another family. As it was, she was very tense and tight-lipped. I could deduce she was thinking, How could you do this to me?

Easter Sunday 1965
L to R: My parents, brother Mark, Susan & sister Clare

Why was what I had done to myself turned into something that I had done to her? Perhaps my mother was experiencing déjà vu; my brother Mark's girlfriend Linda had been pregnant when he was just out of college and she was a junior. However, they were a couple, and they ended up getting married.

I had no one to marry.

I repeated my intention of giving the baby up for adoption, of letting go of the baby who was her grandchild. My mother had no words of sympathy, no kind words of support, no tears for her own loss. No protestations of "Couldn't we help if you kept the baby?" Nothing. On my part, I basically shut her out as I had been taught to do by the best of shut-people-out experts — my parents. I asked for nothing. I told her I had everything all worked out. In this way, mother and daughter, we played out our Yerburgh family dynamics. It was an unsatisfactory way

Shadows and Light

of being a family.

After my mother returned home, I presume she told my father everything, but he did not rush to see me, never called to ask how he could help, and never offered to support me in any way, and I don't mean financial.

I had seen other families in which parents supported their children through difficult times, but these families were not mine. This was indeed a difficult time for me and it was made even more difficult by my family's cold manner of dealing with it.

In the fall when my friends left Cape Cod, I too came back to Boston. I accepted Mark and Linda's kind offer to stay with them in an attic room at their house in Waltham, Massachusetts, until I had the baby. Those last six weeks of waiting were very long. I took walks, read much, babysat my nephew, and watched Red Sox games. (What a great season for the Sox that fall!) Despite his earlier advice that one of my options was suicide, Dr. Murphy continued to be very understanding as well as compassionate during my pre-natal checkups. There was, however, no discussion about medications and whether I wanted any, but he did offer to induce my labor when it was safe to do so.

I was at my friend Kathy's apartment when my water broke. She was nearly hysterical, and in order for her to drive me to the hospital safely, I had to calm her down. For me, the breaking water signaled that the time had come to have the baby, to put an end to this hiatus in my life, to let this baby go into its life. I was not overly nervous. Once in the hospital, I was placed in a wheel chair and pushed down the hallway. The last thing I remember was being given a shot of Scopolamine, a popular drug at the time to induce labor. This drug wipes out your memory, but the mother is awake and can follow instructions. I was told I was very entertaining, thanks to the drug. Also, I remember coming to in the recovery room and saying to the nurse in very explicit terms about what a mess the woman on the bed next to me was in.

The nurse smiled and told me I had had a baby girl.

Since my parents were not there — how could my mother not have offered to come with me when the time came? — I was lucky to have Kathy stay with me and be with me after the birth; of course, she eventually had to go home and I was alone with my thoughts and my hormones. While I had thought I was accepting of what I had decided I must do, pure hell followed as reality hit that I was about to give away this baby that I had carried for nine months. She had lived close to my heart — physically — and now she would live her life with other people and enter into their hearts. I cried nonstop.

How could I possibly give up my baby girl and hand her over to strangers!

Dr. Murphy called my parents with the news and the next day, my parents and my sister Clare came. In her usual not-connected-to-her-intuition way, my mother explained, as if it were totally reasonable, that she hadn't known what to do. When talking to Dr. Murphy during the call when he announced the birth of my baby, she asked if she should come to visit me. She repeated this to me as if it were a perfectly normal quandary that mothers have. He told her to come with my father and to bring flowers. So, following orders and not her heart, she, my father, and sister came for an uncomfortable, short visit. They did not speak about what I had been through or about what I was going to do.

This was their granddaughter that I was giving up, but this fact had not seemed to register.

Fortunately, in the days I was recovering, Kathy, another friend, and my sister-in-law, Linda visited. They were kind and sympathetic. I especially appreciated Linda who had been so good to me when I was living with her and Mark before the baby was born and was now continuing to be so. My visitors put up a brave face for me, but I was told later that, as soon as they left, they cried. I wish we could have cried together. It would have done me some good. Like my parents, I was pretty stoic and could have used the example of a good cry.

I was given the choice to see or not see my baby girl, and I decided to see her. I had a private room at the end of the hall, and it was here they brought her to me. I held my daughter, very briefly, but — oh! — the pain! In my heart, I sent her off to another family and I wished her a good loving home, a better home than I had known. However, I blocked myself from any attachment to this beautiful baby girl. What else could I do?

When the nurse took my baby and left, I sobbed. It had been harder than hard to not bond with her during our short time together. Would I ever see her again? That was not likely to happen! When it was time to leave the hospital, I did not want to impose any longer on Mark and Linda. Kathy and some other women were looking for a new place in a few weeks, and I was hoping they would find an apartment that I could soon move into with them. Meanwhile, I was too tired mentally and physically to look for other options. I had no choice but to ask my parents to take me in and I went to their home for a few weeks knowing it was temporary.

While I was with my parents, I started to work again as a private-duty nurse; I needed income if I was to move away, and for the time being, I liked the flexible hours temp work provided. I had the freedom of working the day shift when I wanted to.

While it seemed on the outside that I was getting my life together again, the trauma of relinquishing my baby did not subside. I had recurring nightmares of babies crying in the nursery and wanting to help them, hold them, but not being able to do so.

Unfortunately, in the weeks and months that followed, I had to deal with the actual process of adoption. That was another knife waiting to plunge into my heart. At some point, my social worker, whom I had been seeing weekly as a counselor, told me it was time to sign the adoption papers. Then ensued days when I could feel, in spite of my resolution, a voice saying, "Don't do it. You can still back out." I knew however that adoption into a good home was the best choice for my baby girl. Later, as I sat at an office desk signing papers, I saw a blank space for the father's name. One awful thing was that I could not remember his last name and so I left the space blank. I suppose I could have done some research with the help of the friend I'd been with on the weekend, but I had made a conscious decision never to contact him. At the time, I accepted it as a weekend fling and the consequences were totally my responsibility. I realize now I was not thinking clearly; knowing her father's identity would have an impact later if my daughter needed to know her genetic background.

As with other major changes in my life, I wanted to close this chapter of the book and never reopen it. This I tried to do with my baby daughter, but I could not do it. I often thought of her. Where was she? Who was taking care of her? Did they love her? These thoughts always brought tears to my eyes. I was isolated in this grief. Only my family and a few close friends knew about her existence, and none of them — including my close friends — ever talked to me about her or asked how I was feeling about the experience.

For the entire year following my giving up my baby for adoption, the nightmares of babies crying and my not being able to help them continued to haunt me. I had thought that, once my emotions were tightly wrapped up in a sealed package, I could function again. This was the reaction to life I had learned at home, and while I had seen how it did not work, it was nonetheless what I hoped would work for me.

Eventually I moved into a new apartment with my close

friend, Kathy, and two other roommates whom I did not know. The apartment was in a new high-rise building in the Longwood Medical area, convenient to many hospitals. Although life was continuing, I was unable to participate in the exciting, changing times of the late 60s: Apollo 7 orbited the earth for several days; the assassinations of Rev. Martin Luther King and Senator Robert Kennedy, and the peace movement around the Vietnam War. I went out with my friends on occasion but was not dating. Dr. Murphy became concerned about my continued sadness and started me on an antidepressant. When that didn't help, he referred me to a psychiatrist.

In time, the private-duty nursing also started to take its toll. I accepted particularly challenging patients, and I wonder now if I did so to assuage my guilt. One day, a physician whose patient I was taking care of asked me out, but believing that I was not ready to date and it would not be fair to him since my emotional state was so precarious, I refused. This is something I have always regretted as he seemed like a calm, caring, and interesting man. One always wonders what life might have been like had one taken a different path!

Following Dr. Murphy's psychiatric referral, I began therapy with a Dr. O'Brien. The visits were 50 minutes long during which time I smoked two cigarettes; the first at twenty minutes past the hour, the second at twenty of the hour. The room was nondescript: there was basic office furniture and no artwork or décor to soften the walls to make the space feel homey and inviting. Next to the chair I sat in was a table with a box of tissues and an ashtray; I reached for the tissues frequently as I shed many tears. Dr. O'Brien was not effective, however, in helping me to adjust to the challenges of my life. (When I ran into him several years later, I discovered he was in therapy himself and was recovering from alcoholism. I wonder if his ineffectiveness was due to being under the influence or hung over in our therapy sessions?)

In the beginning of October 1968, a few weeks shy of a year after my baby girl was born, the temp agency assigned me to a large teaching hospital where I was tasked to give medications to around 40 patients. I took pills from a bottle and placed them for each patient in a small paper cup which was then put on a card with all their meds written on it. Because there were many paper cups and med cards on the tray, it was easy for them to misalign and for confusion to ensue.

As I was walking home one afternoon after the day shift, I started to panic. "Had I given the right medications to the right patients? Did I give Mr. Smith or Mrs. Warren the phenobarbital?" I could not remember.

I was afraid to return to work. This confusion would surely lead me to make an error. I called the agency to say I would not be in and would contact them when I wanted another assignment. I stayed home for at least two weeks. I wore the same clothes day after day and stayed in bed. I was clearly in a bad way. In addition to my paranoia about the drugs, I was sure that no one cared about me or what might happen to me.

"Susan," my friend Kathy said one day, "we are going out to see Funny Girl. Come along with us. You need to get out, and besides, you like Barbra Streisand."

"I am too tired. I'll be all right."

"Why don't you change your clothes; we are leaving in a half hour."

"What's the matter with my clothes?"

I stayed home and continued to isolate myself. Sometime later in the week — this would have been in the evening when my roommates were at work and I was alone in the apartment — the veil of depression covered me so thickly I could not see how to continue to live. Suicide, which had not been an option the previous year, now seemed viable. I have a vague recollection of standing in the bathroom and reaching for a bottle of pills, and, one by one, swallowing them. I fantasized that no one would come to my funeral. I did not care; I wanted to die. Perhaps I had chosen the wrong option the year before and I should have killed myself like the doc suggested. I was totally into myself and felt like an alien in my life on earth — yearning to go home to my planet, wherever it was. Anything would be better than my present life. I felt alone and forgotten with nowhere to go but out. I was more afraid of life than death.

The next thing I remember is being one floor below mine in a friend's apartment, and vomiting in her bathroom. She must have gotten Ipecac for me; it's a drug that induces vomiting in the case of overdose or poisoning.

I have blotted out memories of the evening. Over the years, I have wondered why I never went through with suicide and chose to go downstairs to seek help. It would be many years before I had some insight on why I chose to live.

I do not recall what happened next — whether I was admitted to St. Elizabeth's Hospital in Brighton, just outside of Boston, right away or stayed in the apartment on "suicide watch" until I was admitted. Dr. O'Brien, ever the ineffectual psychiatrist, recommended Electric Shock Therapy (EST) as it was called back then in 1968. It was believed to help with suicidal impulses and severe depression. Since I was 24 years old and of age, I consented. I have no recollection of signing a consent agreement nor of being admitted to the locked inpatient psychiatric unit at St. Elizabeth's. I do remember not caring what anyone did to me as long as they could rid me of those feelings of wanting to die. The vortex they had to help me negotiate was deep, very dark, and could suck me up in a second. As a student nurse, I had had a rotation in a state mental institution and was well aware of what I was undergoing as I had seen EST being given, but I was desperate. When death seems like a solution, EST can seem to be the lesser of two evils. Surely, however, there must have been a less invasive therapy available!

Years later, as I read my medical record, trying to understand what had happened to me, I realized Dr. O'Brien basically did not know what else to do with me. What was officially my record could have been anybody's, as there was no information to indicate my uniqueness as an individual, in spite of the fact that I had been crying in his office for a good while now! How could such a psychiatrist be allowed to practice?

I received EST every Monday, Wednesday, and Friday morning for five weeks. The treatment room was the typical, sterile, hospital room with the machines at the head of the bed. A padded tongue depressor was handy to use if the patient had an event, such as a major seizure. Bilateral electrodes were placed on my temples. After the anesthetic was injected, the electricity was administered inducing a minor seizure which was both acceptable and expected. It happened very quickly. (You can imagine how I looked forward to these sessions!) Afterwards, too dazed to move on my own, I was helped into a wheelchair and pushed to my room where coffee and muffins awaited for breakfast. This was welcome since I was hungry. As a result of these ESTs over fifteen sessions, I was like a zombie, sleeping a lot especially in the beginning.

My memory was severely affected. When my mother visited one afternoon, I said to her, "No one comes to see me; I have had no visitors."

"Yes, you have!" she replied. "Mother Marjorie (a nun who was her friend) came yesterday. Your friend, Kathy, and one of your other roommates — I can't remember her name — came last weekend."

Years later, I asked my mother, "Did Daddy ever come to visit me when I was in St. Elizabeth's? I don't remember."

She said he hadn't because "he was too busy."

I was in St. Elizabeth's for six weeks, and he was living only 20 minutes away. Couldn't my father have come after the school day or on the weekend? I still don't want to believe he didn't come because he wasn't bonded to me. I prefer to think he felt some guilt and responsibility for my emotional issues.

On my floor were patients who were psychotic or hallucinating. They paced back and forth along the hallway, spouting gibberish. It was not uplifting to realize I was with these broken people. I felt like an inanimate object, a piece of furniture. Was I crazy, too? Years later these words came to me.

I am a chair. I am a chair.
How does that feel?
To be sat upon, to be dependent is heavy, but...
I have no say.

Worn and faded, empty and jaded,
Silent and rigid, passive and frigid.
Crazy, crazy.

Yes, it is safe, but I must change.
I am not that weak.
I must be more than just a seat.
Set me free: I am human.
I am me.

I was told, but I do not recall, that one afternoon, my friend Julie came to visit. She was accompanied by a friend of hers, Michael. I had already met Michael three years earlier in 1965 at a Boston College party. Julie, who was dating Michael's friend, David, had thought Michael and I would like each other.

At the time, Michael had been a senior and I, a junior. I had found Michael to be nice looking with dark hair and glasses. I can still see him meticulously dressed in khakis and a sweater. I liked that he was on the tall side, six feet two inches and his weight was normal, but we did not connect that evening. He did not ask me out, and I doubt I would have gone out with him if he had.

I had not seen Michael since we had met at Julie's and David's party. I'm not sure why he came to my room rather than wait in a lounge, but at the time, since I have no memory of his coming, I have no idea how I felt about him. Connecting would come later.

After six weeks, sometime around Thanksgiving, I was discharged from St. Elizabeth's. My memory was so affected by the shock treatments that I have no idea if I went back to my apartment or to my parents' house. It could have been either, but I have the sense that I went back to my apartment. I don't remember interacting with my roommates, but I do recall one scene when I was out with friends one evening. We had met up with a group of guys at a bar and were talking about where we lived. Much to the embarrassment of my friends, I asked, "Where do we live?" Fortunately, lapses in short-term memory like this did not last.

I had money saved up so I was able to keep up with the rent and I had taken out individual health care insurance while I had been working as a private duty nurse so hospital bills were covered.

My feelings about EST remain mixed. I often say it was not as traumatic, dehumanizing an experience as it had been portrayed in such movies as in "One Flew Over the Cuckoo's Nest." EST got me out of a very deep funk and back to work. However, the questions always linger: Wasn't there a better way? What really happened to my brain? What happened to my soul when I was zapped with electricity? Structurally what happened to my brain? And spiritually to my mind?

Afterwards, as I continued my nursing career, in spite of expressing that the EST experience was not as traumatic and dehumanizing as some media have made it out to be, I would cringe when I saw a patient being defibrillated. Any minor electric shock still bothers me; I try to avoid getting the typical shock when opening a door in the winter. And so obviously, at some deep level, the experience remained with me as very difficult.

A psychiatrist later explained it to me. "EST rearranges the brain; in other words, one forgets the unpleasant memories." All well and good, however, what happens to those unpleasant memories? Where do they go? To the trash to be recycled and sanitized or into cyberspace never to return except for an occasional retrieval in another dimension?

That winter, I began my long struggle toward normalcy. I was feeling like I could cope with life again and with having lost my baby girl. My short-term memory returned in full. I decided I did not want to do private duty nursing anymore, and after Christmas, I was hired as a Respiratory Therapist at Children's Hospital, which I could see from our apartment window. My roommates also worked there.

1969 would reunite me with Michael who would be my first husband.

Shadows and Light

Chapter 2
My Wrong Decision

By the summer of 1969, I was working full-time, and to anyone viewing the young nurse I was, I was living a normal life. I was even going to be a bridesmaid. My friend Julie's boyfriend David had returned from Vietnam, and they were marrying. Julie had asked me to be a bridesmaid — what could be more normal than standing for a friend at her wedding? She informed me that Michael was to be an usher for David, and they wanted the two of us to walk together. I had not been dating so it seemed a bit of an adventure to be paired with a man and I couldn't see any reason why it would not work to have Michael as my escort and so I agreed.

To my surprise, Michael and I had a lot of fun dancing and socializing both one-on-one and together with others. There was a get-together after the wedding that the bridal party was invited to. I spent more time with Michael so it did seem like sort of a date. The liquor flowed, and the fun continued until the late evening when Michael gave me a ride home. I had to admit to myself that I had had a lovely time. It had been a while since I could say this, and it felt good to be pleased with my life.

After this, Michael asked me out and I said yes. Soon, we were dating seriously. Michael always proposed doing fun things together, and in the process, he spent money on me. I was not used to having someone treat me this way. Growing up, I had not been made to feel special. My parents had taken care of me out of obligation, I felt, rather than from affection. They were dutiful rather than loving. Michael, on the other hand, seemed to be saying he liked me for who I was. He took me out regularly to dinner. To me the restaurants seemed expensive but in reality, they weren't. I wasn't used to going out to dinner like this.

Even before my pregnancy, I had not dated much and certainly not for any length of time with one man. Since my baby girl had been born, my dating had been sketchy, almost nonexistent. Michael was the first person to want to be with me over a long period, and he did not seem to mind spending money on me. My parents had been very careful about their money. I had had a limited wardrobe as a girl, for instance, and had worn hand-me-downs from people my mother knew; I even had a few clothes purchased from a second-hand shop when I was a teenager sent off to boarding school at St Mary's. In spite of my parents' middle-class income, my mother did not believe in spending money, and I had felt that this was especially true about spending for me. Now, I seemed to be at the center of Michael's attention as he and I went to parties, to dinner, and to an occasional show.

After a while, it felt like Michael and I were becoming a couple. I felt wanted and special, and I liked that. I liked it so much that I didn't pay attention to warning signs that should have made me question the feasibility of this relationship. There were many, but I had been lonely and had had a hard time recently. I could not see that my oversight might have dire consequences for me in the future. For the time being, I was caught up in the thrill of dating.

Michael's spending on me could also be seen as carelessness about money. Given my upbringing in a home where money was never lavished on anything, his carefree relationship with money might have been a warning sign to another woman who was more confident about herself and her ability to attract another man. Instead, I caved in to the attention I was receiving and did not foresee distress ahead. I didn't interpret his spending money on me as a problem — in fact, I loved it. His generosity and expensive tastes could have been perceived as his inability to save. How did I, who was so careful with what I spent and could be said to be an adherent of the maxim "A penny saved is a penny earned," not see this?

When we were out, we always had a drink with our meals. I thought of him as sophisticated for ordering wine. I liked being courted by a man oh-so-much-more sophisticated than my parents! For a long enough time, I saw no dark side to his drinking. One evening, however, as we were at our favorite Beacon Street restaurant in Brookline, I was again sharing parts of my past. Believing honesty was best, I had been open with Michael that I had given up a baby for adoption, and I had told him about the trauma that followed. Of course, he had experienced a slice of that trauma when he had visited me in St. Elizabeth's Hospital. It felt good to be able to speak to someone about my experience. During the meal, Michael had had a cocktail and a few glasses of wine. He drank more than I did, but he always did and I never made anything of it.

As we were finishing dessert, as I was saying something again about the sadness that surrounded the baby girl I had given up, he interrupted me by blurting out, "Julie would never have gotten herself pregnant like that."

I was stunned. I stopped in mid-sentence and could not respond. In my mind came the phrase "Susie slut," which Mark, my brother, used to call me when I was home from boarding school! Did Michael think of me as a slut? Was this what the dating was about? I looked straight at him. I saw a look of disdain on his face that immediately recalled the doctor I had seen for a possible abortion. Suddenly, I felt smothered by his negative view of me and by the trauma of two years previously. I had to get away, be by myself for a moment. Getting up quickly, I escaped to the women's room. I'll admit that getting pregnant was not a high point of my life, but I had handled it responsibly — for my baby girl and for me. People make all kinds of mistakes even if most are perhaps not as tangible and irrevocable as having a baby you can't take care of. I know as I write this that how I handled my pregnancy and adoption is something I can be proud of. That evening as I hid in the women's bathroom, however, I sank once again into the trauma that followed the baby's birth. That time had been harder than hard, and I was not over it yet. It continued to have a hold on me, and I had not expected Michael to be a person who would clobber me with it.

I was in the bathroom a good while before I finally regained my composure and freshened myself up a bit. I realized I could not go back to losing myself as I had done for so many years in other people's view of me. I could not let Michael abuse me verbally as my mother had. I needed to tell Michael about how hurtful and inappropriate his comment had been and so I returned to the table.

He was waiting for me, and we acknowledged each other awkwardly. Then I sat down and said, "You had no right to compare me with Julie. I do not want you to say anything like that to me again. You were hurtful."

I don't recall his reaction but I suggested we not see each other for two weeks. I needed to assess where our relationship was going. I had to admit to myself I had noticed that, after a couple of drinks, Michael's personality changed slightly. He tended to be more self-aggrandizing and self-absorbed. In spite of knowing that, foolishly, because I was ready to be married, ready to have a home of my own, ready to stop being lonely and struggling, I explained his abusive remark away in the next two weeks, blaming it on the alcohol he had consumed at the restaurant.

Shadows and Light

I decided to continue seeing Michael. Other than that painful moment which I decided, conveniently, was an anomaly, the relationship seemed to be going well. I put what he had said out of mind; or, rather I should say I put the cruel side of his personality that had lashed at me out of mind. When I look back on this incident, I see myself as emotionally immature. I was willing to confuse my fantasies with reality, and my vulnerability to criticism undermined my almost non-existent self-esteem.

By the fall of 1969, I had been going out with Michael for a few months. We planned to drive up to see his parents in a small Northern Maine town. We were becoming a couple, and I was being introduced to his parents. It seemed like a milestone was being passed and I wanted to do it right. For some reason I can't recall, Michael sprang on me that he had invited his friend, Rick, to come with us. Rick was a Boston College friend and not someone from the same area in Maine; it was not as if Michael was kindly offering Rick a ride back to see his own parents. When Michael told me he had invited Rick to join us, I didn't want him to come, preferring to be alone on the trip with Michael, wanting to build some intimacy between us. In my usual lack of self-care, however, I did not insist on what I wanted from this trip. Even as early as a few months into our relationship, I knew that if I had said something about not wanting Rick to come, Michael would not have listened to me and I could have jeopardized our relationship. So now there were two people not listening to me — Michael and myself! In my passivity, I participated in setting a precedent in our relationship, and my lack of affirmation would haunt our marriage. It would take me a long time to accept this responsibility and to understand that, if I did not tell Michael what I wanted, how was he to know?

Once in Maine, Michael and I were almost never alone to interact with his parents. Instead he and Rick put on a two-man show. They entertained everyone — Michael's relatives who were there to meet me and see Michael — with their repartee and humor. Their extraversion dominated the visit that ought to have been a quiet time for me to get to know Michael's parents and relatives and they me.

For the duration of our visit, Michael paid no attention to me. It seemed that the congeniality with his college friend took precedence over his relationship with me. I felt like I was an afterthought. He was in bachelor mode, not able to relate to me as the woman in his emotional life. Although I could not express it at the time, I felt that he needed to leave his life with the boys behind and relate to his female partner. Hurt then as I had often been with my family earlier, I went into my ineffective shutdown mode — how often had I seen this in my parents! — and said very little, only speaking when spoken to. As a result of this repression which had started on the drive up, I turned my frustration and anger, as had become my habit, into a muscle spasm in my neck. The spasm inflicted considerable pain on me.

At one point that weekend, Michael's mother and I were alone, and she said, knowing that she might be speaking of me, "I pity the girl Michael is going to marry." As important as an elaboration might have been for my future, I did not ask her what she meant. I assumed she meant that he liked to spend money and could be critical at times. I even recall his father saying, "Michael thinks money grows on trees." Perhaps I was afraid of being dissuaded from a future I had already set the course to attain? Had I not been afraid of what I might learn, her answer might have helped me make a better decision for a husband and the future father to my children.

Michael could be somewhat overbearing at times and I could see where he got it: from his mother. Michael had wanted to go to Harvard, but because the family was Catholic, his mother had insisted he go to Boston College so as to meet a "nice Catholic girl." The irony was that, at Boston College, he met and eventually married one of the only two non-Catholics in the nursing school.

After almost a year of dating, however, in the late spring of 1970, Michael asked me to marry him, and I said, "Yes!" At the time, I thought I was in love with him, but I was not clear on what love meant. Marrying seemed the right thing to do.

Other than getting married, another decision had to be made. Michael had the opportunity to transfer with his accounting firm to its Paris office. He would start in the fall, but could only be out of the US for two and a half years as he had to return to complete his army reserve obligation. This would mean that we would be apart for a long time starting in the fall, and this would probably be the end of our relationship.

I was at a crossroads, and I took what I thought at the time to be a very good option. I would have a husband with a good job and I would live in Europe with no financial worries. I see now that I made the decision to marry without much thought. I was caught up with the excitement of a wedding and of life in Paris, not with whether Michael and I would be good partners in a marriage. This fantasy life provided an antidote to my past problems which I hadn't dealt with adequately up to then.

I had no idea who I was. I wonder what Michael saw in me? Later in life, I thought, "If Michael hadn't been transferred to Paris to work, would I have married him just then?" I might have held him off a while and traveled to Europe with two of my roommates with whom I had planned a trip during the summer of 1970. Would time apart have helped me to evaluate whether or not going into this marriage was a really good idea?

That night after his proposal, however, I was ecstatic, feeling myself on cloud nine, and I couldn't wait to tell my parents. Did I want to be perceived as an adult who was doing adult things? Did I want to redeem having had a baby I had to give up? And certainly, had I thought of what my parents' reaction was likely to be — was I not their daughter who had lived with their emotional disconnection all my life? — I would have realized I had little reason to have been so excited to share my news with them.

When, late the next morning, I hustled myself over to my parents' house with my exciting announcement, I found my mother and my father sitting at the kitchen table eating lunch. Breathless with excitement, ready to take in their response at my level — surely, I must have had some fantasy that getting married would validate me in their eyes and redeem me for all I had "put them through" — I blurted out, "Michael and I are getting married."

"That's nice, dear," my mother responded between bites, as if I had said, "I just bought a new shower curtain."

My father gave me a slight smile. Perhaps he was acknowledging that I was there but had not clearly heard what I had said.

Even if my parents had already anticipated that Michael and I would be getting married eventually, either my mother or my father could have showed approval or disapproval, anything to tell me they had heard me. I felt deflated. What was the matter with these people? Wasn't what I had to announce wonderful?

When I told my friends later, thank goodness they responded with the excitement I wanted to hear. I was in love and excited to soon be a wife and, in the future, a mother.

I had found someone to fill the husband slot in my life. And Michael, was he also trying to fill his wife slot? Years later, I recall him saying that he had thought I was very social and would be a good drinking partner.

Wrong on both counts!

After we set our wedding date for August 30 — just three months away — I began planning right away. I chose my roommate Kathy to be my maid of honor because she had supported me through some rough times and had shown herself to be a true friend.

Shadows and Light

Taking her role as maid of honor seriously, Kathy scheduled a bridal shower at our apartment in Brookline. It was a small event with my mother, my sister Clare, and my sister-in-law Linda as well as a couple of college friends. Other friends who had moved out of the area would not be attending.

After we had been sitting in our living room chatting for a bit, Kathy signaled it was time to open my gifts. The first one I unwrapped was a sexy, blue negligee from Kathy.

"It's gorgeous," I said as I held it up for everyone to see. "Thank you so much." I went over and gave Kathy a hug. I was moved at the special attention she had given to this gift.

The next present I was handed was a small package from my mother. "What lovely little surprise had she found for me?" I wondered — or perhaps more hoped than wondered. Inside the package was a small enamel pot used to make Turkish coffee. It was a two- or three-dollar item I had seen in the store where she must have bought it. I was embarrassed! Such a cheap gift, and from my own mother! She had once again proven herself true to form. I was sure others, too, at the shower must have recognized it for the throw-away item it was. I wished I could stuff it back in the packaging, but everyone had seen it.

My face must have expressed my surprise and disappointment. No one said anything. There were no "oohs" and "ahs!" No "Isn't that the cutest thing!" Instead, there was silence.

My mother quickly protested, "I know it's something small. I'm putting all my eggs in one basket for your wedding gift."

My friends did not respond. The moment was quite awkward. Silence filled the room. It was like my mother was socially inept and did not know how to function in a world where mothers are presumed to lavish care and love on their daughters? My mother's lack of *savoir faire* embarrassed me in front of my friends, but even more, I was sad that I did not have a mother who could celebrate with me. I wanted her to be able to tell me,

"I looked all over for a special gift for you. I so want to help you launch your new life successfully with Michael." Is it possible she had never been to a bridal shower and had not seen how other mothers interacted with their daughters?

Then, thank goodness for Kathy who, with her good humor and tact, handed me another gift. The rest of my gifts were appropriate, but the joy had gone out of the shower for me.

The cheapness of this small enamel pot wasn't really a matter of my mother not having money to spend; she was working full-time teaching. That summer, she also had the disposable money to go to England to visit her sister Clare. It was true my mother had put her "wedding eggs" for me in another basket. She and my father helped me pay for part of the wedding reception, and they gave Michael and me money to buy china. Her problem was a matter of comportment, and it was puzzling to me. She seemed to simply not know how to respond to situations. If she didn't know what was appropriate for a shower gift, she could have sought advice from one of her friends. The embarrassing part was that my friends saw that my mother did not know how to be a mother.

I wanted a mother I could be proud of.

Michael and I had trouble agreeing on a church for the wedding and a venue for the reception. Could this have been another sign of things to come? As I had when we went to Maine to see his parents the previous year, I continued to give in to him as I had given in to so many other people already in my life. Michael would not agree to my suggestions — nor would he compromise. He wanted to marry in a Catholic Church. Finally, we decided on getting married at St. Ignatius, a parish church near Boston College, and on having the reception at Alumni Hall which was within walking distance of the church.

Michael and I went through the mandatory Pre-Cana meetings with the Catholic priest. I was told I had to bring up any children we might have as Catholics. I did tell Michael that if he failed to take our children to the Catholic Church, I would take them to the Episcopal Church. I also insisted on having an Episcopal priest at our wedding to have some acknowledgment of my faith.

The summer, devoted to working, preparing for the wedding, and packing for Europe immediately after our wedding, went by quickly. During this time, my mother went to England to visit her sister Clare and was gone for six weeks. When she came back, she complained about how expensive the bridesmaid dress was that she would have to buy for my sister Clare. She balked at having to buy matching shoes.

My mother may have been as reluctant to dress Clare as she was because she did not want me to marry Michael. She never said anything at the time, but years later, she told me that she could see Michael was not affectionate. (Of course, such an observation coming from the cold woman she was herself would have been surprising had she said anything then.) Had she told me this at the time, however, I doubt I would have listened; I was confused about love and affection and would have denied Michael was not affectionate. This was clearly typical of the dynamics of my exchanges with my mother: I wanted her to give me input, but only the input I wanted, and I was willing to dismiss her input if it was not what I wanted.

In the week before the wedding and the departure for Europe, I stayed with my parents as the lease on my apartment was up. While I was packing the suitcase I would take on our honeymoon, my mother came into my bedroom ran her hand over my clothes. "Why do you need all these clothes?" she said as if it were a question. "You're spending so much!" It was not the actual words but her look and the way she said it that were upsetting. I worked and earned my own money so it wasn't as if she had had to buy the clothes. I was going to Majorca and London for a honeymoon and then on to Paris to live. Of course, I wanted to look good. Somehow, she spoke from the same mind that had told her the cheap Turkish coffee pot was okay. She just didn't seem to know how things were done.

I believe she was jealous of me. How does a daughter incorporate that realization into her relationship with her mother? I was better looking than she had been as a girl and I had blond hair. When I would go out, I would garner attention, especially from men. In spite of this, when I was in college and living at home, my mother, and my sister too, would not hesitate to criticize me by saying things like, "Your hair is such a dirty blond. Why don't you do something about it?"

I also had a better sense of style when it came to clothes. This may have been why, I believe, my mother was criticizing my clothes. My appearance was important to me. Besides spending on new clothes, I had also spent a lot on my gown at Priscilla's Bridal Shop in Boston. Simple but elegant, I thought.

In the weeks and days before the wedding, the stress I let enter into my life was overwhelming; I lost ten pounds the week before the wedding and had a constant headache. How would I enjoy my wedding day if it were encumbered by a headache? I am sure the stress was partly due to my unacknowledged apprehension about the rightness of marrying Michael. I was also always a bit of a perfectionist, which did not help, and the stoic side of me was in full repression. So, I kept

Susan's wedding
1970

my emotions under control, but I believe there was something else going on at a deeper level. Was my body telling me that I should not go through with the wedding, that I was making a mistake? If I had any intuitive insight, I pushed it out of my mind. That week, I was back to my usual *modus operandi*, doing everything myself and not feeling like I should ask for help. Michael was busy doing his own things, recovering from his bachelor party, unable to offer the support I craved and wouldn't let myself ask for — support I secretly longed for. I had created a crisis of sorts and now I hoped that Michael might volunteer to help resolve it. He did not step forward, perhaps sensing I had taken control of the wedding and there was no room for him.

I had no insight into any of this confusion. Instead, it was all something negative that was aimed at me, and like my parents, I trudged ahead stoically, never sharing my feelings nor asking Michael for his. Had I — or he — spoken up we might have gotten to know each other better earlier on.

My mother agreed to have Michael and his family — not the whole wedding party, but only family members — over for dinner after the rehearsal at Saint Ignatius. Surprisingly, the dinner went well. My mother went all out and cooked some of my favorite dishes which were her standbys: Swedish meatballs and an English trifle for dessert

My father walking me down the aisle

Michael and I married on a sunny, warm Sunday afternoon in late August. It was not a fancy wedding by any means, and Michael and I cut costs by not having a proper photographer and by serving a cold buffet meal at Alumni Hall. The wedding and the reception went well except for a couple of glitches. I forgot to bring my "going away" clothes to change into and corralled my brother to go back to get them at my parents' house. The so-called ecumenical Mass at the church was awkward because of the Catholic priest's apathetic demeanor — he was not the one we had chosen — but the Episcopalian priest from my church saved the day with an uplifting, sometimes amusing homily. Since Michael's Porsche had been stolen two days before, his parents drove us to the motel we were staying in for the night. Was the theft an omen of things to come?

Michael & Susan
at their wedding reception
1970

On our wedding trip, Michael and I stayed at a resort in Majorca where we went to the on-site beach. I was looking forward to showing off my new bathing suit. I thought I looked really good in it, maybe even sexy! We were relaxing in our beach chairs when Michael spoke harshly.

"Cover yourself up."

"What?"

"When you leaned over, you exposed some chest."

Rather than take pride in the beautiful young woman he had just married, it was like he could not acknowledge the sexual nature of a marriage. Or, was I wrong? Perhaps my new husband was really ashamed of me and I had truly embarrassed him? It looked like a modest bikini but technically it was a one-piece suit since the front had a panel connecting the bottom to the top. I didn't understand where his comment came from. It did not add fun to the honeymoon, which was supposed to be romantic, wasn't it?

From Majorca, we went on to London. When we got there, we found that our travel agent had screwed up our hotel reservations. Eventually, we did find a place, but it was a modest room, not in the area we wanted. We made the best of it, and I was just happy to be in London to see the tourist sights I had always wanted to see. We did not visit my Aunt Clare who lived outside of Oxford, but we planned to see her when we returned to England later in the fall.

In France, a period of tremendous change was ahead of us.

Chapter 3
Settling into Paris

When we arrived in Paris, we ended up with a housing snafu, much like we had in London. Michael's company had had trouble finding us a hotel room. The city was booked up, and his company could only find us a modest room in a less desirable section of Paris. The room was clean, but I did not like the feel of the meagerness — its thin pillows and scratchy blanket. Even so, it was exciting to be in Paris. Its beautiful buildings were lit up at night, the open-air markets were filled with people, the neighborhood shops offered specialty foods. And then there was all the art and the culture.

We were not tourists, of course. Michael would be working at his new position in the same top accounting firm he had worked for in Boston, and I would be "not working" at home as I was unable to obtain a work permit. As we were getting ready for bed that first night, Michael announced, "I have to leave for the office early tomorrow morning. You can take the Metro and meet me there. We'll have lunch and then I have time to look at apartments with you."

His plan, appropriate as it was, filled me with anxiety. Neither Michael nor I seemed to understand the depth of my sudden unreasonable fear. I was unsettled by being in a new city and in a room that was barebones and not at all welcoming. As irrational as it was, I didn't want to go out by myself the next day. I don't think it was about going on the Metro but rather about the fact that Michael was leaving me to cope by myself. I wanted to be taken care of. Going out alone should certainly not have challenged another 25-year-old college graduate, but it did me and I could not understand why. Today, I think it may have been some sense that I had placed myself in a situation where all my customary fears about not getting the support I so craved would be proven true. I did not appreciate that Michael himself must have had his own apprehension about showing up in an office where he would be expected to perform right away at a certain level of professionalism. He was the "new kid on the block" and he would have to prove himself. It must have been challenging to him to deal with this uncertainty in addition to taking care of a fearful wife.

Seeing that I was over-the-top fearful, if he had just managed to say, "What can I do to make going out alone easier for you?" I would have had a better feeling, one of being part of a couple. If I had not been a person who was still dealing with the trauma of her childhood and of her recent unhappy pregnancy, I'm fairly sure I would have reacted differently. As it was, it felt again like early September 1958 when I'd been dropped off at St. Mary's in Peekskill, New York, for my freshman year of high school.

After living in Minnesota for two years, my family relocated to Port-au Prince, Haiti, where my father, as a missionary with the Episcopal Church, was principal of their boys' high school. I had attended an English-language elementary school, but as the school did not go beyond eighth grade, a boarding school in the States had been in my future.

But the notion of "in my future" was a far cry from the reality of the unfamiliar setting I found myself in that first year and of seeing my mother drive away without me. I was terrified about all the unknowns I would find and anxious about being alone for most of the coming year as I would not be seeing my parents again until the following summer. Arrangements had been made for the Christmas holidays for me to visit the house of the headmaster of the boarding school my brother went to. While the school was only a three-hour drive away, this did not comfort me as neither Mark or I had a means of reaching the other. (I'm not sure why Mark hadn't stayed with my parents in Haiti and attended my father's school.)

My parents had chosen St. Mary's because it was run by Episcopal nuns, and since my father was principal at an Episcopal school in Haiti, I received free tuition for the four years.

I cried myself to sleep for many nights (there were other girls who cried openly) — but, of course, that kind of drama cannot last and eventually I settled into the boarding school routine and made friends. I was elected one of the four class officers that year so I must have put on my façade of everything-is-just-fine even though inwardly I was sad and lonely.

Susan off to St. Mary's School Sept. 1958.

I had been brought up in a religious home where my parents said prayers and the family all went to Episcopal services together. My grandfather had been a bishop in Canada, my father's brother was a priest, and my father had completed his studies to became a priest but was never ordained — I never knew the reason. In spite of this and of going to a religious school, it was during my years at St. Mary's that I stopped saying my prayers at night before bed and gave up on God as my bulwark and protector. What was the use? I had been abandoned and I was alone.

My husband Michael was doing the equivalent of my mother driving away. I offer this flashback as a way to document why I reacted so irrationally.

I did not sleep well in that modest Paris hotel room with the scratchy blankets the night before having to venture out alone to join Michael via the Metro. In the morning, he left early to meet his work colleagues in his new Paris office. It must have been both an exciting and a nerve-wracking time for him, but I was caught up in my own drama and was not able to help him any more than he helped me. After he left, I dawdled in the room, then dressed and went to the lobby for a late morning coffee and a freshly baked croissant. With butterflies in my stomach, I stepped out into the street and started walking to the Metro station, which was only three blocks away. I walked quickly and with purpose so as to boost my confidence and without paying attention to my surroundings. Caught in the vise of some memory, of some past experience, I just wanted to get to Michael's office.

I descended the stairs of the Metro station and bought a first-class ticket as Michael had instructed me to do. By then, I was calmer and the blending of past trauma and the present had lessened. It was easier than I had thought during the night to make my way around. I could actually understand the signs. When I was on the Metro, the names of the stations we passed by — Bastille, Hotel de Ville, Musée du Louvre, Tuileries, Concorde — were familiar from history, politics, or literature. I started to get excited, thinking I would soon be seeing all these new places. This initial sortie helped me to feel more confident about being able to find my way around, but it was an example of the crippling effects of unprocessed memory.

What was this fear about, this sense of the foreboding aspect of Paris? As I was to learn many years later when I finally accessed many past-life memories, I had once had a difficult experience in Paris in one of those past lives — an experience that no one would ever want to relive. This memory explained part of my being fearful, but I did not know that then. Aspects of my past lives were asserting themselves, but I had no idea that was happening.

We did not stay in the wretched hotel room long. Almost right away, Michael's company found us a temporary, furnished apartment until we found one of our own. After my initial negative reaction to being in Paris, I had managed to get around like the adult I was. Someone from Michael's office helped us look for apartments and came with us to see them. We found one quickly but could not move in for three to four weeks. While Michael was working, I spent the day figuring out what I was going to cook for meals and where to buy food. I loathed butcher shops. I have a keen sense of smell and the odor of raw meat repulsed me. I found a small grocery store that had chicken plucked and neatly wrapped up in cellophane. One evening — to my horror when I opened my meat package — the chicken inside was complete with head and neck. I started to cry. I couldn't deal with this. I picked the dead chicken up by its dangling neck, stuffed it in a bag and promptly threw it down the garbage chute outside the apartment.

That evening when I told Michael what had happened, he very kindly suggested that we go out to dinner. This was the kind, understanding husband I had wanted to marry, but on another day, I experienced a different husband who emerged on his way to work.

"I left a pair of shoes out that need polishing," he told me.

"I don't do shoes," I answered, my defensive mechanisms alerted, and feeling commanded.

"What do you mean 'you don't do shoes'?" he replied.

If Michael had asked me politely, in a loving manner, to polish his shoes, I would not have been triggered. It was his expectation that I had to polish them that bothered me. This unfamiliar role of a housewife that Michael expected me to fill for him was too much for me. In the early days in Paris, I was not feeling expansive and I was into protecting my own boundaries. Michael had a purpose — his job in Paris — while I did not. I had no job to go to every day, no purpose to give me meaning. Where another person might have reveled in the freedom of being supported by Michael's job and might have taken up a project of her own, I did not. I saw myself having to relate to being a housewife. My major learning became how to be a homemaker, which was not a role that was particularly interesting to me, nor would I have the camaraderie of co-workers to keep me going. I would have to depend on my own energy and I was hoping it, along with my nesting instinct, would kick in after we moved into our permanent apartment.

 I did not polish Michael's shoes that day nor did I sit with him in the evening to share why I had reacted as I did. Neither did Michael ask me to share what had gone on between us in the morning. Starting married life is perhaps difficult for many people and the difficulty was about to be amplified by living in a foreign culture that constrained us in many ways. Certainly, if I could have gone out to work — which was my instinct for organizing my days — I would have dealt much better with daily life.

 We found a seventh-floor apartment with a skylight in the 15th Arrondissement on Rue du Laos. The apartment was small but it did have the two bedrooms we wanted, as we knew we would be having guests. Michael's brother and his wife, my sister and a cousin, and several friends were planning on visiting us during our Paris stay. Our new kitchen was tiny and had a half-sized refrigerator and minimal counter space. To make telephone calls, which was only possible during the day as there was no service at night, we had to go through the concierge. But living in this apartment, which was close to three Metro stops, would make it easy for me to get around.

Since we had no car, we were dependent on public transportation. At some point we would need one for travel and Michael preferred one for his commute to work. If I needed to drive during the day, he could always take the Metro. On one of the first weekends we were in Paris, Michael went to an auto show with a friend from his firm while I spent the afternoon with his friend's wife at their apartment. This couple and their three children were also from the Boston area and had been transferred to Paris at the same time as we.

The afternoon passed pleasantly enough until Michael and his friend came back and announced, "We bought cars."

I was surprised. I thought Michael was going to look at cars, but was not going to buy one. Just a few weeks earlier, I had been single and had made decisions for myself, which was fine as no one else was affected. Now I believed that a couple ought to discuss major purchases. Instead of that, now I was tied to someone who was, by himself, making decisions that would affect me. Maybe being with his friend had encouraged him to make the decision unilaterally, but since I considered buying a car to be a major decision, I had thought, when the time came, we would make it together as a couple. How had I assumed that Michael had the same viewpoint about how couples make decisions?

Obviously, he thought he was still single! It was similar to when we were in Maine visiting his parents, when he seemed to forget I was there as he clowned around with his friend Rick.

Fearing the answer, I asked, "I assume it is an automatic?" I had learned to drive with a stick shift but I had driven an automatic for the past couple of years and did not particularly enjoy shifting gears.

"No!" he declared.

I protested that I was not comfortable with a stick shift. Why had he bought a standard? Years earlier, when learning to drive, I had rolled a car backward and hit another car. The fear of stalling and sliding backward on a slope was still with me and I must have shown it.

This early on in our marriage, Michael and I took up our defensive positions that were to exhaust us, and, as neither was able or perhaps willing to change, would lead to the breakup of our union.

By way of appeasement, Michael volunteered to take me to practice.

On my part, rather than talking through with Michael what had happened so as to develop a better style of resolving conflict, I persuaded myself by thinking that maybe it wouldn't be that bad since I wouldn't be driving much and Paris did not have a lot of hills. The Metro stations were close by, and using the subway, I could go anywhere within the city.

Early one evening when the light was still strong, Michael took me out for a practice drive to get reacquainted with handling a standard. I was doing well until I saw the Arc de Triomphe in the distance. There, twelve roads converge on the rotary! Entering cars had the right of way and they barreled in from the right at a fast clip!

"Oh, my God, Michael!" I cried.

Panic fluttered in my chest as I was not a person to be energized by a challenge like this. I entered the traffic circle. In spite of driving in Boston, I did not have experience driving in such large rotaries with heavy traffic. Nervously, I maneuvered the standard-transmission car over to our exit. Somehow, I managed to get in, through, and out of the traffic circle without stalling. Michael was not attuned to my fears and hesitations, however irrational they were. He was thinking of the mechanics of driving but he did not ask himself how I was going to feel while driving and what he could do to make a positive experience for me. He

Shadows and Light

did not take the time to ask himself what the best route for me to practice my driving in Paris might have been. Michael was not given, as I was learning, to feeling the emotional nuances of other people. And I, on the other hand, was given to wanting other people to support me. It would take me many years to step up to my power.

Around the same time — that is, when we first got to Paris — Michael and I started French classes at the Berlitz Language School. His company paid for individual classes for a few weeks. I did not particularly like my teacher's impatience. It fed my lack of self-confidence as I believed learning French should have come more easily, but my experience was learning French was, in fact, difficult. I could have asked for a different teacher, but I did not. Perhaps I sensed the problem had something to do with me and I did not want to face it. After a month or so, I quit this Berlitz class and was glad not to have to spend any time with the teacher again. If I was going to be in Paris, however, I needed to learn some French, so I bought audio tapes to proceed on my own. But I did not learn enough French to carry on a conversation, even a simple one. It was embarrassing, and I could not understand why an intelligent college graduate could not pull off language acquisition, especially since she was hearing French on the street every day.

Just moving to France would have been challenging enough for any new relationship, even if we — or one of us — had spoken French. But neither of us did. I still felt confident, however, that we could make a success of our time there — with or without French.

It was only years later that I came to understand why learning French had been so difficult for me. It was for a reason I never would have guessed and which I will share with you later.

In October that year, how could I not be aware that the baby

Shadows and Light

girl I had given up for adoption had turned three years old! I resisted thinking of her as "my" baby girl as I knew she was someone else's baby girl by now, but I could not stop from remembering the brief time I had held her three years earlier. I did not have a name for her, so I had to think of her as "baby girl." Would I learn her name someday? Wherever she was I hoped it was in a loving home.

The early months in Paris passed by quickly. Weekdays, I spent my time shopping, cooking, studying French, and reading. I walked around Paris a lot, getting to know the streets around our apartment. This soon produced my favorite shops. On weekends, Michael and I began a routine of doing as much sightseeing and traveling as possible. We began with France and then planned to broaden our reach to other nearby countries. We understood that traveling would be the best part of living in Europe.

When we went somewhere beyond Paris, Michael drove our car, and I did the navigating. I thought I was very good with a map, but on many occasions, he questioned the directions I gave him. He was no more familiar with France than I was so his objections and corrections did not make sense. Maybe he had an innate sense of direction, but I too had a good sense of getting around. I perceived that beyond not trusting my capability, there was an element of his needing to be right.

I soon realized that Michael also needed to control where we went. On one long weekend, we drove to Normandy where we walked the bluffs looking down on Omaha Beach. Below us, exposed to German gunfire and easy targets, Allied troops had landed on D-Day twenty-six years earlier. When we went down to the beach itself, it was equally sobering to look at the steep cliffs and think what horror the Allied troops encountered as a storm of bullets and mortars came down on them. We went on to pay our respects in a couple of cemeteries where row upon row of white crosses testified to the debt we owed to these young men who died at the age we were that day.

It was a very sobering visit, and I was feeling down. I did not want to return to Paris without doing something less sad. On the way back to our hotel in Caen, I said to Michael, "While we are here in this part of Normandy, I would really like to visit Mont St. Michel."

"I have already looked at the map," he said. "We do not enough time to fit in a visit to Mont St. Michel."

Since I really wanted to see Mont St. Michel, I continued, "It looks like a fascinating place, this old monastery perched up on a tiny island. Can we talk about it this evening and see if we can come up with an alternative plan?"

"Maybe," he replied.

We did not go to Mont St. Michel.

This was not the first time I could not get him to compromise on something I really wanted. Why had I not been attuned to this obstinacy before we married? I had, of course, had the opportunity to notice it, if only I had been more aware! There had been the time we were unable to compromise on a church for our wedding. Then there had been the money gift we had received from my parents for a set of china. While I had wanted one pattern, Michael had insisted on a second and we had ended up with the second. Now, only a few months into my marriage, I wondered about why I had not assessed correctly the kind of man I had married. How could I have made such a choice for one that ruled me out?

Had I married my parents?

When I think of this time now, I see a similarity between my passivity in choosing Michael to marry and my passivity in letting the French lessons go. At the time, I did not see any links — neither to these nor to other choices I had let go.

We met couples from Michael's office who invited us to dinner at their homes. Of course, they expected us to reciprocate with a dinner invitation of our own. I could handle two to four people for dinner, but when Michael suggested a cocktail party that would include a number of the people from his office and a few we had been entertained by — at least twenty people, maybe more — I felt intimidated. An extrovert might have been excited by the possibility of meeting this many new people, but as an insecure introvert, this made me anxious. Besides meeting new people and having to chitchat with them, I knew nothing about cocktail parties and serving alcohol to guests, let alone what wine to buy. I was sure I would be judged and found inadequate. I couldn't let a get-together be just a get-together. Being a perfectionist got in the way of my pleasure as I could not even throw an average cocktail party — it had to be perfect. My parents had occasionally had people over to dinner, but it was not on the scale of the cocktail party at which Michael now expected me to entertain.

But I went ahead with the planning. I put all my energy into our first party, asked other women for ideas for food, and put Michael in charge of the alcohol. It was a success, and I even remember receiving compliments from the guests. Some part of me thought, I fooled them all! What was my hardwiring that I could not accept the compliments and let down my guard? Why did I have to be on the defense all the time? Why did I have to be perfect?

That first fall, Michael and I went back to England to visit Aunt Clare who lived in Woodstock, just outside of Oxford. Next, we visited Cousin Dora, a second cousin of my mother's and Aunt Clare's, in the Cotswold region. I was enamored of the name of her town, Stow-on-the-Wold and of the names of other surrounding towns. We had a delightful tea with Dora before heading to Sleaford, where a father and son combo of my paternal ancestors had been rectors of the local Anglican Church for much of the nineteenth century.

Shadows and Light

That fall trip to England was a fun trip, and I got to see some relatives and learn more family history. Michael and I enjoyed traveling here with its numerous pastoral scenes. Perhaps because everything was conducted in English, traveling was more relaxing than in other countries?

Back in Paris, as months went on, we would be out with other people when I noticed that Michael was drinking more than I remembered when we were dating. Before marrying, it had seemed to me sophisticated when we had gone out to Boston restaurants and Michael had insisted on drinks with dinner. But in the short time since we had been married, although his increase in consumption was very gradual, there came a time when, at parties, his speech was slightly slurred and he said things that were out of context; his behavior embarrassed me.

"Susan's grandfather was a bishop," he would announce without much of a prompt to a group of his colleagues and their wives when we were at dinner or at a party. His assertion would have no relevance to the conversation, but Michael was the type of person who "knew everything." When he drank, his insecurities came out. I was proud of my grandfather, the bishop, and had fond memories of him, but I was uncomfortable with the way Michael threw this information out as if it was a surefire access to social standing. It was as if he was seeking approval and needed validation — and by extension, I felt it must have seemed to the group that I also was seeking attention and validation. I was unsure enough of myself to want to avoid this perception. After a few of these half-drunken revelations, I started to dread going out in a group because I worried about how much Michael was going to drink and what he would say. When we did go out, I would inevitably end up stressed and develop a splitting headache. It would take years before I was able to master these headaches and dispel them — and the cause was not somatic: I never had more than one cocktail or glass of wine, both because

Shadows and Light

I was not much of a drinker and because I felt I always needed to be aware of what was developing with Michael.

Back home, perhaps in the morning after, when I attempted to talk to him about how much he drank, how he acted and how it made me feel, Michael would deny there was any sort of problem and that I was making a big deal out of nothing. (It was the sort of reaction I had come to know from my mother. I so disliked it.) His was the usual drinker's response, and as with many drinkers and their spouses, this conversation often ended up in an argument.

That winter of 1970-71, our first in Europe, Michael and I were invited to a party that someone from his office was hosting. At the party, I was introduced to an attractive, personable young man. At one point, I was sitting on the floor opposite him, flirting a bit. When he offered me a cigarette, I accepted. I knew Michael would disapprove; I had given up smoking because I wanted to and knew Michael disliked it when we got married. But I was feeling defiant. I had almost finished my second cigarette when I caught a glimpse of Michael, walking by. He was not steady on his feet. Quickly, I stubbed out the cigarette, got up, and walked over to the entryway where the host of the party and another man were standing with Michael whose speech was now slurred. He was clearly in a bad way, and I knew I had to get him home right away.

Michael & I in Paris apartment, 1970

What happened during the rest of that evening remains a blank. With so many events in my life that prove to be negative,

I have a gift — or a curse — of being able to wipe bad memories out. Since I do not remember anything about the end of this evening, I was fairly sure that something negative must have happened. I knew that it was not drink that caused me to lose contact with what was going on as I kept to my limit of two drinks and would have not passed out. The rest of that evening was one of my many "forgotten incidents" and it was only years later that I received a glimpse of how traumatized I had been by what happened.

The details would emerge many years later due to psychic information from my spiritual counselor. What is certain is that just as my brother had not been able to protect me from a group of boys when I was twelve, Michael, given his inebriated state, had not been able to protect me.

Chapter 4
More Changes

By the spring of 1971, in spite of the considerable charms of Paris, the growing difficulties of my relationship with Michael were wearing me down. The fantasies of the previous year that had led to my marriage could not see me through the incompatibilities of our lives together nor could they compensate for the inner emptiness I so longed to fill. What's more, the aftermath of whatever happened at the party the month before were still with me — a dark feeling that I could not identify.

I was undeniably unhappy and wanted to go home — to go back to Boston. Wanting to vent my frustration and hoping to receive some support and encouragement to leave Michael, I wrote my friend, Kathy. She had been my maid of honor and my trusted friend during the time when my baby girl was born and after. Perhaps she would have an insight on what was best to do and could support me in leaving.

"I can't stand being married to Michael," I wrote from my little seventh floor apartment on Rue du Laos. "I just want to leave him and come home. His drinking is getting to me."

I awaited her reply as I might have awaited a lifeline. I needed someone to propel me out of this relationship. Not only had my marriage to Michael not filled the void that was always with me, but the stress of living with someone with whom I was incompatible had also increased my unhappiness.

Shadows and Light

When her response finally arrived, I opened it, eager to be supported.

"What is the matter with you?" she wrote. "You can't leave him; you just got married. You have to stay."

I was afraid of public disapproval. Unexpectedly, my best friend had disapproved of what I had told her; how much more "THEY" — other friends, people in general, society — would disapprove! Had she suggested that she could make room in her apartment for me to stay temporarily if I decided to leave Michael, I might have had a different life, but she did not. Instead she admonished me. In spite of my instinct that staying with Michael was far from my best interests, I decided I had to stay to work on our relationship. It was a decision of mind over emotions. I had a need to prove myself a responsible adult. After Kathy's response, there was no way — even though I felt like it — that I would end this marriage just yet. It would be flying in the face of public disapproval and courting ridicule: "Susan chalked up another failure."

Because I was not active in making decisions in my life, but a person who constantly reacted to the cues given to me, I let others decide, or at least have a say in, what was best for me. Wanting to be on people's good sides, I felt I should be happy and be able to adjust to Michael's shortcomings and our incompatibilities. Other women with less reason than I to stay in their marriages had succeeded in making them work. Here we were, Michael and I, living in Paris — an opportunity of a lifetime — and I was feeling despondent and dissatisfied. What was wrong with me? Well, staring me in the face was that, after more than a half-year, I still felt I was living with a stranger. I could see little way of making this marriage a happy venture. That is, I could not see how Michael and I could ever enjoy each other's company. On a lesser level, I was bothered by still not being able to speak French to carry on a conversation. Something in me was

Shadows and Light

feeling permanently blocked.

What was the matter with me?

As a result of the stress of living with a man I knew now I did not love, as I had once thought I did, and perhaps even a man I did not like much, especially in social situations, my headaches seemed to come more frequently. Following Kathy's reproach ("What's the matter with you?"), I began to blame myself for much in our relationship. I know I disappointed Michael in that I had turned out not to be the social butterfly, the extrovert who enjoyed socializing with him, that he had once presumed I was. There didn't seem to be anything I could do about that. It was against my nature and his presumption was totally a projection of his need. I, too, was weighted with my earlier projections on Michael.

There were so many little negatives in our relationship: I didn't like driving a stick shift; I couldn't iron his shirts to his liking; and I wouldn't shine his shoes!

What was the matter with me?

Michael was working long hours, and one night, he did not come home. I knew he might arrive late on any given evening, but it never occurred to me he would stay at work all night. He could not call me because the telephone system in our building was shut down, and I had no way of reaching him. Given this situation, I allowed myself to be worried beyond belief and had not been able to sleep thinking that something terrible had happened to him.

When he walked into the apartment the next morning, bleary-eyed and unshaven, I bludgeoned him verbally: "Where were you? I was so worried."

"I had to stay and finish up a project. It was expected of me."

"Did you know before nine, when our telephone shuts down?"

"Yes."

"In the future, please call and let me know or make sure I know that it might be all night."

This sort of demand was not something that was destined to open Michael up to me. He was exhausted from working all night, and my response to him was to be upset. Rather than offer to create some comfort, I criticized him. Today, I believe my onslaught stemmed from my unhappiness and depression. More than anything, I wanted a husband who loved me and took me into his life, not one who did not think of alerting me when he knew he would not be coming home.

I was not part of any activity that seemed meaningful to me and I felt shut out from Michael, my only contact in France, really, and from his work. I had no idea what he was doing since he was not a person who shared, and since I did not meet interesting people every day and did not have projects that were unfolding before me, I had nothing interesting myself to share. At least, that is how it seemed to me. Where another woman might have volunteered somewhere to find some connection—at an American school, for instance — I stayed home alone and grew more depressed. Of course, the inability to make better decisions was part of the territory of depression.

Michael, too, could be very critical of me at times. This would play on my low self–esteem and I would feel I was to blame, responsible, for not correcting the shortcomings he found in me. Part of the problem was me; I had not been happy much in my life, was often shut down with headaches, and always wracked with insecurity. In addition, the long hours Michael worked did not help. He was either not present with me because he was at work, or when he was home, he was tired from the long hours. To my knowledge, he had no male friends in Paris that he could talk to. So, why didn't he talk to me? Here we were — two strangers, far from everything familiar, unhappily living together in a small seventh-floor apartment and not talking to each other.

After permission to escape Michael that I had sought from Kathy had not come, I had let myself accept the long haul with this faltering marriage. Somewhere it is said that repeating the same actions and hoping to get different results is the definition of idiocy. This is what I committed myself to at the end of my first year of marriage.

When the spring weather arrived — flowers in the planters in front of shops, leaves burgeoning in the park, warm sun — it lifted my spirits a bit. I was no longer stuck so much of the day in the seventh-floor apartment with the skylight. Now I could be out in the full sunshine. One long weekend, Michael took time off, and we went to London with another couple, Bill and Laura. This was our third trip to London since we had arrived in Europe. It was fun to be with other people all day and comforting to hear English spoken around me. Laura and I had a traditional afternoon tea at the Ritz. It was spectacular, and I am glad she persuaded me to go with her — having an English tea was something she had wanted to do. The socializing of that weekend was pleasant all around and, of course, there was London to appreciate.

We began to plan a trip to Switzerland and Italy in the early fall. As a girl, I had read the book *Heidi* and so I was really looking forward to visiting the Swiss Alps where Heidi's story took place.

Michael and I had decided to wait to have children until our return to the US. He could only be out of the country for two and a half years due to his army reserve obligation, so postponing a family had seemed to be a sensible decision that did not delay starting our family by much. Two and a half years was not that long a wait. However, I thought the cause of my headaches, occurring more frequently and intensely, might be due to the birth control pills I was taking.

What to do?

My headaches had started when I was a senior at Boston College. I never thought much about them, as my mother said, "Everyone gets headaches." She went on to say that, for a short time as a teenager, she had had bad headaches. She would get nauseous and eventually throw up. Her brother would stay with her and hold her head. Her headaches resolved spontaneously after a year or so. You would think, if she had had this experience as a teenager, she would have had some empathy for me. She did not suggest at the time that I should seek medical help. My mother's lack of empathy reminds me of another time when I was thirteen and we were living in Haiti. I got diarrhea and I recall her saying, "Everyone gets diarrhea here." After I had almost stopped eating, and most likely had lost weight, she finally took me to a doctor who treated me for parasites!

After I started working evenings as a staff nurse on the burn unit at Massachusetts General Hospital, my headaches increased in frequency and intensity so that by January of 1967, it was time to seek relief. I made an appointment with a neurologist. All the tests came back negative. He put me on a medication — thinking I might have cluster headaches — but it did not help. Migraines were not mentioned. At the last visit, he said, "I am not sure what else I can do for you. Are you having problems or stress in your life?"

"Absolutely," I replied. "I don't like my job here at MGH on the burn unit."

"Then you need to quit and find another one."

I stayed because I wanted to prove that I could do the work. As a new graduate from Boston College and not a hospital nursing program, I was given a hard time — collegiate nursing programs were thought to be lacking in the amount of time spent training on the units. I finally quit after I found myself pregnant. I don't recall having headaches when I was pregnant with my baby girl. For the next couple of years, I was depressed and had memory loss from the EST, so I am not sure if I had headaches or not, but I recall them starting up again when I married Michael.

I wanted to go off the birth control pills that spring to see if the headaches would subside. Michael and I opted to use other birth control methods, which, incredibly (since my goal was not to have a baby), I must not have adhered to or we were careless as I got pregnant. While I was in an unhappy marriage and ought not have committed myself to co-parenting with Michael, I did exactly that by not taking command of the situation. Perhaps a clue to what was happening was that I was overjoyed to be pregnant. Pregnancy allowed me to enter again into a fantasy, as I had the previous year when we had married, of creating a loving home with Michael. This pregnancy happened within the context of a marriage that, incredibly, I wanted to believe would provide me with support.

I also hoped that doing this pregnancy "right" would ease the pain I still felt about giving up my baby girl. In the prior three years, seeing a mother with an infant had always brought up pangs of regret and sadness in me. So, becoming pregnant played a therapeutic role in my life, one that I might have unconsciously promoted by opting for an alternative birth control method.

Michael was not thrilled with my being pregnant. Did he sense that our marriage was not stable enough to support parenting? What he expressed, however, was how much parenting would hamper our lifestyle, which consisted of traveling through Europe. I agreed that a baby might slow us down, but in the anticipation and excitement of having a child, I believed I could deal with anything. I was finally happy. What I didn't fully appreciate was that, with this pregnancy, I was now in for a long-term parenting relationship with Michael. Focusing on my baby, I stopped trying so hard to work out a relationship with Michael, and that led me to start to pull away from him.

Then, Michael's company told him it was transferring him to its Brussels office. This seemed like a lateral move and not a promotion; perhaps his company thought he would be a better fit in the Brussels office or perhaps they had a special need there that he could fill. At any rate, he did not speak to me about it in any detail. Michael didn't seem to need to share anything. He didn't confide in me as a friend would. Michael did not appear to want to get to know me nor did he have a need for me to know him, and therefore, to want to understand me or want me to understand him. It was like being with my parents all over again. Had I married someone who was similar to them, someone who wanted a role and not a relationship? (I sensed this is what my parents had done.) Our relationship might have started off on a better footing if we had stayed in Boston for a year before moving to Paris. We would have had time to get to know each other in familiar surroundings rather than being thrown into the confusion of dealing with a different country and culture. And perhaps it would have been easier to separate had we stayed in Boston.

In late September, we followed up on our spring plans to travel in Switzerland and Italy. I was enchanted by the beauty of the Alps. We had a scary ride through one of the passes when Michael felt the brakes of our car starting to fail. Other than the brakes and my morning sickness, this part of the trip fulfilled my fantasy. From there, we went to Florence and Venice. In Florence, I was sidelined by a head cold. Michael took off by himself one day to visit the city while I rested. Unfortunately, I did not see as much of Florence as I had wanted to. In Venice, I was feeling better and we did the usual touristy things. I was thrilled to find some gorgeous shoes that fit me. I have a notoriously hard time finding shoes because of my very narrow feet, but with these orange suede shoes, I felt fashionable. Michael and I seemed to get along better when out by ourselves, away from his work and our everyday routines. But, then again, I was happy being pregnant so I was in a better mood and maybe that was the reason.

Of course, on the trip and afterwards, I wondered what Brussels would be like. I had mixed emotions about leaving Paris since I was just getting settled in after a year there. Another new apartment and new city to get used to! How would Michael do at his job? I would have to make friends. What would it be like to have a baby there? More change was on the way, once again.

The move to Brussels, it turned out, was logistically easy as we had very little furniture, and after only one year of marriage, we had not accumulated much "stuff." We found a two-bedroom furnished apartment in the Woluwe-Saint-Lambert section of Brussels. I had liked another unfurnished apartment more because of its clean, modern kitchen, where it would have been easy to spend time preparing meals. The apartment was also surrounded by trees. But spendthrift Michael was adamant that buying furniture was "an expense that we cannot afford."

"I am tired of living with someone else's furniture," I said. "It would give me something to do to fix up an apartment."

I was a homebody at heart and my nesting instinct, especially with the baby coming, was in full swing. I needed a place of our own that I could furnish and decorate. But as I had learned not to do from living with my parents, I did not stand up for my need. It was often easier that way as I could avoid a conflict that then would have required that I stand up for myself. I also avoided establishing a more solid basis for a relationship with Michael.

Our second-floor apartment in Woluwe-Saint-Lambert was overflowing with furniture and decorative items, so much so that we asked to have some things removed to make the space feel less cluttered. The few pieces we had would certainly have looked out of place in the clutter and so we stored them. Included in the space was an antique trestle table and carved armoire that I liked. The apartment, similar to the one we had left behind in Paris, was small and the bedrooms tiny, but the kitchen, even if not modern, had more space than I had had in Paris. The apartment's location was convenient, within easy walking distance of a trolley stop that went right downtown and close to a street with a laundromat and all the necessary shops.

When we rented the apartment, the owners told us they had a woman, Marie-Josée, who cleaned the apartment, and if we wanted, she would continue to clean for us. I didn't really need a house cleaner since the apartment was small and I had time, not working, but Michael and I made the decision to hire her. She would take good care of the antique furniture — one less worry — and she charged very little. It turned out to be an excellent decision. She spoke no English so she was a good person to practice speaking French with. As we got to know each other, we would chat in French over a cup of coffee in the morning. She did most of the talking.

Brussels was friendlier and more relaxed than Paris. The population is composed of the Flemish who spoke Dutch — the ones I met spoke English and often French as well—and the Walloons who primarily spoke French. In addition to the Flemish and the Walloons, Belgium had a small German-speaking community that lived in the eastern part of the country bordering Germany. Only French was spoken in the small neighborhood shops I went to, and everyone there was willing to help me. For example, in the laundromat, the pregnant owner always helped me operate the machines and she often chatted with me. She was expecting twins, and we were due to have our babies around the same time in May.

To improve my French, I signed up for a weekly class at the

Alliance Française. There I met a student, Natasha, who was to become my friend. She had come to Brussels from Yugoslavia with her husband. Like me, she was unable to get a work permit. Every week after class, Natasha and I would have a coffee and a pastry together. Her English was good, and her French was so much better than mine that she could help me with my pronunciation. She was patient with me as I would try to roll my r's, something I was never able to accomplish.

Susan in Bruges, Belgium

Michael seemed to be more relaxed in Brussels, and he did not drink as much. He was still busy, and this called for working long hours, leaving me alone in the apartment or to spend hours walking around the city by myself, shopping and getting things for the baby. I found an English-speaking obstetrician I liked and felt comfortable with. His wife would subsequently be our pediatrician.

Several years earlier when I had had my baby girl, I had been surrounded by shame and secrecy. I had a story about my "husband" being in Vietnam. My parents did not acknowledge my pregnancy. Then, I had been knocked out with drugs for the birth and had no recollection of being in labor or giving birth. Now I was more present in my pregnancy. As a married woman living with her husband, I found it easier to be pregnant. I was not afraid of giving birth. My nursing training came in handy. I knew what pregnancy and birthing were all about and what to expect.

Once a week, when Michael was home, we enjoyed walking

to one of our favorite neighborhood restaurants for dinner out and we continued to go on day trips on weekends — or go away the whole weekend when time permitted — to explore Belgium. The Netherlands was another country that had intrigued me from childhood, and being as close as we were, I wanted to see the windmills, the tulips, and the wooden shoes filled with flowers hanging in the front of the houses. By now, when we took trips, Michael was accepting the idea that I could read maps and give good directions.

In November of 1971, fourteen months into being away, Michael's company paid for an annual leave. We went back to Boston where we stayed with my parents and at some point, we saw Michaels' parents. One Saturday, we went with a group of Michael's friends to a Boston College football game. Afterwards, as we made our way over to Alumni Hall for a drink, I found myself walking beside Michael's friend, David, at whose house I had met Michael four years earlier. When David married my friend Julie (who "would not have gotten herself pregnant") that was the occasion for Michael and me to get reacquainted. That fall afternoon, Julie, Michael and the others were ahead of us.

"Michael is doing so well right now, isn't he?" said David. "One day, I think he will be extremely successful and become a partner in his company. Don't you think so?"

I paused for a moment to think it over. "I don't think so. I am not sure why I am saying this." David didn't comment, and the conversation switched to life in Paris and Brussels. I think now that this was my intuition kicking in, but at the time, I did not realize I had this gift of intuition. As a little girl, I had shared some intuitions with my mother, and she clearly did not like my doing that. I had stopped connecting to my intuition and had become disassociated from it. It would still take over three more decades before I could reconnect.

That Saturday at Boston College was the first time I can remember thinking that Michael might not be as successful as I had originally believed or had led myself to believe? Our marriage had started with a sojourn in Europe. Surely, I had dreamed, my marriage would go upward from there. Surely, my promising young accountant would continue to offer me even more. But now after this conversation, I could sense there was a different possibility.

That same evening, we went out to dinner with four other couples. Everything was going smoothly, and I was enjoying the easy exchange when I became aware that Michael and one of his friends, Rick — the best man at our wedding who had come up with us to visit Michael's parents — were getting quite loud.

"Oh dear," I said to myself. "I hope they haven't had too much to drink."

I hadn't been paying any attention to how much Michael had to drink. The scene escalated a bit. Michael and Rick were making inappropriate, annoying — fortunately, not sexual — comments to the woman who was waiting on our table. I looked around and could sense that others were embarrassed by their behavior, which was akin to what immature college students might indulge in but not young professionals in their late twenties.

I breathed a sigh of relief when the time came to leave. This was not the behavior of the up-and-coming successful young professional I had once convinced myself I was marrying.

After I started to show and my belly grew in the winter months, I relished the attention I got. I enjoyed being pregnant and was in a much better mood. My headaches had continued to be absent. Everyone was asking about me and how I was doing. I was even offered seats on the trolley when all the seats were taken and someone had to get up. I was not used to people being this thoughtful with me. Michael was sparse with his compliments and had little understanding of what I needed — and my parents had seemed hopeless cases.

Michael's parents, Ken and Mary, were coming soon and would be staying until after the baby was born. Perhaps they would show more support. The idea of being my own center of support was still far from my consciousness.

Chapter 5
Having a Baby in Brussels

My May 1972 due date was approaching. Michael's parents, Ken and Mary, were arriving the first of April. Michael and I both thought it would be good to have some family around when I gave birth to our baby. Mary was a grandmotherly looking woman with curled gray hair and steel-rimmed glasses. She was slightly overweight and had the appearance of someone a child would want to snuggle up to. She was college-educated and had taught school for a short time before she married Ken. After her four children were grown, she had returned to teaching. Our baby would be their thirteenth grandchild.

Since my relationship with my own mother was always tense, I had hopes of a smoother, more loving one with my mother-in-law. My previous contacts with her had been pleasant enough. Maybe Mary would be a mother figure I could talk to and be understood by.

Despite her appearance, however, Mary was not particularly affectionate — no warm fuzzy compliments or hugs. I found it difficult to have a meaningful conversation with her as she talked a lot about her two daughters and her other daughter-in-law and had nothing but praise for them. In my usual insecure way, I felt I would never measure up to these three women. I soon realized Ken and Mary expected me to be a tour guide and a hostess on top of what I was prepared to do in these final weeks of my pregnancy. I had no issues with preparing meals, shopping, and so on, but my in-laws expected me to entertain them every day. I would offer to take them on errands but they were not interested in joining me. Mary was passive and she would not express her needs. My own tendency during these weeks was to run errands, cook, and curl up on the bed with a book when I had a chance.

Ken did go out by himself a couple of times and take the trolley downtown, but Mary had no ambition to go with him. To make matters worse, it rained during the first four weeks of their visit so it was easy to stay indoors and not explore the city on their own. They were each around seventy years old and had no major physical problems or disabilities to prevent greater activity. Soon, I was asking myself why I had agreed to have them come for an extended period.

The sun finally came out on the fourth week of Mary and Ken's visit. It was just a week or two before my due date and I was ready for some distraction. Michael had one whole weekend off, and the four of us drove to the Keukenhof Gardens in the Netherlands. Late April was one of the best times to see the tulips in their prime. This garden — at 79 acres, one of the largest in the world — was spectacular. These several million bulbs bloomed at the same time and the gardens were ablaze with color. We saw more tulips as we drove in the countryside: There were entire fields entirely of red or yellow tulips. This trip helped energize me for the impending labor and birth. Ken and Mary seemed to enjoy the gardens, and I got along well with them. I am sure the sunshine helped, but I also wondered if they behaved differently in Michael's presence.

Michael and I were having trouble picking out names for the baby, but we eventually came up with a compromise, a name that we both agreed on: Timothy. A girl's name wasn't a problem as we agreed on two.

My contractions started on a sunny, warmish Sunday morning, the seventh of May. I was fairly sure I was in labor, but since the contractions weren't too strong, I decided to finish putting the rollers in Mary's hair and then I would call my obstetrician. When I called, he said, "Susan, come over to the hospital now. I will be there when you arrive." Michael was getting anxious. I kept assuring him that I was just fine, and everything was going to be okay. As we were driving to the hospital, I was thinking how different it was from when I had had my baby girl four and a half years earlier. I was doing it right this time. I was married and my husband was driving me to the hospital. Most important of all, I would be able to keep and raise this baby. I felt such a relief knowing that whatever was ahead of me in the next few hours, I could deal with it. Hopefully, I would be able to experience the birth with my eyes wide open, not knocked out by a drug.

Our son, Timothy, was born that afternoon at 3:30. The birth went along without a hitch, and I was wide awake the whole time, not requiring any medications. I was beaming with joy and was proud to show Tim off to my visitors.

Five days later when I went home, Ken and Mary were still there. I was tired and did not feel up to doing all the household chores. Mary helped out a bit with the cooking, but she wouldn't go grocery shopping. One morning, she saw me stressed out and asked, "What can I do to help today?"

"It would be such a help if you could go to the laundromat for me. With all the baby's things, the clothes are piling up," I said.

"Ken and I don't know how to speak French, and we don't know the money," she replied.

I explained, "It is really not hard. I will give you the coins you need and tell you how many to use for the washer and dryer. The owner is very friendly and will help you out."

She wouldn't agree to spell me however so, without the support I needed, I ended up going to the laundromat by myself. In postpartum hormone swing mode, I was feeling overwhelmed with an infant, in a foreign country, without friends to confide in. My one friend, Natasha, who came to see me in the hospital, wanted to get pregnant and was not able. How could I confide in her about the difficulties of being a new mother?

When Michael came home from work that day, he found his parents in the living room. His mother was crying. He found me crying in our bedroom with Tim.

"What on earth is the matter?" he asked me.

"Your mother says she wants to help and do something, but when I asked her to go to the laundromat today, she said she and your father couldn't do it because they don't know the money or the language. They said it would be too difficult. It is a half-block down the street and I am sure the owner, who is really nice and has always helped me in the past, would have helped your parents as well. Going to the laundromat would have been the biggest help to me."

I just wanted to spend time with my newborn son and not have all these irritations about domestic chores and worries about getting along with my in-laws. I decided I would make the effort in the last few days of their visit to get along with my in-laws and keep my emotions at bay. It worked and there were no more meltdowns even though they stayed in the apartment most of the time. I concentrated on caring for Tim and did not ask Mary to help except where she would not feel threatened, as with meal preparation. My mother and father were coming in two months for their visit. I hoped their visit would be easier, but then again, I knew better. I wouldn't get the attention I craved, but at least they wouldn't expect to be entertained.

After my in-laws left, I settled into a routine with Tim. I took him for walks in his carriage and to the store to pick up something for dinner. Getting around was easy because Michael had by then bought an old, automatic VW station wagon for me. These days were a quiet time that I enjoyed, but it would have been helpful to have a friend with a baby or young child to talk to. When Marie-Josée came to clean, I soon saw that she loved babies and was enthralled with Tim. I asked if she would be willing to look after him when I went out to run errands. I didn't care about how much cleaning she did. She was so pleased when I asked. She told me that she cleaned for another couple who had just had a baby, but they wouldn't let her go near the baby.

Michael was getting adjusted to having a baby around. He wasn't into helping change a diaper — I understood some men wouldn't — but he would hold Tim in the evening while he read the paper and I was cleaning up from dinner. I did leave Tim with Michael one weekend when I went to have my hair cut. When I was walking home, I looked up at our apartment building and could see into the guest room window, which was a large one. Michael was pacing and had Tim in his arms. As I walked in the door, he yelled, "What took you so long? I can't find the pacifier. He won't stop crying."

I took Tim from him and looked around for the pacifier. "It's here somewhere."

I soon found the pacifier and popped it into Tim's mouth. He calmed right down.

I said to Michael, "I am sorry you couldn't find the pacifier. I fed Tim just before I left so I thought he would sleep."

"It didn't work."

"Next time, I will make sure you know where at least two pacifiers are."

"If there is a next time," he murmured as he left the room.

What a disappointment that was. I had hoped Michael would show a little more interest in looking after Tim. Parenting didn't seem to come naturally to him — at least then. Would he ever change?

Shadows and Light

In July, after visiting my Aunt Clare in England, my parents crossed the channel to see us in Belgium. After the uncomfortable visit with Michael's parents, I was looking forward to seeing my parents. At least, I knew their quirks and had learned to work around them, but I was apprehensive about how they would react to their new grandson. I wanted them to be appreciative about how wonderful he was. Despite what I knew about my parents, I still wanted them to tell me I had the most beautiful baby in the world.

To meet his grandparents at the Brussel-Nationaal / Bruxelles-National where I drove to pick them up, I had dressed Tim in a blue sailor outfit; he looked adorable. I couldn't wait for my parents to fuss over him. When we got to the airport, I found a parking place and put Tim in his stroller. Entering the airport lobby, I looked over the heads of the people and searched for the tallest man — my father was six-feet, eight-inches tall. When I saw him in the distance, I rushed as fast as I could.

"Over here, over here," I shouted as I waved my arm. As I approached, I noticed my mother wasn't smiling, or looking even remotely pleased to see me or her new grandchild. My father greeted me with about the same amount of enthusiasm — almost none. It was as if they were thinking of something else. We exchanged our usual semi-hugs, and when it came time to fuss over Tim, they didn't. They did not get down to his eye level nor did they ask to hold him as I imagined most grandparents seeing a grandchild for the first time would have.

Again, I had set myself up to be deflated by my parents. I continued to want something from them that was just not available. While their lukewarm greeting was really not a surprise, it was a disappointment. What did I know about them that would have led me to believe they would react differently? Nothing, yet I wanted more! After not seeing them for some time, it was wishful — and unrealistic — thinking on my part that they might have changed and greeted me and Tim with, at the very least, a big, animated smile. The emotional component was simply not there. I still could not face the fact that I did not have the parents I needed. I still hoped that one day they would be different. I was still not dealing with what it was in me that continued to have this unrealistic aspiration.

The rest of the visit was unremarkable. Since neither one of my parents was demanding, they did not require being catered to. My mother took Tim for walks in the neighborhood in his carriage, which she seemed to enjoy and that helped me. My father took the trolley downtown to spend time touring by himself. My parents were distant with each other and did nothing together. A silent detachment surrounded them. I had always observed the lack of affection between them, and in the several years since I had lived with them, their relationship had clearly deteriorated; they were not communicating on any but a basically civil level. I would not uncover the reason until the following year, after Michael and I were back in the US.

While my parents were still visiting, we had arranged to have Tim baptized with other babies during a Catholic Mass in an English-speaking church. Tim looked beatific in a christening gown from my mother's side. It was what I, as well as others in my family — for at least two generations, maybe three — had worn. We had asked Michael's older brother by twelve years, John, to be the godfather. He had come with his wife, Marilyn. Our friends from Paris, Matt and Rachel, also came. We had asked Rachel to be Tim's godmother.

As I was walking out of the church beside my mother, and as I was thinking that the Mass and the baptism had gone well, she blurted out, "That was the worst church service I have ever been to in my entire life." Fortunately, no one else in the baptism group heard it.

Was she reacting this way because she had not accepted that Michael was Catholic and that we baptized our baby in the Catholic Church? Or was she perhaps merely reacting to missing her music in the high Episcopal church she and my father went to? I had to admit to myself the mediocrity of the organist and the guitarist, but the event was not about the music: it was about participating in Tim's baptism Why did my mother have to complain? She might have expressed her criticism in a gentler way. In my self-conscious way, I took her reaction to be a rejection of me, Michael, and Tim. Keeping her feelings to herself would have been an even better option.

Tim's Baptism

I know we must have had everyone back for a meal, but the details remain in a fog. I assume that my mother's comment had dampened the day. Placing memories in a fog is a response I have to negative events, blocking them out rather than dealing with them. These blanks occurred over decades. I went memoryless and did not know I had done so until later. In the moment, I let others color my feelings rather than take ownership of them. I could not say to myself, "This is about my mother and has nothing to do with me. Why should I let her reaction be an influence on how I feel about my day?" I also had the habit of putting a lot of pressure on myself and never felt that I measured up. I felt that Michael's older brother and his wife were a tough act to follow: he was a successful businessman and she was the ultimate, outgoing hostess that I was not.

After my parents left, I reveled in motherhood and enjoyed looking after Tim. Michael drove our car to work every day and now that I had my own car, I could get to doctors' appointments and out shopping. I had more freedom and independence in my mobility but not in my finances. Up to now, Michael had been in charge of our finances, and at first, that was fine with me; I thought that his being an accountant would make him better at taking charge. This was not proven true. While I saw ways we could be saving, Michael did not. For one example, soon after we came to Belgium, Michael decided to buy a new BMW for himself and have it shipped back with us to the States. He wanted to avail himself of the more advantageous European price, but I worried that, even with the savings of a European purchase, a BMW presented a big-ticket price. We would be left with no down payment when it came time to settle in the US with a house of our own. Michael should have been thinking about holding on to our savings rather than spending it on an expensive car.

My sister, Clare, who was going to be working in Vienna, came to visit at the beginning of September 1972. She had spent her junior year in Austria and had opted to return for work. She had a job lined up and the plan was she would land in Brussels, and then we would drive her to Vienna in the VW station wagon we had bought for me. While it was an older vehicle, we needed the space for luggage and baby paraphernalia. Michael would take his own two-week vacation then so we would have time for sightseeing. It seemed like a good plan. The fact that Clare spoke German would be a help as we were soon to find out.

The first part of the trip went well, and Tim was a good traveler for a four-month-old. While Clare did not show much interest in Tim, she had agreed to look after him when Michael and I went out to dinner in the evening. We would get her something to eat before we left. Her lack of interest didn't bother me as I know some people are not very good with babies while others are always playing with them and doing silly things to make them laugh. Clare was more like my mother in that respect. Traveling with a baby did cramp our style a bit, but we still were able to do a lot. For the most part, Tim was a good sleeper.

The second day, as we were driving in the German countryside, the VW station wagon suddenly broke down. There were no stores or houses in sight. What on earth were we going to do? It was 1972, and there was no such thing as a cell phone. The plan we came up with was for Michael and Clare, who spoke German, to hitch a ride to the nearest town and find a garage while I stayed in the VW station wagon with Tim. During what seemed a very long wait, I let myself think of all the worst possible scenarios. What if they got lost? What if they couldn't find someone to fix the car? What if they never come back? What if, stranded out in the Austrian countryside with a baby and not speaking a word of German, I had to make my own way out? Somehow, as odd as it sounds, worry was comforting. It provided a pattern of response that I was good at and familiar with.

I am not sure how long Michael and Clare were gone — it seemed like forever — but when I saw a repair truck pull up, I sighed with relief. The mechanic got the VW fixed, and we were soon on our way to Vienna. When I look back at this incident, I think I was anxious because I was waiting for the next bad thing to happen. Up to then, I had forgotten a lot of what had happened to me in childhood, but many bad things had happened and these had left me ripe for being anxious. It would be a long time before my past came clear to me.

Just before we got to Vienna, we realized Clare was depressed. When I pressed her for some information, she revealed she was not happy about her potential life and job in Vienna. She regretted having accepted the offer. We talked options: take up being in Vienna and make the most of the work, or quit the job even before she began and go back home to Boston.

We had a few good days in Vienna. Because the hotel we stayed at had a babysitting service, we were able to go one night to the opera to see Carmen. The theater itself was truly magnificent. While our seats were not good due to a partially obstructed view — I stood occasionally to see what was going on below me — the experience of being in a grand music hall and hearing this renowned opera made up for it.

By then, Clare had decided not to stay in Vienna but to return home to Boston. From there, I sent a telegram to my mother saying, "Clare fine; job not. Returning on Flight …."

With Clare now on her way back to the US, I suggested that Michael and I go to Salzburg on our return home. I was attracted by its combination of architecture, culture, and Mozart. As with Mont St. Michel, Michael did not want to go to Salzburg and would not compromise his plans for us to go there, even if only briefly. This reminded me that Michael didn't listen to me or try to understand that going to Salzburg was important to me. This disagreement was another harbinger that did not bode well for our marriage. I felt a return to the days before Tim was born when I was so unhappy with Michael. Motherhood was proving not enough to soften my disappointment over my marriage, and my own temperament was not strong enough to oppose Michael. Now there was a baby in this unhappy marriage.

From Vienna, the three of us headed home.

Eventually, when I spoke to my mother via an expensive transatlantic line when I was back in Brussels, I was surprised to learn that she thought it was my fault that Clare did not stay in Vienna and accused me of persuading her to return to Boston. I assured her that it was Clare's decision and not mine, but my mother would not change her mind. She was adamant about not accepting that Clare was a young adult and a college graduate totally capable of making her own decisions. Again, I was butting

Shadows and Light

up against my mother's narcissism.

The winter passed by quickly. During the days, I was busy at home, and Michael was still very busy at work. I had stopped going to French classes, but I hired a tutor to come to the apartment once a week to teach me. The tutor came in the morning when Tim was taking a nap. We hired a babysitter through an agency for Saturday nights so Michael and I could go out — a woman who lived close by who wanted some extra money while her husband played cards with his friends on Saturday nights. It worked out very well for both sides. I was totally comfortable with her.

Then, in April of 1973, it was time to pack up and move back to Boston so Michael could finish his military reserve duty. I was also looking forward to returning home, but at the same time I was sad to leave. I felt I was just really settling in to living in Brussels, making friends, and establishing some roots. It was especially sad to say goodbye to Marie-Josée. She was very attached to Tim and she cried profusely when I told her we were returning to the US.

Coming home to Boston seemed like the beginning of my real life after the dream life of Europe.

Chapter 6
Unraveling and Putting Myself Back Together Again

Our time in Europe came to an end in the spring of 1973. Returning to Massachusetts without a home of our own to go to, Michael and I were initially grateful to live with my parents in West Roxbury until we could find our own place. Being in their home was not easy, especially with my mother smoldering with anger. I could see her jaw tense as she kept her emotions in control and did not lash out. It was a look I was familiar with, remembering it from so many other times, from when we had first talked about my being pregnant, for instance, as we sat outside my rented cottage on Cape Cod. Hers was a set jaw that had loomed over my childhood. And that jaw continued to harden that spring.

Shirts with a floral pattern were popular for men in the 1970s, but my mother did not like that my father had bought two for himself and would make comments whenever he wore either one. Perhaps having had enough of her remarks, my father asked what I thought of them. Wanting not to take sides but needing to be honest, I said, "They are fine. All the guys are wearing them now. They are the trend."

My mother was upset with me, obviously inferring that I was agreeing with him in some argument they were having. What I didn't know then was that my father had spoken with her about

Shadows and Light

being gay, and she was grappling with that revelation. (She must have thought floral patterns were effeminate and associated that with being gay.) My father's shirts (and this is my best bet) embarrassed her because she believed they shouted gayness. Any woman would have had a difficult time accepting that her husband was gay, but at the time, I did not know what was going on and it was not appropriate to involve me.

Given the tension at my parents' house, I was anxious for us to find our own place as soon as possible. Even though Michael had a well-paying job as a CPA in one of the big accounting firms, we didn't have money saved for a down payment. We had spent our extra money on traveling while living in Europe and on the new BMW. It would have come in handy now. Fortunately, my mother was willing to lend us enough for a down payment on a house in Southborough, Massachusetts, a suburb not far from Boston. Perhaps she wanted the quiet of her house back or perhaps the tension with my father was something she wanted to live privately. At any rate, she helped us buy a house.

The house in Southborough we bought was close to the turnpike. We thought this proximity would make the commute into the city easier for Michael. Unfortunately for me, the isolation and the sameness of a suburban life was a culture shock after having lived in Paris and Brussels. I was isolated in a neighborhood where there were only houses and no stores, no restaurants, no businesses — no coming and going. The big house we moved into needed a lot of housekeeping, which would fall to me as the stay-at-home mother, though Michael did take responsibility for mowing the lawn, and he planted a small vegetable garden. Even food shopping was alienating as supermarkets were time-consuming with their endless choices.

Most of the other mothers in the neighborhood were like me in that they did not work outside the home, but their children were older than Tim, who was still a toddler. They were involved in many activities, and so I made an effort to know a few of the neighborhood women by joining in some of their activities. I took tennis lessons and joined a women's club, but still, there was no one I bonded with.

Soon after moving in, I found myself pregnant with our second child. I enjoyed being pregnant so the pregnancy would not be a problem. My headaches vanished again, and I remembered that this had also happened when I was pregnant with Tim. When I was out in public, just as in Brussels, I got some long-needed attention that I never felt I had enough of from Michael. He continued to work long hours and was not home until late in the evenings. We welcomed our new baby boy, Peter, into the world on December 10, 1973. He was a calm, quiet baby.

Peter's Baptism

What ensued was a long winter of isolation. I was now shut up most of the day with only the company of a toddler and a baby. Michael stayed at the office way beyond supper, which made the evening tasks of getting the children washed and to bed more difficult, since he was not there to share the work. (I would have enjoyed the companionship of doing these family chores together.) Because Michael was absent to me as a friend and helpmate, my life was a solitary one, during the day and through the evenings. I was lonely without much adult interaction. How I needed a good friend to talk to in that suburban life, but I supposed this isolation would be temporary. Life would soon be easier, or so I thought.

By the fall of 1974, nothing had changed. My loneliness had hardened into sadness, and once again, I was slipping into the pit of depression. I knew I was in trouble and needed help. Fortunately, I was always able to take care of my children. I ate with them, as I had given up waiting for Michael to have dinner with when he got home. Once the boys were in bed for the night, I would lie on the sofa, not reading or watching TV, flat on my back. When Michael finally came home, which seemed to be always late after I had dozed off, I would get up, heat his dinner and go right back to the sofa, leaving him to eat by himself. After four years in a marriage that I now knew ought not to have happened, I was understandably unhappy, and Michael must have been as well. Who would want to come home after working all day and deal with a sad, emotionally depleted wife lying on the sofa? He must have wondered what happened to the Susan he thought he had married, the Susan he believed was happy and fun-loving. Even then, he must have had thoughts of leaving me.

He did not seem to understand his hours away left me without enough freedom to rest and explore life more than I could with two little children. He did not sit with me and say, "Susan, what can I do for you?" Instead, he continued to invest long hours at work — where was his family in his work life? — and to leave me to my own devices, which were less and less adequate.

That same fall, after we had been back in the States about eighteen months, my parents decided to split up, but neither spoke to me about what they were doing. Although they lived only 25 miles away and a face-to-face conversation was easy to arrange, instead of sitting with me, they both wrote letters.

My father wrote, *"I don't expect you to understand even though your generation is more understanding than mine. I make no apologies or excuses. I have learned to accept myself as I am, as God has made me and have found inner peace."*

My father had gone on to write, *"You have been such a won-*

derful source of comfort to Mother, and I know you will continue to be so. It grieves me deeply to see her suffering so much, but I feel totally unable to help her."

I was surprised that he thought that I had been so good with my mother.

My father's letter continued, "All I ask is for your continuing love, even though at present I may seem unlovable to you, my dear daughter, and I hope you shall be able to return that love, no matter what happens. We must always keep the lines of communication open."

He was writing in code but I knew he was telling me that he was gay. Finally, he was "coming out." It was then that I realized that I had always known he was gay but I didn't know how or when I knew. When discussing it with Michael, he recalled that I had questioned it a couple of years earlier but I could not recall that conversation. While my father's words seemed to be proof that he loved me, why did I never feel that he did? Was it love he felt or was it more affection because of a shared past?

When I went to talk to my mother, I had no idea if I was comforting to her. She did say later that I accepted their news far better than my brother or sister. Was that what was comforting to her?

Around this time, while I kept thinking of suicide, I knew I would never, this time, try to follow through with these thoughts. I would not put my two sons through the trauma of losing their mother; I loved them dearly, and their welfare always came first with me.

I was in a major depressive episode, and I needed help to get through it. To help assure that I would not slip into killing myself, I made an appointment with my former psychiatrist, Dr. O'Brien. While my faith in him was non-existent after he had ordered shock therapy years earlier, I didn't know anyone else to consult. Perhaps it was because of my depressive mood, but it did not occur to me to conduct a search for a more compatible doctor. I was that isolated, that powerless, that I accepted passively an inadequate connection as my only choice. Of course, being depressed, I had weak will power.

Dr. O'Brien had moved his office to a different location, and the non-descript furniture that had seemed so ugly when I had consulted him during the year after my baby girl had been born had been replaced with more comfortable furniture and some decorative artwork. Fortunately, he referred me to a new counseling group called Liberty Street Associates, and I accepted his judgment. When I showed up at their office in Newton, I was assigned to a licensed psychologist named Gwen whom I started to see for individual sessions.

Gwen recommended that I go after the holidays to Liberty House, a residential program her counseling group ran. I knew I needed help, and by getting help, I knew I would be a better mother for my children. I agreed to go for them and for my marriage. I was faltering in my role as a wife. I knew we had marital problems but before those could be addressed, I needed to delve into my psyche and find out what was causing all this angst.

My identity as a person was almost nonexistent. I felt that no one cared about me. I concluded the reason Michael didn't want to come home early was so as not to have to spend the evening with me. I was sure it would be good for Michael to have a break from me.

Both Michael and I agreed that an intervention would be an opportunity for me to recalibrate myself, but who would look after the boys? Michael could not take the time from work and no vacation days saved up. We probably could have hired a full-time babysitter, but that would have been a squeeze financially. Coming to the rescue again, my brother Mark and his wife Linda — who was the nurturing, quintessential mother — agreed to take the kids in. Since Linda was at home all day, it was really she who made the commitment. I will always love her for her generosity.

While I knew the boys would be in good hands, I wished that Mark and Linda didn't live in New Hampshire, as that meant that neither Michael nor I would see our sons for six weeks. Michael could have gone to see them on the weekend — almost a three-hour drive one-way — but chose not to. I am not sure why. I was not allowed out of Liberty House.

With childcare settled, there was the cost of the program to be considered. Fortunately, Michael's Aunt Eva agreed to foot the bill for therapy at Liberty House. She was a lovely, generous person who had helped Michael out in the past.

With trepidation, now that the logistics were arranged, and as 1974 turned into 1975, I prepared to go. With no idea what I was getting myself into, I was taking a leap of faith into the unknown to have a better life than I was now experiencing.

The Liberty House program was loosely based on a drug-rehab program, as far as I knew at the time. We were pretty much shut off from society and family. No phone calls could be made during the week, and we were only allowed one visitor on Sunday for a limited time. We did leave once to go see a movie; other than that, we did not go outside even for a walk. The rules and regimen were strict: no sex, no alcohol, one pack of cigarettes per day, all meds and drugs under lock and key. Prescription drugs were given when needed. The residents did all the cooking and cleaning. Except for a half hour after dinner, we were kept busy from the time we got up until lights went out at night.

The first week was living hell for me. I had trouble sleeping and eating. I was used to my own cooking, and the food cooked by the residents was often not up to my standards. I had a constant headache and lost ten pounds. I slept in a room with three other women; we had bunk beds and a small shared bath. Fortunately, I bonded with one of these women. After lights out, Pam and I would sit in the bathroom — one on the bathtub edge and the other on the toilet seat — and talk, smoking our last cigarette of the day.

When not working at maintenance chores — cleaning, cooking, and laundry — we were scheduled for a wide range of exercises, games, role playing, art projects, writing, psychodrama, and so on, to get our emotions out so we could talk about them. The process started to work for me. My emotions were freed for the first time in my life and they spilled out in the open. I not only got angry at people for the first time ever, but I also expressed it. Getting in touch with my anger was a profound revelation, and I started to enjoy expressing myself. We used batakas (soft foam bats) to hit pillows to release anger. This discharge felt so invigorating!

One of the assigned work jobs was to inspect the bedrooms for perfectly-made beds and for dresser drawers with aligned and neatly folded clothes. As I was checking one of the men's bedrooms one morning, a younger man, whom I felt a bit intimidated by since he had been in jail for armed robbery, entered the room. He grabbed me and pulled me toward him. As he bent to kiss me, I took my clipboard and whacked him over the head. He never said a peep and walked out; he didn't mention it again and neither did I. I was stunned that I had done this, but I felt great to have stood up to him. I was slowly learning, although I admit that hitting isn't the best response.

One day, I had a really bad headache and so I asked for an aspirin. I was told, "Go think about why you are giving yourself a headache." I was really mad because, in my usual manner, I felt I was not understood. Nobody seemed to realize how severe these headaches were. I wanted the pain relief and not the work of asking myself why I was in pain. Years later, I was to learn the efficacy of asking myself such a question, but at the time I was still hidden from myself — although I was leaving my unconscious cocoon.

While at Liberty House, I was seeing my psychologist, Gwen, who came up on a weekly basis for sessions with her clients. All the residents also had to have one meeting in which both their parents and their counselor would be present. As I approached the room where my parents — still living apart — were waiting, I was very nervous, but I was also excited that I might resolve some issues by bringing them to light. Before I walked into the room where my mother was waiting, I overheard her speaking.

"How inconvenient for me that Susan is here and I had to come; I am so busy right now with my own problems."

Some things never change. Nonetheless I went in determined to speak honestly and bravely. During our time together, I said to my parents, "I grew up feeling that you never loved me."

"Of course, we love you," my mother answered in a matter of fact manner with no emotion attached. Avoidance was her recurring response instead of something more honest like "Tell us what we did that led you to feel that way?"

After my mother said this, I felt so deflated! True to my upbringing, I, too, avoided confrontation. That day, I was a "good girl" for her benefit and to my detriment. As I shared other things with her, she answered with platitudes like, "That's nice, dear." There was no look of surprise or animation in her face, however. And a hug or an excited body gesture? Forget it! I don't recall my father saying anything important either; he probably nodded in agreement. This was odd for a person like him who worked with people every day and yet had so little sense of supporting me.

After a six-week residency at Liberty House, my mood was much better and I felt I could cope with life once again. Coming home, I was overjoyed to see my sons and, to my surprise, to be home with Michael. I would be going weekly to group therapy, to couples therapy with Michael, as well as to an individual session with Gwen as needed. Looking back, I appreciate that I certainly did a lot of work, but I now believe it was a bandage solution. I know that anger turned inward can cause depression, but I still did not know why I was so angry nor how to release that anger so that it would not continue to harm me.

Before an individual session with Gwen one day, as I was checking in, the receptionist told me my mother was coming in the next day to see Gwen. Hearing that sent my emotions running high, as my relationship with my mother was always tense and I was always on the ready to expect a threat. Once inside Gwen's office, I needed to talk about my mother's visit, about why she was coming. I was aware of client confidentiality but that did not stop me from inquiring. Gwen suggested that I might talk with my mother after her visit to inquire about the session. If my mother wanted to share its content, Gwen told me, that was her choice as, she would not be bound by confidentiality.

Apparently, all the counseling I was having was beginning to pay off as I followed through and called my mother at the weekend to set up a time to see her. I was determined to have a face-to-face conversation, but I was also apprehensive because we rarely got together even though we were living less than thirty minutes apart.

That weekend, at her house, my mother told me, "I went to see Gwen about you so she could help me learn how to handle you."

How to handle me? I was into my thirties. Did she still think of me as a recalcitrant child?

"I gave up on you when you were six years old. I didn't know how to handle you."

There it was at last! As I had always known, a shift happened when my sister was born and I was six. From then on, my mother treated me differently from my brother and sister. More than once, I recall her saying, "I like to take you out because you are good with other people. At home, I like Mark and Clare better than you."

Interestingly, I resembled no one in my family — I was the only fair-skinned blonde — which didn't help my sense of belonging with these people. In the winter, because of my coloration, my cheeks were not rosy — the epitome of healthy children, according to my mother — but mottled with red spots. I was reminded about this more than once.

Other than for the holidays and birthdays, I always did the contacting with my mother. At one point, I decided to test her to see how long it would take for her to contact me. It took her three months to call me! She never seemed interested much in seeing me or her two adorable little grandsons. She never spoke to me about what a good job I was doing as a mother. It would have been heartwarming to have some words of support from her!

Susan with baby sister Clare
1950

Of course, I never knew fully what was discussed in the meeting as Gwen could not tell me due to confidentiality and my mother was not about to begin to share since she had never done so. The conversation I had with my mother about her visit to Gwen reinforced the concept that people did not understand me, but it reinforced more than that: it hardened my sense that there must be something wrong with me.

Michael and I saw Gwen for couples therapy. Unfortunately,

in spite of my having been her patient for half a year already, she listened to him more intently than to me, and there was something in how she spoke to him. She was easier on him and far less challenging. What was happening in those sessions paralleled my family dynamics when I was a child. Once again, I felt that I was the one out of favor; I was the different, difficult one causing the trouble. After a while, Michael and I stopped going to see Gwen together since we were doing better as a couple, but Michael continued to consult her from time to time. I was learning more about myself in group therapy and continued to go every week.

Chapter 7
Remembering Trauma and Looking for Maggie

That spring of 1975, after my stay at Liberty House, I started standing up for myself with Michael and with others. My bottled anger was coming uncapped, and I must have been difficult to live with. While getting anger out may be a first stage of healing for an individual, it is not a useful tool for patching a relationship. This state of affairs continued through the summer, and consequently, in the autumn of 1975, Michael and I separated after five years of marriage. I was well aware that Michael and I might not come back together and our separation might lead to a divorce. In that case I would need to work, so I took action to prepare myself. I hired a babysitter — the children had stayed with me at the house — so I could take a refresher course in nursing at Boston College. I hadn't worked as a nurse in five years, and I would need this course to land work. I also needed the stimulation of people and learning.

After Christmas, after three months apart, Michael and I agreed that we would try to make our marriage work again and we got back together. I made a conscious decision to postpone working until the boys were a bit older and in elementary school. I would have worked if I had had to but staying with them seemed a better decision while they were so young.

In the summer of 1976, we moved from Southborough to Newton. Newton was closer to Boston, and Michael would have less of a commute. I hoped the move would be a new start for us as we were both committed to working on our marriage and making it a success. The new house was roughly the same price as the one we sold and so the move was not a change in our financial set-up. Since there were several young families in our immediate neighborhood, I hoped I would make a close friend among the mothers.

Newton House

That fall, I signed up for a weekly yoga class. Michael supported this by committing to coming home from work earlier on my yoga evening. He would put the boys to bed while I went off to the class. At the end of the first session, when doing the total relaxation, I had an epiphany. Lying on my mat, I was conscious of my body being relaxed. This was a new sensation, and it felt so good! In each subsequent yoga class, I tried to relax totally but always some body part or muscle would not cooperate or I would retain just a bit of a headache. Unfortunately, the total relaxation didn't happen again for a long time, but the experience was enough to hook me into continuing the class.

As I persisted in my yoga practice, my overall flexibility improved. I felt stronger and more toned. After a few weeks as I was trying once again to do the total relaxation at the end of class, rather strange images popped into my mind. One was of basement windows in an apartment. I recognized the scene as the cellar of a school dormitory where my family lived when I was eleven and twelve years old; another image was of straps in a desk drawer and of a curtain blowing in the breeze.

There were no words, just images coming to me as I relaxed, or as I would say, "Let down my guard." What were these images about and why were they coming to me? What forgotten — or obliterated — memories were bubbling up at last to consciousness? Since my electroshock treatments eight years earlier, I knew I had lost a few memories of my life before that time and so the truth of parts of my life were hidden from me. Was I emotionally ready to learn the meaning of these images now, which might be why the unconscious was releasing them to me, or had the shock treatments started to wear off and memories of what I had always known were now returning to me?

Slowly I came to understand that something traumatic had happened to me in that basement.

In 1956, my father taught at Shattuck Military Academy in Faribault, Minnesota. It was a boy's preparatory school, and our family lived in a small, three-bedroom apartment on the first floor of a dormitory. There, I shared a room with my sister. We had twin beds with wrought-iron headboards and a single dresser. The single dresser was not a problem as neither Clare nor I had many clothes. My mother was not teaching at Shattuck as she did later when we moved to Boston. I assume she spent time going out with friends she had made and volunteering at the local Episcopal church. Since we ate our meals in the dining hall with the boys, my mother didn't have to cook or go food shopping. Even though she had all sorts of free time to shop and cook, often there were no snacks — either bought or home-made — in the apartment when I came home from school. I had a friend over one time, and when I looked in the cupboards for a snack to share

Shadows and Light

with her, I was embarrassed to find the only thing there was dog food. To avoid this sort of embarrassment — "What kind of mother does Susan have?"!"— I usually went to my friend's house if I could. I mention this to underline how my mother was not a nurturing woman who was vigilant about caring for her children. Why didn't it occur to her that growing children often need snacks between meals?

What actually happened in that Shattuck School basement that came to haunt me in images on the yoga mat? It had to do with a group of boys, and evidently, I was raped. I say "evidently" since I do not remember the circumstances. I did tell my obstetrician, Dr. Murphy, about it before I had the EST treatments which wiped out my memory and I verified having told him later. In that way, I had held on to these memories.

I do recall having a heated argument with my mother — this was unusual so I suspect it was right after this basement incident — because I refused to go to dinner in the dining hall. While she insisted that I eat there, I was adamant that I would not. I did not want to see the boys who had been in the basement, and I held my ground. My mother, for all of the moments of psychic insight she claimed to have had, was not really intuitive. Rather than sensing there was something that "Susan needs from this," she saw only the inconvenience that I was creating. Rather than speak kindly to me when she saw how adamant I was — "surely something must have disturbed Susan deeply!" — and offer to bring me a tray, she said, "All right, you can stay home but you'll have nothing to eat for dinner except bread and water."

And so, I had no dinner that night. While I had not told my mother about what had happened to me, I wanted her to guess that something out of the ordinary must have happened for me to be acting this way. But it was not in her nature to be sensitive, nor was it in mine to ask for what I needed.

That evening, hungry and scarred from an experience that I

could not speak about, I felt totally alone and uncared for. Looking back, I grieve for that twelve-year-old who had to submit later to facing her abusers day after day for breakfast and dinner.

I have no idea if I ever told my mother about what had happened. I doubt it, and if I had, I don't think she would have believed me. My brother was fourteen at the time, and if I was home, he probably would have been home as well. I wonder if Mark could have been involved as well in the basement scene with the other boys?

Another memory recapture I experienced came back to me at a different time. I mention it here because I believe it influenced the depression that characterized these years in the 1970s. Around 2010, I was revisiting some of my life's memories when I realized that I did not recall my entire seventh-grade life, when my father taught at the Shattuck School, with two exceptions: a vague recollection of being in the music room playing a clarinet when we lived at Shattuck School, and a memory of sewing a skirt in Home Economics. But I have no picture in my mind of the local school I went to nor any teachers or classmates. Interestingly, I have a clear picture of my sixth-grade school and of my teacher, Miss Mandell. She was dark-haired and very pretty. Much to her students' delight, she got married that summer. She asked me and another girl in my class to help serve refreshments at her wedding reception. I felt very privileged and wore my best dress. The princess-styled dress was made of pale blue linen embroidered with little flowers that my mother had made for me. (I believe it was the only dress I had at the time.) She had made a similar dress for my sister in a different color. (It was typical of my mother not to have asked herself why a twelve-year-old would want to look like her six-year-old sister! It was as if my mother lived in fantasy world where she had never met other people and so had no idea how she herself might behave.)

If I could remember these details from sixth grade, why is

almost all of the seventh grade gone from memory, the seventh grade when I have memories of basement windows below an apartment where we lived, playing the clarinet and sewing a skirt

I continued with my group therapy. In the fall of 1976, while in a group-therapy session, I told my story about my baby girl. One of the members knew about a birthmother who went to a support group of birthparents and adoptees. At the time, I had two lovely boys, but I was also still emotionally unsettled about my baby girl who was now nine years old. My thoughts were always with her. A woman who has given up a child for adoption always fantasizes: What does he/she look like? Are they being treated well? Where do they live? Naturally, my need to alleviate my continuing pain got the better of me, and I went to the birth-parent group meeting I had just learned about.

Adoptees Liberty Movement Association [ALMA] was comprised of adoptees searching for their birthparents and of birthparents searching for their surrendered children. We birth mothers are women who will never be understood by the rest of society. Only we know the pain involved, the shame, and the guilt. Not much is currently written about the women of my generation who gave up their children, since today it is acceptable for a single mom to raise a child.

Two women in ALMA — Sara and Paula —both of them adoptees, were well acquainted with Boston City court records. Under some guise, they were able to get to the birth certificates that were changed from the original to the amended ones showing the names of the adoptive parents and the name they gave the child. This was before the Internet when all the records were sealed — so what they did was remarkable. Through their help, I was able to find my daughter's name and who her adoptive parents were. I was on cloud nine.

At last, I had a name for her: Maggie!

Just as when Michael had proposed to me, I wanted to share the news with my parents. I went first to my mother who was still living apart from my father.

"Mother, you won't believe this. I found out about the baby I gave up and where she is."

"What baby? What are you talking about?" she asked.

"Nine years ago! I had a baby that I gave up for adoption!"

"Oh! I had forgotten."

How could she have forgotten a grandchild lost? How could she have forgotten visiting me on the Cape and at the hospital when Dr. Murphy had told her to bring me flowers? How could she have forgotten the main reason for my depression, my suicide attempt, the electrical shocks, Liberty House. How could she have forgotten everything I had gone through. I was deflated and angry.

But, even as I thought this, I also realized that, in some way, I was the same as she. Had I not chosen to forget that my mother was emotionally illiterate and would never rise to the occasion of being the mother I wanted and needed? Why did I keep going back for more misery? What would it take for me to remember this?

In my excitement, however, I went on to tell her some of what I had found out about Maggie. "This should make you happy. Maggie's adoptive father is an Episcopal priest. They used to live about a mile away from your school, but they moved to Martha's Vineyard two years ago."

"Oh," she answered. "That's interesting."

I told her their last name and asked, "Does it sound familiar?"

"No, but I will ask Father Beecham, the rector, when I see him next at church."

"Let me know if you find out anything. Any scrap of information would help me."

When I went to my father later, I hoped that he might be more sympathetic than my mother.

"You haven't forgotten that yet?" he said as if I could forget if I wanted to. Did he think remembering a baby you have given up for adoption is material to be forgotten, like forgetting the bad seat you had at a theater and remembering it all these years later. "Forget about that bad seat! It's not that important."

When pressed, he said he thought he had briefly met Maggie's father at one time and did agree to find out more about him. That appeased me somewhat.

When I talked to my new friend Sara, the adoptee, some more, I said, "I really would like to meet Maggie's family and talk to them, but I don't think it would be good for Maggie at nine to have me barge into her life all of a sudden."

She answered, "Others have met the children they surrendered. You could, too. Maybe I can think of some way to make it happen."

A week later, Sara had come up with a plan: "Do you remember the woman, Paula, that I go to city hall with to get the amended records?"

"Yes," I said.

"She has a Jeep. I thought the three of us could drive down, get a ferry to Martha's Vineyard next Sunday and see where Maggie lives."

"Whew, that sounds pretty risky," I sighed.

"Her family might not even be around," Sara went on to assure me. "It is February, and I don't think the weather will be good. It is supposed to snow over the weekend." Reluctantly, I agreed. What harm could it possibly do to see the house where Maggie lived? This could really help put my mind at ease. That next Sunday, with Michael in charge of Tim and Peter, Sara,

Paula, and I drove down to Cape Cod to catch the ferry to Martha's Vineyard. It had snowed the day before, and the driving was hazardous. I kept thinking, Why are we doing this and taking such a risk going to the Vineyard in February, with such poor driving conditions? What are we going to find out?

We crossed over to the island. I remained relatively calm until we got to the town where Maggie lived and then I started to get panicky, feeling we shouldn't be there. We drove by the Episcopal church where her father was the rector, and soon, we were in front of the rectory.

"I am a wreck," I said. "I've seen the house, so we can leave now."

"Not so soon," Sara replied. "We are going to see if anyone is home."

"I am staying in the car. You two can go."

Sara opened the door and practically dragged me out.

"What if I look like Maggie?" I said.

Sara grabbed a pair of glasses from her pocketbook and put them on me. My legs were shaking as we walked up the front steps.

"I am not talking at all; I can't tell any lies about why we are here."

A tall, thin woman — presumably Maggie's mother — answered the door. Sara and Paula started on their cock-and-bull story about visiting the Vineyard next summer and wanting to see the church. Maggie's mother said that her husband, the rector, was not home to show us around, but hopefully, she could help us. She showed us into an office adjacent to the foyer and left to get some literature about the church. We all noticed a picture of Maggie — at least we thought it was Maggie — about nine and wearing glasses.

"Now she is going to know who I am. Maggie probably looks like me with the glasses."

"Stay calm, Susan. We will be leaving soon," Sara said.

Maggie's mother returned with the information. Sara and Paula thanked her, and I nodded in agreement. Leaving, my head was spinning as I tried to navigate the front steps without falling.

I couldn't believe what we had just done. A gamut of emotions coursed through my body. On one hand, I was grateful and happy to know Maggie was being raised in such a comfortable home by outwardly competent parents. On the other hand, I felt guilty to have barged in under pretenses, and terrified that we might be recognized and the police might be trailing us.

I made a conscious decision not to contact Maggie's family. It was in Maggie's best interests that I not come popping into her life. Knowing she was in good hands made waiting until I might actually meet her easier, but even so I took several steps to allow a possible meeting to occur one day. I left my contact information with the agency that had handled the adoption and stated my desire to be reached if Maggie tried to find me. I also left my name on a national registry for adoptees searching for their birth parents. I always hoped Maggie would find me first. I would welcome her with open arms. On the other hand, after she had reached adulthood, if I not heard from her, I knew I would try to contact her. It would be easy now that I had her name. It was very healing for me to know who Maggie was and where she was being raised. In hopes that I might see some pictures of her and/or news about her family, I subscribed to the local Martha's Vineyard newspaper.

Would Maggie and I ever get to meet?

Chapter 8
My marriage Goes Its Inevitable Way

Having seen where Maggie lived unleashed something in me. These words came into my head one evening. I knew they were important so I wrote them down and subsequently they were published in the ALMA newsletter.

A child is born...and surrendered.
The mother is left
alone and forgotten, grief ridden, guilty...and very angry.

"Forget, forget," they said
  to me
as the current of electricity
  entered my brain.
Am I crazy...or is this my
  punishment
for a brief encounter one day
  in the midst of February's
  bleakness?

These repressed feelings are my burden...
the core of my existence these past nine years. But,

I never forgot as I withdrew into the safe confines of
  depression.

As I break the silence,
I now see the hypocrisy of it all.

Besides my family and some close friends, only a few people knew that I had had a baby girl. Now that I had talked about her in two different groups, I thought I was ready to share with others.

I was enjoying my new neighborhood where there were several families with boys who were Tim and Peter's age. Peter was friendly with one of these boys, and I liked spending time with his mother, Sharon. When Tim was in kindergarten, we would arrange what is now called a "play date." As Sharon and I got to know each other a bit, we also started to share more personally. One day I asked her if she could look after Peter. I explained that I was going to court to support a young mother who had given up a child for adoption. It was a minor case — the details escape me — and I said to Sharon I was going since I had been involved in an adoptee group.

I then revealed that I had given up a child for adoption a few years earlier. It was the first time I had shared this information with someone I didn't know well. Sharon did not respond but I could detect how she felt from her look of disapproval. While she took care of Peter that day, after this, her son wasn't available to play, and she basically ignored me for the next nine years until they moved out of the neighborhood. Any conversation we had was limited, and our sons ended up with different groups of friends. While I could say that she was a disappointingly limited person, I also understood that I had not assessed her accurately. After this, it took me a long time before I would talk about Maggie to anyone I did not know intimately. There were times I had to endure being in a group of people when the subject of adoption came up and someone would say with disdain, "How could someone ever give up a baby?" At these moments, I wanted to disappear with the shame and grief I felt. Would I ever get over feeling so vulnerable? I could have spoken up to educate people, but I didn't. My guilt was still strong, and I was riddled with insecurity.

It would be a long time before I would go beyond the amnesia of EST and know what had really happened to me.

In time, Sara, the adopted woman who had brought me to Maggie's home, became a friend of mine. I grew comfortable talking about my past with her as she did hers with me. Recently divorced with a teenaged son and a low paying job, she was having emotional difficulties. Being the concerned friend I was, I suggested that she contact my psychologist, and when she did, Gwen took her on as a client. I myself was not seeing Gwen at the time.

It turned out that Gwen and Sara both loved dogs. Gwen had a West Highland Terrier, and Sara had three Poodle-Schnauzers. They decided to mate their dogs. I thought this personalization of their relationship a bit inappropriate on Gwen's part. Wasn't she crossing a professional line with a client?

Michael and I had been living in Newton, Massachusetts, for a couple of years when these puppies were born. Our house had a fenced in yard, and my sons were anxious for a pet, so taking one of the puppies seemed reasonable. And none of us could resist the runt of the litter! The dog was a small, black, fluffy ball of cuteness. We named her Muffy, and she was with us for many years.

My parents were only separated for a year or so before they got back together. I was not privy to their reasoning for resuming

Shadows and Light

their marriage, but it did not seem that much had changed between them. They rented a house for a while but then began looking for one to buy — still in West Roxbury. My father had retired from teaching but worked in the library at Roxbury Latin School where he had taught. I believe my mother was still teaching. When I discussed the move with them, I suggested, "It would be good to have a one-story house. You will be in the house you buy for a long time and neither one of you is getting younger. It would be easier not having stairs."

"I don't know," my mother replied. "It depends on what is available."

"At least, think about it."

Of course, they bought a two-story house! It was a small colonial with three cramped bedrooms upstairs. There was no garage. The house was in pretty good condition except for the old, dark, flowery wallpaper in the three bedrooms. I don't know what possessed me to offer to strip the wallpaper and paint these three rooms. I had the time that summer since I was not working yet, and Tim and Peter were both in a summer day camp which was close by. I would drop them off in the morning and go to my parents' house to start working until it was time to pick up the boys.

I did not see much of my parents as they were not often at home. True to how they thought, neither of them took advantage of the opportunity this redecorating might have been for us to work together. So that summer I worked alone on their house.

It was hot and removing wallpaper with a steamer in the upstairs of a small house with no breeze spelled discomfort. Somehow, I managed to get the three rooms done with little disruption to my parents. The bedrooms seemed larger, and the whole upstairs was brighter due to the light color I had applied. I was proud of the work I had done.

"Yes, the rooms look nice," was all the feedback I got from

my parents.

There was no real accolade. No "Thank you! What a great job you did. The whole upstairs is transformed." A minimal smile and a murmured "thank you" was all I got for the hours of hard work I had invested. After I had finished the last of the painting, I drove over to pick up the boys from their day camp. I thought about what I would like to have heard.

"We would like to give you something for all your hard work."

"We are so lucky to have a daughter like you to help us out."

"Here is a money gift as a token of our appreciation. Go buy yourself some new clothes."

Why had I offered to do the project? While I do like to help people out, I must have known that I would get nothing from it — neither money, which had not been my goal, nor heart-felt praise, which would have been welcome. Perhaps, even as I approached forty, I was still seeking their approval on some level? Was I hoping they might have changed and become the parents I had always wanted?

Was I ever going to learn?

Ever since I had taken the refresher course in nursing when Michael and I were separated in the fall of 1975, I knew I would start working again once the boys were both in elementary school. After taking the refresher course, I realized that nursing no longer appealed to me. I had changed a lot since my BC days. My motivation for being a nurse had been somewhat unfocused to begin with and was not really what I wanted to do — or be — in the future. I attended a couple of career counseling sessions wherein computer programming was identified as a good match for me. Combining computer science with my nursing background would assure I had marketable skills. I signed up for the two required programming courses at Boston University, which would lead to a certificate in computer science.

One of the programming courses was way over my head. I decided to drop it, knowing I would need much personal tutoring, which was not available within the course. I stuck with the second programming class and managed to pass with a C. From this experience, I learned that I did not especially like programming and, therefore, decided against pursuing this BU certificate. When I look back, I understand my decision to study computer science was a mistake. Both my confidence and my background were inadequate. I did not even pick up enough information about how computers could be used in hospitals. This might have enhanced my job prospects. I had simply made another decision without considering how it would truly impact me! Does that sound familiar as my way of acting?

Somewhat sobered by the advanced computer material, I decided to take an introductory computer class to learn the basics of how to use a computer and an algebra class to beef up my math skills. I took these classes at Northeastern in night school and aced both of them with a grade in the high 90s. I had never felt I was good in math. This negative assessment of my talents went back to my high school years at St. Mary's. My teacher, Miss Rodgers, a former officer in the Marines, would often make fun of me when I was in front of the class at the board trying to work out a theorem. So, my two As were a rebuff of Miss Rodgers and a vote of confidence for me. These two courses, however, did not really inform me about what I might do for work.

Michael and I had enjoyed traveling in Europe, and we both wanted to do more sightseeing, so I signed up for courses to become a travel agent.

It was another shot in the dark.

By late 1978 and early 1979, Michael and I had fallen back

into poor communication and seemed unable to work things out. Both of us were unsettled. I was trying to figure out without much success what I wanted to do for work, and Michael was dealing with career disappointments that had syphoned off energy that might otherwise have gone into our relationship. Since he would not talk about what was happening, I could not help him emotionally. I tried to talk with him from time to time, but to no avail. It was clear that we did not have a supportive relationship where we might have reacted as a couple to our situation.

When he realized he was not on a partner track at his accounting firm, he decided to leave the company for another. Interestingly, when he told me about the company that he was considering working for, my intuition, which was to be so important to me later, kicked in. I told him I did not like what he had told me of this company. I had no idea why it did not seem like a good choice, but I had a clear sense that it was not. Of course, as with Mont St. Michel and so many other things, he paid no attention to me and accepted the position. He was operating as a "lone ranger" and that left me even less confident about our marriage.

The death of Michael's mother Mary might have been another factor in our marriage taking a downward turn. Mary had died of cancer in the fall of 1978 at the age of seventy-five. She had said more than once, "It will kill me if you two get a divorce." Now that she was gone, it freed Michael to rethink his options about leaving me and not having to worry about the effect on his mother. Ever since we had separated for the three months in 1975, divorce had always been in the back of my mind. I was unsure how our marriage would play out, but I had tried to think positively and hoped time would be my ally. I don't recall thinking then that the death of Michael's mother would precipitate an end to our marriage. This conclusion came to me

Shadows and Light

much later. Michael's father was still in good health following a heart attack and bypass surgery three years earlier. He never expressed his feelings so I never knew how he felt about Michael and me.

I was not doing yoga anymore because the yoga teacher I really liked was not offering classes and I did not want to continue with someone else. But, I still needed to do some sort of physical activity so I took up jogging. Jogging had started to be trendy around this time, and I thought that it was something Michael and I could do together. Generally, however, as one of us had to stay home to babysit the kids, we would go out alone, individually. Still thinking jogging might be an activity that would help us to get closer, I would sometimes get our neighborhood teenager to watch the boys. On those occasions, we'd go together.

When out jogging together one day, Michael said, "Look at the way you are running."

"What do you mean?"

"Your feet aren't hitting the pavement correctly."

"How do you know that? I am built differently from you so wouldn't it be natural that I should run a bit differently?"

"I know for a fact that you are not doing it right."

From the early days of our marriage, I had been aware that Michael always had to be right. As he criticized my jogging style, I thought to myself, Here he goes again telling me how to run when I know he really doesn't know much about jogging. Soon, we stopped jogging together. It wasn't fun to share it. I needed encouragement, not criticism. I continued to go out by myself, and Michael stopped running. That failure only confirmed that we were no longer able to work as a team.

We were not successful either at playing board games which, when I played with Michael, turned out to be highly competitive. At one time, Michael tried to teach me cribbage, which he had played frequently when growing up. He was willing to show me how to play, but I soon discovered he was not able to do so because he was too impatient. He expected me to learn rapidly in spite of how little he explained the game and how little practice I had. I required things to be broken down — to have someone teach me — to understand what I was doing. My failure at cribbage fed into my thinking I was not smart enough. My math success at Northeastern evening school, however, showed me this was far from the truth. Our learning styles were different; this was the challenge and not my lack of intelligence. This difference in our style of approaching not only cribbage but also life was dooming our marriage.

However, hope, as they say, springs eternal. Ignoring the breakdown of our marriage, we took a second mortgage to pay for a kitchen remodel. It was a big project as the kitchen had to be gutted and a wall removed. Michael and I were forced to compromise and make decisions about many issues, including on cabinets, appliances, hardware, and lighting. In the end, the transformation created a kitchen that was both easier and more pleasant to work in, but when I thought about this kitchen remodel in later years when I lived in the house alone, I wished I had insisted on doing things differently. As in so many areas of my life, I had not spent enough time thinking about what I needed. In this case, I had not thought enough about the layout and the cabinet choices. It was I, after all, who would be spending the most time in the kitchen. (This lack of thought during the remodeling was a repeat, I realize now, of how I had approached marrying Michael and so many other things in my life!)

One of the two contractors who did the work on our kitchen was a down-to-earth man, friendly and easy to talk to. I wouldn't have called him handsome, but he was easy on the eyes. Michael would be gone all day and I was at the house to make sure that the work was being done as we had decided. As such, I had many

Shadows and Light

opportunities to chat with this man on the fly. Then, we'd chat over his lunch break. In this way, we got to know each other. He told me he was recently divorced and he talked freely about the failure of his marriage.

"How is your marriage?" I recall him asking.

"It's fine," I answered, perhaps deflecting what might have been an overture on his part. "We have had some rough spots but we got through them."

I was aware of a spark between us. Under different circumstances, he might have been a good fit for me. He seemed genuinely caring and interested in me as a person. This was at a time when Michael and I were strained and so this man's attention was particularly appealing, but he never made a move and nothing ever came of this relationship. It did, however, give me confidence that maybe in the future, if I had to, I would be able to find romance with another man.

Conversing with this man made me aware of how Michael and I were unable to chat freely. A hidden agenda of resistance always seemed to be looming in the air between us.

Initially, Michael had been supportive of my endeavors to increase my skills and had even helped me with the work of the programming class at Boston University. Now that the children were older, I was feeling a lot of pressure from him to go from preparing for a job to landing one. My salary would obviously have helped with the kitchen remodel and all the extra expenses that came with it. He had his own job issues and had recently had to find another job as the small start-up company he worked for after leaving the accounting firm (the one I had intuited he should not go to work for) had gone bankrupt. I had finished the requirements for becoming a travel agent but had come to realize that working as one would be an unwise decision. I needed both better pay to boost our financial status and regular weekday hours. I started applying for jobs in which my nursing skills would be utilized, but I did not want to do clinical work. Instead, I applied for jobs with a research bent.

I had some interviews but no luck until the early fall of 1981, when I was hired at Newton-Wellesley Hospital as a full-time staffing secretary. I was over-qualified for this position but the hospital was only a mile from our house and I wanted to get back into the workforce both because Michael wanted me to and because I had a sense of the handwriting on the wall concerning our marriage. After not working for eleven years, I accepted that this would be a good re-entry since I was not sure what I wanted to do.

My new day started at 6:30 a.m., so Michael would get the boys off to school before he left for his own job. Then, just after 3 p.m., before the boys walked home from school, I was home again. In the coming year, I was so wrapped up in adjusting to working again that I did not see the signs — or conveniently chose to ignore them — that Michael was pulling away more and more from me. By then, he was barely speaking to me. I imagined I was not much fun to be with. I needed some slack and much support to get me through the challenge of working again. It was not forthcoming.

One evening in the fall of 1981, after I had started at Newton-Wellesley Hospital, Michael said to me, "I don't like you anymore."

I could accept that he no longer loved me — in fact, I no longer loved him either — but saying he didn't like me was a different story. How could two people who not only did not love each other anymore but who had grown to dislike each other live together?

I could discern no way we could reconcile our differences. I wasn't the affectionate, loving, sociable wife that Michael wanted, but to my credit, if not to his satisfaction, I had tried my best. This avowal on Michael's part was a clear statement that I had to acknowledge that we were at the beginning of the end. That night, eleven years into my marriage, I realized I did not want to be married to Michael. The next day, I told him we needed to think about a divorce and learn how to go about doing one. I removed my wedding band shortly afterwards.

In keeping with a pattern that had been in effect since I had had electroshock treatments, I look back on those months before and after Michael and I separated, and I recall very little. I seem to have repressed all my emotions and a fair number of memories. I realize now that it was at times like this that I turned inward and depression prevailed. The depression that fell on me then was not as bad as the two major ones I had already survived to date.

But depression was my way of coping, and the only way I knew.

We planned that Michael would continue to live in the house for about six months. At some point, we began sleeping in separate bedrooms. That would take us to late spring of 1982. We would wait until much closer to the actual time before separating and telling Tim and Peter, who were then in the second and fourth grades. I am sure they probably knew that we did not get along well but we wanted to wait until we had specific plans, including where Michael was going to live, how often they would see him, and so on. I was emphatic about one thing: I told him, "If we are going to go through with this, I want neither one of us to speak negatively about the other under any circumstance. This is going to be hard enough on the kids, and I want no added stress on them by having them be caught in the middle of our issues."

Michael thought along these lines as well. To my knowledge, we were able to keep our pact for the years to come. There were times, especially in the first few years, when I had to bite my tongue to keep from saying something, but I held true to my word.

Shadows and Light

In the months after our decision was made, I was a depressed, emotional wreck and knew I needed professional help. I made an appointment with Gwen, the psychologist I had seen in the past. As I talked about what was happening with Michael and me and how I was feeling, I said, "I need your help to get through this."

"I am not going to be able to see you as a client," Gwen said. "I am already seeing Michael on occasion and cannot meet with both of you. Since Michael is a continuing client, I have to stick with him. I also can't see you and your friend Sara, also a client, at the same time."

She had a referral for me, a Dr. Cohen, whom she said was very good, but I started to cry and just wanted to get out of her presence as soon as possible. However reasonable her words were — and they concurred with my own understanding of professionalism — I felt abandoned. I beat a hasty retreat. Through my haze of tears, I knew I shouldn't drive so I sat for a few minutes to collect my thoughts. The more I thought about Gwen on the way home, the angrier I got. Thoughts of suicide popped up. By now I knew I was done with that option so I pushed those thoughts aside. In spite of being thirty-seven, I couldn't help but feel it was like my mother preferring my brother and sister to me. I felt as abandoned as I had when my mother dropped me off at St. Mary's. Everyone appeared not to understand me. There must be something wrong with me! When was I going to find out what it was? At this point, I convinced myself that I would refuse to give up. What I could not see was that I had placed my happiness in other people's hands.

The years that would follow, years alone, would teach me much.

Chapter 9
Living a Single Life Amid Recovered Memories

Michael and I had not been able to work out our differences and stay married. I wish we could have done this for the boys' sakes, but we could not. While it is easier now to look back to uncover where either of us could have done things differently, at the time, we were committed to the best we knew how to do for each other and that was not always good enough.

I regret that I did not postpone marriage to Michael; I had not been ready for it. At the time, I was weighed down with mental health problems. Twelve years later, my mental health was again precarious. It would still take me years to understand how to address the hurting.

Michael and I managed an amicable enough divorce as we continued to focus on the welfare of our sons, who were clearly the best part of my twelve years of marriage to Michael. A decision for me to stay in the house was an easy one; Michael had no interest in maintaining the house and looking after Tim and Peter full-time. My main reason for staying in the house was the boys. I had moved around enough as a child myself, and I had always wanted them to be able to grow up in one neighborhood. As long as I could afford to stay, I was going to. We agreed that Michael would take the boys every other weekend and have them over for dinner one night a week. Subsequently, he was faithful

Shadows and Light

to this commitment except for when he moved to Connecticut for a few months. Even then, they would take a train to see him for the weekend. Michael was also faithful about paying child support, so it was financially possible for the boys and me to stay in the house.

The few months between the time we decided to divorce until the late spring of 1982, when Michael was to move out of the house for good, remain a blur in my mind. I was busy with work which fortunately kept my mind from obsessing about the upcoming split. I had been separated from Michael before so it wasn't that I didn't know what to expect, and I was also in a different place in my life — my sons were older, I was working full-time, and thanks to counseling, I did know myself a bit better.

A few months before Michael moved out, my brother, Mark, suddenly left his wife, Linda, and their five children to move to Vermont to live with another woman. It was a total surprise! I couldn't believe that he would move away from his children, and he ended up paying minimal — and mostly no — support for the children ranging from a toddler to a twelve-year-old.

Mark, Linda and their 5, 1979

My sister Clare had gotten a divorce a few years earlier, from a man she had met when in London. After they had married, they moved to British Columbia whereupon they split up and Clare came back to

130

Boston a year or so later. Neither Clare nor my parents ever mentioned his name again. In my family, any emotion was kept under tight wraps and was not discussed or dealt with. It seemed like my family was falling apart. How my parents coped with all of this — three children and three unsuccessful marriages — I don't know because they never spoke about it. Surely, they must have wondered what the model of their own marriage had provided us?

Once Michael was gone, I decided to hire a graduate student to babysit in exchange for room and board. This student would be available not only for babysitting but for light housekeeping jobs. In the beginning of September in 1982, Fiona, who was starting her master's degree in social work, came to live with us for the next two years. She was easy to get along with, worked hard, and was good with the boys. Since I left early for work, she made sure Tim and Peter were up, dressed, and at school on time. Also, she did some house cleaning on Saturday mornings and was available in the evenings if I wanted to go out. The babysitting option was good to have, but I rarely took advantage of it because I was so tired, emotionally and physically, from work and adjusting to the role of a single parent.

That September when Fiona came to live with us, I had been working in the Newton-Wellesley Hospital staffing office for a year. When an opportunity for a promotion as staffing coordinator came up, I decided to apply. All the interviews went well except for the one with the nursing vice president, Sheila, whom I would report to if I landed the new position. For some reason, our personalities clashed, and although I don't recall the details, I assumed she picked up on the fact that I was uncomfortable with her. Instead of putting me at ease, she continued on as she had been and appeared to be annoyed with me. I felt sure I was not going to get the job.

When I thought about it that night at home, I decided to try to repair any damage that the interview might have created. I overruled my intuition that this woman and I might not get along. At the time, I did not have the skills to pick up on the possibility that our personalities might conflict and understand what might happen if we worked together. I let my need to have better pay and more responsibility sway me to continue pursuing the job instead of waiting for another. But I also felt I should have congratulated myself on being proactive in securing a better future by pursuing this job. Taking action was a new approach for me. In the past, I would simply have assumed it was my fault when an interview went badly, or convinced myself that I shouldn't actively ask for what I wanted.

With my courage in hand, the next day, I went to see the nursing vice president.

"I am not sure what happened yesterday, Sheila," I said. "Our meeting did not go well, and I would like to start over as I still want this position."

To my pleasure, she responded, "I agree. Do you have time? We can talk again now." She pointed to a seat, and I sat down. This time, the tone of the conversation was totally different. She offered me the position immediately, and I accepted.

In retrospect, I know I dismissed my intuition that this woman — an emotionally distant female authority figure reminiscent of my mother — and I were not a good mix and this did come back to haunt me in a couple of years. They say you repeat experiences until you finally learn what there is to learn from them.

Christmas of 1982 was the first one at which my family was not intact. My emotions were still raw, fluctuating from anger to sadness, but I made an effort to keep them at bay when around others. I knew Christmas wouldn't be easy. Michael would have the boys for Christmas Eve, and I would have them on Christmas Day. We collaborated on buying gifts so we would not get duplicates and the boys would not be overloaded with presents. So far, our plan to keep in mind what was best for our sons was working.

Since it was the first Christmas without Michael and Linda's first without Mark, I invited her and her five kids to come for Christmas Day as they had in the past. I wanted the day to be as normal as I could possibly make it. I decided to ask my parents and sister to be with us as well. The more family the merrier, I thought.

When I called to invite my mother, she said she would get back with an answer in a couple of days. When she did, it was to say, "We want to have a quiet Christmas here at our house." She also told me Clare, who had moved in with them while in grad school, would not be coming either. She would be spending the day with them.

"We want a quiet day. With the seven grandchildren, it will be very noisy. You, Linda, and all the kids can all come the next day in the afternoon for a visit."

Both Linda and I had had a tough year. I would have thought that my mother would not only welcome the opportunity to have Christmas dinner cooked for her and be able to see her seven grandchildren, but she would also have real concern for all of us who were going through a traumatic time. But, as usual, my parents' response was about them. When would I stop asking them to be different than the inadequate people they were?

Leaving my disappointment behind, I put my energy into cooking and buying presents. While we had a sit-down dinner that day served on a white linen tablecloth — I was determined to stick with all the traditions — and ate our typical turkey dinner, I was deeply aware that Michael and my brother were absent as was the man Clare had been married to.

What other changes would happen by this time next year?

Shadows and Light

How would I cope with any other major changes?

The next day, Linda and I and our kids went over to my parents' house in the afternoon. I didn't want to make a scene and not go and I wanted the boys to see their grandparents, but it wasn't the same as if we had all been together on Christmas Day. Any joy I might have had spending time with my parents had dissipated into the cold, winter air.

A year after Michael and I stopped living together, in the spring of 1983, I was walking through the dining room one day when I saw a book on the buffet against the wall. Fiona, my resident graduate student, was reading it for her social work degree. It was on sexual abuse. I started to read how victims of sexual abuse often had issues with depression, were likely to have unwanted pregnancies and often became addicted to drugs and alcohol. I flashed to the time when I was twelve, in the basement when "something happened" with a group of boys. Had I been sexually abused? Even though — according to this book — I had a lot of the symptoms, I was not allowing myself to be totally convinced, since rape did not seem real to me. I had connected this incident to a vision of the basement windows, but the other images that had come to me while doing yoga — a curtain blowing in the breeze and the straps in the drawer — still remained a mystery, but they would not remain so for long.

Shortly afterwards, on a Sunday afternoon, I was visiting my parents in West Roxbury, in the house whose upstairs rooms I had slaved over! Since they were both working and I was a single working mom, we didn't get together very often. I had taken my two sons along as it had been a while since we had seen my parents. We were sitting in the living room, and the boys were on the floor playing a game. Mother served tea with a plate of biscuits. We were enjoying both and chatting when Clare came in to join us; still single, she was now no longer living with our par-

Shadows and Light

ents but had come for a visit.

We were talking about old times, and the subject came up about when, one summer, I had babysat for a family who had a cottage on a lake in New Hampshire.

"I was never at a lake in New Hampshire for a summer. You must be thinking of someone else," I said.

"Susan, it was definitely you," my mother insisted. "It was 1961, and Daddy was teaching for the summer at the Hotchkiss School in Connecticut. We all went there for the summer and then you went off with one of the faculty families for a babysitting job."

"I just don't remember it at all. Wasn't it you, Clare?"

"No," said Clare. "I was only ten. However, I do remember the family. The man had a brain tumor and was short in stature."

My mother added, "I don't think you wanted to go, but we thought it would be good for you to earn some spending money."

My father nodded his head in agreement but didn't add anything otherwise to the conversation.

I decided to drop the conversation as they obviously had different memories than mine.

Over the next few weeks, however, that forgotten summer, when I would have been turning seventeen in September, kept popping up in my mind. My inner voice was telling me I needed to look into it. What could that summer possibly have been like? It was odd that I couldn't remember anything about the school my father was teaching in nor any of the people I had met. It was a blank slate with no pictures or words.

Why couldn't I remember? Was this another example of memory loss from the shock treatments?

This missing memory of a summer by a lake in New Hampshire came with a vague and threatening feeling. I began to accept that, in the summer of 1961, I had babysat in New Hampshire for a Hotchkiss School faculty family. At the end of

Shadows and Light

that summer, my family would be moving again, the fifth move in nine years. The previous two and a half years, my father had been at Hoosac School just outside of Albany, New York. He was new to Hotchkiss and so did not really know this Hotchkiss faculty family. It amazed me that my parents had let me go away with an unknown family for the summer. It was so like them, of course, not to understand what being a parent should entail. Had something happened that summer? What was I keeping from myself that I had "forgotten" but which was leaking back?

I made an opportunity to visit my parents again so as to look through family photo albums of the time when we were at the Hotchkiss School and my father was teaching summer school. Fortunately, my mother was well organized and every picture was in sequence with a date. There was one picture of me wearing a dress that I did not recognize and I was in unfamiliar surroundings. Since I wore uniforms for the school year at St. Mary's, I just had a few basic outfits for the rest of the time. Because of that, I felt sure I should have recognized the dress. Looking at these photos as much as I did was of no help. No new information surfaced.

I wrote to my brother who was still living in Vermont at the time with his new woman (he married her at some point after his divorce from Linda). Perhaps, he would remember something? In his letter back to me, he said, "Yes, I do remember that you went on that babysitting job to NH, and when you came home, you were very closed mouth about it. You seemed upset and would not talk."

He had no other information to offer me as I continued to piece memories and information together. After my father finished summer school, my family moved to Boston where he had accepted a teaching post at the Roxbury Latin School in West Roxbury, a suburb of Boston. I went from the summer in New Hampshire to my family's temporary rental apartment in Boston.

In later years, I had to ask myself, "Why did my father change jobs so frequently?" I can only surmise that he was dissatisfied with his life and/or it was something to do with his being gay. My mother must have been upset by having to uproot the family so many times. I do recall her being very angry when living in Haiti. The reasons for the moves were never discussed in the family. That, of course, led to my imagining that something untoward had happened and my father was asked to leave his teaching positions.

Many changes were then taking place in my life, and I was not coping very well. During that brief week back from New Hampshire with my family, during which I shared a tiny room with Clare, I was feeling very lonely. I had been gone all summer and now, after a week in an apartment that had not felt like home, I would be gone all the rest of the year. Why had it seemed a good idea to my parents, I ask myself, to have me go away for a summer after I had been gone all year and would be going away again for another year?

This question did not have a happy answer, but I kept my feelings to myself. My practical self was in full swing. I had to get the next school year over with since it was an important one. I would need to focus on keeping my grades up and getting into college. That week, I packed my school uniforms to bring back to St Mary's for my senior year, which I was very anxious to leave behind and begin a new chapter in my life.

The fact that I had forgotten the New Hampshire summer would come up, go away, and then I would ask myself again, "Why had I forgotten it?" I could not ignore it, and I resolved to talk about that summer with Dr. Cohen, the psychiatrist whom I had been seeing every week since Michael and I had split. Dr. Cohen was a Harvard-trained psychiatrist who was totally different from Dr. O'Brien whom I had seen earlier. While Dr. Cohen's waiting room was a small, windowless room, it had an

Asian mural, plants, and a few art pieces to make it welcoming. Dr. Cohen was always punctual. When it was time for our session, I'd hear the doorknob turn and soon see Dr. Cohen greeting me with a smile. He was short — a few inches shorter than I — and had straight, dark brown hair. His glasses had dark frames, and he was immaculately dressed in a jacket and tie.

The afternoon when I had decided to talk about that forgotten summer in New Hampshire, I sat in Dr. Cohen's office in my usual place on a comfy, soft sofa. He sat opposite me in his chair. With its muted watercolor prints on the neutral-color walls and plants throughout the room, this office was so different from Dr. O'Brien's, and its atmosphere soothed me.

By now, I had connected the image of the curtain blowing in the breeze to that summer in New Hampshire. It felt to me that the same sort of thing had happened there as in the Shattuck School basement.

"Susan," Dr. Cohen said to me, "you need to talk to your parents again to see if anything else comes up for them to share with you. Visit them with an open mind and remember to question and challenge them in a way that is non-confrontational."

I heeded Dr. Cohen's advice and went to my parents' house by myself, intent to talk about that summer. We had our usual tea and biscuits and chatted for a bit. After taking a few deep breaths to relax myself, I felt ready to get to the difficult conversation. My heart was still pounding as I said, "About the summer I spent babysitting for a Hotchkiss family in New Hampshire? I have a feeling that something bad happened with that man; do you remember anything about the family?"

My mother's neck and upper body went rigid, and her jaw tensed as she abruptly turned her head away from me.

"Nothing could have possibly happened to you!" she insisted dismissively, not inquiring about the feelings that surrounded this missing memory of a time when she had not been there to protect me.

My father said nothing. I assumed he agreed with my mother, as he usually did.

Their denial of what I perceived to be real was so much like so many other times when they had denied my reality. I ran upstairs to the bathroom, whereupon I had violent diarrhea. I was shaking with emotion and crying.

"This is very significant," I thought to myself, "this physical reaction is telling me something. My body needs to get rid of some old garbage." After twenty minutes or so, I went downstairs.

"You were gone a long time, dear," my mother said. "Are you all right?"

This weak, polite inquiry was all I got; nothing else — nothing substantive — was said. Knowing I would get no more information from them, I left for home because I felt like they had slammed an important door in my face, but there remained the question of what had happened to me. Did something happen? Did my parents know something about this family and would not share it with me or had they "forgotten" as well?

At a follow-up session with Dr. Cohen, I told him about the visit to my parents. No new insights had popped into my head in the intervening time; the facts of that summer were still unavailable.

He said to me, "The important thing is not the actual facts but the emotions connected to that summer, how they affected you and how you are dealing with them."

"You are telling me it is not important to remember the facts. Correct?" At the time, I did wonder, "How can I deal with these emotions if I don't know what happened?"

He suggested hypnosis, but I felt it was too nebulous and I had heard bad things about it.

In the first year or two of therapy with Dr. Cohen, I had many memorable dreams. For a few months, I had nightmares — violent ones of terrorists in my kitchen ready to shoot me or of threats to my life under other circumstances. Fortunately, these nightmares did not last, but two recurring dreams started. The first dream was about teeth. In it, I was conscious of my teeth being loose and then, one by one, they would start to fall out. I do not recall all of them actually falling out, but I dreamed that many did before I woke up. My other recurring dream had to do with dirty bathrooms. Needing to use the facilities, I would enter a public restroom, open the stall door and find feces and urine on the floor. I would close that door and go to another stall only to find similar conditions. After a few of these attempts, I always gave up and left the bathroom. These dreams continued for about the next twenty years or so. Fortunately, as the years passed, fewer teeth fell out and the bathrooms got cleaner.

It would be many years before I would access psychic vehicles for understanding what had happened to me.

When I recall my Aunt Clare, my mother's sister, I see us walking down a quiet country lane in England. The meadows are dotted with multicolored wildflowers and grazing sheep; the small cottages are far apart and each has a garden. Aunt Clare lived in

Aunt Clare

Woodstock, just outside of Oxford. I never knew much about her except that she had never married nor had children. There was one story of a fiancé killed in the Second World War. However, since my parents were not storytellers, I did not know the details from them and I had not asked her while I was on visits to her house. She lived in a cottage which was in disrepair and had no central heating. She made her living teaching for the Anglican church and raising Tibetan Spaniels. At one point, before Aunt Clare became a pensioner, my mother had given her money to rebuild her house. With these improvements, Aunt Clare had a more comfortable place to live. My mother understood that my aunt, in her will, would leave the cottage her.

I always enjoyed visits with my aunt even though they were infrequent. Michael and I had seen her twice when we lived in Europe as it had been an easy long-weekend trip from Paris or Brussels, even before the Chunnel. After my return to the US in 1972, I didn't see her again until the fall of 1983 when she came to visit my parents in West Roxbury. During that visit, she stayed with me, Tim, and Peter for a weekend. She said she had come in the fall to see the New England foliage. She didn't have to go far as there was a glorious maple bursting with shades of red and orange just outside the guest room she slept in. She was enamored of its autumn splendor.

Other than taking her to one of the kid's soccer games, we didn't do much. I got the sense that that was what she wanted — just to spend family time with us. Having some time together by ourselves that weekend was special, as my mother or my father or my sister Clare would otherwise always be around. After Aunt Clare went back to England, my mother told me she had an inoperable brain tumor.

Knowing this, I saw that her visit made sense: it was the last time she would see her family. I often wonder why she didn't want anyone but my mother to know about her tumor. I can only

Shadows and Light

imagine that it was the family stoicism. She kept any suffering to herself and wouldn't want anyone feeling sorry for her.

It appeared to me that Aunt Clare had lived a relatively solitary life and would continue to do so until the end. Thanks to the United Kingdom's National Health Insurance, she was well taken care of in a nursing home and died in the spring of 1984 — roughly a half-year after her visit.

A month after her passing, I received a letter from an attorney stating that she had left me some money: $16,000. After she visited New England, she had changed her will to include me.

I was touched, but my mother was incensed.

"How could she leave you all that money? It was meant to go to me."

"I think, when she visited me, she had a good time and she saw what my life was like as a single working mother," I ruminated. "Perhaps she decided a small inheritance would help me out."

My mother was not appeased; seeing what my life was like had never moved her to compassion.

"It's my money she gave you," she insisted. It was true that my mother had given Aunt Clare money, but surely Aunt Clare had more money than just what my mother had given her. In my mother's way of understanding things, I had no right to an inheritance from Aunt Clare.

"Her brain tumor had caused her to change her will. She was not in her right mind," my mother declared.

"What are you saying?" I answered. "She was lucid and gave absolutely no evidence of abnormal brain behavior."

My mother continued, "You have no idea what I am going through right now. I lost my sister."

"She was my aunt, and I am feeling her loss as well," I added. It was evident that, if I said anything else, it would make the situation worse. My mother was so wrapped up in her sense of entitlement and the wrong that had been done to her that I could not comfort her in any way.

Soon afterwards, I received a letter from both my parents trying to persuade me to forgo this small inheritance of $16,000 — not a fortune by any means, although, at the time, it added up to almost one year's net income for me. In his letter, my father wrote me how upset my mother was and could I please change my mind. It would make things so much easier. I can't recall what my mother wrote; I imagine it was more of the same. She probably repeated how my aunt made a mistake leaving me anything.

I stood my ground and did not give in to them or apologize for anything. Besides, I really needed the money. With my small salary, even with the increase in pay from the promotion at Newton-Wellesley Hospital and with Michael's child support, I was just able to get the bills paid. When all the paperwork was finalized and Aunt Clare's legacy dispersed to my mother, she mailed me a check. She could have kept the legacy as it was she who was writing the final check, but she did not. The practical side of me deposited the money in a savings account. It didn't occur to buy myself a gift of any kind. Eventually, the money would be spent on much needed repairs that would include painting the house before putting it on the market in a few years.

I don't think my mother ever forgave me for accepting Aunt Clare's gift.

Around the time Aunt Clare died in the spring of 1984, the fact that I had not listened to my intuition when I interviewed for my staffing-coordinator job caught up with me. I started having work problems at Newton-Wellesley Hospital. By then, I had been there for almost three years, I felt comfortable in my position — I was now called nursing systems coordinator, as we used a software program to determine staffing levels — and presumed

I was doing well. The staffing office had run smoothly under my charge, while my boss Sheila, the nursing vice president, was on maternity leave for three months. Shortly after her return, Sheila gave me my annual performance review. It was a scathing one. Her negative comments unnerved me, as I was not used to unfavorable evaluations. Essentially, she took all the comments I had shared with her about where I thought I needed to improve and turned them against me.

"Why did you change the hours for the positions on this unit?" she asked me.

"As you saw, I split the hours of one full-time position into two part-time positions. I didn't think it would be a problem and I sought out the approval of the vice president in charge of the unit," I responded.

She was fixated on this staffing change. "You never should have done it. It screwed up everything."

Perhaps she hadn't done her due diligence, and this was her way of getting the evaluation task done quickly! I believe, if she had talked to the nurse managers, she would have heard praise.

She put me on probation with a warning that I had to improve in the next three months. I was reeling from shock when I left her office that afternoon. I was so distraught I couldn't even think rationally.

Why hadn't I listened to my intuition during my first interview with Sheila, when our personalities had clearly not meshed? I ought not to have accepted the position! Was it even about me? Maybe Sheila was taking out her frustrations on me for her not being able to stay at home with her new baby? Years later, it came to me that Sheila was a non-caring, emotionally distant female — just like my mother. At that time, I assume that I still needed this type of female authority figure in my life. I did not know myself well enough yet to ascertain what I was doing.

After obsessing with the unfairness of this situation for two days and coming down hard on myself for not having seen the confrontation coming, I calmed down and started to think about how I was going to deal with it. Obviously, Sheila wanted to fire me because I would never meet her expectations. In addition to my being on probation, I knew it wasn't a good job for me as, contrary to my expectations when I took it on, it provided very little satisfaction. I was caught between Sheila and the nursing staff. Staffing levels were based on a patient-acuity system — how much nursing care each patient needed. The nurse managers were mad at me when their units were understaffed, as this caused more work for the nurses, and the administration was annoyed with me when the units were overstaffed, as this caused the budget to go into the negative. I had good relationships with some of the nurse managers. In fact, one was always asking me to come and work on her unit.

In spite of the problems, there were some aspects of my work that I did enjoy. My job offered me an introduction to a computer program that would prove very useful later. I gained confidence with systems issues. At times, I had a phone in one hand — talking to the help desk — and a screw driver in the other—taking the back off the computer to take a look and make any necessary adjustments. The good parts of the job, however, were not enough for me to stay and try to rectify my unwarranted probationary status.

I decided to leave, but I was not going to do so without speaking up for myself. First, I went to speak with the director of Human Resources. I voiced my concerns about my boss Sheila — how I had been singled out and put on probation unfairly. This was the deal I proposed: I would leave quietly and not file any complaints, but I wanted two things: to be able to collect unemployment and to have a letter of recommendation from Sheila. Secondly, I spoke to the President of Nursing and again voiced my concerns about Sheila. The president thanked me for keeping quiet and dealing with everything in a professional manner. Once my requests were accepted, I gave my notice. It would not be until September that I would leave, however. It took that long to get in hand a strong letter of recommendation that I was satisfied with.

On my last day of work, September 6, 1984, my co-workers threw me a going-away party at the hospital and gave me gifts. I knew I was appreciated by many of the nurse managers I had worked closely with for all my hard work and tact. Surprisingly, Sheila was at the party and must have been saving face as she was pleasant to me and gave no indication that my work performance had been subpar. That final day happened to be my fortieth birthday, and while walking home that afternoon, I felt a shift had taken place in me and change was coming. It was a pivotal time in my life. I was elated but still anxious. A multitude of thoughts were swirling around in my head. It was a warm, late summer day, and a few leaves were starting to turn. I had a bounce in my step and felt like a burden had been lifted from my shoulders. I no longer had to put up with Sheila who had given me such a hard time. I had taken a huge risk as I had no job to go to. With unemployment and child support, I was confident I could support myself and my sons for a while until I found another job. My divorce was now two years in the past, and I was starting to get used to being on my own. But I still had a long way to go to figure out my identity

By the spring of 1985, while I had had several job interviews, I still had no luck finding new work. When my unemployment ran out, I started to panic. To bring in some income, I did temporary office work with an agency. One day, I was assigned to go to a local ophthalmologist. Dr. Goldberg liked me and after my first day there, he offered me a full-time office job — knowing it would only be for a year or two — which I accepted. Before accepting the job, I had decided to enroll in the Health

Record Administrator Program at Northeastern University. This was a two-year program, for which I would be taking classes two evenings a week. There were lots of job opportunities in the field, and I would start looking for a job as soon as I had completed enough courses.

Chapter 10
Surviving a Crisis and Deciding to Date

"You do not deserve to live," some pesky voice kept telling me. "You would be better off dead."

The thoughts were perhaps a bit self-indulgent, but they came with much pain. Although I would think thoughts about dying, I knew that I would never kill myself. Tim and Peter were far too important to me, and I would never inflict that loss on them. Even so, when a neighbor with young children had died of cancer, I wished I had been her.

"Why can't I die of cancer, too?"

This was my way of thinking about suicide without executing it. I wanted to get rid of the depressed feelings and painful angst for good. Even though I repeatedly told myself I would not commit suicide because of my children, I always kept a large stash of assorted pills in my house. I had told no one about this.

I was still seeing Dr. Cohen once a week. One afternoon as I walked up the stairs to his office, I could smell a familiar odor — most likely a cleaning product of the condo building his office was in. It wasn't a bad smell, but it reminded me I had been coming every week for about four years. How much longer will I have to come? It is getting to be a drag, I complained to myself as I reached the top of the stairs. The floral and striped wallpaper caught my eye. I wished it could be changed to something brighter and more inviting.

Once seated in the consultation room, I started talking about my week and how things were going. In these sessions, I did most of the talking. Dr. Cohen was the silent observer, interjecting when necessary to lead me in a therapeutic direction. He took a neutral stance so I never knew what he was thinking. I must have been talking about my neighbor dying and how I wished it could have been me instead. Then suddenly, without planning to, I blurted out, "I have stocked enough pills to kill myself."

"What do you mean?" he asked. I could see a tremor of surprise in him.

"For some time now, I have collected assorted meds, pain pills, and tranquilizers," I said.

"This is very serious," he replied rather sternly.

"I am well aware of that."

He wasn't going to let this go.

"This is what I need you to do," he continued. "You are to bring me those pills and hand them over to me tomorrow."

"OK. But when? I have to work tomorrow."

"Come after work. I will be at the hospital tomorrow afternoon. When you get there, have me paged, and I will meet you in the lobby. Will you do that?"

"Yes."

I had never seen Dr. Cohen so emotional and even a bit upset. The following day, I went to the hospital and handed him the pills. I wrote the following words afterwards and showed them to him at the next session we had.

> In a web of confusion, you called my bluff and I surrendered…
> Exposed and vulnerable, I must now trust you and my own instincts.
> The trap door is now open and I await your kindness

and support
To help me through.
... in hope that we can go on
As partners in discovery of my past.

I saw this interaction as a turning point in my therapy. Unconsciously, I had tested Dr. Cohen to see how he would react. Finally, after four years, I felt I could trust him. I knew that he cared about me.

This experience with Dr. Cohen reminded me of a conversation I had had with my mother a few years earlier. We were talking about a cousin in British Columbia. My cousin's wife, Paula, had been hospitalized in the past for depression, so I asked my mother, "How are John and Paula doing? I remember that Paula was in the hospital for depression."

"Yes, she had a more difficult time than you."

"What do you mean?"

"Oh, Paula's problems were much worse than yours."

I thought to myself, My mother has no idea what I have gone through. She continues to dismiss me, as when she refused to talk to me about the summer I "forgot." Why would I want to open up to her when I can't trust her? It is apparent she does not even care for me.

An honest, frank conversation with my mother about Paula and about my experiences might have taken our relationship a step up to a higher level. But the mother I would have to have had for such a conversation was not the mother I had.

Late in the same spring of 1985, I visited my parents at their house since it had been a while since I had seen them. We were in the living room having our usual cup of tea and biscuits when my mother announced, "We are selling the house and moving to England to live in Auntie Clare's house."

Shadows and Light

I almost dropped the mug I had in my hand. After I caught my breath, I replied, "I understand your ties to England, but I don't think it is a good idea at this stage in your life. You are 71 and 74 years old now. You will not have any family around for support and help if needed."

"Daddy has a cousin near where we will be."

"A distant cousin you do not really know is not a substitute for two daughters who live close by to you." My brother was still living in Vermont at this time.

My mother said, "I am sure we will be fine."

My father nodded in agreement but had nothing to add.

"If you don't want to sell Auntie Clare's house," I persisted, "why don't you rent it out? You could always visit at least once a year for a month or two. Another option would be to sell the house and rent a house in the same village for a month each year. This way, you get the best of both worlds."

"No, our minds are made up. We are going to live in her house."

"I just want to be clear that I do not agree with your move. And besides, won't you miss your grandchildren?"

"You can always come to visit."

"Maybe Clare will," I said. "I won't be able to afford the air fare for myself, let alone for the boys as well. Money is tight right now and has been for a while. I have a low paying job while I am back in school."

My parents had a tendency to get uncomfortable when I didn't agree with them and any further conversation became pointless. Their minds were made up, and I knew I was not going to persuade them to stay. Maybe my reasons for wanting them to stay were selfish. I knew I still longed for the family that I never had. My dream family would be what I called "close-knit" — supportive and nurturing. They would be composed of people who would welcome me with open arms when times were tough.

I knew by now my parents were never going to change, and I had to accept that.

I didn't know when I would see them again. And once again, the feelings of abandonment that had so often plagued me in my life cropped up. When I thought about it, I was reminded once again of the time long ago when my mother had dropped me off at boarding school for my freshman year at St. Mary's before going back to join my father in Haiti, where he was teaching in an Episcopal high school. I had felt so abandoned then. Although I was a lot older now and wiser in some ways, the feeling of rejection was still pervasive. Did they ever really care about me and my children? I continued to think, it was more common for children to move away from their parents and explore the world, than for parents to up and leave their grown children and move three thousand miles across the Atlantic?

Haiti, 1958
L to R: My father, Susan, Clare, my mother, & Mark

Fortunately, I was in counseling with Dr. Cohen, so I was able to work through the remaining issues of anger and abandonment I had with my parents. I knew I had to separate myself from them and continue on my own path. I would see them in a few years, but by then the tables were turned in a new direction.

Almost three years later, my mother came back for a visit in the summer of 1988. My father, who didn't accompany her, wanted me to know that she was having a "bit of a memory problem." When I picked her up at Logan Airport in Boston, we waited at the baggage carousel and watched the bags go around and around until only a few were left and then those were removed. The exact details elude me, but my mother could not recall what her suitcase looked like. After searching through many bags in an abandoned-luggage room, we found hers by the luggage tag.

It didn't take me long to realize she might have Alzheimer's. She was lucid most of the time and knew who I was, but I noticed that she had forgotten little things. Her personality had changed as well. She was different with me; she no longer had the familiar tenseness that had so often been present when we were together in the past.

After she had visited my sister for a few days, she came back to my house and I took her to Logan Airport for her flight back to England. We were driving on the Massachusetts Turnpike into Boston when she said to me, "I am having a little chest pain."

My heart sank. Now what was I going to do? I knew she had angina after a recent heart attack in England, but she had not mentioned any chest pain until now. I suggested she find her nitro tablets in her purse. She managed to get one out and put it under her tongue. Thankfully, it seemed to work. We got her bag checked, and as we were approaching the gate where I would have to leave her, I did not feel comfortable letting her go on by herself. There was still an hour left before her flight, and I was afraid she would forget what she was doing and wander off, missing her flight altogether. I pleaded with security — explaining her mental status — to let me stay with her until she boarded. They did. Fortunately, in the 1980s, security was far more lenient than it is at present.

My mother did not want to sit — she was antsy — so I walked around with her. I would not let her out of my sight. At one point, she said in a very loud voice, "Why are you following me around?" I mumbled some excuse that I needed to be with her. I was very relieved to hand her over to the flight attendant and see her get safely on the plane. She definitely was not her usual self. She showed no emotion when saying goodbye to me; I could have been a stranger she said goodbye to. I wondered whether I was ever going to see her again and what was going to happen to her. And, I wondered how my father was going to cope with my mother after the personality changes caused by her memory loss.

Also, in 1988, I completed the Health Record Administrator program at Northeastern and began working as a supervisor in the Medical Records Department at Brigham and Women's Hospital in Boston. BWH is a large teaching hospital in a congested area. Since nearby parking is very limited, I had to park off-site in a garage and take a shuttle bus back and forth. The garage was right next to the Mass Pike across from Fenway Park. On game days, we had to get our cars out early. However, there was a small compensation for this inconvenience, as the aroma of sausages cooking on the food carts wafted through the air and into the garage. One spring afternoon in 1989, I got off the shuttle bus to retrieve my car. It was a warmish, sunny day about a year after I had begun to work at BWH, and I had a bounce in my step as I relished the thought that spring was finally here.

When I got to the upper level, I paused for a moment to look at the traffic beneath me on the Mass Pike as it whizzed by. Suddenly and for no particular reason, the thought of wanting to die again popped into my head. I thought, How easy it would be, Susan, to hurl yourself into that rapidly moving traffic beneath you. Death would be immediate.

Why did I have a thought like this? I had a job I had been preparing for and now had enough money to live relatively comfortably. My two sons were doing well and had no major problems. For once in my life, everything was going pretty smoothly. These suicidal feelings were certainly familiar but why now? I was doing everything I knew how to help myself and this included continuing to see my psychiatrist, Dr. Cohen, weekly.

This incident proved to be a turning point for me. At that moment, I made the decision to go on antidepressants once again (I had stopped taking them at some point after the shock treatments). These feelings were beyond my control, and there was simply no reason for them — or to put up with them. At my next appointment with Dr. Cohen, I asked him to put me on antidepressants. He prescribed Prozac, and very gradually, my mood improved and these suicidal feelings subsided once again.

By 1990, I had been divorced for eight years, and Tim was eighteen and Peter almost seventeen. That is, they were approaching adulthood, and with my really active parenting largely behind me, I decided to make a serious foray into the dating scene. I longed for a lasting relationship and I had always thought I would meet someone at some point. Up to then, I don't think I was ready. Although I had been very busy during those eight years, I was lonely at times and wanted a constant friend and partner by my side. Although I had already dabbled a bit by going to some singles events and answering ads in a singles magazine, nothing came of the resulting encounters.

In 1991, after a year of short-term dating, I met a man through a singles ad. Ironically, he was named Michael, but he went by Mike. He was pleasant to look at with a short white beard and hair, on the thin side, and slightly taller than I. He lived in an apartment in Cambridge and had a modest job working for the state of Massachusetts. He had neither been married nor had children. I soon found he was a quirky person and I did not feel at home in his apartment. The unusual layout did not bother me as much as there was no real comfortable room to hang out in. He had a whole room devoted to travel memorabilia that he was very particular about, a room meant for show, but not to live in. I was willing to put up with some of his issues because we did have some good times. He showed me all around Cambridge, and his neighborhood had a lot of ethnic restaurants that we enjoyed.

That summer of 1991, my father wrote to say that, after six years away, he and my mother were returning to the US. He reported that my mother's memory was getting worse and they needed to be closer to family. I was not involved with any of the planning. They and Clare decided that my parents would buy a house in Manchester, New Hampshire, close to where my sister and her family lived. Remarried and now the mother of two school-age boys, Clare was going to help them out and be the primary caretaker, if and when needed. By now, neither one of my parents was driving, so Clare would be taking them to doctors' appointments, and other needed errands. Since she worked only part-time, Clare was able to commit to that.

Since my background was in healthcare, I felt I could have done better with helping my parents with their medical issues, especially with dealing with my mother's Alzheimer's, which she clearly had. But New Hampshire was a less expensive place to live than the Boston area and generally quieter with less traffic and congestion, so it made sense for them to move there. Plus, my parents were closer to Clare and, obviously, preferred to have her to look after them. They bought a house about three miles down the street from Clare's.

Again, they had expressed their preferences, as they had when I was a child and then an adolescent. I was sure that if my brother Mark were still nearby and not now in Oregon and remarried to a third woman, they would have placed him second in their order of favorite children. Imagine approaching fifty and still feeling this stab — not as acutely as before but still feeling it.

How long would it be before this lack, this penury of nurturing from my parents, would be healed?

I was glad to have stayed in Newton for the boys' sakes as I felt it was a favorable place for them to grow up in. The schools were excellent, and downtown Boston was accessible via a half hour ride on the MBTA.

I always knew that I would have to sell the house when the boys went to college because, in the divorce agreement, part of the house had been put into an educational trust. Although half of the proceeds of a sale would go to me, the other half was entailed for Tim's and Peter's college educations. Since Michael was responsible for their tuition, he needed money from the trust. In the late spring of 1992, he let me know that the time had come for the trust to contribute to Peter's tuition.

When Michael and I had bought the house in 1976, the sellers' realtor had made an impression on me. The reason was very simple: I could tell she liked our house and I had a good feeling about her. I always remembered that and, more importantly, I remembered her name. When I had to put the house on the market, I was thrilled that she agreed to be my realtor and sell it for me. The house sold within a week at asking price. I couldn't have asked for more. I took two vacation weeks that summer to pack up and get rid of a lot of stuff.

Subsequently, my realtor was a huge help in finding me a two bedroom condo, still in Newton. I had to get rid of a lot of furniture, old appliances, and other things. It was quite an undertaking, but I got it done. The paperwork went smoothly for the house and condo. I used the money I earned from the sale of the house for a down payment and began to pay the remaining mortgage monthly; I invested the rest of the sale money.

Peter was entering Villanova University in Pennsylvania

Shadows and Light

that September. For the next four years, since he wanted to stay in Newton to be close to his friends, he would be living with me during the summers and while on breaks. Tim would be starting his junior year at Hartwick College in Oneonta, New York, and would be living with his father when he was home on breaks.

I loved having a smaller place to live in and care for. It was all mine, since it was in my name only, and I could decorate and paint it as I wished. I had no more lawn to mow or leaves to rake. I was not going to miss those chores at all. Even though my sons, when they were older, had helped me over the years, I was the one who had to think about it and prod them to do it. My condo did have a small deck at the side and a place to plant a few flowers. I had everything I wanted.

I was still dating Mike on and off. I had my doubts about him and some of his behavior was bothering me. He was a borderline obsessive-compulsive. He had to have things just so and done in a way he had always done them.

I had vacation time coming so Mike and I decided to spend a week in Puerto Rico. After one day in Puerto Rico, Mike was extremely rude to a bartender for not having the kind of beer he wanted. He reminded me of an obnoxious, demanding tourist, and I was embarrassed by his behavior. I enjoyed driving around the island and seeing the sights, but was disappointed that Mike did not enjoy spending any time on a beach, which was a priority for me. We finally did get to one beach but only spent about a half-hour there.

One day, after finishing our breakfast and morning coffee on the balcony of the dining room at our parador, we walked to our car to start the day. The left front tire was flat. Mike started to go off on a rant. Clearly agitated, he paced around the car. He had no idea how to change a tire; in fact, he didn't even own a car, which had always been a bone of contention with me. While I

Shadows and Light

could probably have studied the car manual and changed the tire, I had not wanted Mike to lose face.

"This is what we will do. You stay here, and I am going back to the inn for help," I said.

He agreed. I found a man who worked at the inn to help change the tire, and before long, we were on our way for the day.

Then, on our way to catch our flight home, I said, "I think we have a flat. You had better pull over."

"This is not happening," he said. "What are we going to do?" Mike's face was getting red and he was starting to get agitated again.

"I see a gas station just ahead on the right."

When we pulled into the gas station. Mike jumped out of the car, yelling and waving his hands. You would think by his actions that we were having a medical emergency instead of a flat tire. I had to suppress a laugh as my father's words echoed in my head, "Always leave extra time when you are going somewhere, in case you get a flat tire." It had actually happened after all these years! We had left for the airport with plenty of extra time, so we would make our flight. A man from the gas station came right over to us and said he could change the tire. Then he looked from Mike, who was still ranting, to me and said, "Are you okay?" I assured him I was.

After this experience, I knew I no longer wanted to date Mike. A few days after getting back home, I invited him over to my place. I was sensitive when breaking it off with him and did it in the best way possible. Even so, he did not take it well and cried copiously. When I think of this trip with Mike now, I realize I learned a lot about myself and what I needed in a relationship. My communications skills were clearly improving.

Having disentangled myself easily enough, I was now alone again and that was fine.

Chapter 11
Reaching Out for a Life Companion

The mid-1990s were important years for me. They included a relationship that was very satisfying, but before we can get to my time with Johnnie, I have to write about several other important things.

In April of 1993, my godmother, Lydia, died and left me an inheritance. Because she had lived in British Columbia, I had not seen her since I visited my relatives when I was 24, more than two decades earlier. She was a friend of my mother and had never married. Her family was wealthy (at least by our family's standards), and my mother had always said that Lydia planned to leave me some jewelry. I had pretty much forgotten about this jewelry. Lydia had a long, slow decline with dementia, and when I learned she had died, I figured I no longer was important to her or she would leave all her jewelry and money to charity. Then, two months after she died, I received a phone call from her attorney informing me that Lydia had indeed left me six diamond rings, as well as about $100,000!

I was overjoyed to be the recipient of this windfall! I was told it would take a while for the will to be probated and the money released, but even so, this was exciting. It was more money than I had ever had.

Concerning the rings, I thought, "Who needs six diamond

rings?" Even so, I was jittery with anticipation and very curious about the value of the rings I was going to receive. Perhaps they were also a windfall!

In spirit and not in person, I thanked my mother, who was herself now ravaged by Alzheimer's, for being Lydia's friend and selecting her for my godmother. At last, for all the grief I had gone through with my mother, I had something to be grateful to her for.

The rings turned out not to be valuable since they were "mine cut" and small, therefore not worth a lot, but the money was something else! With the last inheritance that I had received from Aunt Clare, I had spent nothing on myself. When Lydia's bequest arrived after about a year, I bought myself a new TV and a gas grill for my son, Peter, who lived with me during college vacations. Other than those two small purchases, true to my nature to be conservative about money, the rest of the inheritance went in the bank. At least this time, I had honored myself with a gift.

Linda, who had been married to my brother, had remarried and she and her husband Zack had bought a cabin on Maidstone Lake in the Northeast Kingdom of Vermont, an hour away from where they lived in Wheelock. When they invited me up for a visit one weekend in the summer of 1994, I found the drive up there, which took about three and a half hours, seemed endless. The last twenty-five minutes was on a curvy country road and then the five miles to the lake was on a dirt road that was full of potholes and ruts. I had thought, Why would they ever do such a thing as put themselves in a place like this?

The lake, however, when I came upon it, was gorgeous, very clean and quiet. There were no commercial buildings, condos, or high rises anywhere. Over the weekend, I learned that friends of Linda and Zack who had come up for a visit had been so drawn to the beauty and calmness of the lake that they had put money down on a place of their own. I found myself to be increasingly hooked, and I even started to think how, since I now had some disposable income thanks to Lydia, it was also possible for me to invest in a place of my own.

Back in Newton, my financial advisor was against the idea; he thought vacation homes were not a good investment. As he said, "Everyone gets excited about a summer place and dreams of owning one. However, they are money drains. Taxes, repairs, extra appliances. In the long run, owning a cottage does not make sense from a financial standpoint."

Here I was, single, and I needed this for myself. Ignoring my advisor, I decided, for the first time in my life, to take a risk and defy conventional wisdom. I began looking for a place on Maidstone Lake. In October of 1994, I signed papers on a small cabin. Built around the mid-forties, it was rustic, its stove and refrigerator ancient, and its water pumped from the lake. At some point, a bathroom had been added. The cabin, situated right on the water, offered a fabulous panoramic view of the rolling hills in the distance. At the time of the purchase, I made a promise to myself: I would sell it if it ever became a burden.

I spent the larger part of the next 15 summers at Maidstone Lake. I went up most weekends, and every year, I took my two-week vacation there. How I enjoyed it! I would drive the three and a half to four hours up almost every Friday evening. Once through the traffic, I would start to relax. The trip that had been so wearisome when

Maidstone Lake

I had first done it at Linda's invitation now became a time to let go of the tensions of the week. When I entered the White Mountains, I was even more relaxed, knowing I would soon be at my haven. I always stopped for groceries in a town twenty miles from the lake because, once I was at Maidstone, I wouldn't want to take the time for shopping, especially as the nearest general store was fifteen miles away.

The lake became my refuge. A place all my own where I could do anything I wanted to, yet I had friends close by to do things with if I liked. The community of Linda's and Zack's became the core of my new group. We had our famous potluck dinners, which we held in a rotation of cabins, and everyone brought what they had or wanted to cook. It was fun and some of the meals were interesting! Any family or friends up for the weekend were always welcome.

The beauty of the lake was so peaceful. I could spend hours sitting on my deck just staring at its ever-changing moods, from clear and calm to choppy and windy. There is the saying in New England that, "If you don't like the weather, wait a few minutes." One of the most beautiful mornings at the lake was in the fall when my son, Tim, was up for the weekend. When we woke up, the lake was totally fogged in. As fog started to slowly lift, there was soon a crystal-clear reflection in the lake of the blue sky and the brilliantly colored fall trees on the other side of the lake. It was nature at its finest. Just stunning.

Because of my cabin at Maidstone Lake, I met a man who was to add much to my happiness — and who would then leave me. In the summer of 1995, Johnnie came into my life. I still smile when I think of him. He came into my life after years of my being single. While I had dated Mike and had met a few other men on occasion, I had not felt the urge to make a deep connection with any of them.

Shadows and Light

One Saturday in early June of 1995, at my cabin on Maidstone Lake for a weekend, I was sitting on the deck relishing my second cup of coffee. The expanse of lake before me was perfectly still except for an occasional jump of a fish. I would be turning fifty-one in September, and my life was better than it had ever been. I was so lucky to have this place in Vermont. Peter was a senior in college, and Tim was on his own now and busy with his job and friends. Divorced from one another for many years, Michael and I had nonetheless managed to stay in the relationship enough to support each other in doing a good job of raising our two boys.

I knew life was good, but I sensed it would be even better with a special man to share it all with: my cabin in Vermont, my condo home in Massachusetts, my whole self. But then, would dating again be worth the aggravation that my sporadic forays into finding a relationship had brought into my life? As I looked back on my most recent one, I knew I had spent more time worrying about him and his behavior than having a good time. It was clear that he had not really cared about me. Maybe if I cared more about myself, I thought sitting on my deck at the lake, I could find someone who would love and appreciate me for who I was.

At that moment, serendipity came paddling toward my dock in a kayak. Linda came from her place a mile down the lake, bearing news. After Mark had left her and their five children, I had wanted to keep a good relationship with Linda whom I now called "my sister." Going down to the dock, I helped her out of the kayak.

After I had prepared her tea, we took ourselves out to the deck. After a while discussing plans for our potluck dinner that evening, Linda said, "I know this teacher from school. I would like you to meet him. He would be a good person for you to see while you are up on the lake."

Shadows and Light

I was hesitant to agree to anything.

"His name is Johnnie, and I think you would enjoy his company," she persisted. He had just retired after twenty-five years teaching English at the same coed boarding school in northern Vermont where Linda taught, so she knew he was well liked.

"He loves to read and enjoys the outdoors."

Then, as if moved to honor truth and not mislead me, she said he had been married four times.

"But, give meeting him a try," Linda said. "It can't hurt."

She was right. There was not much point in not giving meeting him a try. I told her to have him call me. When Johnnie called a few days later, I invited him over for dinner the following Saturday evening. I am always nervous meeting a man, a potential partner, for the first time, and so I kept telling myself this wasn't a "real" date. Thinking it wasn't a date lessened my anxiety and expectations. After all, I was just meeting Johnnie to please Linda.

That Saturday, I finished preparing the meal early — my *pièce de résistance* was an apple pie. Then I had an hour to wait until he came. As I usually do when I'm anxious, I paced for a while; I walked from one room to another straightening out a pillow or rearranging the table setting. Why was I feeling so nervous? Were my hopes of hitting it off with this man high? I feared to admit this to myself, but I did have some sense that I would be a better person within the context of a relationship. Making an apple pie was perhaps my way of showing Johnnie that I was worthy of a relationship. Perhaps, in the back in mind was the old saying, "The way to a man's heart is through his stomach." This hope was an unconscious one at the time, but then again, maybe it wasn't and I really wanted to impress this unknown man and have the relationship I was so ready for.

Finally, I heard footsteps on the walkway! Johnnie turned out to be friendly, talkative, and easy on the eyes. He was about five feet, eleven inches, trim, and muscular, with graying hair and a moustache that was still dark; he was casually dressed in shorts and a tee shirt. Any fears I had about meeting him vanished. When we walked into the living area, which faced the lake and whose windows provided a full view, Johnnie said, "What a lovely place you have."

"Come outside to the deck and you can see more," I said as I opened the screen door to the deck.

Our chatting proved so easy. When it was time for the main course, Johnnie helped me grill the chicken, and we stayed on the deck to eat. I had a round table so, while eating, we each could have a view of the lake. Through the meal, I was looking forward to serving the apple pie, which I was sure would receive his warm praise.

When it came time for apple pie, however, Johnnie passed on it!

I couldn't believe he could do that. My ex-husband Michael had been especially fond of apple pie, and I assumed that Johnnie, too, would have liked it. Clearly, I would have to adapt if I wanted a relationship! What I had known with Michael was not what I would need to know with Johnnie.

I felt a bit deflated, but I decided to let it go. We continued to sit on the deck and talk, exchanging stories about work and children. When Johnnie realized it was time to leave — he had an hour's drive home — we said good night without making any plans to get together again. I had enjoyed his company and had even felt a tiny spark of chemistry. When standing next to him, I had felt warmth emanating from him, and we had flirted a bit.

Take it easy, Susan, I reminded myself. You have just met this man and will have to wait to see what happens. Even as I was feeling hopeful there was potential for a relationship, I felt fine with our lack of plans. It would give me a chance to at least enjoy a fantasy about a fling with Johnnie in case he did not want to see me again.

I had not taken it easy with my first husband. Not that we got married fast but that I had failed to give it enough thought. I should have postponed marriage as I was not ready for it and my mental health was precarious. During the late spring of 1970, when Michael asked me to marry him, in spite of being aware of significant personality and values differences, I had said yes. What ensued was what usually does when two people who don't really know each other marry for unsound reasons. We set ourselves up for twelve years of struggle.

I did not want that in my life ever again.

With caution born of experience, I agreed to see Johnnie again when he proposed an outing. Our first "date" was a hike on Mount Pisgah. Unfortunately, the day was excessively hot; the exertion of climbing Mount Pisgah depleted me — my head was pounding as I had not had enough to drink. I should have known better and set limits. Anticipating trouble, I asked Johnnie to take me home early so I could lie down. After he had done so, I went into the bedroom to sleep. Twenty minutes later, I woke up to knocking on the front door. When I staggered out of the room, there was Johnnie!

"You left your pocketbook in my car," he said as he handed it to me. "Are you okay?

I did get better soon and I did see Johnnie again. He told me later that he thought I had feigned the headache to get rid of him!

Our relationship progressed through that summer. When we were apart, we wrote breezy, funny letters to each other. Every afternoon after work when I picked up my mail, my heart fluttered. Was there going to be a letter from Johnnie today? I was ecstatic when there was one. When there wasn't a letter, I knew one would be coming soon. One weekend in September, when I was up at the lake and Johnnie was away on one of his fishing trips that were a passion for him, I told Linda how well things were progressing with Johnnie and that we were seeing each other almost every weekend.

"When I introduced you, I thought you might see a movie or do something together once in a while. I did not expect it to turn into a relationship," she said.

But it had. After the cabin was closed for the winter, Johnnie and I continued to spend as much time together as we could on weekends. Often, on Friday afternoons, I would drive up to Vermont to be with him or he would come down to Newton to see me. When I visited Johnnie, I found the rustic ambience of his house relaxing. The finish was all wood inside. There was a large wood stove. I especially enjoyed lying in bed and watching the snow fall, as it did frequently all winter in Vermont, from the huge picture window in the master bedroom.

I was enjoying getting to know Johnnie and having some fun with him. Johnnie had retired at fifty-five from teaching and was selling his Vermont house. He had no set plans for the future. I was glad because, if our relationship progressed, I would not have wanted to move in with him in cold and isolated northern Vermont. I much preferred the thought of his joining me in Newton.

When thinking of a commitment with Johnnie, however, I was always naggingly aware of his four previous marriages. Is there something off about how he relates to women? I would wonder, but I was having a good time and did not push the thought.

In March 1996, Johnnie and I had become comfortable enough with each other to travel to Grenada. After months of cold New England weather, we enjoyed the Caribbean sun and warm water. My life seemed to be opening. This was the first time I had traveled outside the continental US since I had gone to Puerto Rico with Mike. It felt good, and I hoped that it foretold a bit of my future.

We had a few disagreements, however, about where to go and what to do. I wanted to spend time on the beach and Johnnie wanted to fish. But for the most part, we were able to compromise and have a good time — a much better time than I had had with Mike. A local fisherman, whose boat was moored on the beach in front of our inn, took Johnnie and me out one morning. It was fun, and I caught some fish! Johnnie, in turn, spent some time on the beach with me.

These pleasant days in Grenada were followed, however, by my brother's sudden death in Oregon on March 30, 1996. Mark was only fifty-three and had had coronary artery disease for a while. For some time now, I had sensed he was a lost soul, floundering in the bog of life, unable to free himself. I believe he died from a broken heart. He had been living in Oregon for about seven years with his third wife, Grace. I had not seen him in at least three years — and that visit of his to New England had been a quick one and I had only seen him while he was visiting our parents.

Of course, Clare, her eleven-year-old son, and I flew out, but when we called from the hotel to say we were in town and would like to come by the house, Mark's widow Grace said she did not want me to come to her house! We had never met, and I was after all her

Mark, 1965

Shadows and Light

husband's sister! What kind of strange person would not want to meet her husband's sister, one of only two siblings?

That afternoon, Clare and her son visited Grace at the house, but I did not. It felt very off-putting — and wrong!

The next day, after the service, everyone was invited to Grace and Mark's house for a reception. Grace, whom I had spied at church as obviously the widow and whom Clare had pointed out to me, was nowhere to be seen. Just before Clare and I had to leave for the airport, Grace made her appearance. I gave her a brief hug and offered my condolences. She was awkward with me, saying nothing and giving me only a hint of recognition with a slight smile. How had my brother married such a strange woman! It made me feel sad for him that he had apparently settled for so little. Then she walked away without offering me any condolences in return.

On my return flight to Massachusetts, I had plenty of time to think about Mark who was two years older than I. I hadn't really known him as an adult, but as children, we had spent a lot of time playing together. We drew apart when I was at St. Mary's boarding school. When I was either a sophomore or a junior at St. Mary's and saw him when I was home — which was not for long since I was away working those summers — he would call me "Susie Slut" at times. This, of course, did not endear him to me. What was that about? Did he remember something that I couldn't? Was he projecting something that was really about him? In what way was he promiscuous?

He had married Linda right out of college and they had moved away to Connecticut where he got a job, like our father, teaching in a boy's boarding school. After that, we never spent any significant time together. We both were struggling emotionally, and I am sure that contributed to keeping us apart. I also wondered, as I flew across the continent, what he had told Grace about me that had made her behave so erratically. I also couldn't understand how he had left Linda and their five kids to end up in another marriage which did not last and finally a third marriage with a woman like Grace.

When I got back to Massachusetts, it was good to have Johnnie not too far away so that I could connect with him and unload a bit of Grace's boorish behavior and to process some of my grief.

By the summer, my relationship with Johnnie was still going well, and I was up at the lake with him as much as I could be. We had now been dating for a year, and our relationship felt like it would last.

In August of 1996, while I was on vacation at the lake, my father called to let me know my mother had taken a turn for the worse. Wanting to be with her one last time, I had driven down by myself to the Manchester nursing home where she had been a resident for more than two years. My mother's death would be a blessing after her long time with Alzheimer's. I sensed she knew Mark had died just over four months earlier and she wanted to be with him.

I drew up a chair and sat beside her bed. At such moments, memories flash by — some of the good times and some of the other times. I was overwhelmed by so many bad memories that I stayed for only about fifteen minutes. Kissing her goodbye one last time, I left to drive back to the lake. I wanted the comfort of being with Johnnie.

My father called the next morning to say that my mother had died a few hours earlier. I did not feel any remorse or sadness. Instead, I felt a sense of calm. I had done my grieving over the years while coming to terms with how she had abandoned me.

Linda remembered my mother saying good things about me. She spoke so well of me that, as Linda was entering our family, she said she was intimidated by me. My mother often talked to her about how competent I was, how hard I worked, how proud she was of me.

Why couldn't she have said these things to me?

Talking to Linda has helped me sort things out, but my mother still remains an enigma to me. Why would she have given up on me? Maybe she didn't even know herself. After all, much later when I was communicating with the afterlife, she acknowledged from there that she had said cruel things to me and didn't know why she had done this.

Her funeral service was at the Grace Episcopal Church in Manchester, New Hampshire, which my parents attended. In the last years of my mother's life, my father had been living by himself and he had done the best he could, but the house was not clean. Because we had planned to have people gather at his house for lunch, I expressed to Johnnie that some cleaning was in order. Later, I could see that Johnnie was not around. Setting out to look for him, I found him down on his hands and knees cleaning the bathroom. This made me feel nurtured by Johnnie who, I felt, was attuned to the support I needed.

Wow! I was impressed. Was this what I might expect long-term from a relationship with Johnnie? It was different from what I had known with Michael who had not had this kind of feel for what to do next to support me.

My mother circa mid 1930's

I was so busy with preparations that, for several days, I did not think about my mother having died. But on the day of her funeral, I got a bit weepy when I greeted people on the way out of church. Other than that brief moment, I did not shed any tears for my mother.

It is always hard to know about someone else's life, but I will offer my thoughts here. I do not believe my mother was mentally ill. She was depressed especially around the time when she and my father split up in the 1970s. At least, that was when I became aware of her depression. She lacked self-confidence and had a poor body image. She had wanted to go to college and did not because she took care of her mother who had rheumatic heart disease and was confined to a wheelchair.

My mother, 1976

In the first few years of my parents' marriage, my father was away in the army, and my mother was alone to care for Mark and me. When I was a married adult with children, after she and my father had split and were back together, she said she knew that her marriage, while we were still living in Canada, was not good. Unfortunately, she had seen a counselor who told her to stick it out. During these years, I can imagine she did not acknowledge to herself that he was homosexual. In keeping with the family tradition, as she had done so many times with so many

My parents wedding, 1941

other things, I can imagine it was easier for her to deny or "forget" this fact. I can also surmise that knowing that he preferred men had not nurtured feelings of security in my mother.

For the sake of his teaching career in boys' schools, my father was a gay man who had lived as a heterosexual man, and perhaps that was one reason my mother either did not know or had "forgotten" that he was gay.

My father and my sister came up with a plan to put a second story addition on his house. The new upstairs addition would have bedrooms, a bathroom, and a den for Clare and her family. On the first floor, my father would have his own bedroom, bathroom, and office so he could maintain his privacy. They would share the kitchen, the living room, and the dining room, which were also on the first floor. With this arrangement, my father would not have the upheaval of having to move, but he would also not be spared of all of the disruptions and the irritations that accompany a renovation.

In the fall of 1996, fourteen months after we had met, Johnnie moved into my condo with me in Newton, Massachusetts. He had sold his house, and it was a logical next step for him to live with me. I was also more than ready to live with him full-time. He seemed to be all that I was looking for in a partner. He had made it clear that he was never going to marry again and that was all right with me. Marriage at this stage in my life was not important to me. Our children were grown, and we would never have children together. To me, children were one reason to get married. Also, I felt I was not ready for another marriage right then, since despite being in my early fifties, I did not yet know myself well enough when it came to men and relationships. My parents had not been good role models for marriage. Theirs was distant with no display of affection. What's more, my father preferred male lovers.

Although I was still wary of Johnnie's four marriages and all the baggage that this might dump on a relationship, I was willing to make a commitment — although not to one as binding as marriage. I agreed to live with him. I had found nothing amiss in our relationship thus far. I was financially stable so I did not need his support, although the money he contributed monthly to the household expenses allowed for some extras. A shift had taken place in me; I was more accepting of myself and was starting to put the insecurity of my past to rest. But I was still plagued by nagging but buried memories of my childhood.

Was that wishful thinking that those memories would stay buried and never resurface again?

Chapter 12
A Surprise Ending

It had been fourteen years since I had shared my life with a live-in partner, and I was up for the companionship. I was ready to enjoy life.

Johnnie found part-time work at an after-school program nearby in Newton, and in season, we continued to spend as many weekends at Maidstone Lake as possible. He enjoyed the quieter, carefree life we had there as much as I did. Together we were able to make repairs more easily and quickly and to do fixing-up projects on the cabin. He also was a man's man in many ways. He loved hunting and fishing, and at the lake, he was in his element.

Johnnie was also good at bargaining. When a few pieces of furniture arrived from my godmother's estate, I had no idea how to sell those I did not want. He located an antique dealer to appraise the pieces and sell them for me. I was impressed and sighed with relief as he took care of this. I had been doing everything myself for the last fourteen years, so it was a balm to have someone share the work of my life.

There were several lovely things in my life that fall, my birthday on September 6 being one. It was my second birthday with Johnnie, but this was different, since we were now a couple without the tentative play of doing enough but not too much so as not to give the wrong message.

Kayaks were popular on the lake. Linda would often kayak over for a visit. To my surprise, Johnnie bought me a bright red kayak for my birthday. I was overwhelmed with his generosity and his thoughtfulness. I had wanted a kayak for some time, and now I could go out with either Linda or Johnnie.

Susan kayaking

With Johnnie at my side, with the lake friends I had made around Linda, and with my sons who were now adults and living on their own but keeping in touch with me, I felt less alone than I had in years, and I sensed I was part of a supportive family. The pain of my childhood, my years with Michael and the years alone since Michael and I divorced, were all in the past. I felt the present was good. Johnnie and I laughed a lot and kept up the humorous banter we had had when exchanging letters. There was a joke about a lamb — I cannot recall the details — so for Christmas that year, I gave Johnnie a cute stuffed lamb. "Lambie" became an alter ego for us as a couple and provided many laughs.

Johnnie enjoyed cooking and would occasionally prepare dinner. This was a new experience for me — to be catered to and thought of. I usually did the grocery shopping and most of the cooking because I enjoyed it, but it felt comforting to come home from work to the condo to find the preparations for dinner underway. Some days, Johnnie would bring me a pastry or cookies leftover from his after-school-program. These were not run-of-the-mill goodies but scrumptious ones donated to the school by the local bakery.

In March of 1997, we took another trip together, to Florida to visit one of his sisters and her husband. The plan was to stay with them for a couple of days and then go off by ourselves. While there, I asked Johnnie's sister, "Do you have any idea why your brother has been married so many times?"

Incredibly, she said, "I have no clue."

Perhaps she didn't know him well enough to know or perhaps she was not a perceptive person about feelings — not, as I was learning, unlike her brother. Or again, perhaps she didn't trust me enough to tell me the truth. Perhaps she feared that, if I knew why Johnnie had been married so many times, the answer would lead me to leave Johnnie and he would be alone and she did not want that. I was also self-conscious enough to wonder if she thought, "Johnnie is introducing another new woman to me. Is this parade of women ever going to stop? I don't want to invest in yet another woman until I know they are going to remain together."

After we left his sister's, Johnnie had planned for us to go to Captiva Island as he had been there before. I was up for anything; this was my first time in Florida. So we took off in our rental car. Johnnie had booked a place to stay in Fort Myers close to Sanibel and Captiva Islands. The motel Johnnie had found through some organization — possibly a church — was a no-frills place. I felt some sense of loss since it would have been pleasant, on a vacation, to be at a more tropical, beachy resort. The motel he had selected wasn't much fun to be in, but at least it was clean.

Captiva Island was more built up than he remembered it, and he was disappointed. On Sanibel Island, I was thrilled at the prospect of walking its beaches and I wanted us to spend time on the beach looking for shells to bring back home. Johnnie, of course, wanted to fish and had no interest in shells. We only had one full day left, and so we came up with two plans. Johnnie would drop me off at the beach to do my shell hunting and he

Shadows and Light

would go off and do his fishing thing. We agreed he would come pick me up at a designated spot in three hours.

I was entranced with the beach on Sanibel Island where I found lots of shells. As I walked along, the sun felt warm on my back. I was in tune with nature and sensed this was a special place for me. The magical feeling continued as I walked and walked. The trance broke when I looked at my watch and thought, I've got to get back. Johnnie will be coming soon. On the walk back, I realized I was a bit deflated; I would have liked to share this shell-seeking experience with him. In exchange, I would have gone fishing, but we had not talked about how to meet our own needs and still do things together.

On this vacation, it disappointed me that we had not done many things as a couple. It wasn't as if he did not have enough time to do things by himself when we were home that he would begrudge me an afternoon of togetherness in Florida. My customary fears of abandonment kicked in, and I wondered if there something in Johnnie that already needed distance from me? Or, was I beginning to experience the reason for his four marriages — perhaps he was good at beginnings and not so good at maintaining relationships?

I was still getting a lot out of being together, which had proven, in spite of the Florida trip, to be mostly a salve to my abandonment fears. I chose not to dwell on negatives.

Michael and I had traveled a lot in Europe. He had always dominated making our plans. In particular, I remembered wanting to go to Mont St. Michel and Salzburg and because it had not been a priority of his, we had not gone.

It was with these memories of France that, almost two years into my relationship with Johnnie, the Florida trip as well as the trip we were soon to take to Prince Edward Island became a kind of harbinger.

In the summer of 1997, the Confederation Bridge connecting Prince Edward Island to New Brunswick had just opened. When Johnnie and I, separately, had been to Prince Edward Island before, we had taken the ferry. He wanted to see the new bridge. I wanted to go to PEI itself. When I had gone with Michael many years earlier, the Anne of Green Gables house was not open to the public. I told Johnnie the Green Gable books were a favorite of mine in childhood, and I was eager to visit the park with him. I wanted to go together to the house and share with him how much the story had meant to me.

We were getting ready to leave Vermont where we had been staying when I saw he was loading his fishing gear into the car. Naturally, I thought, We'll go to Anne of Green Gables together and then he'll go fishing. I'll either go with him or I'll do something else. Of course, this was my presumption since we had not spoken about it.

Johnnie and I drove to PEI from Maidstone Lake. It was a long drive across New Hampshire, Maine, and finally New Brunswick, where we stopped at a charming B&B for the night before driving over the new bridge. It was an amazing sight. The eight-mile wonder was a graceful, curving concrete and steel structure that was stunning to view from a distance, but when driving on it, because of the fencing, I could only catch a glimpse of the waters of the Northumberland Strait below. We only had two nights on the island, and there was a lot both Johnnie and I wanted to do.

"When can we go to the Anne of Green Gables house together?" I asked Johnnie now that we were on PEI.

"There is no way I'm spending one of my two days there. I am going fishing," he announced.

"It would mean a lot to me to share this experience with you," I said.

He would not help me on this one. Johnnie said I could drop

him off at a bridge to fish from and I could take the car and drive to Green Gables. This arrangement made me feel like a single person who did not have a loving partner. Abandonment issue screamed from all over me, but I refocused myself and decided to make the best of the situation and enjoy my time at Green Gables.

The site was all I had wanted from it. I listened for noises as I walked in the "Haunted Woods" and I pictured Anne in her bedroom and what life was like for her growing up in that house. I would have enjoyed turning to Johnnie to tell him how these Green Gable books had been a lifeline at times when I had been so unhappy. One of those times was when my father taught at Christchurch, a boys' boarding school in Virginia, and life was confusing and I felt my mother did not care for me. Another time was when my father taught at Shattuck, a boys' military boarding school in Minnesota and there again, I felt alone and misunderstood. It was at that school that something had happened to me, and I had always wondered whether it was the incident where my brother was present and knew what had happened.

Anne had given me hope and a bit of comfort when I had desperately needed it. Fortunately, I also had friends — ironically, one called Anne — at both these schools who provided distraction and helped keep me going.

The abandonment I felt from Johnnie on the PEI trip picked up on what I had felt at Sanibel Island, and more. Was I in the relationship I had bargained for? Is this what I could expect? It was beginning to feel like my time with Michael when I was either not listened to or when I did not assert myself sufficiently to be listened to — or perhaps both.

Starting when I was a senior at Boston College, I have been prone to severe headaches. In the summer of 1997, my headaches had gradually become frequent. They weren't the bad, migraine-like ones I have had in the past. These were less intense. The pain would start in my shoulders and creep up into my head. Even though I slept soundly at night, I would wake up with a slight headache in the morning that would slowly get worse as the day progressed. As the summer of 1997 unfolded, I had an almost constant headache. I woke up with one and went to sleep with one.

That summer, I saw my first headache specialist. She was a caring and knowledgeable neurologist, but the drug for migraines she prescribed did not provide relief. Then I heard about another neurologist, Dr. Jansen, who also specialized in headaches, but he did not accept my health insurance and wanted cash up front. The constant pain of the headaches was wearing me down so much, mentally and physically, that I agreed to pay out of pocket.

Dr. Jansen insisted that I stop taking over-the-counter drugs, which I had been taking a lot of. He thought I was getting rebound headaches — headaches from taking too many over-the-counter drugs. Next, I had to keep a daily headache chart. He started me on a low dose of Tofranil, from a tricyclic class of antidepressants. By then, I had been taking Prozac for nine years. For pain, he gave me a muscle relaxant and a non-narcotic suppository as needed. This combo worked! At last, I had some relief when I needed it and the quality of my life improved.

A few years earlier, after reading an article, I had diagnosed myself as having migraines. Now, finally, Dr. Jansen had diagnosed me professionally with a history of migraines and had given me validation that my headaches were real! I had thought I had brought these headaches on myself; that it was my fault.

Dr. Jansen also told me, "You inherited bad muscles." Evidently my shoulder and neck muscles were very tight, which he presented as the cause of my current headaches. He sent me for physical therapy, but PT really did not seem to help the muscular tension, other than temporarily. The headaches, however, were much less intense and frequent for the next several years, and I eventually stopped taking all drugs except for an occasional muscle relaxant. Finally, I was in control of my headaches, and they did not control me.

I did not connect these headaches and this muscle tension with my past or the fact that I had had two major losses — the deaths of my brother and mother — in the previous year. Johnnie seemed to roll with the punches and be an easy-going person and not be put off by my headaches. Although I wasn't a complainer, I must have been irritable and grumpy at times.

The two trips we took that year that had been unsatisfactory at times were now joined by another unsatisfactory distancing experience. While we had both enjoyed going for a walk or a short hike together even when it was cold, now, when I asked, "Would you like to go for a walk today?" his answer was sometimes, "Not today, I am going fishing." In the past, he always said "yes" and was willing to go with me. Fishing now seemed to have taken up the whole front seat of our relationship! It began to feel like I was living alone, and this was only after one year of sharing the condo.

By the winter of 1997-98, I was doing things by myself more and more often. The fun of our relationship seemed to have become a memory. When I think about 1997 now, I realize it is possible that Johnnie was not sharing how he really felt about my headaches. That year, we continued to drift apart and perhaps the burden of my headaches on Johnnie contributed to our distancing.

The following summer of 1998, the third since we had met, once again, Johnnie and I spent as much time as possible up at the lake in Vermont. Our relationship had slipped into a routine that had its comforts but in which we were doing little together. Our intimacy was on a downward spiral.

It was not easy talking to Johnnie about the distance we were developing. I would have to drag the words out of him. When we did talk, the mood between us improved for a while and then we were right back where we had been for the last year, not communicating.

I would remember his four marriages and wonder again if he was good only at starting a relationship but not so good at sustaining it.

By the following summer, in 1999, I could feel that the dynamics between Johnnie and me had deteriorated seriously, but I could not get a grip on what was happening. Johnnie seemed to be significantly unavailable. I still wanted our relationship to work and I did not know how to make our lives together better. We were having disagreements more often. Talking to Johnnie about our dynamics, which were unsatisfying to me, was nonproductive as he simply would not talk things out.

In August of that summer, when his nephew was getting married in New Hampshire, Johnnie told me he was thinking of our staying the night in a college dorm.

"It won't cost much," he said.

Since I was better off financially than Johnnie, I replied, "If money is a factor, I will pay for the night at the motel."

"No, it's not the money," he said.

I could not understand why he would want to spend a night in a college dorm in separate beds when we could be in a comfortable hotel room and perhaps have a romantic night. It seemed like the Fort Myers motel room all over again. But perhaps he was no longer interested in romantic nights with me? I had to ask myself.

In early October, after we closed the cabin for the winter, Johnnie had a cord of wood delivered to the lake and then had his adult son come over to stack it. I thought it strange because we didn't really need the wood and, if we did, we could have stacked it ourselves.

I had spent a lot of time trying to figure Johnnie out, and up to then, I had not been able to. Nor was Johnnie any help. For an English teacher who dealt with literature and its meaning, Johnnie was neither verbal nor insightful.

We had had a lot of fun in the first years, but Johnnie was now turning out to be as inarticulate as my father and Michael were. Did I have a gift for choosing men who could not nurture me? What was that about? Was Johnnie unable to take responsibility for his part of keeping a relationship going? I was beginning to think he might not be, and that was not something I could change.

After so many years of counseling and trying to figure out my own life, I was getting better at it, but I could neither figure Johnnie out nor figure what I might do about making our lives together better.

Later in the fall of 1999, Johnnie, the man I had shared my life with for the previous four years, announced that he had decided to go fishing in Belize for a few weeks and to work there teaching English as a second language. He often went on fishing trips and came back after a few days. Now he was going much farther away, and he was going to work, too. Why hadn't he discussed his plans with me? In the days before he left, Johnnie was acting very strangely, almost secretively, as he bustled about packing his things for the trip to Belize. My foreboding was growing that something was not as it appeared. One time, standing with him in the upstairs hallway of the condo, I felt the urge to speak to him.

"You are planning to come back, aren't you?" I asked.

He nodded yes, but a bit of a shifty look on his face made me wonder if he was telling the truth. Our lives together had become difficult, but he was the first man I had lived with since

Shadows and Light

my divorce from Michael some seventeen years earlier and I had enjoyed much of it. I wondered how I would fare if I were alone again.

How long would he be gone?

He would not tell me.

"Be back by Christmas at least," I had asked.

Several days later as I stood in the doorway of my condo watching Johnnie leave, not knowing how his leaving would play out, I could feel the chill of the early October morning. I pulled my bathrobe tighter around my shoulders, but the coldness in the air was nothing compared to the cold that had penetrated my heart.

It was as if I were a girl again and my mother was dropping me off me at St. Mary's for another year in a boarding school I did not enjoy. I would watch her leave knowing that she and my father would not come for parents' weekend, not for visits "just because we miss you," not for the Christmas Pageant I would be in. There had even been school years when I had worked away from my family all summer at jobs that my mother had gotten. Then after I had been away all summer, my mother would bring me to St. Mary's again. Or, as it felt at the time, abandon me there.

Now in my fifties, I was again trying to ward off feelings of abandonment. Would this sense of estrangement never go away? But Johnnie, my intuition told me, was a wild card.

Two days after he had left for Belize, it dawned on me that Johnnie wasn't coming back.

As the days passed, I noticed there was no mail coming in addressed to him. Had he set up a forwarding address? Also, there was that look he had given me and there were other little things I had noticed he had done around the house. For instance, he had packed some of his belongings. When I noticed that, I had a shot of adrenalin. I blasted off an email.

His response did not come that day, nor the next. Finally, a couple of days later, he emailed to say he had had a problem getting online. Then, he announced in this email and not in person, "I have no intentions of coming back to live with you. I'm moving on."

Mr. Communicator had announced the end of our relationship in an email! I was furious! This was shabby! When I saw pictures I had of him, I erupted with anger. I had taken those pictures in moments of joy and I could not have known that he would sneak away as he had. In my anger, I ripped those photos up and threw the pieces away. I had no idea if he was still in Belize fishing, but if he were, I wished that his fishing boat would sink.

I cried and I raged for a couple of weeks. When I would come home from work and find the house empty and no one but me to make supper, I sobbed endlessly. This drama could not last indefinitely, however, and one afternoon, I walked around from room to room to see what he had left behind. Finding "Lambie" — Johnnie had not packed him up — caused a huge pain in my heart. I picked up "Lambie" and threw him in a box with some other things that Johnnie had left lying around. I thought, What will Johnnie's reaction be when he opens up this box and finds Lambie? Will he get emotional when he sees it?

Earlier, when his son was stacking what I still considered at the time as "our" wood, I had thought the arrangement odd, but I was nonetheless grateful. In retrospect, I realize Johnnie must have been guilty knowing he was going to leave me in the lurch. At least, he must have told himself to relieve a guilty conscience, Susan would have wood for the coming cold weather.

A few weeks later, Johnnie came to the condo in Newton to pick up his belongings. When he got out of the car, he couldn't straighten up, and I could see he was in a lot of back pain, but I was in no mood to sympathize. After I let him in, I proceeded to follow him around, talking constantly, asking questions, and generally letting him know how I felt. He was silent as he gathered his belongings and carried them to his car. He had also left things at the lake, and at some point, his daughter made arrangements to come for them.

What had happened? I can only surmise that dropping out when a relationship needed nurturing was his *modus operandi*.

Johnnie's leaving the way he did shook me to the core. I had been abandoned a number of times in my past, and I desperately wanted it not to happen again. It was as if he had brought someone with a fear of heights to the top of a wobbly tower and left her there.

I would spend the next ten years learning how not to ever be abandoned again, and in the process, I learned that a lot about not being abandoned was about me.

Chapter 13
A New Era Begins

In the weeks after Johnnie left in the fall of 1999, I was very vulnerable and I wanted very much to be important to someone. So, I made the hour drive up to Manchester to spend time with my father perhaps a bit more often. In his late-eighties, he spent most of the day in his recliner and no longer went out for walks. My sister, her husband, and their two school-aged boys had moved into his house as the renovations were completed.

As I continued to process my new singlehood, I kept reminding myself that Johnnie had been married four times — yes, four times — or in a long-term relationship, and that when the going got tough, his modus operandi was to cop out. With me, his copping out had led to leaving with no explanation, never looking back to see the tears of the woman he was abandoning. There was a dark side to him that, if he was aware of it, he was unwilling to acknowledge, or ask for help with. Something was missing in him, and I had to reassure myself that his leaving surreptitiously — yes, I would call it that — was about him and that I was just the latest of a number of women he had abandoned. I could only assume that checking out of a relationship was far easier for Johnnie than taking the responsibility to make it work or being thoughtful about another person's feelings. Still, for all I told myself it was about him, the abandonment theme in my life screamed at me.

Had he said to me, "I will want to abandon you after a few years and you mustn't let me," I might have been more alert to the possibility, and together we might have averted it, but to do that, he would have had to be another person.

But, none of that had happened. He had played out his part of abandoning me, and I guess I had played mine out of being abandoned. Johnnie was another mystery man that I was not able to figure out, another man who gave up on me and was unwilling to change and/or support my emotional issues. Superficially Johnnie and my ex-husband, Michael, were polar opposites — a teacher and outdoorsman versus a conservative CPA — but they were similar in their emotional detachment and in their inability to take responsibility for their part in a relationship. Michael had gone to couples' counseling whereas Johnnie made no effort whatsoever. Then again, Johnnie and I had never had children together, which might have forced us to make a serious attempt at staying together.

What did I learn from this relationship with him? I learned to loosen up and have fun, which is why I smile when I think of him. I also learned it was possible to fall in love again. I rediscovered the pleasure of letter writing and grew to have a greater respect for nature and the outdoors. I went fishing and hunting which I had never done before. Johnnie taught me a lot about Vermont, especially the Northeast Kingdom where he had lived for many years. But the most important thing I learned was that I had to be more aware of the men I went out with. I needed to determine whether they were emotionally unavailable and/or mysterious in any way.

I felt I had been hung out to dry, but instead of being folded and stored in a drawer to be worn again, I was discarded in a bag to be given away. In the past, I would have turned my anger at being abandoned in this way against myself and, most likely, gotten depressed. Instead, that fall of 1999, I displayed my anger outwardly and talked about it. This was a breakthrough for me.

I believe people come into our lives to teach us something, and this was the case with Johnnie. Maybe there was a soul contract between us. One day, I will know that for sure, but what I realized then was I could handle a fairly successful relationship with a strong intimate component. Even though this had been a painful ending, it gave my confidence a boost. I felt I had done my part right. I knew, when the time was right, I would again seek a long-term partner.

The winter of 1999-2000, I went at least every two weeks, unless it was snowing, to see my father at his home. Even though it was an hour's commitment to drive up to Manchester, New Hampshire, and another hour back, I felt just visiting him was not sufficiently "big." Although I was emotionally detached from my father, I felt I owed him, as his daughter, a certain respect and caring. During the winter of 2000 and the spring that followed, his appetite was almost nonexistent so I decided to make delicious soups to bring him. Homemade soups, in my mind, were far superior to canned ones so I searched for recipes that were nutritious, tasty, and easy to eat.

On my visits to his home, I would pull up a chair next to him, and we would chat about the events of the week. When I look back at these conversations, I realize they could have been an occasion to really talk about important matters — about our lives, our choices, and our disappointments. I was in a much better place than I had been when I was younger and would have been able to listen rather than react to whatever he said.

"Do you believe in the afterlife?" I asked once, the question having just popped into my head.

After a moment of thought, he responded, "Yes."

Then there was silence, and he didn't say anything more. This could have been the perfect opening to talk at a deeper level, but he was unable or unwilling to talk and I was unable or unwilling to push him. I will always regret that I let the opportunity go. I had given him the bait, even though at the time I didn't realize it, and he could not or would not find the hook. That had been the story of our lives together. That missing connection had characterized my childhood home.

I had very few earlier memories of being with my father, of sharing experiences. But one involved walking with him to the woodshed on our property when we lived in Canada. Also, while in Canada, there was a family story of him chasing me around the house trying to catch and spank me.

Another vague memory was accidently walking in on him in a bathroom of our Virginia home. It was disturbing because I knew it was something I should not have seen. Then, there was the time much later in 1975 when he "came out" and had temporarily separated from my mother. I knew at the time that I had always known he was gay. I just didn't know how or when I knew.

How can one have so few memories of a parent? I suppose it comes from that parent having been absent, but I do have another memory of my father's absence, of my parents' absence really.

Every fall, St. Mary's hosted a Parents' Day. My parents never came to any of the Parents' Days nor to the Christmas Pageants which were always a big affair and something the girls looked forward to. For the first, when I was a freshman, they were unable to come because they were still living in Haiti. But they left the country suddenly around Christmas time of that year. A Duvalier spokesperson had come to our house in Port-au-Prince and told my father he had 48 hours to get out of the country. I never knew the exact reason. (Coincidently, the bishop of the Episcopal Church in Haiti was also forced out of the country

Shadows and Light

at gunpoint about two years later.) My father had gotten a teaching job at The Hoosac School near Albany, where my brother was a boarding student while I was at St. Mary's.

For the next three and a half years while I was at St Mary's, my parents were only a three-hour drive away, and a day trip from the Hoosac School to see me on Parents' Day would not have been overtaxing. Other parents undertook this trip.

When parents attended Parents' Day, they took their daughters out to dinner. The result was that the school population was emptied, and the remaining girls were left to fend for themselves — read a book, study, or take a nap. In my first and second years at St. Mary's, I was invited to dinner with the family of one of the girls. In my junior year, however, I had no invitation to dinner. I am not sure how this happened. Perhaps it was simply an inadvertence, and each of my friends thought I must have been invited by the others, or my emotional neediness was keeping people away.

On Parents' Day, I felt abandoned by my parents. The ironic thing about my parents was that they had taught in and lived at three different boys' boarding schools. Each of these had Parents' Days. Could they really not have known how much young people need to share their school lives with their parents? Did they really not understand how supportive of their children it was to have parents attend these functions? The only thing I can answer is that they had a hole some place inside themselves — and they were not aware of this hole. I was left to deal with their emotional lack, and it resulted in a hole of my own.

It is the third year that I vividly remember. Parents' Day fell on a cold, gray day. I was sad my parents would not be attending again, and sad that no one had invited me out to alleviate the loneliness. The weather only added to my gloom. There wasn't any activity to plug into that day at the school, and I found myself too distraught to initiate anything on my own. I suppose I could have gone out for a walk or gone to the gym to shoot baskets or read a novel that I had not had time to read, but I did not have the energy for any of that. I was caught in a quagmire of sadness. The more I thought of my abandonment, the more abandoned I felt. This was a pattern I would live in for a long time in my adult life.

There were two other girls besides me whose parents had not come, so they were stranded like me at the school. I had nothing in common with them except that we had no parents come that day. These two were the least popular girls in the whole school of around a hundred. I am sure I was being judgmental, and we probably did have some things in common, but being an adolescent and concerned with social image, I did not want to be dragged down by them into the realm of the unpopular girls. I had enough problems already.

Even though, on that day, I felt like a misfit right along with them, I knew I was somewhat attractive and popular since I had almost been elected vice president of the school that year, losing after a recount of the votes as it was so close. I was elected as an Athletic Association Representative — again the whole school voted for this position — and being an Athletic Association Representative that year was the reason I was on the Student Council. Even so, I had really started to withdraw from people, and girls who had been closer to me the previous year were feeling the effects of my distancing. Perhaps that is why no one invited me out that year. This withdrawal manifested itself on the Student Council to which I had just been elected: I never spoke at any of the meetings. I remember thinking that it was odd I had nothing to say or add to the discussions. I must have had something to say but thought that whatever I wanted to say would be insignificant and that no one would want to hear it. Years later, I realized that I was probably depressed and that was the reason for my lack of participation and close relationships. I simply lacked the

Shadows and Light

emotional energy.

That Saturday, loneliness took over, and I retreated to my room. I tried to concentrate on reading a novel, but being in the mood I was in, it failed to interest me. Finally, it was time for lunch. There were only the nuns, some lay teachers, and the three of us girls for dinner. It was a quiet meal, and I was glad to have it over with. Afterwards, I went back to my room and waited for everyone to return. It was a very long day.

Of course, I wondered if my parents had any idea how it felt, in spite of their extensive private school experience, to an adolescent to be one of three out of a hundred girls whose parents had not gotten it together to spend the day with her? This feeling of abandonment and despair was so familiar.

Finally, I heard the excited, joyful sounds of girls returning from their day. Their voices brought an end to this silent and lonely day. But, if the day did end, the sadness resulting from my realization my parents had not chosen to be with me persisted. I had felt that I could not depend on them at a time when I felt I needed to.

So much for another memory of my father's absence.

In the spring, my father's health took a turn for the worse and he was hospitalized once more. One visit to his hospital room stands out as deserving some mention. My father and I had been talking, facing one another, for about a half hour when a nurse entered my father's hospital room. She said, "Hello," and I reciprocated and added, "I'm Susan." She turned to my father and told him she had come for a brief procedure. After she had helped my father from his chair back into his bed, she pulled the curtain around the bed.

"Is Susan your eldest?" I heard her ask as she moved around him.

"Yes, Susan is my elder daughter," he replied, ever the

teacher seeking to champion correctness of language.

"So, she is your Number 1 daughter."

Strange how sitting just on the other side of the curtain, I made the easy but potentially unsettling juxtaposition from "Number 1" as in "older" to "Number 1" as in "favorite." Even in my 50s, I wanted the reassurance that my father found me significant in his life, that I meant something important to him. I had had a long history of being somewhere at the bottom of his list of concerns.

My language leap from "older" to "favorite" was apparently not so outrageous, since my father then did the same thing. I heard him respond, "Actually, she isn't. Clare, my younger daughter, is Number 1. She is great and does everything for me. She cooks my meals and takes me to my appointments."

He went on to extol all of Clare's many other virtues.

Their conversation ended, and before I knew it, the nurse pulled the curtain open. She shrugged her shoulders and whispered on the side to me, "Sorry I asked the question!"

On the drive home, I found it oddly assuring that my perception of not having been special to my father was proven correct — I had never been the preferred daughter. What's more, I felt fairly certain that I simply didn't rate. Since it had been a long time since I had expected anything from my parents on an emotional level, my father's words did not upset me. Even so, I thought how different it would have been for me had my father, when he was talking to the nurse, said, "I am lucky to have two such caring daughters. Both are Number 1 in my eyes. I live with my younger daughter and her family. My older daughter lives an hour away but she makes the effort to come to visit frequently. Her visits mean a lot to me." The words would have been very simple, but even now that my father was getting ever closer to death, he could not speak in a way that would create a loving legacy for me. I felt much taken for granted even as I shrugged the words away.

As the time of my father's death seemed more imminent, I didn't have knowledge yet of what a dying person goes through and how I might have been able to help him in the process he was clearly engaged in. By then, my mother had been dead four years and my father seemed ready to take his own next step.

During the spring of 2000, I went through some job changes. My position as Quality Report Coordinator for the Department of Quality Measurement and Improvement at Brigham and Woman's was tenuous. I had been in this department for several years by then and had enjoyed the independent nature of the job and its research and data collection components. But the department had undergone a lot of changes, including layoffs and reorganization. I was now reporting to the director of the department who was a physician. In a recent performance review, she had told me, "You don't have a Harvard Medical personality." I wasn't sure how to respond so I nodded my head. It puzzled me because up to then, my lack of a "Harvard personality" had made no apparent difference in my getting or maintaining a position within the hospital. I had to assume it was important only to some people? As I thought about it later, it all made sense why I felt I wasn't really accepted in this department. I was on the quiet side and didn't have the intellectual, humorous repartee some of my colleagues seemed easy with. I kept my words to a minimum, to what was needed or necessary. At a meeting, while I did share ideas, I wasn't sitting on the edge of my seat bursting with ideas, anxiously awaiting my turn to talk. Most importantly, I was never good at schmoozing — something I would have to do to get ahead in this department — and I didn't want to pretend to be someone I wasn't, so I decided to look for another job.

In May of 2000, I found a different position as a clinical auditor still within Brigham and Women's Hospital. Ten days after

I had started this new job, Clare called me at home early in the morning to say that our father had died. Again, as with my mother, I did not feel particularly sad and cry on hearing the news. His death was expected, and that it had finally happened was a blessing. I called my boss to tell her I would not be in and drove to New Hampshire to say goodbye to my father.

Later that morning, when I was in the hallway of my father's house and saw a picture of my father next to my brother, a wave of emotion hit me, and I shook briefly as my eyes filled with tears. It dawned on me that both my father and my mother were now dead. Mark, too, was gone. I was now the oldest not only of the siblings but of the larger family.

As was my mother's four years earlier, my father's funeral was held at Grace Episcopal Church in Manchester, New Hampshire. It was a small gathering: my boys, my sister Clare, her husband and their boys, Linda and Zack, along with the headmaster and two faculty members from the Roxbury Latin School where my father had last taught. The headmaster gave a moving eulogy. He spoke of my father's chief love — the theater — and about his deep social conscience and Christian faith. At six foot, eight inches, thin and dignified in his bearing, my father, the headmaster emphasized, was known for his remarkable appearance. When he walked, he gave the appearance of gliding. One boy, said the headmaster, described him as "God on wheels."

Sitting in the front pews of Grace Church, I realized once again how little I really knew about my father as a person. He

My father

was as distant as my mother had been. How sad it was for him to conceal himself from his family. What had happened to cause this? Why was he never able to share his life with me? It was a natural leap from my father to Johnnie, who had not been able to share something of his life with me, and then to myself, asking why I did not share parts of my life that needed to be shared if people were to know me.

I was no longer as angry with my father as I had been in the past, but hearing his eulogy, I did feel remorse. I understood that he had had a tough childhood, which he did not like to speak about, and that he was a gay man who had to function in a heterosexual world as a heterosexual for most of his life. As a teacher in boys' boarding schools, he had had reason in his day to conceal his homosexuality. As a result, he had learned how to be secretive. But, if I was able to makes changes so as to have a more emotionally sound life, why hadn't he made changes that he needed to? I had to conclude that he just hadn't been able to.

My father in later years

I had not appreciated my father for who he was beyond his role of being my father. It would take a few more years until I gained a fuller sense of him and a better understanding of how he had influenced my life.

For me, the timing of his death at the start of a new century signaled the end of one era and the beginning of another new one. When I look back, that winter and spring of 2000 was like a rebirth for me. And change had only started. A lot of growth that I could not anticipate was ahead for me, and best of all, my family, which had shrunk with the recent deaths, would soon expand to include daughters-in-law and grandchildren.

I needed the closure on the unsatisfying relationships with my parents that happened with their dying. Their deaths allowed me to forge ahead and become the person I was meant to be, freed from parental shackles.

Chapter 14
Expanding After Johnnie

In the summer after my father died, I was spending a lot of time at Maidstone Lake and was still missing Johnnie. It had been over nine months since he had left and I thought I should have been over him by then, but I wasn't. I had been unrealistic thinking I would get over him so soon. He had done a lot to help me and now I was on my own again. As I walked around the cabin, I would see things that reminded me of him: a souvenir from Grenada, the Hoosier cabinet he got for the kitchen so I would have more storage, the more efficient wood stove, and the full woodshed.

The solitude I found at the lake always led to reflection on my situation. I spent time on the deck just being still and gazing at nature surrounding me. I also enjoyed walking the three miles of road along the east side of the lake where my cabin was.

Although I had tried online dating and met a couple of men, nothing came of it. Would I ever form a relationship again? One Sunday morning when I was out walking, I saw Douglas, a friendly man of about eighty, outside of his place. Douglas had helped me in the past by doing odd jobs in the cabin.

"Hi, Susan," he said when he saw me. "I hear you are alone now."

How had he known that Johnnie and I were no longer together? Then again, he seemed to be one of those people who always knew what was happening.

"Yes, Johnnie and I broke up last fall."

"You know I take Viagra now," he said with a lascivious look in his eye and a big grin.

Oh my God, I thought. I looked Douglas in the eye and said, "I am not interested." I turned and beat a hasty retreat down the road toward my place. Was it possible he was teasing me? I didn't think so because his look said otherwise. The tears were rolling down my cheeks. Here I was in my mid-fifties — recently rejected after a four-year relationship — and the only man interested in me was an eighty-year-old.

After I got over this encounter with Douglas, I decided to meet more men and pursue online dating with a renewed spirit. I felt I did better in a relationship and did not want to spend the rest of my life alone. However, meeting men online was terrifying. I had read about women having bad experiences and these I tried to keep out of mind. I felt I could trust my instincts. I resolved I would always keep safety in mind, and if I felt uncomfortable for any reason, I would cut off contact with that man.

During that fall and winter, I dabbled in online dating and met a few men but no one I wanted to pursue. I tried to keep my spirits up by taking care of myself. I did my yoga videos to remain in shape. Also, through a friend of mine, I met two women who were interested in going to the Boston Lyric Opera. I bought season tickets and would meet them for dinner downtown before the performances. I loved it! I had forgotten how much, when I had been a few times in the past, I had enjoyed opera.

My season tickets got me out of my comfort zone because I had to take public transportation regularly to reach the Boston Lyric Opera. There was an MBTA stop near my condo where I could park. Going downtown in the late afternoon was fine but coming home I was apprehensive. I was never very adventurous and I had had an experience in Paris when a weird man sat near me on the Metro and followed me when I changed lines. I lost him when I went into a department store, or perhaps, he gave up. I continued going to the opera with these two women, whose company I enjoyed, for three years, and of course, I got used to taking the MBTA into Boston.

In the spring of 2001, I met Henry online. He was about my age and lived nearby in Waltham in an apartment. By then, I relished my independence and I knew I was comfortable being and living by myself, but I also knew I preferred living with someone — eventually. I am a homebody at heart and need companionship and affection on a day-to-day basis.

I was immediately comfortable with Henry. He had been divorced for enough years for his marriage to be well behind him and he was easy to talk to. Besides that, he was tall and I liked being with someone taller than I. From the start, however, there was something about him that I was not at ease about. He had been let go from his job and was living off a settlement from an age discrimination lawsuit. I admired his tenacity in fighting for his rights, but the forced retirement had not led him to any engaging activities. He had few, if any, interests. Was he never going to work gainfully again or pick up some volunteering? I asked myself, realizing I really did not know what he did all day — that is, how he could fill his time in an interesting way. I knew myself better by then and suspected that someone with an intellectual curiosity and the ambition to do something more in life than Henry was exhibiting would be a better fit for me. I kept this apprehension in the back of my mind and, in the meantime, I decided to see how things developed as I was not ready to write him off.

Henry was a good dancer, and when we went to some local dances, it was apparent I could use some classes. I had always

Shadows and Light

wanted to learn how to ballroom dance and I had never been with a man who would take classes. I did not yet have the gumption to go out and do it on my own. For some reason — maybe the style and music attracted me — I wanted to learn how to swing dance and found a one-time class. Henry agreed to accompany me, and I was thrilled that he wanted to go. Henry and I were doing well learning the steps, when the instructor said, "It's time to switch partners." I now had to dance with a perspiring stranger. This put a damper on the dance class, so much so that I never signed up for another class. It was typical of me not to speak up to insist on dancing with the partner I came with. Instead, like a good girl who was pleasing her parents, I obeyed the instructor's wishes and griped about it. It was dropping language class in Paris all over again. There was something here for me to know about myself, but I was not yet ready to learn it.

My sons, Tim and Peter, were now out on their own, working or getting a graduate degree and living in an apartment with roommates. I was lucky that they were independent, financially and emotionally.

Sometime in the summer of 2001, Tim told me he and his girlfriend, Amanda, were getting married the following summer. I was thrilled to hear this news and said so. I had felt deflated when, years earlier, I had told my parents I was going to marry Michael. So, when Tim announced his news, I made it a point to show my enthusiastic support for his decision. Because Michael and I had divorced when the boys were young, I had always had this fear that they would make poor choices for a marriage partner. They had not had good role models growing up. My fear was soon allayed as I got to know Amanda better. From Concord, Massachusetts, she was an attractive, slim young woman with short, dark brown hair. She worked as a graphic designer. She turned out to be a delightful daughter-in-law.

What kind of mother-in-law would I be? I knew I was not going to be like Michael's mother whom I had experienced as critical on so many occasions — as when she had shown me the unflattering photo she had taken of me when Michael and I were visiting them one summer with the boys. I never forgot her brusque words, "This is what you look like." She was not volunteering information in case I did not know what I looked like. No, she was telling me I did not look good. I recall being angry at the time. Why did she have to show me an unflattering photo? Her tone was almost accusatory. Then there was the time when she had visited in Brussels and had volunteered so little help to me after Tim was born.

I was not going to be the kind of mother-in-law to my sons' wives that Mary had been to me.

Sitting in silence with Henry one day as we watched the replays of the horrific events of 9/11 on television, I wanted to snuggle up to him and feel secure that our relationship was headed towards a possible commitment. Henry and I had had fun together over the summer going to dances. He took me to a concert — Jimmy Buffet whom I had never seen before — but, the spark that might have led to intimacy was just not there. Knowing this, I decided not to lead him on in any way but to continue to see him as I waited to see how my life played out.

Since Henry was easy to talk to and we had been dating for a few months, I shared how, when I was twenty-two in 1967 and just out of college, I had gotten pregnant. It should not have been a total surprise, I explained to him, as I had done what one does to get pregnant! However, my denial mechanism, which I had learned so well at my parents' School of Total Denial, was well entrenched and so, unreasonably, I had been surprised. Perhaps my denial had to do with my abandonment issues, with the sexual abuse at one of the schools my father taught at, and my always wanting to please.

"Even today as I sit here," I told Henry, who was actually an understanding man, "I do not know how I could have let this pregnancy happen. It wasn't that I was so young."

Telling Henry this story was intimidating because it involved sharing some information that did not paint the best picture of me and difficult because it brought back the pain of those days when I had set into motion the thing that seemed the best to do: letting the baby go to a family that could take care of her as I knew I could not. There was also the memory of the time I had told the mother of one of the boys' playmates when we lived in Newton and she had ostracized me for hearing the truth about me.

I teared up a bit as I told Henry about the baby girl that I had given up after only a few days. Talking about the wrenching moment when I let her go always brought back searing memories. Even though everyone told me I would forget, they were wrong. I told Henry I had found out where she lived but I had made no effort to contact her. Henry was empathetic; he had a grandchild die of SIDS so he was familiar with the loss of an infant.

Later, toward the middle of October, around Maggie's birthday, I told Henry I might look for her. At that time of year, I'd think of her more often and I'd become a bit depressed. It was never a good time of year for me. Henry was supportive of my trying to meet her. After all, Maggie was now in her mid-thirties, and since she was an adult, I could presume her to be able to handle any difficult emotion that might arise.

I had waited a long time to make the move I was now contemplating. I felt I was in a stable place, emotionally, except for an occasional bout of mild depression that did not last. I was no longer seeing Dr. Cohen for therapy but met with him every six months for a medication review since I was still on Prozac. I was a curious person by nature and thought Maggie might be, too.

But, if she was, why hadn't she tried to find me? I had to consider what I might find. Was she even still alive? It had been over twenty years since I had learned where she lived with her parents. What had adoption done to her psyche? Had she been abused like me? Was she a drug addict?

Thanks to an internet search that fall, I quickly found three recent addresses where Maggie had lived, but the addresses were not dated. With trepidation, I wrote to the one I thought was the most recent. Months went by, but I did not hear from her. My hopes were dashed, and I wasn't sure if and when I would continue to look for her.

Meanwhile, for the most part, I was enjoying my job as clinical auditor which I had held since May 2000. I liked the independence and the interaction with the physicians, but there was a snag. Marie, my boss, was an unhappy soul, obese with a myriad of medical issues, though at times, she could be pleasant and helpful. I had realized from the start that it was best to have little contact with her, and only when necessary. It helped that we were in separate areas of the department. I realized by then that female bosses presented problems for me. In the past, one had put me on probation for no good reason; another had denied me a promotion for which I was qualified, again for no apparent reason. None of these women had helped me advance in my career.

After dating Henry for over a year, I knew it was time to move on. While Henry was understanding and kind and we were good friends, I knew the relationship lacked intimacy. It was missing, and I knew that intimacy was important to me in a commitment.

Although he was a kind soul and had been good to me in many ways — he was far more attentive than either Michael or Johnnie and would go out of his way to please me — his lack of

Shadows and Light

ambition and interests bothered me. I was always bursting with ideas, and he seemed to have none. He had no desire to travel, and travel was important to me. His focus was on me, which wasn't bad in a way, but I found it smothering. I felt he was sucking up my energy.

One evening, I broke the news that I thought it was best that we didn't see each other anymore. Henry showed no emotion and appeared to accept my words. Since he said nothing, I had no idea what was going on in his mind. Maybe it was a relief for him as well? Had I chosen another emotionally detached man, another Johnnie or Michael? At the time, I didn't think I had, but in retrospect, I realize I may have. His emotional detachment came across in a different manner.

Untethered from Henry, I decided I was not going to give up on a partner for a long-term relationship. I resolved to pay much closer attention and not end up with a man who gave up on me emotionally. With Henry, I had made progress. He did not give up on me. I was learning to choose better, but still had a way to go in knowing how to make a great choice.

Later, in a self-serving moment, I thought I should have strung Henry along so I would have a date for Tim and Amanda's wedding which was coming in June 2002. At the wedding, I would have to interact with Michael and his current partner, Carol. Without a date, I would be a woman who was alone again when Michael had been in a successful relationship for a number of years. Would people think that it was I who had not been able to make our marriage work? What was that going to be like? After my initial insecurity, I realized being at the wedding alone would work out.

For Amanda's bridal shower, I gave her an appropriate gift from her registry and did not embarrass her as my mother had done to me. Tim and Amanda's wedding day was on a cool, drizzly Saturday in mid-June. Despite the weather, the wedding, in an old Congregational church in the center of Concord, was beautiful and elegant. I was so proud of Tim and Peter, who was his best man, and looked forward to knowing my new daughter-in-law. I had been worried about seeing Michael, his partner Carol, and some of his relatives, but I need not have been. Everyone was friendly. However, I did sigh with relief when it was over because I hadn't realized how tense I was even though I went to it with an open mind and feeling comfortable being by myself with no significant other to lean on.

For the wedding, Peter had invited his new girlfriend, Erin. She was an outgoing, lovely young woman who was a special-education teacher. Before I knew it, they announced their engagement and were getting married the following August in 2003. How fast my family was changing!

Tim & Amanda's wedding 2002

Chapter 15
Putting Many Things Together

After I stopped seeing Henry, I continued to engage in online dating. I was really ready to find someone, but it was not happening. After a while, I wondered if I were too restrictive in the distance I was willing to travel. I decided to broaden my search to an hour's drive from Newton. It proved to be a good decision.

In the summer of 2003, just before Peter and Erin got married in August, a profile caught my interest: the man, whose name was Stuart, was attractive and pleasant looking, and it appeared we had a lot in common. I wrote him a friendly introductory note, and he responded immediately. Five years older than I, he lived in Kingston, New Hampshire. When I looked Kingston up on the map, I saw it was at the limit of my one-hour drive stipulation, but that was okay.

Keeping to my rules for meeting men online, I insisted we exchange a couple of preliminary emails. When these raised no red flags, I suggested a phone call. Then, because I had felt comfortable chatting with him, I let the conversation evolve into a plan to meet for dinner in Burlington, Massachusetts, halfway between our houses.

Before that could happen however, I drove with Tim and Amanda down to Long Island for Peter and Erin's wedding. It was another beautiful wedding on a warm, sunny Saturday in

August, but the scale was grander, as the marriage ceremony was in a Catholic cathedral. Again, my heart swelled with pride as I saw my sons standing at the altar. I felt Peter had made a good choice with Erin, and I couldn't have asked for more in a daughter-in-law just as I could not have asked for more from Amanda.

My life was looking up, I realized. My sons were in their adult relationships and were well launched in the world. While they had been on their own for some time now, seeing them married seemed to bring a symbolic end to any responsibility I had for them. Now it was up to them and their wives.

Peter and Erin's wedding
2003

My life also seemed to be on the upside, because — and I realized, of course, I had to protect myself against fantasy — of the very, very interesting man I had recently met online. Maybe my hard work had paid off and I was finally ready to meet someone with whom I could create a long-term relationship?

The date with Stuart happened on a warm evening in August just after Peter and Erin's wedding. In the year since I had broken up with Henry and had been dating online, I had come up with a first-time-meeting outfit. Looking good gave me confidence, and driving to our meet-up, I was hoping that maybe, just maybe, this man could be the one!

I was tired of being alone. I wanted someone to be with,

Shadows and Light

someone who would want to be with me. Even so, I was determined to remain cautious and not jump into something I would regret later. I was not in the least bit anxious meeting Stuart since meeting men on blind dates had become routine, even a bit tiresome in the year since I had broken up with Henry. Was this date going to be another meeting where the man was nothing like his photo and profile, or where the chemistry was nonexistent and we would proceed through a wooden conversation until it was mercifully time to end the encounter?

Always trying to stay positive, I entered the restaurant and looked around. There was no single man there who looked like the man in the photo Stuart had sent. I sat down to wait, sure that he would pop in at any time. After fifteen minutes, prizing punctuality as I do, I was growing irritated, but I had already invested in this date, so I decided to wait a little longer. Perhaps Stuart had gotten held up in traffic. (While I had a cell phone, I did not have the habit of using it and anyway I didn't have a number for Stuart.)

After about a half hour, a man rushed into the restaurant, breathless, and looked around the room. I waved gingerly, and he responded. Arriving at the table, he was apologetic, explaining he had gotten tied up with a client at work and then there was traffic.

I smiled, having decided to give him the benefit of the doubt.

Stuart was of medium height and build with curly gray hair; later, I often thought he had the "mad professor" look as his hair was regularly unruly and his thick white eyebrows always needed a trim. Stuart had grown up in England and had graduated from a top university there. His prestigious education impressed me. When he was about thirty, he immigrated to the Boston area with his first wife and their two little girls. One of his daughters needed medical treatment that was not available in the UK at that time. Since Stuart was a software engineer and the computer industry was in full swing in Boston in the early 70s, getting a job had not proven difficult.

That evening, the conversation flowed, and we talked non-stop over dinner. Stuart was intelligent and had a dry wit. We had many common interests. I liked that he was British as those were my roots, too, and I thought perhaps, because of that, we would understand each other. We were both readers, enjoyed traveling and liked to go to self-help workshops. I had my place on Maidstone Lake in Vermont, and Stuart had a log cabin only 45 minutes away on a river in Bethlehem, New Hampshire. By the time we said goodbye in the parking lot, we had already made plans to see each other again.

I had forgotten how good it felt to have chemistry with a man. In spite of having warned myself, I was on the inevitable "cloud nine" once again. Stuart was funny, smart, and compatible. I was happier than I had been since I was first with Johnnie; it felt good to laugh a lot and be silly. I was impressed that he was in a men's group and had been for many years. To me, this meant he had close friends he could talk to. He was also involved with a group that did a series of workshops on self-awareness, and at times, he would help run these on weekends. While I could not be sure until I knew him better, it appeared at the time that he was interested in learning about himself and doing self-growth work. This was right down my alley. These were signs that we could be good together.

Stuart had been married twice already in addition to having had two more long-term relationships. This was in the same range as Johnnie's marriages, but Stuart did not seem to be carrying "baggage." He readily talked about all the women who were or had been in his life and expressed no anger towards any of them. In fact, he saw his first ex-wife, the mother of his two daughters and the woman he had come to the US with, and her current husband, at family gatherings. He had no contact with his second ex-wife since that marriage had been a short one and there were no children to attach them to one another. Ever wanting to protect myself, I looked for red flags, but I could see none. I was especially on the lookout for a drinking problem because I did not want to repeat my experience with Michael. But there were no signs of any issues with alcohol. Nor did Stuart appear to be emotionally distant as my father and both Johnnie and Michael had been.

    I liked that Stuart still had a bit of an English accent. I was slightly nostalgic for England and remembered fondly the several times Michael and I had been there while we lived in France and Belgium. If Stuart and I did end up in a relationship, I hoped a trip to England was something we could do together.

    That fall we continued to date. We went out to dinner, hung out watching movies, and showed each other our vacation places — Stuart's cabin in the woods by a river and mine on Maidstone Lake. Stuart explained at length how he was involved with a nonprofit organization based in California, with branches in other parts of the country, that presented workshops on love, intimacy, and sexuality. Stuart had participated in a series of these workshops and had even served as a workshop assistant. Since these workshops sounded interesting, I decided to participate in a Level I weekend a few months after I had met Stuart. I was taken completely out of my comfort level and learned a lot about myself and how I interacted with people. Following on this successful experience, it was an easy decision for Stuart and me to sign up for a couples' workshop.

    At the workshop, it was interesting to see Stuart interact with the people he knew. While I was new to the group, Stuart was not. I could see that something prevented him from fully relating to these people, but I couldn't put my finger on what it could be. There was something else I couldn't put my finger on: a couples' weekend was a chance for us to spend time getting to know each other on a deeper level, but Stuart did not pay any particular attention to me. In a social event, many couples accept it as normal that when they are in a group, they should devote their time to meeting and interacting with others rather than to each other, but this was not a social time. It was an opportunity for the two members of a couple to deepen their relationship. Complicating this task was my tendency to feel left out in a group. That issue compelled me to want Stuart to be attentive to me. To my credit, I put this desire aside, and for the most part, the weekend went well — but it was more of a personal experience rather than a couples one.

As we drove home, I felt that his not connecting with me more was a form of holding back so I would not know him as his true self. But only time would tell if the exercises Stuart and I had done together would help us form a more intimate relationship. Years later when I thought about this workshop, I realized I should have sought to understand how Stuart interacted with other people and me and I should have asked myself if his way of interacting would work for me. It was similar in ways to the time Michael and I had visited his parents before we got married, when he and his friend Rick dominated the weekend and I had felt left out, somewhat ignored. I had not spoken out then at Michael's parents' house and I had not spoken out at the workshop. And mostly, I did not ask if the sort of interaction I was having was what I was looking for.

By the time the holidays came around in 2003, we had met each other's families and everyone seemed to get along. That January, we went to the Caribbean, our first trip together. I always thought a trip was a good way to observe a man's reactions to life once he was out of his comfort zone and how compatible he and I would be in resolving problems that arose while traveling. The challenges of a trip together had certainly propelled me to stop dating Mike with whom I had traveled to Puerto Rico in the 1990s.

With two of his friends, Stuart had bought a one-week timeshare in St. Martin and he had access to it that year. Since he had been there several times, Stuart knew the island and how to get around. Once there, this made it easy to find restaurants, beaches, and activities. Stuart and I had a great time exploring both the French and Dutch sides of the island. I loved the beaches and, of course, the blue skies and the warmth, which always offers a great respite from the New England winters. By the end of the week, my travel rule had proven helpful again, and our relationship was cemented.

After our return to New England, since we lived an hour apart, we continued to date and see each other on weekends only. By the end of our first year of dating, the distance and the separation became onerous, and we decided to put an end to it by living together. I was definitely not ready for marriage since we hadn't known each other that long, but I understood moving in together was a big commitment — and almost like getting married. Stuart was entrenched in New Hampshire and would not budge, and while I had lived for twelve years in my condo in Newton, I was not attached to it. I had lived in Newton for over thirty years by then and I anticipated a change might be good for me. My sons were both married, and with work and now with a baby apiece, they had busy lives that did not need me — except for some babysitting. If I moved to New Hampshire, both families would still be within an hour's drive.

I agreed to move to New Hampshire but not to his house, which I did not care for. It had an odd interior layout and needed updating. A tenant lived in a basement apartment and would come up to Stuart's floor to do laundry and take a shower. I was not comfortable with that arrangement. But this was not a problem since Stuart wanted to sell his house. The exterior consisted of a large tract of land that required extensive maintenance. Stuart was amenable to moving so as to avoid all the yard work and not to have to plow a mile of driveway when it snowed. The downside of the move was that I would have an hour's drive daily to and from Boston. I had never had a long commute before, but at the time, I felt full of energy and was willing to give it a try.

We bought a spacious condo, a townhouse attached to only one other unit, close to the Massachusetts border in Atkinson, New Hampshire. It probably had more space than we actually needed, but we wanted the dedicated office, the family room, the workshop, and lots of storage space. The development had a New England feel as all the condos were capes or salt boxes with white picket fences. Our private deck overlooked a wooded area, and I had plenty of space to plant flowers. While we planned to share the cost of the condo, the price was a bit more than Stuart wanted to spend. However, when I convinced him that it needed no work, and I would be happy living there, he agreed to the purchase.

We moved in together in November 2004, fifteen months after meeting. It was hectic to sell our respective houses and merge our belongings into one household. But, we did it relatively smoothly with no major meltdowns on my part — I was the emotional one in our relationship. My commute into Boston every day was bearable, and I took it in stride. The transition to living together seemed easy from the start. Money issues were not serious. We kept our money separate except for one joint account; each month, we deposited a sufficient amount to pay for expenses we incurred in common. The system worked well. Since I had more savings than Stuart, if I wanted something like a piece of new furniture or drapes, he would say, "Buy it. You have the money." I was always conservative with my spending, however, and sometimes found it difficult to buy something I wanted as opposed to needed. We had also written an informal cohabitation agreement that stated our wishes if something happened to one of us.

Shadows and Light

I was still seeing Dr. Cohen for a Prozac check every few months. Since I had had no issues with depression for a while and my life was headed in the right direction, I decided around this time to come off Prozac for good and make a break with Dr. Cohen. I came off the drug with no repercussions and I said goodbye to Dr. Cohen. He had stood by me and cared for me for many years now, and for that I was grateful.

At first, I didn't mind getting up at the crack of dawn to drive into Boston; it was only an hour ride as there was no traffic at that time. Coming home, however, I encountered the afternoon traffic and the commute took longer. Listening to NPR and books on CD helped pass the commuting time. Eventually after a year or so, I only had to drive in four days a week as I was given the option to work from home on Fridays. By then, I was ready for some relief from the grind of commuting daily and the Friday break was a huge help.

Most weekends during the summer, Stuart and I went up to Maidstone Lake. Stuart enjoyed being there but was not too keen on some of my favorite things to do: swimming, kayaking, and walking. He preferred relaxing on the deck, though he said he was thinking about buying a small sailboat (which he did not do until the following summer). One Saturday when the lake was very calm, I wanted to introduce Stuart to the pleasures of kayaking, so I said, "Come for a ride with me."

"No, don't think so. I would rather sit and read my book."

"Please, just for a little while."

"You know my knees are stiff from playing tennis all these years, Susan. It's hard to get in and out of the kayak. I really don't like the struggle."

I said I could show him a new way of getting into the kayak that was way easier on knees. He was clearly uncomfortable to try even that.

"Okay" I replied. "How about going for a walk down the

road after supper when it has cooled off a bit?"

Stuart agreed to a walk. After about half a mile down the road, he said, "I have had enough. Let's turn back."

I was just getting warmed up. When I walk by myself, I usually go for three to four miles. While I agreed to go back, I was disappointed. After all, Stuart had always played tennis, and I thought he would be fit enough to go farther. I didn't really know if the problem was his stamina or his knees. After this time, when we went on a walk together, I adjusted myself to his pace, but I was not getting the exercise I craved.

In spite of these small blocks in our interactions, we were getting along well. In the fall of 2005, a year after moving in together, Stuart asked me to marry him. With joy and enthusiasm, I accepted. After 23 years, it would feel good to be able to say "my husband" again. Something more permanent than "partner." To me, marriage was permanent, and I felt sure at the time that Stuart and I would be together forever — at least until one of us died. It never occurred to me that we could eventually not get along and a divorce might ensue.

We chose the afternoon of New Year's Eve 2005 for our wedding. We both agreed to a very small ceremony, attended by immediate family and a few friends and performed by a Justice of the Peace. I was glad because I did not want to repeat the more formal church wedding I'd had when I married Michael. New Year's Eve was a date that we hoped those we invited would be able to keep. We chose a local restaurant with a function room for the ceremony and for the dinner to follow. The ceremony and the reception went without a hitch, and everyone appeared to have an enjoyable time.

We had planned a two-week honeymoon in St. Martin a few days later. We would spend a week at what was now our timeshare — we had bought his friends out — and the other week at two different hotels. I was looking forward to it. I planned not to

Shadows and Light

work the four days before leaving so I could rest up from the stress of the wedding and the holidays. I recall not feeling very well; nothing specific except for one glaring, unusual symptom indicating a possible bile problem, which I promptly put out of my mind.

The wedding trip to St. Martin was delightful, and we appreciated having the extra week to linger there after the timeshare was over. During that second week, however, I began to have upper abdominal pain. I brushed it aside, thinking it was probably something I had eaten. In fact, the pain would go away, but then it would come back. This went on until we had only two days left before our flight home.

St. Martin timeshare

We went out to dinner that night, but I could not eat and the upper abdominal pain persisted through the evening. Back at the hotel, Stuart fell asleep, but I could not as the pain was getting worse. Finally, about five hours after we had returned to our room, I was bent over with pain and hugging my knees for relief. I knew I needed help and I woke Stuart up.

We were staying in a very small inn in Philipsburg, the capital of the Dutch side of the island. There were no cruise ships in the harbor that night so it was quiet and I was worried there might not be anyone to help at the front desk of the hotel. Stuart went down and mercifully found help was available. In only a few minutes, Stuart returned to our room and said, "The ambulance is on its way."

"Oh no, I didn't want you to call one," I said without thinking, not wanting to bring attention to myself. I realized immediately, of course, an ambulance making a hasty trip to a hospital might be for the best since I didn't know how much longer I could stand the pain. I was very wary, however, of being admitted to a hospital in a foreign country where English might not be spoken. Stuart helped me down to the lobby where we waited for the ambulance. It was now about 3 a.m. and raining.

Arriving at the hospital, I found myself assigned to a good doctor who spoke English well. After a thorough examination, a CT Scan and blood work, he announced I had pancreatitis and cholecystitis. Further workup was needed.

"But, I have to be on the flight home tomorrow afternoon. I must be on that flight. Take good care of me while I am here so I can leave tomorrow," I said.

He assured me that he would do his best to alleviate the pain but that this fix would be temporary. I was given antibiotics, pain meds and, feeling less in pain, discharged from the hospital the next morning with several instructions: I could have nothing to eat, only clear fluids to drink; I was to tell no one at the airport that I had been in the hospital since we might not be allowed to board due to my medical condition; and I was to seek medical care immediately upon arriving home.

The trip home, while it seemed to take forever, was thankfully without a flare up in the pancreatitis. I was getting hungry, of course, but I had no pain. Once home, the next morning, I saw my primary care doctor in Boston and she admitted me to a local hospital for further treatment, an endoscopic procedure to remove bile duct stones. The medical staff taking care of me laughed when I told the story of being in St. Martin on my honeymoon. At the time, I didn't think it was particularly funny because of the intense pain and the fact that we had lost two days of our trip.

Later, when I was more in touch with my intuitive powers as I was to grow to be in the coming decade, I wondered if this medical emergency on my honeymoon had anything to do with a warning that I shouldn't have married Stuart. Why did the pancreatic attack happen when it did? But, I was already married at the time and so I put it in the back of my mind.

Chapter 16
Expanding My Horizons

In the spring of 2006, I began an exploration of the paranormal that was to change my life. Over the next years, my study of psychic phenomena provided the key to transforming my personality from a woman who suffered from post-traumatic stress to a woman who would be able to take control of large parts of her life. At the time I did not know that I was embarking on such a powerful adventure of liberation. Perhaps, I should write, an adventure of centering as I had been thrown off kilter by so many experiences in my life — beginning, and especially, with my childhood and my parents.

Stuart and I, it turned out, were both interested in metaphysical phenomena which, of course, is comprised of a lot of vastly disparate elements. Stuart's main interest was in UFOs, and about a year before we married, he had started writing a book about how aliens had a part in designing human beings. In other words, is God connected to ETs? Other than reading a couple of books by Brian Weiss, M.D. on past lives, my own exploration of the metaphysical world had been minimal, but I had enjoyed Weiss's *Many Lives, Many Masters* and I thought Stuart would also enjoy it. He found it fascinating, so much so that he went online to read more about Dr. Weiss. On the internet, he learned that Dr. Weiss was presenting a workshop in our area. After discussing it, Stuart and I decided to sign up together.

Shadows and Light

The workshop was held one beautiful sunny, warm Saturday in April of 2006. Brian Weiss spoke in the morning to an audience of several hundred people. His presentation was much as I had anticipated. He told interesting stories that held the crowd's attention and had each of us do a psychic exercise with a stranger in the audience. Then he led everyone in a past-life meditation. I got glimpses of mundane past life experiences that had little significance. I find large audiences to be distracting and so I didn't gain much from the meditation.

During the lunch break, Stuart and I ate outside, soaking up the spring warmth. Then came the afternoon when a speaker named John Holland was presenting. He gave a talk on mediumship and how it worked. This was a totally new topic for me, and I found it fascinating. Before long, as John stood in front of the audience, he received messages and shared these with the pertinent people. Men and women gasped in recognition, and some cried as the messages came through while others laughed as they remembered their loved ones. The reactions of these people seemed genuine. Then, there was a break during which I went into the bathroom. As I came out, I started to feel a little odd. I was overcome with a feeling that was not at all familiar. I started to think about my brother, Mark. This feeling became stronger as I went back to my seat; I told Stuart about it. By then, I was feeling shaky and emotional but I had no idea why.

John Holland walked out to the front of the audience, and the afternoon session resumed. All of a sudden, he said, "You with the blue sweater, please stand up." He was pointing to Stuart who was seated next to me. Someone came over and handed him a microphone, and John proceeded to ask him questions. Nothing was resonating with Stuart, and by this time, I was standing up as well. Although I don't remember the questions John asked me, I knew my brother was there in spirit as he had identified himself to me.

Shadows and Light

John told me Mark had five children and was sorry that he put gum in my hair, which had to be cut out. All true. There remained, however, the BIG question I had long wanted answered, ever since Mark was found dead in a hotel room while attending a conference. I had been told his heart had taken him. He had suffered a prior myocardial infarction so a natural death was definitely possible. Since his wife, Grace, controlled all the data and she disliked me for some reason, I had a lingering doubt about the veracity of her report.

Had Mark killed himself?

"I didn't," Mark said to me through John Holland.

Now, I knew for sure. The tears were flowing down my cheeks.

The last thing John said to me before I sat down was, "You have psychic abilities."

I was speechless from what Mark had communicated to me — and now to hear that I had psychic abilities!

Being told I had psychic abilities that afternoon would become a major turning point for me. I had never thought about my place in the universe and how I fit into the scheme of things. A whole new concept of an afterlife had opened up and it was to lead to my spiritual awakening. Who was I beyond the here and now and what was I capable of finding out about myself and my role in the universe? This psychic life that John Holland had opened up for me was something I had to explore. I was chagrined when he said he was not conducting individual sessions at that time.

After this experience of hearing from Mark, I was buoyed by the possibility of hearing messages from other deceased members of my family, especially from my parents with whom I still needed more closure than I had had. I wanted some acknowledgment that they had felt and/or perceived me as an important person in their lives. Because John Holland had proved to me that

Shadows and Light

communicating with the afterlife was possible, I wanted to pursue contact with them. While John was not offering individual sessions, his website had a list of mediums he recommended. That is how I scheduled an appointment with Diana who lived about a half hour from Atkinson.

About six weeks later, not knowing what to expect, I was nervous as I rode over for the appointment with Diana. Would my parents come through with messages for me? Would hearing from them help me to feel better, or would what they had to say make me feel worse, as it often had when they were alive? I consoled myself with thinking that any information I got was better than none. When I drove into the large housing complex where Diana lived, it took a few minutes to find her building, whether it was due to my nervousness or to the complexity of the layout. With trepidation, I walked up the steps and rang her doorbell. An attractive, vivacious woman opened the door and announced herself as Diana. She was warm and welcoming, and I soon felt at ease. Without much delay, she led me into the room where candles were lit and the aroma of incense was subtle but not overwhelming. She sat across from me at a small table covered with a silky, purple cloth and began the session.

My mother came first with a message for me. "I said things to you that were cruel and I am sorry. I don't know why I did it." She did blurt out things that were hurtful and sarcastic on occasion. Often there was no reason for her words; we might simply have been speaking and weren't arguing with each other. For example, after I had graduated from Boston College and started as a staff nurse at Massachusetts General Hospital, I had bought myself some new clothes: a plaid dress and a pink coat to go with it. When she saw me wearing the outfit, she ran her hand down my arm, and with a sarcastic tone and a slight curl to her lip, she said, "Nice new coat. How much did *that* cost you?" The tone was clearly that she thought I had wasted my money and had been fooled into spending so much. How good it would have been to hear my mother say instead: "What a pretty coat. You look so good in pink. I am glad you can afford to buy yourself some lovely, new clothes; you deserve it after all your hard work."

I knew it was my mother in spirit as I sensed her personality. Diana said my mother spoke with a slight British accent voice. My mother had always maintained her accent so this was more evidence that it was my mother Diana had contacted. My mother was born in England and had immigrated to British Columbia with her family when she was a teenager. Also, Diana had given me bits of information that confirmed it was my mother who had contacted me. My mother had actually apologized for something she had done to hurt me! I was blown away!

As I was driving away from the session, I felt a wound had been healed. Although I had not made a second appointment with Diana, I headed home resolved to understand my life via this new medium that had opened up for me and to remedy the hurts I had been carrying with me. A few weeks later, I called Diana to make a second appointment.

In the beginning of our next session in July, Diana said, "Your grandson, Ian, was just born."

My face must have dropped when she used Ian's name. I replied, "That's right. Ian was born in June." Diana aced two family dogs — a silky haired Golden Cocker Spaniel, and a black mustached Scotch Terrier—but she didn't get their names, which were Taffy and Angus.

Next, my father who was to be the main visitation from the afterlife that day came to us and had a lot to say. He told me, "You were lonely for a long time so I am happy you found Stuart. You are soulmates and had a past life together." After a while, he continued, but as in life, it was hard for him to get his message across. "I felt the emotions but could not get the words out," he told me. He went on, "I was toxic to you, and you need to let that go. I was ashamed. I lingered over dying. I went over a couple of times and came back. I wanted to clear up some things, but in the end, I was unable to arrive at some resolution with you." He added one more thing:, "Your self-esteem is still too low, and you need to love yourself more." My father's voice from the afterlife was different from that of the father I knew. It was wiser, more in tune with what I needed to hear. Everything he said resonated with me. He had an esophageal stricture as an adult, and every few years, it would have to be dilated. He had a problem with swallowing at times but was always able to speak. The fact that he "could not get the words" out made sense as the throat is the communication chakra — or energy point — and he could not speak about how he felt.

I was now convinced that my parents did come through via Diana with messages for me. Their personalities were present, and the details were accurate. There was absolutely no way Diana would have known all of this beforehand. All I really needed was to hear that my parents were apologetic for their handling of my upbringing or for the unsupportive and sometimes cruel words they spoke. I didn't feel angry with them and could accept them for who they were, but I felt sad as they had not been able to be more understanding while they were alive. How beneficial it would have been to me if they had more insight into our relationship as they would then have had sympathetic understanding for what was happening to me.

That afternoon, my brother also made a brief appearance and mentioned the pearl necklace he had given me one Christmas when I was around ten years old. To this day, I am filled with joy when I remember it; he must have spent a dollar or two of his allowance on it in Woolworth's. He talked about when we rode bikes and how free he felt when riding.

These sessions with Diana would prove to be a major factor in my healing process and gave me a lot to think about.

In September of 2006, nine months after Stuart and I married, a long-cherished dream of mine came true: to travel with my husband in England. It had been over thirty years since I had visited there with Michael. That had been a touristy trip, but these two weeks in the fall of 2006 were to be weeks of discovery that would reveal to me something about Stuart — and about myself. I was excited to have Stuart show me his old haunts. For Stuart, visiting friends and his cousin were, of course, a priority. In addition, I wanted to revisit some of the places that had played a part in my family history. Not only revisit but understand something about them that I was sure would tell me something about myself. These included finding my maternal grandfather's grave in London. (It was he who had been the bishop Michael used to tell everyone about when we lived in Paris.) I also wanted to visit Sleaford, the Lincolnshire County town where the rectorship of two of my paternal ancestors had almost spanned the nineteenth century.

As I had grown older, I had spent more time thinking about my past and trying to discover how I fit into my family. So it was important to visit places where my ancestors had lived their lives and to imbibe the spirit of these places. While I was definitely searching for answers, I was not sure what it was I was looking for.

Michael had put up a few resistances when we were in England together in the early seventies. And later in the nineties, it had been the same with Johnnie in Florida and PEI. Their intransigence had lessened the pleasure of my experiences there. Traveling with Stuart, however, was different. I was grateful because Stuart agreed to do all the things I wanted to. In exchange I agreed to what he wanted to do. (Isn't that the way it's supposed to be?)

Stuart and I drove into London and found St. Mary's church near Lambeth Palace, the official London residence of the Archbishops of Canterbury, where my mother's father was buried. Walking up to the church, I said to Stuart, "Something doesn't look quite right. Why is there a sign about a museum?" We soon learned that the church had been turned into The Garden Museum. After some inquiries, I found someone who told me, "The area of your grandfather's tomb is being used for an office, and there is nothing to see." They did not know anything more about his tomb or even if he was reburied on the premises.

My grandfather, the Bishop
The Most Reverend
Walter R. Adams

I had no desire to visit the museum. As we walked around outside, I told Stuart how I remembered my grandfather from childhood. Those early scenes were the only memories I had of him. I tried to picture him walking around the churchyard at St. Mary's attired in his cassock and collar with his large bishop's cross hanging from his neck, but I couldn't summon the vision.

We stayed with a couple of Stuart's friends. I really liked them and was comfortable with them. Then, we had lunch with his cousin and his wife. Next, we headed for his university. Stuart showed me around his old college and then he took me punting on the local river, a typical thing to do when visiting his university. A punt is a small, narrow, flat boat with a square-cut bow propelled with a long pole. I got in the punt and sat down feeling a bit nervous. I was wondering how Stuart was going to manage this very long pole standing up — his balance wasn't the best. It was a warm, sunny day so there were a lot of punts out. After a few near collisions, the hang of punting came back to Stuart, and I could sit back and relax. He pointed out the different colleges that formed the university as we floated by. We passed under bridges, charming neo-Gothic covered bridges. Some of the low hanging trees provided a couple of laughs as Stuart almost got tangled up in them. After this fun excursion, we had a delicious English cream tea complete with scones, jam, and clotted cream.

Our next visit was to Sleaford to see St. Denys' Church. I vaguely recalled it from being there with Michael years earlier, but we had been in a hurry then. Michael had us rush in, look around, and leave. We had seen a stained-glass window dedicated to Susan Mary Yerburgh whom I was named after — or so I thought. I was a lot younger when I had gone there with Michael and not particularly interested in my family history. This time, I had a totally different experience and was able to appreciate my ancestors. As Stuart and I drove into Sleaford, we saw St. Denys' Church, a prominent presence at the far end of the market square. It is a medieval parish church dating to the twelfth century. My great-great- and my great-grandfathers, both Richard Yerburghs, served as vicars at St. Denys from 1809 to 1882. We found a parking spot and walked up the steps of the church.

Visiting at a slower pace with Stuart, I noticed immediately, on opening large carved wooden doors, the stained-glass windows. My ancestors had seen these windows every day, I felt with a certain thrill, and had played an important part in the life of this church. As we walked around, we saw more windows dedicated to the memory of the Yerburgh family. As I stood in front of my great-great-grandmother Susan's window, shivers ran down my spine. Who was this woman? What was she like? On the altar floor, my great-great-grandfather was commemorated by inscription.

Stuart said, "I am impressed with your family."

I was buoyed by Stuart's praise both because I had come to realize giving praise was a rare occurrence for him and because I was not used to being the object of praise.

A man entered and, seeing we were examining the church, asked if he could help us. When we told him we were looking for graves of the two Richard Yerburghs, he told us the graves had been moved from the churchyard to another location and the vicarage next door would have been where my grandfathers had lived. He was not the vicar so he could not invite us into the vicarage. What a disappointment!

St. Denys' Church

When we left the church, we took time to walk by the vicarage. I thought about what it must have been like to live here in the 1800s. I think this trip to Sleaford was the first time I felt connected to my ancestors. This was a big step for me because,

St. Denys' Vicarage

up to then, I hadn't. I imagine this time was a combination of being older and of having come to accept my family. Feeling closer to my roots and wanting to know more about them seemed a natural development.

We had a pleasant stay in Norwich with more of Stuart's friends before heading to Cornwall on the west coast. We didn't have much time left but Stuart did promise me we would get there. I had read many English novels and wanted to see the dramatic Cornwall cliffs and quaint harbors — perhaps filling a romantic need since a lot of the novels I had read had been set there. Also, I wanted to see a moor. A line of Emily Dickenson's poetry has always remained with me over the years. *"I never saw a moor, I never saw the sea; Yet know I how the heather looks, and what a wave must be."*

In Cornwall, we stayed in a quaint B&B on a cliff. It had access to a beach below. A long walk on the beach and a Cornish pasty — a meat and root vegetable pastry that I wanted to try — completed the day. Heading back to London, we drove though Dartmoor, and I got a sense of its desolation and expanse, imagining what it would be like to get lost in a rainstorm or have a romantic encounter as women in Brontë novels did.

My Aunt Clare had lived in the village of Woodstock near Oxford for as long as I could remember. Now, my aunt was no longer with us, but driving in England and seeing the occasional signage for Oxford led me naturally to reminisce about Aunt Clare. Poor Aunt Clare had probably not wanted the family brouhaha her bequeathal to me had occasioned, but come it had, I thought, as we headed back to Heathrow, passing again not far from Oxford to catch our flight to Boston.

On the flight, I thought about what a great trip it had been. I had met some of Stuart's friends and family, I felt closer to my ancestors, and I had seen new places to whet my appetite for things British. Although it didn't provide any answers about my

Shadows and Light

past as I had hoped, my sense of worth was enhanced by the pride I felt in my forebears from the 1800s. Also, I felt I knew Stuart better having seen the house where he grew up and the university where he had studied.

After Stuart and I returned from England, I decided to do something about those blanks in my memory that were still nagging me. In particular, I wondered why I had ended my suicide attempt by going downstairs to my friend's apartment for help. This was in 1968, about a year after I had given my baby girl up for adoption. I also had not answered why and how I had always known that my father was gay and why he said to me from the spirit world that he was "toxic" to me.

About my father's being gay, I had a vague memory from when I was around nine years old. I had walked in on him in the bathroom and saw him naked. I have no recollection of what I saw, just that it was something I was not supposed to see and it was more than seeing his nakedness.

Also, I had been thinking a lot about Maggie since coming back. October 19 was her birthday. It had been about five years since I had written and she had not answered. Perhaps she wanted nothing to do with me?

To help me with both these questions, I scheduled another session in October with Diana, the medium. During that session, I asked her if she could get any information on why I had changed my mind about dying. She said, "I see someone pushing you back. They don't want you to cross over."

When she spoke to me, I had a clear vision of someone, presumably the spirit guide whom I had recently become aware of and called Simon, telling me, "Go get help. You need to live this time. You were in a similar situation in a past life long ago, and you did kill yourself. This time, you need to experience living and mending your life."

Shadows and Light

Next, through Diana, my father's spirit spoke to me again. He verified that I had seen something but not what it was. "I am ashamed," were his words. "It was a family contract not to talk and speak up. It has been so for at least four generations." I finally connected the dots. When I walked into the bathroom and saw my father, he was with another male. That is why I had always known he was gay, and now he had acknowledged that I had seen something and he was ashamed. This made sense to me, as this would have happened when my mother took my sister, who was three and still quite attached to her mother, and went back to British Columbia for a visit. My brother and I, who were around nine and eleven, were probably left alone a lot during this time to fend for ourselves, and it is possible my father thought I was out playing with Mark or at a neighbor's house. At the time, I was told "not to tell." His words scared me so much that I was rendered speechless. I was only nine years old and knew nothing about sex, so this scene would have disturbed and confused me. This memory was among the many obliterated by the shock treatments I received after my suicide attempt and that is why I remember certain incidents only up to a point. I could remember without much detail being somewhere and doing something with someone, but such a fragmented memory too often could not answer my questions. Even with all the therapy I have had and the passage of time, some of these memories remain only snippets that do not provide enough information to cast meaning on my past.

Before I share what else was revealed to me from this session with Diana, I need to share more about my father. He was a thin, dignified gentleman whose towering height at 6'8" was sure to mark him out in any group. Mild mannered, reserved, and honest, he was not one to swear or get angry. His emotions were always well contained, which made him stoic beyond belief. Once when he had abdominal pain, he decided to walk to the local GP a few blocks from our house. Fortunately, my mother insisted on driving him. He had *volvulus*, a condition in which the bowel gets twisted around itself and causes obstruction. That day, his bowel was completely obstructed, and he was rushed to Mass General Hospital for five hours of emergency surgery.

Born in the small town of Alix, Alberta, over a hundred miles northeast of Calgary, he came into the world with two strikes against him. His mother died giving birth to him, and his father was devastated by his wife's death. She had previously given birth a year earlier to a baby boy named Robert who had died soon after. My father was also named Robert after that baby. My father never told stories of his childhood and what it was like growing up.

My mother had told me that when his stepmother, who was my "Gran," came into the household my father at four was almost non-communicative. I recall Gran as a gentle, kind woman who played the piano. I would sit on the piano bench next to her as she sang. I am sure she had a positive influence on my father.

My father received his M.A. in Latin and Greek from the University of British Columbia in 1940 and taught both languages for many years. He also spoke fluent French. Teaching at Roxbury Latin School in West Roxbury, he directed his students in a play in Greek, nonetheless! My father liked hiking and the outdoors. He founded the Roxbury Latin School Outing Club and enjoyed exposing the boys to the outdoors in the wilds of New Hampshire.

Wherever we lived, my parents attended the Episcopal Church on a regular basis and got involved with church activities. However, my father went over to the Roman Catholic Church around the time Michael and I moved back to the Boston area in 1973. I am not sure of his exact motive for doing so except that there was something about women being allowed to be ordained

Shadows and Light

in the Episcopal Church, and he did not agree with this. I thought that was his reason for doing so and naturally I was incensed. By the early seventies, women's liberation was in full swing, and I took his move as being that of a misogynist.

When I was a teenager at St. Mary's, my father had taken seminary classes to become an Episcopal priest. While I am fairly sure he finished all the requirements, he was never ordained.

He was always a mystery to me, and I never got the chance to know him. He was also gone a lot from the house in the evening at various school or church activities. Even when he was present physically, he was distant emotionally. Years later, I realized he must have been going to downtown Boston some of those nights to pursue his gay life.

Now, I come back to my session with Diana.

Besides providing the insight on my father during this October session, Diana saw one of my past lives, which tied into my communication issues and my silence. Evidently, I was a red-haired bar maid during the French Revolution who was passing information on to counterrevolutionaries. I was caught and guillotined. It sounded very dramatic to me at the time, but when I thought about the details later, this story made some sense of my head and neck issues. When living in Paris in the early 70s, I had had an inordinately difficult time speaking French. I could understand what was being said but I had trouble getting the words out in response. This particular past life of mine helped me to understand my difficulty speaking a language that had been spoken around me when I was guillotined almost two hundred years earlier. Reference to this past life has come up more than once in psychic readings. I can only conclude it must have been an important one for me. I picture this red-haired bar maid as feisty and competent and maybe that's where I get those characteristics from. My own feistiness, however, lay dormant for many years while I was in a shut-down mode. Even now, it only comes out once in a while.

Ahead of me now was coming to terms with who Maggie was in my life and whether we would ever have any relationship.

Chapter 17
Maggie and Settling Issues With Work

I was determined to get to the source of my inner conflicts. I knew I still had many issues to resolve and one of them that continued to weigh on me was what to do about Maggie. My relationship with her remained unresolved. Would it ever be resolved? On my next visit to Diana, I gave her Maggie's name and details about giving her up for adoption. I wanted Diana to get information about contacting Maggie. Was there a spirit guide out there who could help me?

We sat in silence in the room Diana had set aside for her medium work. The scent of candles and incense filled the room. Nervous with anticipation myself, I could see Diana's face reacting as she received information. This was exciting! Before long, she said Maggie's adoptive father's spirit was present — he had died when Maggie was in high school. This is what he said to me:

"You do need to contact Maggie. Be patient, as it will take her time to come around. Give her the gold chain that belongs to your family. Thank you for the sacrifice you made; I know it hasn't been easy for you."

Wow! I nearly fell off my chair. The tears of relief streamed down my face. This had to be Maggie's father speaking as there was absolutely no way Diana could have known about the gold chain — my paternal grandfather's watch chain. It was in a jewelry box that sat on my dresser. From the gold chain hung a pendant of an agate heart. Where the pendant came from, how he got it and from whom, I did not know.

The words of Maggie's adoptive father had a profound effect on me; his acknowledgment of my sacrifice and of how hard it had been to relinquish my baby was a balm. His words of reassurance were ones I had always hoped to hear from my own father — and my mother. Maggie's father made me feel I was not alone in thinking I had done something right in giving Maggie up for adoption. I congratulated myself. His words also made me believe she had been brought up in a loving family. This was a relief since I couldn't face the alternatives. The guilt would have been too much to bear. I would find out later that Maggie had had a happy childhood and had been comfortable growing up with her family.

I liked the suggestion of giving her the gold chain. It was a symbol of connection to her biological family. While she had been given up to another family to raise, her biological family was still where her DNA had had its origins. At the same time, giving her the chain — with its pendant — would affirm my connection to my ancestors, which had not been strengthened over the years during which I felt I did not belong to my family. What I felt was being abandoned. Now after my visit to England, I felt a connection and perhaps giving this chain to Maggie would continue that connection into another generation.

Encouraged by her adoptive father's words, I decided several weeks later to write Maggie the following letter at an address that I believed was current. I sent it and the gold chain by certified mail to assure me that she had received the chain. I wanted her to have it, and I did not want to simply lose the chain to an undeliverable address.

November 13, 2006

Dear Maggie,

I am not sure if you ever got the last letter I wrote to you a few years ago. At any rate, I wanted to send the enclosed necklace so you have something of mine. It comes from my father's side of the family. The chain was my grandfather's watch chain but I am not sure the origins of the agate heart.

No matter what happened in the past or what the future brings we will always have a piece of each other within ourselves. It is a bond that can never be broken.

This is sent with love and with the hope that all is well with you.

Love and blessings from your birth mom,
Susan

I included my contact information in the letter. A few days later, Maggie signed for it, but I did not hear from her.

The waiting was to continue. When would it end?

That fall, encouraged by my meetings with Diana, I read several books on past lives, mediumship, and the afterlife. I was fascinated by the afterlife and wanted to know more about it. One book stood out: *Journey of Souls* by Michael Newton, Ph.D. He had developed a system he called Life Between Lives Regressions. I found his work thought-provoking as I got a glimpse of the spirit world, the nature of our souls, and the purpose of the life we are in today. I felt not only ready but compelled to take

Shadows and Light

this journey of my soul. Why had I chosen the life I had?

In my quest for this answer, I sought someone who might help me. I found Pam, a hypnotherapist who had studied with Dr. Newton and was certified to do the Life Between Lives Regressions. In January of 2007, I scheduled an appointment with Pam. As on the day of the first appointment with Diana, I was anxious from not knowing what to expect. Would I be able to relax my body enough to be hypnotized? I had read that not everyone doing these regressions reaches the deep level hypnosis required. My self-confidence was nagging at me.

After some preliminary conversation, we got down to business. Pam led me through a ninety-minute relaxation and regression exercise. Even though I was in a hypnotic trance, I was aware of my feelings and of my surroundings. At one point, I came to an impasse and could not get into the spirit world. I was floating around looking for my soul group and was unable to find it. Suddenly, I became hysterical and started to cry. I thought I had murdered someone! I knew I hadn't murdered anyone so what was going on? Pam told me I had a spirit entity attached to me. Her name was Jill. Pam said Jill — after she left the earth plane — went to a dark place where she had been hanging out for a long time. I sensed her coldness and her big, round, vacant eyes. When Pam confronted Jill, the spirit said she had been attached to my mother before me, and possibly to my mother's mother before that. Jill was seeking revenge for a child of hers who was murdered by a man called Simon, sometime in the 1850s.

Pam and I had a ceremony for Jill. We recognized her role in my life, visualized tying a golden cord around her body, and with the help of my spirit guides, sent her back to her soul group.

This initial session with Pam lasted just shy of six hours! When, at last, it was over, I was exhausted. My emotions had run the gamut. One minute, I felt peaceful and relaxed; the next, I was sobbing and tense. I knew this whole incident with a spirit entity would seem unbelievable to most people. I was even skeptical myself, but because I felt I had been carrying a burden on my shoulders and could never figure out what it was, the experience made sense. Also, I had felt recently that something was holding me back.

However, I was encouraged to find out about Jill. This knowledge was important and might be the catalyst for me to open up more on a spiritual, psychic level. Pam wanted me to write a farewell letter to Jill once I got home.

The following day, this is what I wrote.

Dear Jill,

> *I think yesterday was a significant day in both of our lives. I got to meet you and understand the role you played in my life. You got to go back to your soul group in the spirit world at last.*
>
> *I am truly sorry that you lost your daughter at such a young age. It was a despicable crime that Simon committed. I don't really understand how you got attached to me and my family, but whatever the reason, I am glad we got it sorted out yesterday. You had me so confused when I was doing the Life Between Lives Regression. A murder in my life did not seem real to me, however, all the emotion was there. And the pain — I have felt your pain for so long and hope now that it will ease. I can be assured that you will no longer have pain in the spirit world.*
>
> *I can't imagine why you wanted to hang around for such a long time. I suppose, like other things in life, one gets used to something and letting go is very challenging. In the end, we confronted you. It was difficult, but I am sure it was the best for you. Sorry we had to tie you up in*

the golden rope, but I really needed to have the answers. It felt good to see you go into the light and perhaps, one day, we will meet in the hereafter.

For now, I need to keep developing my soul, and hopefully, it will be easier to do so without you.

Blessings,
Susan

Meanwhile, that winter, Stuart had changed jobs and was now working part-time from home writing software for a start-up firm. I envied his new freedom as I was still commuting into Boston four days a week. I had been doing this for more than two years. He was enjoying his virtual job and the time it saved from not driving to work opened his days to writing a book about his favorite topic, Extra-Terrestrials, that he had started the previous year. On weekends, we enjoyed attending a spiritual class of some kind as spirituality was a topic in which Stuart and I were both interested. Diana sometimes gave a class. Stuart and I took one of hers about becoming a spiritual warrior. This class gave us a lot to think about.

One Saturday, I wanted to do something fun. We couldn't agree on anything, and since a new toilet was something we needed, we ended up at Home Depot. My intent in proposing an outing together was to connect with Stuart, but this outing produced an unexpected wedge. At Home Depot, the toilets were on shelves up above our heads. With time, looking upwards caused my neck began to hurt. It was a familiar neck issue, possibly due to arthritis.

I told him about it. "I can only look upwards for a minute or so before it is painful."

"It won't be much longer."

"I don't think I can last another minute. Could we please go to another store to look at toilets?"

He took off in a huff. I went after him.

"I am not mad at you," he insisted, but I was not sure. I wanted him to have been a bit more sympathetic — to not be like my mother when I had a bad headache. I have a real neck issue and cannot look up long without having pain. I couldn't help but wonder, "Where are these communications and listening skills we had supposedly learned at the couples' workshop we went to?" I tried to talk it out with him and come up with a solution but it was useless. I felt he wasn't listening to me, but I also had to ask myself, "What role was I playing in his shutting down?"

Maybe I had to change how I related to him.

The winter of 2007 had some difficult moments. Commuting was frankly wearing on me and taking its toll. The rigid position required of sitting at the steering wheel for so long tensed the muscles in my neck and shoulders even more than they already were. If traffic started to back up in Boston and I knew the commute would be longer that day, I would get weepy and depressed. The commitment of entire days away was getting to me emotionally as well. I could see that Stuart was more relaxed and he had more time for his project. I started to have trouble falling asleep.

Stuart had bought some meditation CDs, and I listened to them most evenings, hoping they would relax me and help me fall asleep. They didn't have the desired soporific effect.

Something strange happened after I listened to these CDS for a while: I began to see a blue light.

"Are you seeing anything when you listen to these CDs?" I asked Stuart.

He said he wasn't.

I told Stuart about the blue light I kept seeing. It did have meaning but it would take me a while to understand what that was about.

That same winter, another difficulty arose around Stuart's book. After he finished the first draft, he wanted me to offer him some feedback.

"I would be happy to read your book," I replied. Since I do better with uninterrupted time when I am not tired and can give my full attention to something, I told him I would pick it up shortly, but not at the moment.

He gave me a copy of the manuscript, and I put it on my bedside table. I could see he was reluctant to wait but he said nothing more. At the time, my response seemed reasonable — at least to me — and with his silence, he seemed to agree. A couple of weeks later, with an unscheduled weekend before me, I read through his manuscript.

The book did not seem to have been written with a particular audience in mind. When we sat down in our living room for a discussion, I began by praising his writing — he does write well — and then I went on to ask, "Who is your audience?"

I presumed his answer might help us to arrive at some useful feedback.

"Curious people like you," he replied.

One problem with his answer was that I was not actually curious about extraterrestrials. Because of his generic reply, it was obvious that he had not put much attention into asking himself who his audience was as he was writing. It certainly was not me.

Being as non-confrontational as I could, I offered, "As you have written this, your book's audience doesn't seem to be the average person actually. It's a bit scientific."

Then, to soften what I hoped he would not have found too harsh, I added that I might not be the best reader for a book on extraterrestrials since I normally wouldn't pick up a such a book. Then, something — call it the devil — made me throw in that the title was a bit confusing. I ought not to have said this. By the changes in his body language, I could discern the title critique had been too much for him to take in, in addition to the comment on the audience. He was obviously upset. However, when I suggested we brainstorm a title, he agreed and we came up with several options. Eventually, Stuart chose one of his alternatives to replace the confusing title.

That weekend, nothing more was said; I could see he was sensitive about his manuscript and I did not want to repeat the tension of our initial discussion. What he needed was an editor with whom he had no emotional connection and from whom he could accept criticism. What he had was a wife from whom he wanted praise. Unfortunately, his wife was too honest!

In retrospect, I had to admit to myself that I had not realized how important it was for me to look at his book both immediately, when he had asked me to, and uncritically. The easy rapport we had had early on in our relationship was becoming strained and this manuscript critique did not alleviate that. We were entering a time when we had to weigh what we said to each other. The future — the near future, at least — promised to be less fun than our early years.

To add to the tension of commuting, I had some growing tension with my boss, Marie. I had realized from the start of my employment that it was best to have minimal contact with her, and only when necessary. Because of the issues I had had with my mother, I knew by now that female bosses presented me with problems. I decided to relate to Marie as a learning opportunity and to try to discover any additional insights on the conflicts I had with bosses of my gender. From the beginning, I had not expected much from her, although she had not appeared emotionally distant like my mother. For the most part, we got along just fine, and at times, she could be pleasant and helpful. But I continued to believe having minimal contact with her was best. At first, there had been two nurses working part-time with me under Marie. Then, these two women quit, creating two downsides for me by their departure: first, being a hard worker and a pleaser, I took on the whole workload by myself, and second, I was alone to bear the brunt of Marie's attention.

Marie and I had a couple of significant conflicts in which she yelled at me. Once, when her door was open, and it appeared she was merely chatting with one of the other employees and not having a private conversation, I started to walk into her office.

"Get out," she shouted immediately. "It's very rude to walk in like you did."

I was taken aback as I stood in the open doorway. All day afterwards, I brooded about her active reaction, and my passive one. The next day, having resolved to defend myself, I went to her office again. She was alone and I walked in. I told her that I felt I had done nothing wrong the previous day. "The way you spoke to me was inappropriate, and I was upset by it," I said. She didn't apologize, but that was not what I needed at the time. What I needed was to learn to articulate my issues in a conflict. In this way, I could learn to stand up for myself and not let anyone — neither Marie nor anyone else — get away with speaking rudely to me. As time went on, I realized how little work Marie did. It was true she only came in twenty hours a week, but I could see hardly any results from her twenty hours which added up to half a regular work week after all. After the two nurses had quit, I was the only person Marie "managed," and I hardly needed management. It frustrated me to know she was getting paid more than I to do nothing, when it was I who was not only responsible for getting the workload of the sub-department done, but getting it done well.

That spring, armed with my frustration and my sense of injustice, I went to Ted, the director of the department and Marie's boss, and told him my concerns. I presented the facts in a non-confrontational, rational way. I summed it up by saying, "I think you might want to check to see what Marie is doing for work." Nothing much more was said at the meeting, but I left feeling relief and thought, I am glad I did this because I am tired of people taking advantage of me.

It was another step toward standing up for myself. This has always been hard for me, but continuing practice has made it easier.

A few weeks later, I came to work one morning to learn that Marie was gone. There was no explanation offered. I heard from others that Marie had also been rude to them, and they asked me, "How could you stand working for her?" Knowing that her manager position was now open, I planned to apply as soon as it was posted. After several weeks, Marie's management job had still not been posted. I went to Ted, to whom I had been reporting since Marie's departure. Basically, I told him, "Either post the position and hire me, or I will look elsewhere for a position."

He hired me, and I was thrilled since it also provided a good raise. To think that Marie had been getting that salary while I was doing the work!

Even with the new promotion and its pay raise, not long after landing the position in the beginning of the summer of 2007, I had had enough of the commute, which was feeding a lot of the pain in my neck and shoulders. Around this time, I learned we were getting new auditing software for the physicians. All the patient information that I would need to do my work would be accessible online. Might this be an opportunity to work remotely and do away with most of the commute? I was already working one day from home and I could see how good that was for me. When I spoke to the tech people, they told me this new software could be put on the hospital network enabling me to access it from home. With their confirmation, I realized with some pleasure that, while I would still have to commute some days to meet with the physicians, this new software, if placed on the hospital network, would allow me to work mostly virtually. With this in mind, I asked Ted if he could arrange for the tech people to put the new auditing software on the hospital network. This would allow me to do more — even much — of my work from home. I shared with Ted how distance work one day a week had proven productive for me and how, with the new software that could be connected to the hospital network, I could work virtually for additional days.

Without explanation, Ted refused my request. It wasn't as if he didn't know what the networked computers could accomplish, but there was no changing his mind.

Knowing that commuting was hurting my health, I gave Ted my notice. As is often done in these times, I told my co-workers I was leaving. One of them told me that the hospital's Radiology Department was looking for a medical coder, a job I had done in the eighties. The job was for twenty hours a week, and it could be performed from home. The job also included all the benefits I was currently collecting. This news was almost too good to be true. While my income would be reduced and I would have to watch expenses, gaining the freedom was well worth the loss of income. I applied and was offered the job.

I was happy to be leaving my old job with all its office politics and its endless commute. I was leaving on a good note since

I was pleased with the quality of the work I had done there and knew I had stood up for myself many times. I had come a long way in the world of work and no longer needed to prove myself.

Working from home, I would have time to take classes and workshops and do the things that I knew I needed to do.

Chapter 18
Some Things Change But Not My Marriage

In the summer of 2007, when I left my full-time job at Brigham and Women's Hospital for part-time medical coding from home and ceased commuting to Boston, I had the good fortune of having accrued eight weeks of vacation time, which allowed me to spend these two months at the lake. It was the longest uninterrupted period I had ever spent there. Without an agenda, only kayaking and sitting on the deck reading and just generally relaxing, I unwound from years of working.

The internet connection Stuart needed to do his job was not yet available at the lake, so he stayed in Atkinson during the week to work, but he joined me at Maidstone Lake on most weekends.

After a weekend or two of his visits, I realized that I was more relaxed without Stuart. I didn't have to question whether I should ask him this or that, and I could eat anything I wanted when I felt like it. Any two people living together are faced with constant compromise, but these compromises are usually not important to a couple. What is more important is being together. However, after almost three years of living with Stuart, I was feeling more myself without him than with him. This was an ominous sign that our relationship was not where it needed to be and where I wanted it to be.

Shadows and Light

Inevitably, I had to ask myself: if I was more comfortable when he was not around, what was life going to be like when I started to work from home and we were in each other's presence every day, all day?

In the spring, in order to clear the power lines, the utility company had chopped down trees and overhanging limbs along the main road in front of the cabin. While the crew had taken the big pieces, they had also left a lot of debris. In between periods of "doing nothing" on my deck, I would go out and clear some of this debris. While clearing brush — and perhaps only when clearing brush — I wished Stuart could have been around more to help me, but when I wasn't cleaning the area, I was glad to be by myself!

As I write about this long idyll at water's edge, another time long ago, when I had spent an entire summer at a New Hampshire lake, comes to mind. This memory was obliterated by the electroshocks I endured as a young woman after Maggie had been born. Only after the conversation with my parents, which I have related earlier as occurring in the mid-eighties, did this babysitting job, of which I had no recollection, begin to haunt me. I could envision a curtain blowing in the breeze. It was that image that had come to me during yoga class in the mid-seventies, but I had not fixed it to any particular event. It was characterized, however, by an unpleasant feeling — no, I have to say it was more than unpleasant. It was a terrible feeling of being abandoned again. At some point later in the early eighties, I connected the curtain blowing in the breeze to the forgotten New Hampshire summer, but I had no insight into that experience.

When the year at St. Mary's ended and I had come to spend the summer with my family at Hotchkiss School where my father was teaching, my mother announced that she had arranged for me to babysit for a Hotchkiss School family through the summer. She said it would be good for me to have spending money for school, so she and my father had sent me off. How had my parents thought it appropriate to let a girl who had been gone all winter at a boarding school be away from her family again for the whole summer? My parents stayed at Hotchkiss while I travelled with this faculty family to their cottage on a lake in New Hampshire. What I needed was to reconnect with my family more than I needed spending money. It was so much like my parents to have little sense of how they ought to build on their relationship with a daughter who was gone nine months of the year.

Something bad had happened that summer, but I could not remember it.

These thoughts came up as I lived alone week after week at Maidstone Lake. When I was quiet, perhaps sitting on the deck, perhaps falling asleep at night, or when I had my guard down — as when I was clearing brush — these thoughts kept insisting that I ask myself, What steps am I going to take to free myself from a past laden with dark events? That I had little or no memory of these dark events was not helpful. Even so, it was important for me to improve my life by searching to understand what had happened. How was I going to go about doing that?

This is when what John Holland had said about my psychic abilities came to be useful. If my mind and my memory had not led me to answers, perhaps psychic work could. If I improved my psychic abilities, could I arrive at memories that would solve the mystery of my life?

As I pondered this, I also sought physical relief from my pain. In addition to mediumship, Diana offered hands-on healing sessions. In the beginning of August, a month after I had left my position with the wearying commute, I was still having my usual neck and shoulder pain issues. What reason was there still to have these pains? I made an appointment with Diana and went down to Atkinson for an overnight. I don't recall much about the session with her except that I felt relaxed and I coughed when she used incense. Diana suggested I try craniosacral work to get relief from my neck issues and referred me to a woman named Cassandra who did this work. The therapy uses a gentle touch to enhance the function of the craniosacral system. This modality sounded vague, but I was willing to try anything to alleviate the tension and the pain in my neck and shoulders; I made an appointment to see the new therapist in early September when I would be back in town.

After I returned from my "sabbatical" at the lake and before I could see Cassandra, I began my work as a virtual medical coder. I felt energized after so much time off and was resolved that Stuart and I could work out any issues that arose from sharing a common office. The work itself was not challenging, but I had good benefits and the luxury of more time. I also loved not having to get up early for the drive into Boston. More than half of our home office was taken up by computer equipment Stuart needed for his job. Both our desks faced the wall so our backs were to each other. I am a morning person and I liked to be at my desk by eight and work until noon. This schedule gave me the rest of the day to do other things. On the other hand, Stuart slept in and would not start working until ten or eleven in the morning. Because of this disparity in our preferences for work time, we did not overlap long in the office.

When I met Cassandra in early September for my craniosacral session, I liked her energy. Lying on the table as she worked on me, I felt very relaxed. I enjoyed this energy/healing session because I felt lighter in spirit and body afterwards.

After this first session, Cassandra told me that she also taught how to become a Reiki practioner. I was immediately interested as the word "Reiki" had been popping into my head for a while. Was my inner guidance, whom I called Spirit, urging me through Cassandra to do something in order to move my life forward? I asked her when she would be teaching Reiki 1 next. When she said she could give me an individual lesson anytime I was available, I took her up on the offer to learn to administer Reiki and booked a day for the following week.

Reiki is a Japanese system of relaxation which consists of the laying on of hands to transmit the universal life force energy (Chi) to the client. The basics can be learned in a weekend workshop. I was fortunate to have it taught to me on a one-to-one basis. As I was practicing the hand positions on a person whom Cassandra had brought in for learning purposes, she asked, "Have you done Reiki before?"

I had not.

She replied that I seemed to know instinctively where to place my hands.

I was pleased to hear this.

I took a few weeks to absorb this healing work and the Reiki 1 lesson. I like to take time to think about what I have learned before rushing to committing myself to something new. Initially, my neck and shoulders felt better but the improvements were fleeting and my symptoms came back. Even so, I was hopeful that, in time, the improvements could be lasting.

Reiki was something I felt strongly I needed to do, but I wasn't sure why. To learn why, I decided to pursue Reiki seriously. As much as I liked the individual attention with Cassandra's tutoring, I realized I might benefit from having more students to provide me with a variety of subjects to work on. In mid-November 2007, over two months after returning from the lake, I found a local metaphysical store that offered classes and signed up for the Reiki Level II class given by a woman named Sandra. The weekend class was informative, and I liked Sandra's style of teaching. I met a younger woman, Rebecca, and we decided to meet after the holidays to practice on each other.

Shadows and Light

Two thousand and eight was to be an active and eventful year for me. Getting rid of the spirit Jill must have played a part in my surge of activity as I searched for answers about myself and pursued new activities.

In the winter of 2008, my fellow student, Rebecca, and I made good on our promise to work together to practice Reiki. I would go to her house one week, and the next week, she would come to mine. I found these sessions with her to be very relaxing. One day, when I was at Rebecca's house — it was a cold but sunny winter morning — Rebecca lay on her massage table in her living room, and I was standing giving her Reiki. As I looked out the picture window in front of me, I saw a cardinal alight on the snow-covered bird feeder outside. Thoughts about Rebecca's mother came to me. I wondered if they might be significant, but I was not sure what to do with them.

After the session, I said to Rebecca, "I kept thinking about your mother and I am not sure why."

Rebecca replied, "I am having a problem with her that I need to resolve. I don't have a very good relationship with her."

Thinking of how John Holland had said I had psychic ability, I wondered, Is Reiki a vehicle for giving me a message for the client I am working on? I started to think that more was involved with Reiki than I was aware of. Rebecca and I continued to practice on each other for a couple of months until we had to stop due to Rebecca's changed schedule, but we both agreed that we would take an advanced Reiki class the following May when Sandra would be offering it.

I was more determined than ever to find out about my alleged psychic abilities. Stuart and I had learned of the Pete Sanders Free Soul Method, which was psychic and soul work that accessed the brain's joy center and emphasized opening up to Spirit. It sounded fascinating. Stuart found a person, trained by

Pete A. Sanders, Jr., himself, who gave classes locally once a week for about eight weeks starting in early January. Stuart and I found the classes to be interesting, but, since I can't recall much about them, I am not sure of the effect they had on me.

As we attended these "Opening Up to Spirit" classes, it helped me to have Stuart to bounce ideas off of and to discuss our experiences, but I soon noticed that, when I had an insightful experience that he hadn't had, he was irritated with me. If Stuart had been able to relax more and stop his tendency to analyze and/or rationalize everything, he, too, I believe, would have experienced more. Although I was not aware of it at the time, this Free Soul class started a crack in my marriage that would widen and deepen over the next years as my psychic interest grew and Stuart was not able to develop his.

I was learning how much more there was to know, and I was encouraged because, at least, I was getting significant glimpses into psychic phenomena. I thought, Maybe, I am opening up to Spirit and to Reiki because of my psychic ability.

While Stuart and I were taking the Free Soul classes on "Opening up to Spirit," I also started training to be a hospice volunteer. For many years, I had heard the words in my head that sounded in effect like: You need to volunteer in a hospice. Over the years, I put volunteering off because I was too busy with paid work or with being a single mom or finding there was no program available. In January 2008, I found a ten-week hospice-volunteer training program which was starting almost right away in Exeter, New Hampshire, about a half-hour drive away from home. The times and location were perfect, so I signed up.

We were a group of fifteen men and women in this training class. One group exercise stood out. We were asked to list on each of five separate slips of paper one important feature in our lives. I wrote things like my sons on one piece, my independence on another, and my financial security on a third. These had given me meaning and direction. We soon found out why we were we doing this exercise when the group leader announced she would come around to each of us to collect one slip at a time. She said that whatever we handed over we would be done with for the rest of our lives. In the first round, I gave up my independence. Then I proceeded to health, financial stability, friends and, lastly, my sons. Giving up these important aspects of our lives was sobering, and I could feel the emotion pervading the room once we had forfeited every one of the things we had cherished.

"And now," said the leader, "you have a sense of what a dying person is facing: letting go and giving up what has been the most important to them."

By mid-February 2008, I realized that my head and shoulder pain had to be more fundamental than commuting and the difficulties of my last job. At one of the Free Soul "Opening up to Spirit" classes, a woman gave me the name of someone who did deep myofascial massage. I had always avoided massages. In fact, I didn't even like back rubs, but I needed relief and was willing to try anything, even a massage. While still taking the Free Soul class, I signed up for deep myofascial work with a massage therapist named Jerry. One day, as Jerry was working on my shoulders, I started to get weepy. I said to him, "Something is going on. I'm getting emotional and thinking about death."

He said, "I sensed something about death with you. This morning when I came in, I saw something around your neck as you were lying on the table. I thought it was a necklace, but as I got closer, there was nothing." I told him about my past life in France and being guillotined, my suicide attempt, and the shock treatments.

"You must be holding a lot of old stuff in your muscles."

He told me he was psychic and had done extensive work with a shaman. I felt lucky to have found this man who might understand and help me.

At another session, when Jerry had me turn on my back, I thought about death again, as if I were going to die. He proceeded to spend a lot of time on my head and when finished, he said, "I think your father might have told you that he would kill you if you told anyone." That was amazing because I had not told him anything about my father.

My time with Jerry helping me, however, was not long-lived. After about four sessions, he told me, "Susan, your muscles are so tight that I cannot release them. You are still holding back, and I cannot go any deeper. I am sorry but I can't help you anymore."

While it didn't surprise me that he was having trouble releasing my tension as I felt I was tied up in knots, I had hoped to find someone who had the skill to work with me over the long haul. Clearly, Jerry was not that healer. Of course, by this time, the incessant pain and the lack of success in finding help caused me to be often depressed. This was not helped by my also having a major problem sleeping. I never felt refreshed when I awoke to the challenges of a new day.

Again, I was at the start of a search for someone to help me. When would this beginning again end?

Toward the end of February 2008, I received a letter from Maggie! After one year and three months, she had written back! My hand was shaking. I was afraid that she might ask me not to contact her again. This is what she wrote:

Thank you for your kind words and for the necklace. I never imagined that I would hear from you. I have never felt the need to look for you, although I had wondered if a time would come when I would look for you, but it hadn't happened yet. I grew up being very thankful to be where I was. I thank you for making the decision you thought was best for me. I consider myself to be lucky to be part of my family, and at the same time, believe that your reasons for giving me up were the right ones.

So, hearing from you was a shock of my lifetime. It has taken some while to get used to the idea that you are out there and have a name. I wrote a version of this letter a year ago and tucked it away. I haven't had the courage to send it until now. Any information I learn from you (the unknown) will change my life and that scares me.

How do we navigate through this situation of contacting one another? I would prefer any further contact to be through written letters. It makes me appreciate the respectful way you contacted me.

I wonder how you found me, and what led up to your decision. How do you know that I was the baby you gave up for adoption? I also want to know…why you are contacting me now?

I have never known my medical history. Will you share your family's medical history with me?

I was overjoyed to hear from Maggie and to know she had felt lucky to be part of her adoptive family. I knew I needed to write a response very soon and had to be careful with what I said. After all, I had abandoned her as a baby. It would take her a long time to trust me.

I began my answer to Maggie's letter this way:

It gave me great joy to hear from you at last and to know that you are happy with your family. I am truly sorry that I caused you so much upset by contacting you. I could not think of a better way to do it and I had no way of knowing what your situation was or whether you wanted to know me.

I went on to explain about how, through the Adoptees Liberty Movement Association (ALMA), I had found two women who had helped me trace her. Then I wrote:

You asked me why I am contacting you now. There are several reasons. I am in a much better place in my life and felt that I could handle anything that came up if I contacted you. There is much pain and grief involved when one has to give up a baby. Even though those feelings subside somewhat over the years, they never go away. I wanted to tie up any loose ends and know that you were well. Also, if you were looking for me, it would make things a lot easier for you. I have always been someone who likes to have things out in the open.

I included a copy of her birth certificate and said that her maternal medical history had nothing really important in it — no genetic diseases. Of her birth father's history, I knew nothing. Then I told her she could ask me anything about me or my family.

As we continued to exchange letters over the next months and as we slowly got to know each other, I hoped that we would eventually meet.

Time would tell.

In March 2008, I turned to my primary care doctor for help. She sent me to a rheumatologist, Dr. Schmidt. When I went to Dr. Schmidt, I was almost convinced, based on self-diagnosis, that I had fibromyalgia. I could feel the knots that Jerry had not been able to release. They had settled in my shoulders, neck, and hips and were painful when rubbed. In fact, if I rubbed a particular knot in my neck, the pain shot up into my head and a headache soon ensued. As she was taking my history and performing a physical exam, Dr. Schmidt seemed sympathetic and thorough. I was feeling that, at last, maybe I had found someone who would be able to help me. After the examination, Dr. Schmidt walked out of the room without giving me any specific instructions about what I might do by way of alleviating the pains. I got dressed and headed out to the front desk where I asked the receptionist, "Shall I wait here for Dr. Schmidt to talk to me before I leave? I'm looking forward to her explanation of what she found and what she is prescribing."

"No, you're through with your session, but she wants you to get a neck X-ray and try pool therapy Here is a prescription for a drug she wants you to take to help you sleep."

This was quite a letdown as I had believed that Dr. Schmidt was going to enter into a more personal relationship with my health care. I was disappointed. Once home, I looked up the drug she had prescribed. To my great irritation, I discovered the drug was an antidepressant. I was livid. She had not asked me about modalities of treatment I might prefer and about what I thought of taking drugs. I felt like I had been treated as a cookie-cutter patient!

I had had enough of antidepressants in the past and wasn't going to start them again. They were the last thing I was going to take! Yes, I was feeling down and not sleeping well but that was due to the discomfort I was in. Since I had a referral, I did have a neck X-ray taken to see if there was something structurally wrong. When the woman from Dr. Schmidt's office called, she told me the results did not indicate any skeletal problem.

I never took the antidepressant and did not see Dr. Schmidt again. Having had some positive results with stretching exercise in the past — yoga, for instance, in the seventies — I did follow through after my visit with Dr. Schmidt with pool physical therapy. Growing up, I had always loved to swim and had enjoyed the feel of water. I sensed it would be soothing to get in the water as regularly as I would have to if I signed up for pool therapy. The water would help my sore muscles. It turned out to be so, and after the official physical therapy course was over, I continued to swim at the health club. It helped me, both to soothe my muscles and to boost my confidence, which exercising did for me. There was a hot tub by the pool, and after swimming I would go in to let the warm water relax me.

One day as I sat in the hot tub, I was gratified to realize, Here I am sitting in a hot tub with three others — men I don't know — and I am not feeling self-conscious about being in a bathing suit. It was a change in the right direction.

After three months, I realized the chlorine in the pool was making me feel headachy — not my usual kind — and a bit odd at times after swimming. Reluctantly, I stopped going to the pool. Would I ever find a solution to my persistent neck and shoulder pains!

At about the same time that I had pool physical therapy, I finished my hospice training and started to see hospice patients occasionally. I thought I might offer Reiki to those patients who wanted it. My first encounters as a hospice volunteer were unremarkable: the patients were either demented, unconscious and in the active stages of dying, or didn't want to see me.

In the meantime, I continued with Reiki and took an advanced class from Sandra the first weekend in May 2008 in the local metaphysical store's meeting room. Rebecca, with whom I had practiced one-on-one in the winter, took the class with me as she had promised. As I continued to learn more Reiki, I felt my confidence as a potential practitioner grow. A special additional feature Sandra offered was a monthly Reiki "share" where a group of us would practice Reiki on each other. In that way, we got to practice skills in addition to getting a free session.

The local metaphysical store at which I was taking the Reiki class from Sandra offered a variety of classes and psychic readings. I had not forgotten that John Holland had told me that I had psychic abilities, but I had not known what to make of this notion which intrigued me. The "Opening to the Spirit" class had not answered my need. In the spring of 2009, a psychic-development class was listed on the store's schedule for June. I was still skeptical about my psychic abilities, but perhaps this class could help develop what John Holland had been so sure I possessed. Before signing up, I asked the teacher for a reading to check her out. She was scattered, lacked enthusiasm, and her demeanor was mild. However, she provided some interesting information. She said both my grandmother and my mother were psychic but they were ashamed of this power and kept it secret. She saw my grandmother reading tea leaves and cards. (I don't remember seeing my grandmother doing that when I was a child, but my mother had talked to me when I was an adult about premonitions that she had had of things that had subsequently happened.) In spite of the teacher's perceptions, I sensed this woman would not be a good teacher for me. With some disappointment, I did not sign up for her class.

At the same store, I saw a posting for another psychic-development class being offered by a Kevin Ross Emery that June. Next to the posting were copies of a book he had written, *The Lost Steps of Reiki*. After I glanced though this slim, spiral-bound book, I knew I had to buy it. Evidently, there was a totally different approach to Reiki. The little I had read appealed to me. I bought the book and read it through that evening.

From the book, I learned that, in 1996, Kevin had channeled a 5,000-year-old Tibetan shaman called Wei Chi. Wei Chi wanted Kevin to teach the ancient Wei Chi System of Natural Healing. Because of Kevin's *Lost Steps of Reiki*, I knew I wanted to learn

Shadows and Light

more about Wei Chi, as the system was now called. I felt that here might be the something I had felt was missing in my knowledge of Reiki — that there must be more to it than met the eye — and Wei Chi might just be that missing element. But, I would have to wait since Kevin was not scheduled to offer a class on Wei Chi until November.

As with the previous medium, I wanted to check Kevin Ross Emery out with a psychic reading. Calling the number posted, I made an appointment to see him at the store. When I walked in for my appointment, I saw a slightly overweight man who stood in the retail section looking at books. He had a mass of bleached, tousled blond hair and was dressed in shorts and a tank top. Around his neck was a string consisting of a crystal and beads.

When I inquired if Kevin Emery was present, the man turned around and said, "Hi. I'm Kevin."

I was expecting to see someone who was dressed in a more professional manner, a manner that I was used to. What was I getting myself into? I wondered when I was introduced to Kevin, who looked much younger than his almost fifty years.

In my first session with him, I was blown away by how he seemed to understand what I needed and who I was. During this exploratory session, my mother's father, the Bishop, came in from the afterlife to speak to me through Kevin. My grandfather talked about my parents and told me he knew my father was gay. In the Anglican Church around 1940, he said homosexuality was known and permitted but not exhibited. He was tolerant of my father but did not like him. He thought my parents should not have married, but they had since my mother was pregnant; subsequently, she had a miscarriage.

Then I got a possible answer to a question that I had always had: Why did my parents leave British Columbia and move to Virginia when I was turning eight? My grandfather stated that my father's gay life commenced when he was in the army during

WWII and had his first encounters with men. Up until then, he had been confused. He had had an administrative job and never went overseas. The story I heard was that he was too tall and his feet too long; both of these traits would have required custom-tailored uniforms and boots. My grandfather offered to pay my father to leave his family and even offered to assume responsibility for looking after my mother and the three of us children were my father to have left. My mother wanted to stay with my father (I assume she preferred staying with him to being a deserted wife, a divorcée, or having to make a new start.) We ended up moving to Virginia where my father got a teaching job in a boy's boarding school and where no one would know us. Finally, the move made sense for such a drastic upheaval in the family.

I wanted to know one more thing before my grandfather faded out, so I asked, "Are you psychic?" He answered, "I communicate with God in different ways. One is what you call psychic today." So, my grandfather was psychic and maybe that is why I have such a close bond with him. In addition, my grandfather said I was a lot like him but had my father's "flair" — I am not sure what he meant by that. Although I did not get all the details that would have given the reasons for my parents' move to Virginia, I did get enough information to help me put things into perspective.

After this startling and most informative session, I knew Kevin could be the teacher I had been looking for and that this psychic exploration could really help me. I signed up for his weekly psychic-development class. Any fragment I might get about my past was bound to help me fill in the blanks I had "forgotten" and understand who I was.

Over the next six weeks as I attended Kevin's psychic-development class, two things stood out. The first was the automatic writing that we had to do at home each day. This consisted of writing whatever came into our heads for ten minutes. Although I did it faithfully, I always wondered about the purpose. Five weeks into class, I asked Kevin, "I don't understand this automatic writing; it seems that I am writing nonsense."

"Go back and take another look at what you wrote," he answered, "and then come back to tell me about what you learned."

I was amazed to read that some of the things I had written were directives for me to do explicit things. For example, "Sell the cabin" was one such directive. I had been struggling with whether I should sell my lake cabin for some time, so this message made sense. After class when I revealed to Kevin about being told, "Sell the cabin," he said, "You have the gift of automatic writing. Everyone gets psychic information in different ways; this is one way you will get it." In other words, when I just sat down and wrote whatever came into my head, I would get psychic messages, not only for myself but for others, too.

The second thing that stood out from this class was a specific homework assignment. We were to visualize going over a bridge and to note what came to us. The bridge I thought of was the one in many of Monet's Giverny paintings. While I didn't "see" an actual painting, words came to me. The following is the visualization I experienced:

> It is a beautiful, warm day. The sun is shining, and I hear the birds singing in the background. I see a bridge in the garden. It goes over a large pond which is filled with water lilies. Flowers are everywhere. I am at ease crossing the bridge and feel the strength of the bridge coming up through the soles of my feet. I see someone waiting for me on the other side. It is Simon, my spirit guide, dressed in his striped robe with his arms outstretched to meet me.
>
> Simon takes me by the hand and leads me down a path until we come to a large rock. There is a bench by

Shadows and Light

the rock where we sit down. He compliments me on the changes I have made in my life and on the spiritual life I am working at. He says that I still have a way to go and that I have a special gift I have not yet acknowledged. I must have faith in myself and love myself. Perhaps then, it will come to me. As usual, I am too hard on myself.

"Let it go! Relax," he tells me. Simon has me look into the pond that is in front of the bench where we are sitting. "See your beauty, see your grace. It has always been there. You are a divine spark of light like the rest of us. You chose a difficult path on earth. However, you will get to the place where you want to be soon."

We hug and say our goodbyes and I go back to the bridge and cross over.

The Water Lily Pond by Claude Monet, 1899

When I did this meditation, I believed it was speaking to me about what was happening in my life at the time. My self-esteem still needed work. I needed to feel comfortable asking for help especially from my spirit guides and angels. The gift I received was learning that I was more of a healer than I thought I was and that I had psychic abilities that I had not yet tapped into.

These ideas were to be tested in the following years.

Chapter 19
Making a New Friend and Meeting Maggie at Last

As I continued with the psychic-development class, I learned Kevin also did medical intuitive work. Hoping his medical intuition could provide some insight that would help resolve my pains and headaches, I made an appointment for an individual session with him. The day before I met with him, I had a really bad headache and took a Percocet — left over from a surgical procedure — hoping it would give me some relief. Instead, I felt even worse and started vomiting. On the day of my session, I almost cancelled, but looking white as a sheet and feeling nauseous, I decided to keep the appointment.

That day, by scanning my body, Kevin was able to come up with a list of foods that were better for me than others and a list of diet supplements that might help. He asked me, "What happened 16 months ago? A shift happened in you." When no answer came to me, he encouraged me to keep doing the automatic writing that I had been doing most days. "Perhaps an answer will come to you then," he said. I left the session glad I had kept my appointment.

On the way home, I realized it had been exactly sixteen months earlier that, in a past life regression with Pam, the spirit entity Jill was detached from me. This had released me to continue on my healing path.

Shadows and Light

My work with Kevin was to continue on and off for the next couple of years. In him, I had found someone at last whom I could trust. He was a man of many talents: a spiritual counselor, a psychic, a teacher, a medium, an energy worker, a medical intuitive, and more. With this combination of skills, he was able to tap into my higher self or soul consciousness. Part of each session was spent talking; the other part was table work. While I was on the table, he would give me energy where he thought I needed it. During this time, he would often get psychic messages for me and/or lead me though a visualization. Some of these visualizations would take me back to past lives when something had happened to me; he would find pieces of me from those times that were stuck and could not move ahead.

In a memory snippet from my earliest childhood, someone was holding a picture up to a light. I connected this image to a story my mother had told me. I was around three years old, and she was driving our babysitter home. Mark and I were in the back seat. Evidently, I was fussing and whimpering, and she admonished me, "Be quiet! We will be home soon." When we got home, to her horror, she realized that she had slammed the car door on my hand! She then took me to the hospital where I must have had an X-ray, as I have that vague recollection of someone holding a picture up to the light. A mother with a stronger sense of her stewardship as a parent would have checked out my whimpering, but not my mother.

The bigger question remains: Why didn't I cry out in pain? It would be a normal reaction for a toddler to scream her head off.

When I was six, my sister was born, and I have always felt that the family dynamics changed after her arrival on the home scene. It was when my mother said she "gave up" on me. When I thought about it more, another memory — an up-to-a-point one — poked its way to the surface again. At around six, I recall being with older neighborhood boys that Mark and I sometimes played with. I was lying on a hard surface in the basement of our house. One of the boys was on top of me saying, "I am going to make a baby." That fragment of memory has always stayed with me, but the details remained a blank. If I had been molested by one of these boys — who would have been a young teen — I assume that, after this incident, I was acting out my anger in some way and maybe this was why my mother didn't know how to handle me? Again, a mother with more instinct would have seen that something was wrong and would have attempted to address it.

Kevin had me continue to do automatic writing each night. I was sure I had been molested, and I was sure this had occurred more than one time. I wrote about the frightened, lonely little girl who cried a lot wanting it to stop. Despite these negative aspects of my childhood, I was otherwise happy and carefree at times as I lived in my own psychic world. When I look at photos taken of me up to the age of six, I see a little girl who was smiling most of the time. My favorite memories were from the summers when my family went to a nearby lake in British Columbia with our cousins and family friends. We spent the days swimming, fishing, and going out in a rowboat; there was always someone to play with.

Susan, 1947

In our backyard in Salmon Arm, British Columbia, we had a catalpa tree, which was a favorite place of mine to climb or sit

Shadows and Light

under. It had masses of fragrant white blossoms in the spring and large heart shaped leaves in the summer. I would retreat there to be in my psychic world where I felt free and in tune with nature, and I dreamed of the future to come — a future with no fear, no pain, no worries, but filled with hope, passion, and love. As I was writing about the catalpa tree, these words came to me:

Tea with Mark under catalpa tree 1948

I was sitting under my special tree waiting for my security blanket to dry. My "Pet" as I called my ragged baby blanket — once pink and now greyish from wear — was hanging on the clothesline nearby. It was a balmy late spring afternoon, and when I looked up into the branches, I saw my friend, the owl. He was magnificent in his mottled brown plumage, and his piercing eyes shone. I waited to hear his words of wisdom and hope. The owl looked down at the frightened four-year-old girl.

"Why can't I be like you?" I asked.

He replied, "You are not ready yet. I can see what you cannot. I can hear what you cannot. I can feel what you cannot. I fly at night and touch people's souls when they need help. I will do the same for you."

"I don't think I will ever have your wisdom. I try so hard and nothing changes."

"It takes a lifetime to be like me. Remember I am always with you. Don't ever give up as there is always hope," the owl said and then flew away.

Now, I understand that my being psychic as a young child upset my mother. I wasn't supposed to "know" some things. This behavior was unacceptable and shameful. Therefore, I had to hide it. I assume that, at some point, I stopped talking and sharing much of anything with her since I was put down time and time again. I began to speak only when spoken to or to speak only when necessary. My brother told me when I was an adult, "You were an odd child."

Susan and her dolls
May 1950

Kevin assigned homework for between sessions — probing, uncomfortable questions to answer. For example, "Where does the practical Susan interfere with the spiritual Susan?" "What would Susan's life look like if she laid down the burden of being Susan?" His work was not for the faint of heart. I had to be ready to take a good hard look at myself, understand and accept the negative aspects of myself — the pain (neck and shoulder pains and headaches), the emotional upsets, the tendency to withdraw in uncomfortable situations (my toilet escapes!), poor self-esteem — in order to make real change. I was willing to do anything to get myself in a better place.

The following is a journal message I got from Spirit: "Patience, patience, and more patience. You cannot undo all that was done to you in such a short time. You were abused emotionally and physically and downtrodden for a good portion of your life. It does not come back easily nor without a lot of pain. Have faith — Kevin will help you work through it."

In July of 2008, I began an experience that was to prove very important to me. I was assigned by hospice to visit a woman who lived two towns away. When I arrived at Ruby's house, I saw a typical, big, white New England colonial situated near the road, with large oak trees along the front. The house looked like it had been there for many years. I found a place to park, and seeing a door ajar at the side of the house, walked over to it and up two steps. After I rang the doorbell, I heard a woman say, "Come in." I entered a small hallway and heard the voice again. Following the sound to the left, I entered the living room. Before me was a petite woman with short grey hair. She was hooked up to oxygen and was sitting in a large recliner at the end of the room. She introduced herself as Ruby.

Ruby was alert and mentally sharp. She asked, "Who are you? Why did you want to be a hospice volunteer? What is your background?" I knew then she was a good match for me; she was as curious as I was.

After a couple of visits, I asked Ruby if she would be interested in a Reiki session. I had just completed the advanced Reiki class with Sandra and wanted to practice more. Again, Ruby asked many questions: "What is it? How does it work? What does it feel like?" I explained the Japanese system of hands-on healing that promotes relaxation and the concept of universal, life-force energy.

"It doesn't make any sense," she replied. After some thought, she was still skeptical but she decided to give it a try.

Every visit started by my sitting across from her in her living room. She always sat in her large, comfy recliner, and I sat across

Shadows and Light

from her on a sofa. Her son, daughter-in-law, and two grown grandchildren lived upstairs on the second floor. Once in a while, one of them would pass through to get to the family business, which was connected to the main house, or greet us as they went in and out through the front door.

We would spend the first fifteen or twenty minutes catching up. Ruby would tell me what her week had been like. We would discuss major current events, and, since she was an avid Boston Red Sox fan, we discussed sports. Both of us were readers so we also talked about books. After this initial chat, we would proceed to her bedroom for a Reiki session. Walking was a struggle for her. Her diagnosis was chronic obstructive lung disease; after many years of heavy smoking, her lungs were shot. Ruby was on morphine and continuous oxygen and could take only one or two steps before she had to stop to catch her breath. A long tube connected her to an oxygen machine. It was long enough so she could get from her bedroom to her living room and her kitchen. The bathroom was accessible as well.

Entering her bedroom took me back many years. Filled with old furniture, it had four large windows, two of which faced the front of the house. Flooded with light, the room was dimmed slightly by the darkish floral wallpaper. The room was cluttered with furniture; knickknacks and mementos were on every surface. A hospital bed took up a commanding place in the center of the room. I would prepare for the Reiki session by opening a window, weather permitting, or cranking up the AC on hot, humid days when breathing was much harder for her. I would get Ruby comfortable in bed, covering her with a blanket if needed for warmth. Once she was settled, I would pop a CD of relaxing /meditative music into the player. Next, I washed my hands in the bathroom and warmed them by rubbing them together. Standing outside of her bedroom to say my prayers — a custom before an energy session — I would ask that Ruby receive whatever she needed in her best interest and highest good for today's session. Then I would walk to the head of Ruby's bed, do some deep breathing exercises and enter her energy field by laying my hands on her shoulders. It would take about a half hour to go around her body. At some places my hands would linger longer indicating she needed more energy in those spots.

She was deeply relaxed when the session was over and she talked about things, she said, she had never told anyone before. It was also a time when I would share any intuitive messages I got for her. For example, I had a vision of a little girl in a red coat. Ruby said, "I had a red coat as a little girl and I was wearing it when playing with a neighborhood boy, a friend of mine. He ran out into the street and was hit by a car. He was injured badly but not killed." It led to a long conversation of the guilt she felt. In our sessions, she was processing and reliving what she needed to. What I was experiencing gave me confidence in my ability as a healer.

After a couple of Reiki sessions, she told me, "My nurse was here yesterday and said my blood pressure was lower."

I continued to visit Ruby every week, and she always wanted me to give her Reiki. After every session, she would tell me more about herself.

When I bought the cabin at Maidstone Lake, I had said to myself, "If it ever becomes a burden to me, I will sell it." That summer of 2008 when I was involved with Ruby and with Kevin, owning my cabin was feeling like a burden. I was thinking about putting it on the market the following year but had not yet made a final decision. I knew I would miss the lake terribly and telling Linda would be hard — her husband Zack had died that May and my proximity would be comforting to her. Selling, however, seemed a reasonable choice. Even though I had replaced the roof, had bought a dock, and had a more functional deck built, there

Shadows and Light

was always work to be done. The taxes were increasing, and my income was lower as I was working only part-time.

Stuart was not contributing anything to help with expenses, although he spent time up there and enjoyed doing so. I got the feeling that Stuart thought it was "my place" and, therefore, did not have to contribute to expenses. I could understand that he would not help when he still had the expenses of his log cabin in the woods, but he had sold it the previous year. Afterwards, he could have helped me out, but Stuart thought differently. He had gotten a lot less than he wanted for his cabin and was upset because he thought the extra money he did not get from this sale would have helped fund his retirement years.

That summer, the individual sessions with Kevin were stirring up my emotions. To ease anything that might arise between us, I told Stuart, "This pain I am having and the moodiness you are seeing are temporary. They have nothing to do with you. Please be patient with me."

When I told Stuart about selling the cabin and my reasons for wanting to, he responded with, "What am I going to do with my sailboat?" Had he offered to help with the finances or to help me with the chores, it would have enabled both of us to enjoy the place for a longer time.

If we had a disagreement, we would talk, but the conversations never resolved anything. It helped me to talk about selling my cabin. I was trying to understand what I needed to do and so I would talk about the situation. If I told Stuart something once and repeated it later — or needed to add to a story — he would say impatiently, "You told me that already."

Instead, of asking him for what I needed and thus cueing Stuart clearly to "please listen to me," I would stop talking or change the subject. It was not a formula for settling things. I was still the little girl who would not speak for herself even though her finger was in the door.

That autumn of 2008, I still was having my usual shoulder and neck pain, with an occasional headache thrown in. I cried a lot as I worked through my past in the sessions with Kevin. These were providing me insights into incidents that I had forgotten or that had been erased by the shock treatments.

A big component had been missing in my childhood: the emotional connection with my parents. I felt it odd that I didn't recall feeling love coming from either parent. I know my mother read aloud to me, but I don't recall any closeness, the warmth of snuggling up to her to hear a favorite story. Our family had a piano in the house we lived in when I was four to seven years old. My father played the piano, but I don't recall sitting on the stool next to him listening and feeling happy hearing the melodies. I have always liked to bake and cook but I can't recall helping my mother in the kitchen nor smelling a freshly baked chocolate cake we might have made together.

Was I just tolerated as a child? Was I merely a needy little person who needed to be fed, clothed, and kept from harm? I had to wonder.

It was if a tractor had run over my childhood, plowing all my emotions deep into the earth. To survive this deep, dank soil, I had to protect myself and keep my anger, sadness, and love knotted in a tight root ball. The practical Susan emerged. I felt I had to keep order and try to please everyone to keep them at bay. I felt downtrodden and not able to express myself. These repressed emotions were now gradually coming to the surface with Kevin's help. They needed light and attention to survive the next growth cycle.

I don't remember playing any games with my father, or going to a movie with him, or his reading to me or teaching me anything. He never bought me a gift, took me out for an ice cream — and the list goes on. I do have fond memories, however, of doing things with my maternal grandfather, the Bishop, when I

Shadows and Light

was visiting my grandparents. I recall walking in the garden with him when we smelled a fragrant peony together. More than once, we walked to the downtown section of town and went to a small café. We had to go down a long stone stairway. When we got to the café, he ordered custard pie, and I had a strawberry milkshake. Were these memories vivid because my grandfather was an important person in my life and our bond was a special one?

As I mentioned earlier, my one memory of doing something with my father when I was between the ages of five and seven was going to the woodshed with him. It is a fragment of a memory; the details are lost.

When working with Kevin one day, this is what came from his intuitive: "There had been an incident with your mother, and she was annoyed with you. Your father sensed that you needed to get out of the house so he took you for a walk. He was empathetic with your plight, and you talked while walking hand in hand toward your woodshed. Evidently, you told him you had seen and/or known something that really upset him. It was something you should not have known about. When you got to the woodshed, he took you inside, and the atmosphere of being together changed. He took you by the scruff of the neck and banged you against the wall, hurting your neck."

Perhaps, this is another reason for the neck issues I have today? It made sense that something untoward did happen and that is the reason I can remember it only up to a point. Also, it made sense that my father did threaten me with punishment. He was the principal at the local high school, and I knew there were straps in his desk and had been told many times they were used to beat unruly students. I have no idea if they were actually used, but at the age I was then, I would have had a mortal fear of being threatened with those straps. Hence, the floating image of straps in a drawer that came back to me later in life was indeed a repressed memory coming into consciousness.

I do recall, when I was living at home and going to college, a scene with my father. My sister Clare was in her teenage years and, quite frankly, moody. At times, she was borderline abusive to me, scratching my bare arms for no reason. Why would she want to do such a thing? I was busy working and going to college and felt put upon by her behavior. Verbal altercations ensued in which I exhorted her to stop abusing me. I would also implore my mother to "please, stop Clare from scratching me!" She would admonish her slightly by saying, "Dear, you must stop it. Let's have the saying, KHOS (Keep Hands off Susan)." It was said with no conviction. It clearly didn't work; Clare continued to scratch, and my mother took no other steps to protect me.

After one of these assaults from Clare, my father came to talk to me. It is one of the few times I recall his doing so. He was very empathetic, saying how hard it was to be a middle child. Gee, he actually gets it, I said to myself. Although I don't recall the details, I thought how good it felt for him to talk with me like that, but the good feeling bubble didn't last long. It was burst when my mother revealed she had made my father speak to me. Even though he seemed so understanding, it was deflating to hear that comforting me wasn't his idea.

Kevin's Wei Chi Level 1 course called for a commitment of two weekends. Even though I felt compelled to take the course, I was a bit apprehensive about investing the time because I doubted my ability to receive messages for the client. What if nothing came to me?

Kevin had said of another woman who was going to take this workshop, "Like you, Linette is interested in death and dying. I know the two of you will get along."

I am always a bit wary when I hear someone tell me that another person and I will like each other. What if I didn't like her?

What would that be like? However, since she lived in the southern part of Massachusetts, I reasoned, if I didn't like her, I wouldn't have to see her around much.

I wasn't that impressed with Linette when we met at the first weekend training; perhaps I was in my contrarian mood. She was pleasant enough but appeared a bit flighty and was very much into clothes and makeup. Besides, she was about eighteen years younger than I. Another much younger woman than I, Kim, took the workshop as well. She was very friendly and easy going, and I felt more rapport with her.

That first weekend of the Wei Chi training was exhausting, yet rewarding. When I practiced on the other students, I was gratified to experience messages that came to me for them. The second weekend of the training raised the ante. In addition to the challenge of learning new material, we had to practice on outside volunteers. I was assigned a Reiki Master who had been doing the work for a while. So, being one to connect to my insecurity, my anxiety level soared up. It needn't have, as I received messages for him that proved to be meaningful. As a result, I felt that I really might be able to do this healing work. It was a heady time for me.

Now, I need to catch you up with Maggie. From the time Maggie had responded to me in February 2008, she and I continued to write long, thought-provoking letters — maybe one every two months — to get to know each other. In July 2008, five months after Maggie had finally felt right about responding to my letter, we exchanged photos of ourselves. Maggie saw similarities in us when she first saw pictures of me. When I saw pictures of her, she reminded me of someone in my family, perhaps one of my cousins whom I hadn't seen in a long time. I also couldn't help but think, Did she look like her birth father? (Of course, I had no recollection of what he had looked like.) There was one of her at about four years old that did remind me more of myself when I was that age. Seeing pictures of her made her real all of a sudden, and I felt scared and procrastinated writing to her again. When I did write, I explained the reason for the delay. Soon after my response, Maggie broached the subject of meeting. I had always wanted to meet her, but our relationship was so emotionally charged that I wanted to make sure she was really ready to meet me. It would still be a few months before we met.

"I feel peaceful about the idea of meeting you," Maggie wrote in October. "A while ago, I was feeling overwhelmed. All of a sudden, I knew that I was going to be okay because knowing you will add to my life as I have known it. You gave me the gift of life, and I will be forever grateful for that. I understand that what I learn from you gives me more insight into myself."

After I read these words, I felt it was the right time to meet. We arranged to meet for lunch at Legal Seafoods at the South Shore Plaza in Braintree on December 2. The night before, I was nervous, but it was a good nervous of not knowing what to expect and preparing to do my best. What if Maggie didn't like me? Would she want to see me again? Then I thought about all that we had shared in our letters. We knew a lot about each other and shared similar interests, so conversation would not be an issue. I decided to go with no expectations — just let it happen.

Maggie at 4 years

I dressed with care in the morning and left early to make sure

Shadows and Light

I would get there in time to be the first to arrive. In fact, I arrived at the mall at least a half hour early so I walked around and window-shopped to work off any energy, even though I felt surprisingly calm. At the designated time and place, I recognized Maggie immediately from her shoulder length blond hair and height of six feet. We walked toward each other and hugged. How to describe the feeling of hugging a daughter you have not held in over forty years! And how to describe the holding back I felt, the stark thought that she was really someone else's daughter — in every way but biological. But, this reality didn't matter as I knew she had my DNA.

Lunch exceeded any expectations I had tried not to have. We talked for two and a half hours straight. I have no recollection about what I ate — only that everything went smoothly. In the parking lot, we parted on good terms, and I said to Maggie, "Take time to think things over and decide what the next step will be." Driving home, I was on an emotional high but felt physically drained. Lunch with Maggie had played out in the best possible scenario and I hoped we could have some sort of relationship. It was a strange feeling seeing Maggie that first time. Here was the person I had carried for nine months and had given birth to. She had played a role in my imagination and in my psychic life, and yet I did not know her — how could I? I did not raise or nurture her to adulthood as I had my two sons. Technically, she was my daughter, yet she wasn't.

That evening, I sent Maggie an email to say how much I had enjoyed our time together and appreciated the opportunity to get to know her — even if only a little bit.

"Thank you for your kind words," she responded four days later. "I thought it was great to meet you and am amazed by how comfortable our time together was. I found our conversation to be very interesting and I have been thinking about our meeting a lot. I am still taking it all in. I would like to keep the line of communication open and also would be interested in spending more time with you."

I couldn't have been happier but I still had to be cautious with her. Even though I had to have come across as a very caring and thoughtful woman, at a cellular level, Maggie knew that I was that woman who had abandoned her.

It was an interesting time in both of our lives. I was going through a huge emotional upheaval revisiting my past, trying to salvage a marriage that I was no longer sure about, and dealing with my pain issues. I hoped I was not going to screw things up.

When I thought about our conversation at lunch in Braintree, I was aware that our lives were running in a slightly parallel manner. Up to then, neither one of us had been able to finesse a loving, life-long relationship. It would be interesting to see how exploring this topic might play out after we got to know each other better. Maggie had recently broken up with a boyfriend. She was forty now and still wanted to get married and have children — even though her biological opportunity was beginning to run out. There were two other stressors in her life: she was jobless as she had had to quit her job due to allergies and she had unexpectedly had to deal with her birth mother entering her life.

It would take time to see what effect our knowing each other would have on her and on me. Our relationship had brought up emotions for her that were painful and needed to be taken in, but only time would tell if this healing would happen. It was interesting to see how different Maggie's life was from what it would have been had she not grown up in her adoptive family. Of course, her birth father's family was completely unknown, but I knew mine well: it was fraught with silence, emotional abandonment, and abuse.

Would knowing each other change our lives in any way? Everything seemed comfortable now but would it stay that way?

Chapter 20
Realizations and Mattie Enters My Life

Sometime after meeting Maggie in Braintree, as Stuart and I were approaching our third anniversary on New Year's Eve, I realized, for the first time, certainly at a deeper level, that what I took to be the usual marital glitches and misunderstandings might instead point to something major happening.

That December, Stuart published his book on extraterrestrials via Create Space and placed it for sale on Amazon. I had given him a lot of support during the previous two years to help make this happen. I had listened to his ideas and I had accepted that he would spend hours in the office working on it, having little time for me. If I found a relevant article or piece of information, I had shared it with him. I had celebrated with him when an agent expressed interest in representing the manuscript. When the agent's interest waned, I commiserated with Stuart.

When he showed me a hard copy, I flipped through it, wanting to seem involved in his excitement. Looking at the layout, I worked my way to the front of the book, to the acknowledgments page, to see my name in print. How would he acknowledge all the support I had given him over the past few years to make writing this book easier? I had seen to it that he had time to write without having to do grocery shopping, cook or do odd projects around our home.

To my surprise, there was only a perfunctory mention in his credits. He had lumped me with my sister, his first ex-wife, and others who had read his book and given feedback!

When I expressed to Stuart that I was hurt by the scant acknowledgment that did not take into account what I had really contributed to his book, he replied, "Well, I was hurt, too. I wanted you to collaborate with me on the book. When you didn't want to, that was upsetting to me."

"What do you mean 'didn't want to,' Stuart?" I asked. "You never said you wanted me to collaborate."

He went on to explain he had wanted me to do more reading about UFOs and aliens so we could discuss ideas for his book.

"How could I help you if you never told me this was what you had wanted?" I said.

Quite frankly, I felt his expectation was rather unrealistic. Why would he think that these were subjects that I was interested in? Why would he think I would ever have wanted to explore extraterrestrials at length? When I looked back on this, maybe Stuart thought since he was supporting me with my Wei Chi work that I should have supported his writing more enthusiastically? He did support me and I always appreciated him for it, but I never expected him to take the Wei Chi class with me or get involved if he was not interested.

The space between our two worlds was widening and it occurred to me something might be amiss in our marriage. A healthier couple might have responded by reaffirming their affection for each other, but Stuart and I were already so far apart that we were unable to alleviate our hurt; all we could do was present our sides.

Around this time, we had another argument. When talking it through later, Stuart said, "You are so involved with the work you are doing with Kevin that I am feeling left out."

"I'm sorry you are feeling this way, and I understand why

you would feel left out," I offered him, and then I went on to say how I had been going through a lot of changes that seemed important to me that fall. In my recent individual sessions with Kevin, I had been dealing with my abuse issues. I had started the Wei Chi training and had met Maggie. "It's no wonder I have been distracted and felt down at times. This work is something I have to do, and it will be over before long."

He continued, "I have a lot of love to provide and you don't take advantage of it." As if to prove his point that I was not reciprocating, he said he had been keeping tabs on how many times I was affectionate with him — and it wasn't enough for him! I couldn't believe he was actually counting.

"It is hard to know your love is there,' I replied, "if you don't show it. Talking to me as you are now helps me to understand where you are coming from. I would like you to talk to me more. Our dynamics as a couple aren't the best. We have come to a point where we are not communicating and neither of us is getting what we want from the other."

Stuart appeared to listen to what I was saying but had nothing to add. I couldn't help but doubt that the parallel lives we were leading were ever going to intersect at some point.

As the year ended, in spite of the tension in our relationship, we decided to celebrate our third anniversary with a trip to St. Martin for a week — we had bought out Stuart's friends and the timeshare for the first week in January was ours. I hoped that this trip would get us back on a loving, marital track.

The trip down proved to be a long one. It began at 3 a.m. in Atkinson, when the shuttle arrived to drive us to Boston's Logan Airport. As we had to change flights twice, the day grew to be a long one. Although we made all the connections successfully, there were the inevitable waits during the layovers and so the trip seemed endless. Adding to my stress was that, during the flight to the island, Stuart made remarks about my "failures." By the time we got to St. Martin in the late afternoon, the combination of the stress of the long flight and of my resistance to Stuart's "quips" about my "failures" had given me a terrible headache. Once I had time to relax — sitting on the balcony of our condo looking out on the sandy beach and the swaying palm trees and writing in my journal — my headache dissipated.

In the days that followed I came to a realization that Stuart and I had always bantered back and forth, but what I had noticed happening on the plane was different. Previously, our banter had seemed to be in good fun. The repartee was funny even if it could be a bit sarcastic. In the relaxed atmosphere of the resort, I noticed that so many of his comments were focused on me and were now negative. In Atkinson, I had not paid much attention to the tone. However, I noticed now how he railed at how imprecise I was with words, how I required food on a trip, how I looked tense — who wouldn't if they had shoulder pain and a headache — and the list went on. Suddenly, I realized these comments were not repartee but hurtful criticism.

I decided to call him on his behavior. "Stuart, I have always enjoyed our back-and-forth banter. However, on the way down to St. Martin I noticed a change in your tone and content. It feels negative to me. Moreover, the focus of these negative remarks is on me and my quirks. I am upset by this. Going forward, is there something you could do to keep the focus off me?"

"I don't think I am doing anything wrong," he said as he turned away from me. When I requested to talk to him more about it, he refused to continue. He had, however, understood what I was telling him because he stopped the comments. The habit of repartee was suddenly gone from our relationship, but at what cost! He shut down even more from this time on.

After this fiasco of a conversation, we did our usual day trips on the island, and I stayed relaxed, enjoying the sun and warmth

Shadows and Light

again. As we drove around St. Martin, we noticed changes. The traffic was worse, and everywhere buildings and high-rise condos were going up. We thought maybe it was time to sell our timeshare. The island was changing. Stuart and I, as a couple, were also changing and I was concerned.

The following February 2009, Kim, Linette, and I repeated the Level 1 Wei Chi training workshop. We were joined by a couple of others taking it for the first time. The three of us thought the additional practice would be helpful as we consolidated our understanding of how powerful this healing system was. Katie, who joined us in taking the training, seemed to be a natural. She was intelligent, vivacious, and she fit right in. By this second round of Wei Chi, I was warming up to Linette. While we gave each other sessions, we learned about our personalities, issues, and quirks. I began to believe that my estimation of her had not been entirely fair.

This second round of training sessions beginning in February was powerful. During one, the work had made me feel something dark and fearful. I sought to escape the feeling by hiding in the bathroom where I had a mini-meltdown and cried. I remained there for a while, not wanting to go back out to face the others in my distraught condition. I had a history of running to bathrooms to hide. I had done it with Michael when he told me our friend Julie would not have gotten pregnant and I had done it when my parents would not share with me what they knew of the summer in New Hampshire when I was seventeen. How many more times would I be doing this? As then, finally, I summoned up my courage, wiped the tears off my face and returned to the others in the practice room.

Linette came to sit beside me. "Are you OK?" she asked. She was really concerned. This was a new response to my bathroom escapes. I liked it.

My lower lip was trembling as I replied, "Yes, but I don't know what happened. This work is so intense and is stirring up emotions in me that I don't understand. I feel so inadequate, isolated from our group, and am not sure if I can do this work."

Linette acknowledged my feelings by giving me a hug. I knew then that she was a loving, caring person, a person I could invest in friendship with. That weekend, I had no idea what an important role that Linette, Kim, and Katie were going to play in my life.

Had I finally found a group who would support me in my quest to be myself?

As a result of my commitment to Wei Chi, most evenings, I did a Wei Chi self-healing and sometimes I would ask Wei Chi for a message. I continued automatic writing in my journal and having individual sessions with Kevin. It was in these sessions that some light was shed on the "forgotten" summer when I was turning seventeen and had gone to a lake in New Hampshire with a family to babysit.

Kevin seemed to be able to access everything he needed to know through his psychic ability. In one particular session, he "spoke" to me just before I turned seventeen. At this age, this is what I told him:

> At first, this couple befriended me. The husband made me a confidante, and the wife was amiable to me. He was dying from a brain tumor, and she didn't want to have sex with him but he still wanted to have it. The wife knew what was happening — that he desired to have sex — and created opportunities for me to be alone with her husband so that sexual contact could happen. In fact, this was why they wanted me to come with them to New Hampshire. But it was the psychological manipulation and abandonment — not so much the sex — that made that summer

traumatic for me.

This "babysitting" job was damaging to me. When I first learned about that forgotten summer from my parents, my mother did say she had a recollection of my not wanting to go. Did I suspect something was amiss with this couple before I went? Did I express this to my parents? The sad part is that they must have known how negatively I was reacting and did nothing to explore whether I had any basis for my misgivings. I was a sacrificial lamb who became a solution for my parents about what to do with me for the summer. While they never said so, I believe my parents did not want me around. At least after Kevin's message, I had some idea of why that summer was traumatic. Living in the memory of abuse, I once again — even if it was 2009, years after my parents had died — felt alone and abandoned by my family. Again, I lived within the anguish of my parents not hearing my plea about not wanting to go. No wonder, in those July and August days in the mid-eighties when I had plied them with questions, they had not wanted to answer me! I had asked them many times to speak to me about what they knew of that New Hampshire season I had erased from my memory. When I tried to speak to my parents, my mother would turn her head, refusing to acknowledge me.

As I lived with Kevin's communication and kept seeing the curtain blowing in the breeze that I now definitely linked to the forgotten New Hampshire summer, I was sinking into the pit of despair again and would have to pull myself out; but the grip of guilt and shame made it difficult. I had to ask myself, Why does the victim bear this burden? It was also impossible not to wonder, Why didn't I just run away from these horrible people? I have to remind myself that I was in New Hampshire where, at the time, I knew no one. There was nowhere to go and no one to turn to for help. My parents had solved their problem for the summer and, conveniently for them, wouldn't have believed me had I told them what was happening.

When I did come home from that babysitting job, it was to a temporary rental apartment in a suburb of Boston. My parents had just moved there to situate themselves, as my father was to commence a new position at the Roxbury Latin School. I do not know why he had to go from one teaching position to another so many times, but at Roxbury Latin he came to a stop and finished his teaching career on its faculty.

Nothing felt stable in the new rental. My parents were making do with the situation as they looked for a permanent home in the Boston area. I would be leaving in two weeks for my senior year at St. Mary's. The school, as unsatisfying as I experienced it, offered stability in my life. In that short time in Boston, I was in a precarious mental state, reeling from the emotional aftermath of that babysitting job.

In the spring of 2009, because I was opening up psychically, I started to have visions before going to sleep. They occurred when I was very still in mind and body, in that lovely hypnagogic time before sleep. My eyelids would get heavy and my limbs relaxed. The visions were often just blobs of energy taking on various geometric patterns, similar to a mandala, or they could be people, objects, a butterfly, angel, or script; in other words, anything. Their appearance was always in black and white; color was a rarity but it could happen. The first image was crystal clear lasting for a second, the second image was not as clear, and by the third the image was blurry.

One night in April as I was falling asleep, I saw an image of an old-fashioned woman who had something familiar about her. She was sitting with one arm resting against her cheek and had a book in her lap. Her dress was a dark, silky material with lace cuffs and a high collar. She looked solemn yet attractive with her tight, light-colored curls. Sitting on those curls was a small dark cap edged in more lace. I thought, Who could this be? I knew her image was important to me but I didn't know why. I decided to leave it to the morning so I might get some sleep.

The following morning as I was relaxing over my cup of coffee, it dawned on me that I had seen the woman in family photos. Later that day, I went to the attic to find a box of old family photos. Inside, I soon found a photograph of the woman I had seen in my vision! I turned the photo over and saw her name: Ann Mathilda Vertue. She was my paternal great-great-grandmother. Why did she appear to me?

Fortunately, the following week I had a session with Kevin and when I showed him the photo of my great-great-grandmother — hoping that he could get some psychic information about Ann Mathilda — he showed amazement and asked, "Do you know her?"

"She is my great-great-grandmother. I call her Mattie," I answered.

My great-great-grandmother
Ann Mathilda Vertue
(age unknown)

"She is a past life of yours," he informed me. Using his mediumship skills, he received Mattie's spirit that came to him with messages. She was a very bright, articulate, and outspoken woman — quite a character — who also wrote diaries and poems. She spoke about how one day, after she married, she and her husband were riding horses in the park. He was encouraging her to talk about herself and about ideas she had, but when she did, because he did not like what she said, he proceeded to back-

Shadows and Light

hand her. She fell from her horse and broke her shoulder. He was apologetic and felt badly, so there was some good in him. (Is the shoulder pain I have related in some way?) I have read that one carries issues from one lifetime to another until they are resolved. Now Kevin said that Mattie's daughter, Emma, also showed up. Mattie was now speaking to Emma:

"Pain is something we learn to live with or we stop living." Emma observed, "You have not been yourself since Father died seven years ago."

Mattie replied "I have been exactly who I am since your father died. There are many things I wouldn't have done if your father was here."

Mattie loved to have flowers all over her house. One spring day, it was raining, and she went out to pick flowers. Flowers brought her joy and asked for so little. Hummingbirds and bees filled the garden with delight, but that day she got soaked and caught a chill. It was the chill that probably caused her death.

Her daughter went on to say her mother was brighter than her father, but her father needed to appear brighter.

Mattie also talked about her grandson, Matthew, when he was in his teens. "He has delicate leanings," she said, indicating that he was possibly a homosexual. She told Emma, "Accept your child for who he is. He is different; allow him to be himself. Your father did not understand such things. He beat children and had a corrupt relationship with God."

Kevin also picked up that Mattie called her husband a "foul bastard" in her head. When she died, Mattie felt she had failed Matthew because she had not communicated to him that nothing was wrong with him.

Apparently, Mattie was very outspoken and had gotten in trouble for it so she learned to speak to others in a more diplomatic way. By responding less forcefully, she was able to help people, though they did not know she had done so. She mentioned a female friend — possibly a sister — who may have been institutionalized. That woman could have been psychic and would have understood Mattie.

Then Mattie turned her focus to me and said, "You chose to be born with a contract with your father. He struggled with being different and had much internal angst. He was supposed to help you around the time your daughter, Maggie, was born and to prevent you from having shock treatments. Your father broke his contract. Also, he was supposed to talk to you before he died. Matthew was to bring your father peace before he died.

"Now that you can truly hear, dear, you can fight better and wiser. Your purpose in life is to fight stupidity and to bring healing. As much as others will allow, make everyone a winner when possible. Use your voice as it was meant to be used."

I wrote all of this so fast that I did not have time to reflect on it, but I was so excited to have all this information about Mattie that I couldn't wait to tell someone. As soon as I got home, I ran into the house to tell Stuart. In spite of all that had become negative between us, I still retained some connection with Stuart that wanted to express itself. Of the people I knew then, he was the one I wanted to share this wonderful experience with.

"You won't believe what just happened," I said to him almost as soon as I saw him when I got home. "I have just learned my great-great-grandmother is a past life of mine." Without waiting for a response, I went on to tell him how her spirit came to Kevin and shared some of the information I got.

Then I stopped and waited for a reaction.

"That's nice," he said with no hint of emotion in his voice. Of course, I could not expect news about a past life of mine to be quite as exciting to him as it was to me. "But, how do you know it is for real?" he asked.

"I know what you mean," I said. "Actually, I was a bit skeptical. Kevin even told me this type of visitation was a rare occurrence. Even with all his psychic, mediumship, and channeling skills, having a past life of a client come to him in spirit seldom happens. But, Stuart, Mattie felt so real. I want to take the time needed for the experience to sink in, and I plan to do some research to see if I can find out more about her."

What did I expect from Stuart? Perhaps he could have asked, "How will you use this information?" or "Do you expect Mattie to tell you something about your father's side of the family?" Stuart, however, contributed nothing beyond his skepticism and, having nothing to say, exited the room, leaving me alone and feeling deflated. Why wasn't he interested in what was happening to me anymore? What had happened to the excitement of laughing together and discovering more about each other? But, the disinterest was mutual: I was not about to learn more about his extraterrestrials. When I thought about this more, I recalled how interested Stuart had been in past lives. After all, he was the one who initiated seeing Dr. Weiss and John Holland speak. Afterwards, he even had a couple of sessions with Diana, the medium. It was as if he were shutting this part down and investing more in ETs. Or, maybe he saw that I was having some good experiences and he wasn't, and therefore his jealousy was continuing to bubble up.

This contact with Mattie was healing for me. Her presence had made me feel that someone cared about me and understood me. I had not gotten that from my parents and I was not getting it from Stuart. I was like a plant starving for nourishment and Mattie had come and had given me some feeding. It meant a lot that she told me my father was supposed to help me but was unable to or chose not to. I felt comforted to have found Mattie and her connection to my life, even though it was only in spirit.

When I went on Ancestry.com, all I could find out about her were dates of birth, marriage, and death. She did have a daughter, Emma. Interesting to note that her birth certificate did not have a father listed so I assume that Mattie had Emma before she married her husband. Was this a lesson for me to have in my lifetime? To have the experience of not keeping a child born out of wedlock? She had kept her daughter even though she was not married at the time. Very interesting to ponder. Would I find other parallels?

At times, especially when I want some information or need to make a decision, I still do my automatic writing, hoping to get some advice or clarification. The day I was writing this story about Mattie, I sensed she was around and had something to say so I started to write. This was our conversation:

Me: Mattie, I have the feeling you are close by. I have been thinking about you since I started to write about you yesterday for my memoir.

Mattie: Woe is me; I wish I could have had your experiences. So little time left and you are making something of it.

Me: What do you mean little time? It sounds like I might die soon.

Mattie: Little, as it is towards the end of your life; not the beginning, nor the middle. In other words, the last part. Remember, time is irrelevant to me. Hope that sounds better.

Me: What would you like me to share about you in my book?

Mattie: What you already have. I am here to help you. So far you are off to a good start. Write from your heart and your soul will come through. I will come through to guide you. Let it flow, forget the words and style for now. You always were afraid to write and for a good reason. Your words would have been stilted and untrue to yourself. Now that you have matured and dealt with the past, it is the time most suited for your words of wisdom. Continue to seek information and grow like a flower newly planted in the spring. Ask for help when needed. You, too, need nurturing and a sprinkle of fertilizer from time to time to fully bloom. Your words will be your voice, not only to help others but to help you, as well. Shed those secrets and pain of the past. Relish your growth of spirit, never forgetting the other realms.

Me: Anything else?

Mattie: Stick to it. Write most days. Ask for help. I am always with you to guide you in the process. Oh yes, don't read too much; instead write, write, and write some more. The words will say it. They will tell your journey. Many will shed tears. However, your tears for the most part have been shed.

What difference would it make to have Mattie in my life? I ask myself as I wish Stuart had asked me on the day I came home with so much excitement. Will it change me in some way? The connection between two lifetimes was made. It continues to awe me as I wait to see how it unfolds.

Since Maggie and I had met the previous December, we had continued to write letters to each other. Our letters were newsy — "This is how we spent Christmas and I cooked…" "I like these HGTV shows" — as we were getting to know each other. I was pleased when Maggie suggested we see each other again the end of April. We met again at the South Shore Plaza in Braintree for lunch at the Cheesecake Factory, instead of Legal Seafoods. Maggie did most of the talking and again we seemed comfortable with one another; but this time, our sharing seemed to have a reserve. Then, toward the end of lunch. I noticed a change in Maggie and wondered if I had said something that bothered her. I hoped I had not blown it with her. I had just gotten hearing aids which magnified background noise and I was having trouble hearing Maggie. Therefore, I was reluctant to enter into a more substantive conversation than we had had.

We parted on good terms, but when I was driving home, I recalled how she had looked uncomfortable. Had I said something that she could have misconstrued?

I didn't have to wait long. The following are excerpts from the letter she wrote me on May 14.

> I had been feeling a bit nervous about meeting with you and just decided to come with an open mind and see what came up. I did have one question for you ... remember? I asked you what it meant for you to have gotten to know me? Maybe you do not have an answer and that is okay. I just noticed you never answered my question. Why not?
>
> After reading your email, I really am curious about what you are thinking. I am glad you are comfortable with me, but what do you mean when you say, "Whatever you decide to do is fine with me." Do you need a break from emailing, because you said that you would understand if I did, but I don't remember suggesting that I needed a break from it? If we have something quick to say or just check in, I think emailing is fine. That is why I sent you a short email last week so that you knew I had questions and would be writing a letter soon.
>
> We may have had a miscommunication during lunch. I was telling you about how people respond differently when I tell them that I am getting to know you. One person will ask, "What's the big deal?" Then someone else will say, "Wow... that's a big deal, an emotional experience!" Then, I told you about my friend who kept talking

about how exciting our first meeting was going to be; she talked about my new family and how exciting it would be to meet everyone. I was a bit overwhelmed by this conversation.

Maggie went on to question why I had talked about not wanting to be called a stepmother and how it related to her. I forget the details of why I said it — probably a random thought. It was not intentional to upset Maggie. She continued:

> I began thinking that I am not really your child, because you didn't raise me as your child. However, we are related biologically. I wonder how you view me and if there is a place for me in your life and family. You told me that you contacted me because you wanted to know if I was happy and had a good life … or something along those lines.
> Do you want to continue to get to know me because of our biological connection or have your questions about my well-being been answered? Do you still have an interest in knowing me? I guess I need to know why you are continuing our communication. If it is because you are my birth mother and would like to know me and have me be a part of your life, that is something I am interested in. It would make our communication worthwhile to know that we are building a relationship.
> I have been forthcoming with my thoughts and have asked questions when I have had them. It sometimes feels like you are holding information back and perhaps are waiting to see what I ask.
> I am interested to know what the future will bring and I sometimes wonder if I will meet your family someday. I am open to the idea, if and when you think that time is

Shadows and Light

right. I have no idea what your thoughts are about this. Do you think you might like to meet my family someday?

I sent her an email saying I had received her letter and would need time to think. She could expect a letter in two weeks. The following is what I wrote:

I was upset after reading your letter because I feel there has been some miscommunication and, somehow, I have let you down. Now I would like to clear up some of the questions you had. I appreciate the fact that you are direct and do not have a problem asking me difficult questions.

First of all, remember that I gave birth to you and you always will have a special place in my heart. Because I did not raise you does not mean I don't love you. I always have and always will love you. I have always wanted to get to know you and have a relationship with you and then at some point (when ready) meet our respective families.

I have tried to focus on the present with you and wait to see what happens before talking about the future. I think what is happening between us is that we are each doing a separate dance around each other and at times not always meeting. Also, I realize that I might be using you in some way to meet my needs. My mother used me in this way and I am afraid I might have done it with you.

I know I can appear standoffish at times and that turns people off. I have never been a gushy, feeling type who is easy to get to know. That does not mean I don't care; it is the way I am. I was fearful of being rejected as I had been so many times in my life. Because of this, I hold back with a person before I get to know and trust them.

I have never withheld information from you. No, I have not told you all the details of my childhood but that doesn't mean I would hold anything back. I had every intent to talk about it at lunch but had the feeling when you said you came with an open mind and had no questions, that you did not want to talk about it and/or anything serious. I consider talking about my childhood as pretty serious.

We just were not connecting at times. No one's fault of course; the circumstances are pretty overwhelming and emotional for each of us in a different way.

As for our conversation about Stuart's children, I do have a problem being called a stepmother. I can see now how it would upset you and make you wonder how you fit into my life right now. I actually did a lot for one of Stuart's daughters and offered to be her mentor in getting a job in healthcare and paid for her to take a Medical Terminology course online. She works in Walmart and cannot seem to get herself out of a rut. It ended in a failure because she took none of my advice, did nothing about changing jobs and is still at Walmart two years later.

The question you had for me about "what is like for me to get to know you" that I did not answer. I don't remember you asking me the question, so it is possible I did not hear it? It is not like me not to answer a question, so am not sure what happened. I have recently gotten hearing aids. I find restaurant background noise comes across as very loud and it is still difficult to hear — even with hearing aids.

To get to know you has been amazing for me! It has closed a gaping hole in my life. I am very proud of you, how intelligent, thoughtful, and attractive you are. It never ceases to amaze me how tall you are and how many things we seem to have in common. I want to share you with my family.

Maggie emailed that she was relieved after reading my letter and would write soon. I felt we had straightened out our miscommunications and would have to wait to see how our relationship played out. I believe Maggie was testing me. After all, I had abandoned her as a baby and this was in her cellular memory. Would things go smoothly from now on or would there be other issues?

As I continued to visit Ruby as a hospice volunteer every week throughout the winter of 2008 into the spring of 2009, she always wanted a Reiki treatment. Was this why Ruby rallied? Her breathing and mental status kept improving, so much so that by the spring of 2009 she came off hospice services. I thought, "Is Reiki this powerful?" As a result of my relationship with Ruby, I was starting to see myself as a healer and wanting to believe that, maybe, I could really help people.

As a result of improvements in her health, Ruby was now off hospice, but she retained the services of her home-health aide who came in twice a week. Since Ruby was officially not having hospice services, I was no longer allowed to visit her as a hospice worker, but we decided that I would continue to see her on my own accord as a friend. Additionally, around this time, I decided not to continue to volunteer for the hospice program. I wanted to concentrate on Ruby and my work with Kevin and Wei Chi. Also, I had hoped hospice might provide a community that I was looking for and felt accepted in, but that didn't happen. I did learn a lot about hospice work and myself in the time that I had been there. I could always go back. When I visited her one Tuesday in April, I had never seen Ruby look better or in a more chipper mood. She was dressed for the first time in months! She said, "Maybe when the weather gets a bit warmer, I can sit outside for while by the front door."

I said, "I will be able to help you do that. Your oxygen will reach. Would you like me to buy some flowers? I have some planters, and we can plant them together."

By now she was beaming. "Can you get some impatiens? They are one of my favorites."

"Of course," I told her. "When the time comes, you can tell me what you want."

Is it really true that all marriages start in pretty much the same way: with hope that this marriage, this love, will prevail and create transformation and lead to lasting happiness? Whether or not that is true, it certainly seems true that all marriages fail in the same way: first, with the growing effects of a lack of communication, then with growing effects of divergence which leads to both spouses going off in a different direction, and finally with an insurmountable breakdown of trust.

I don't think how my marriage to Stuart started or ended was any different from this. However, a shred of hope turned up that spring. Perhaps my enthusiasm for my work with Kevin and how much I was learning prompted Stuart to think. He told me he was looking for a mentor and would go see Kevin on his own. Recently, I had given Stuart the Susan Howatch's novels on the Church of England to read. I had already reread them and thought Stuart would enjoy them as they had spiritual mentors and father figures in them. Stuart felt cheated that his father had divorced his mother and moved to Africa when he was twelve. Stuart never saw his father after that, nor did his father make contact — Stuart did know however that he had a half-brother. Over the years, no one had fulfilled that father mentor role for him.

The first time Stuart saw Kevin, he came back smiling and happy because Kevin had asked him to be on his radio show. Evidently, they talked about his book and how to market it. I must say that this stirred up some old negative feelings in me from when Michael and I had both seen Gwen, the psychologist, and

Shadows and Light

I had felt she preferred Michael to me. I had no way of knowing if, in this instance, Kevin preferred Stuart to me.

After Stuart had seen Kevin a couple of times, he seemed to be more present in our marriage and with me. He even agreed to see Kevin with me for marriage counseling. During that first session, Kevin gave us exercises to do and a lot to think about. To my great relief, I saw no evidence of him giving Stuart preferential treatment.

The previous fall when Stuart and I had closed up the cabin on Maidstone Lake for the winter, I had not yet made up my mind whether to sell it. I had mentioned to a local contractor who had replaced two leaking windows that I was thinking about putting the cabin on the market in the spring. This contractor must have spread the word because in December, I had a call from an interested person. I contacted the local real estate woman, Ann, who had sold me the cabin and had also helped Stuart sell his place. Everything happened quickly, and soon a Purchase and Sale agreement was signed at the price I wanted, and the final passing of papers would take place the following May. It was almost too easy, and I couldn't help thinking that I was really meant to sell at this time. Fortunately, Ann took care of everything, and all I had to do was do the final cleaning, pack up my personal belongings — the cabin was sold with furniture, contents, and boats, except for Stuart's sailboat — and show up when papers would be passed.

In May, the hard part came when I packed the last of my things and said goodbye to my refuge of the past fourteen years. On the first trip up to collect our things, Stuart came with me and we hauled his sailboat back. On the second trip which was the last, I went by myself. I was glad to sell, but sorry — I would miss Linda and our friends, the lake and its moods. I would not miss all the work and upkeep involved. As I walked around pack-

Shadows and Light

ing up my personal items, I saw a lot that reminded me of Johnnie — the work he had done and things he had bought. I saw nothing of Stuart and what he had done. With Stuart, there had been a lot of "mine" and "yours" and very few, if any, "ours." Why had he not contributed anything? Had he felt entitled not to because I owned it? I looked out and saw a loon gliding by the dock. I would miss the loons but solace came when I thought maybe we could rent a place next year on a lake. That would be the best of two worlds, I thought.

Linda had not answered a recent email and didn't come to see me when we had planned to meet earlier. I sensed she was avoiding me. I knew she was angry at me for selling, and therefore would not come around that day. It was probably for the best. If I saw her, I am sure we would both be in tears. We had both gotten divorced around the same time — my brother had gone off with another woman and Michael and I had split up — and Linda's second husband, Zack, had died just over a year earlier. I couldn't help but think, Did that mean something would happen to Stuart and me? Were we running parallel lines in our relationships?

Slowly, I walked through for the last time, I reminisced some more, and then it was time to go. I locked up quickly because the tears were starting to come. As I pulled out of the driveway, my vision was blurry, and the tears flowed. What on earth had I done? I knew I had to make more changes in my life, but why did it have to be so hard? I was weepy all the way home. I wish I had had an understanding, loving partner to go home to. I would not get any comfort from Stuart but I did have a lot to look forward to: an unplanned summer with no more driving back and forth to the lake every weekend, and the Wei Chi practitioner training — the next level that I had decided to take along with Linette, Kim, and Katie — was starting soon.

Chapter 21
Progress with Kevin as My Marriage to Stuart Wobbles

In June of 2009, Kevin taught the practitioner level Wei Chi that Linette, Kim, Katie and I took together. It was a big financial and time commitment involving a tuition of around $1,500 — maybe more — and a training of over a thousand hours. The four of us were motivated to learn more since we had an idea of what a powerful healing system it was. The practitioner level involved learning the seven-session treatment series, which was divided into several parts. For the first part, we each had a volunteer client with whom we met for seven weekends. These were not, however, consecutive weekends, in order to give the client time to integrate the work. When I gave a session to my client, Katie, Kim, and Linette were present. One was designated to record the session, while the others listened and took notes in preparation to give feedback. Kevin was always present guiding, teaching, and bailing us out when we were stuck in the weeds.

Somehow, we all got clients who challenged us on a personal level, and I soon found out what my weaknesses were. I tended to hide behind a traditional therapy mode — the one I was familiar with. I recall that, for feedback, someone had counted the times I said, "Ah-huh." That was sobering and certainly not effective for my client. To gain her trust, I had to change my ways and shed the clinical/therapist mode I hid behind. Slowly, I learned to be myself.

Another difficult part of this training for me were the visualizations we had to lead our clients through. Again, similar to receiving intuitive messages for the Level 1 training, I didn't think I could possibly do them. I worried over them, but when the time came, the scenario for the visualization materialized and the words flowed into my head. It amazed me how it happened. As with anything else, the more I did, the easier it became; but even so, there were times when Kevin had to step in and help continue the visualization.

These weekends were emotionally draining, but we all supported each other as we faced our challenges and climbed out of the weeds. We learned more about each other's personalities and foibles. We were in it together and we managed to get to the end of the seven-session series in late August. It was encouraging to us to see changes in our clients. The process for my client to trust me was slow, but in the end, I think she did. By the last two sessions, I had her full attention and she chose to hope and to continue on her journey of self-improvement.

Wanting to celebrate Stuart's turning seventy at the end of July 2009, I invited family and a few close friends to a birthday party. It seemed like the wifely thing to do, and I hoped that, if we played our roles, the fantasy of a successful marriage would play out again. When the time came for the planning and executing, our persisting marital problems, however, had drained me of motivation and my heart was not in doing something special for Stuart; but a promise was a promise and I felt I had to deliver. Besides, I did not want to call people to tell them not to come!

If I was going to work setting up a party, how could I make it more fun? I decided on including a piñata. The grandkids would enjoy it, and it might be fun for the adults to watch the frolic. When I shared my plans with Stuart, his response was,

Shadows and Light

"This is my party, not the kids'. I don't want the attention taken away from me." Despite his comment, I went ahead and bought a piñata, since I wanted some fun myself and seeing the kids enjoy it would do that for me.

Even though I was feeling distant from Stuart and not invested either in him or in his childish comment, I devoted my energy to the party set-up and decided to keep my emotions to myself. I vowed to keep calm. While the party was to be held at Stuart's daughter's house — she and her husband had a large deck where we could grill and where the adults could hang out while the kids played on the lawn — I took on the majority of the work: buying food, the birthday cake, paper products, the piñata, and so on. Stuart's daughter and her husband were responsible for appetizers and drinks.

Finally, it was party day, and the guests had assembled and the barbequing was underway. I took some satisfaction in knowing both that it had come together and that Stuart could not complain that I had slighted his seventieth birthday. During the party, Stuart gave me a couple of compliments, which should have warmed me but I noticed he did not look me in the eye when he spoke. One of the times, he actually touched me — patting me on the shoulder, but again he didn't look at me. By this time, I was more in tune with his behavior than I had been in the past, and I was resigned to his lack of affection.

The kids enjoyed the piñata, as did Stuart who took a couple of whacks at it. Afterwards, Stuart's daughter gathered people to take pictures in the front of the house. I had been included in a couple, but when I was standing off to one side, I heard Stuart say, "I want one with me and all the women in my life." I presumed that that was my cue to step up, but then I noticed that Stuart gathered his two daughters, two granddaughters, and his first ex-wife for the picture, but not me. I waited, but he made no gesture to include me. I could have stepped forward and spoken up but I decided not to. I kept to my decision of remaining calm, but the fear of rejection loomed over me. This fear had been honed over years of being rejected. It kept me quiet as he positioned the women and girls around him. My mouth was agape. Was I more astonished at not being included or more embarrassed at being singled out in front of his relatives? It was as if he were sending out a public message to his family that our marriage was not good. That was hard for me, I suppose, because I was not ready yet to give up on it. I decided to wait until after Stuart and I were home before saying anything. It was Stuart's party, and I didn't want to make a scene and upset him. In the past, I would have withdrawn and not spoken to him, but I had learned that silence did not solve any issues.

I also thought, How much longer will I be this woman who remains caught in the dynamics of her childhood! Despite all the work I had done with Kevin and with other therapists, here I was in my mid-sixties and still struggling with a negative self-concept.

An opportunity arose the next day when Stuart and I were looking at the party pictures. I said, "I don't mind not being in a lot of pictures, but when this one was taken, which you called out as 'me and the women in my life,' you did not include me. What about me? Did you intentionally intend to exclude me? Were you not sending me a message? Aren't I one of the women in your life?"

"It was a generational picture," he answered curtly, as if I had pointed out something unreasonable.

"So, as your wife I am not part of your generation in your family?"

"Of course, you are," he replied, but he did not apologize or offer to make sure it never happened again. He might have said, "Oh my goodness, I can't believe I left you out. I'm so sorry! Of course, you are one of the women in my life. In fact, the most important one. Let's regroup with you and my daughters and granddaughters for another picture the next holiday we are all together."

But, of course, he said this only in my imagination. The experience of speaking to him, rather than resolving the issue, left a bad taste in my mouth and made me think even more that I was not important to him.

As a late-in-life wife, I did not have a track record with his family, and feeling ever the girl who was left behind on Parents Day, I feared that I might never be included. Had Stuart offered some comforting words — even better, had he looked me in the eye as he spoke these words of inclusion and then hugged or kissed me — I would have felt that he was investing in me and was concerned about our future together.

But he did not say anything. Was he perhaps thinking of what his life after me might be, his life when he would not want to have a photo with me in it?

The dissolution of a marriage calls for much realignment of how we think of ourselves and of our recent experience. I could have asked myself a lot of fundamental questions. Had I made Stuart up? Had I been so out of touch with myself that I had made such a choice? When I thought about these negatives, I also knew that, over the past year, I had started to face myself and my choices and had come to many positives; but I was not ready yet to make any major decisions regarding Stuart and me. When I have a big decision to make, I like to take time to think about all my options. It was no different with my marriage to Stuart. I didn't want to merely react: I wanted to understand deeply how we had gotten so distant with each other and how we could get back on track, if that were even possible at this point. I had taken the same slow deliberation when my marriage to Michael seemed to be ending. As then, I now wanted to make sure that I would not regret a decision to finish my marriage too soon and that I had given as much as I could to make it work.

Two days after the party, still feeling distraught, I sought comfort in a self-administered Wei Chi treatment. I asked for guidance concerning how to react to Stuart and about how to continue to be with him. What Wei Chi said to me went beyond what I was prepared to deal with.

"He will go away. You need to speak your truth. You will be OK. Listen to Mattie's words about fighting stupidity."

What a scary message that was! Now I would have to figure out what "He will go away" meant. Perhaps it signaled divorce or his death? And what about "fighting stupidity" — well, did I really want a fight or to fight? Somehow, I had to figure this out. I had to see Stuart for himself and not what I might have been projecting on him. I don't think Mattie really meant that I had to fight in the literal sense, just that I needed to be aware of what was happening and to stand up for myself. I had to do this in a way that would not intimidate Stuart or leave him realizing what I was doing.

After Stuart's seventieth birthday party, I became aware of more instances in which Stuart was excluding me and — I might say — ignoring me. In the ignoring category, I kept seeing how he really had a hard time giving me a genuine compliment. It was as if he would lose something of himself if he honored an achievement or action of mine. It reminded me of my father. I know it was not fair to project this yearning for a response from my father onto Stuart, but it was also true that I yearned for a response from Stuart himself. I yearned for a sense of a true marriage. More and more, I was feeling like a roommate.

When Stuart realized, or it was pointed out to him, that he had done something negative, his rationalization was to tell me why his response was completely appropriate given something I had done or said that had misled him.

My way of resolving a dispute was to sit down and hash it out. This caused an impasse because it was not Stuart's style. His response to a request to talk a problem out was minimal and negative since he never wanted what seemed to me a real discussion. While I needed for Stuart to listen to me, he did not need the same sort of interaction. Talking issues out helped me to feel better and understand them, but it did nothing for him. If he had been critical of me or had upset me and I felt it was truly his fault or uncalled for, I expected him to apologize. It was my way of gauging whether he was taking responsibility for his actions or words. Unfortunately for me, he had a different way of dealing with conflict, and it was not satisfying for me. Stuart walked away and liked to use his mind to process a conflict, categorizing facts into little boxes to be worked on in the future. After time passed, he would come up with an idea or plan that sometimes made no sense to me. For example, he had told me, "Relationships don't need to be worked on. They just happen."

Another major issue was that neither one of us was able to nurture the other since we spoke different emotional languages. Stuart wanted affection — primarily through physical touch — which I was unable to give him because in order to be affectionate, I needed to feel emotionally connected to him. I wanted evidence that he cared for and understood me and that I was an important person in his life. I didn't need as much physical affection as Stuart but I did need to be heard and, on occasion, be complimented and have little things done for me

Everything was adding up, so much so, that we could not work our way beyond all these negatives. I was facing the realization that I was with a man I did not want to call my husband — nor claim him as such. I was sensing that, beneath the intellectual sophistication, there was a boy who did not want a relationship with a woman. At times, he was stuck in a defiant teenager response, walking away from me, saying, "To heck with you."

I was sensing that I had once again chosen a man who was not willing to be a husband, to be a peer who was happy to go through life with me at his side, as his wife. Even worse, I asked myself if there were something in me that actually feared a man who would step up to being a husband such as I said I wanted? If so, wasn't this lack of affiliation between us a problem I had helped to create?

These realizations added up to a whole picture that I did not like and got me thinking that I needed to make decisions. I could feel a fear stirring from within and starting to poke its way to the surface.

How would I summon the energy to do what I was more and more aware I needed to do?

I was comfortable with Kevin's style of energy work, his use of visualizations, and his exercise of psychic abilities. Slowly, over a year's time, I had begun to put my trust in Kevin. He seemed to understand me as a person and know what I needed to do to heal. My work with Kevin had not been easy, and in the previous year, at times, I had been depressed, weepy, and in pain as I worked through my major issues of abuse and emotional abandonment.

Now that the hardest work in individual sessions with Kevin was over and my inner children, who were at various stages of maturation, had been integrated, I was having fewer sessions with him. Kevin was openly gay, and to see a gay man who was emotionally present, affectionate, and caring — the antithesis of my father — had a positive influence on me. In fact, after taking Wei Chi classes and having individual sessions with Kevin, I was sure he represented a father figure, a corrective one at that.

That summer, Kevin led me through two memorable visualizations — in different sessions.

The first one took place on Tortola in the British Virgin Islands. I was at a beach bar that I had gotten to by swimming from a boat — the only way to get there. I was wearing a bathing suit and a pareo. On my wrist was Linette's bracelet of chakra stones that she had given me in real life; around my neck, I saw a necklace made of shells. A white flower was tucked behind my left ear. For a long time, I danced with a hot, sexy, handsome man who was about my age. I thought that I would end up with him. When it came time to leave the beach bar, I had to choose between two boats. Interestingly, I did not pick the boat with the sexy man I had danced with. There had been another group of people at the bar who had come on another boat. There was a man in this group that I knew was interested in me and would be the best for me at this time in my life. I chose his boat. This visualization was indicative of how I was changing. In the past, I would have gone with the mysterious, handsome, sexy man. Instead I chose the man who would be far better for me.

On another day, the second visualization started with Kevin getting me into the setting and saying, "Hug an old oak tree and see if it has anything to tell you." When I did, this is what I heard: "You are strong, you will survive, and you are love." In the visualization, it was a warm, sunny day, and I was lying down in a meadow full of wildflowers but could not feel the love I was supposed to. Why couldn't I accept this love coming from nature? Why couldn't I love myself? I started to feel pain in my shoulders and then it came to me, "My parents didn't love me." I got up and went for a swim in the nearby creek. A big, old turtle was swimming beside me. I saw an old wooden bridge ahead of me. I swam to the edge and got out to walk on the bridge. When I got to the middle of the bridge, I looked to the left and saw my father; my mother was on the right side. I walked over to my father, and he gave me a ring. I turned around and walked toward

Shadows and Light

my mother. She gave me a necklace. I accepted the love they were able — under the circumstances — to give me. I dove in the water and started to swim back. After a hundred feet, I turned around and looked. The bridge blew up with my parents on it. I went back to the meadow and lay down. This time the flowers were different; hummingbirds and butterflies were settling on the flowers. I was able now to feel and accept the love of these creatures. The pain was gone.

These visualizations were symbolically important to me. In regards to the beach bar scene, was I finally learning what type of partner was best for me? As far as the function of my parents in the visualization, maybe I was finally able to come to terms with them and this opened me to love myself more. At last, I was getting rid of some old baggage that had weighed me down for so many years. Around this time, one night as I lay down to meditate, I asked Wei Chi what I needed to work on. Immediately, I knew it was going to be a visualization and this is what transpired:

It was a sunny, warm day. I could feel a slight breeze as I walked along a path in a meadow which soon came to a forest. I continued along the path into the woods. I was surrounded by trees and it was dark, but as I looked up, I could see the light filtering through. I noticed a patch of moss to my right and saw something twinkling. I reached down and picked up a gemstone — rough and unpolished — that had a bluish hue. As I continued walking, my spirit guide, Simon, joined me. We came to a pond and sat down on a rock beside it. He spoke, "Throw the stone in the water; you don't need it anymore." I did and at first saw the ripples it made but then I saw my reflection. It was my new self, happy, relaxed, free from tension, with light surrounding me. I was in the light, I would walk in the light, and I was in the process of becoming my new self. By this time, I noticed Simon had left, and I jumped in the pond for a swim. I felt at peace and at one with the universe, the person I was meant to be.

I felt this was a breakthrough for me. Not a major one since I knew I had a lot more work to do, but I was changing and starting to see myself differently. I was more aware of my interactions with Stuart and others and needing less validation from them. Overall, my confidence level was up and my aches and pains, although still there, were in the background.

I had a long pattern of projecting my needs onto others. For a while I would confuse the actual person with the inner figures I was trying to take care of. By projecting outward, I was imposing on a living person the job of fulfilling me. As I have mentioned, Kevin became the affectionate, thoughtful father I had not had and whom I had been looking for. Projections, however, have a way of dissolving, and one is left with an actual person, a person one may or may not need or like.

In the beginning when I was getting to know Stuart, I thought he was emotionally intelligent, enthusiastic, full of life. He seemed to be someone who would understand me and listen to me. I was so wrong! I realize now that I was projecting all of what I needed on him. Going to self-help workshops and belonging to a men's group for years did not mean he wanted to work on himself and/or our relationship. Slowly, he shut me out to the point where he did not want to listen to me. Attempts to socialize as a couple — other than for an occasional party —fell flat.

On the flip side, I think Stuart projected things onto me. In a marriage counseling session with Kevin, he said he was attracted to me because I was intelligent and happy — lighting up a room with my smile as I walked in. Michael had mistaken me as being sociable and fun, liking to drink at parties when we were with friends. Stuart, I think, mistook the fact that he deemed me intelligent to mean I would be someone who would have similar interests as his — enough so that I would discuss ideas and col-

Shadows and Light

laborate with him on a book project about extraterrestrials. And happy? Of course, I appeared happy when we first met and for a while after that, but as I dealt more and more deeply with my past, there were times I was weepy and sad.

As I became aware of projection energy between Stuart and me, there were little things that also I started to notice about Kevin. When he wanted something — a ride to the airport or a place to stay for a night, he would take advantage of those unwilling to say "no" to him. Then there were the times he would cross a boundary ever so slightly with a client. In my previous counseling experiences, the boundaries were extremely strict and the therapist would not divulge any personal information about themselves to me, the client.

With his psychic gifts, large ego, and grandiose ideas about his next project, it would have been easy to place Kevin on a pedestal, but I was not about to. Ironically, the inner work I had done — some of the very work Kevin had instigated — started to have its effect, and I took back some of my projection on him.

Toward the end of the 2009 summer, Stuart gave a talk at the local library to promote his book. As far as I could tell, Stuart hadn't done anything to publicize his presentation — not even talking it up to neighbors or making and putting up posters. As a result, only two persons showed up — one was on time and the other walked in when the talk was almost over. I could tell from his facial expression that Stuart was upset, but as usual, he did not want to discuss it so I had no idea how he felt. I commiserated with him saying, "Maybe it was the topic. After all, we live in a small town, and it is a subject only a few people might be interested in."

A bit later, I read in the local paper that a nearby town was holding a UFO festival in September. Stuart signed up to give a talk and was accepted. On the day of his presentation, I went with him. This time, thanks to the crowd already at the festival, he had a decent audience and sold some books. He was pleased with the outcome, and I was, too. It was heartening to see his ego get a boost after it had been crushed at the library.

The middle of September, Stuart and I had another marriage counseling session with Kevin. It was very emotional as I broke down and cried, thinking all our problems were my fault. This was an example of my going into a negative space — taking all the blame for our marriage failing — but this unrealistic appraisal was not addressing our issues. Stuart was visibly upset. Paradoxically, even as I assumed I was to blame, I hoped that perhaps he could see the importance of doing something about our deteriorating marriage himself and that he needed to step up to the plate to improve it. I can't recall what happened during the session except that I did pull out of my dark mood. I think now that I was feeling overwhelmed at the time and frustrated that Stuart and I could not move ahead. I watched Kevin closely in his interactions with the two of us. He was skillful and I did not feel he treated me any differently than he did Stuart.

I had some hope that maybe Kevin could help us salvage our relationship.

In late September, I went with Stuart to a weekend conference called "Cosmos and Consciousness." While he wanted me to come, I was not interested enough to pay for it. I said I would go as long as he paid my way. To my surprise, Stuart agreed. I think that was the first time he had ever paid anything extra for me—other than gifts. Was this a gesture on his part to improve our relationship?

I was nervous about attending because I knew there would be a lot of intellectual people at this conference — one of them was an astrophysicist Stuart knew from Harvard University.

The five-hour drive was long, and we chatted some of the time. The first part of the weekend went well as I found some

Shadows and Light

people to talk to. They were interested in the energy work I was doing with Reiki and Wei Chi. I even gave a quick Reiki treatment to one of the speakers. Since I got an intuitive message that was meaningful to him, I was feeling like a successful person in what was a foreign element. The next day, when Stuart and I had breakfast with his astrophysicist friend, I felt comfortable and not intimidated by him. Dinner that evening, however, was as I had feared: I sat at a table with Stuart and five other men, all with scientific backgrounds. I don't recall if the tables were assigned or if the arrangement just happened, but I would have been more comfortable with at least one other nonscientific person at the table — even a scientific female would have helped. It wasn't as if there weren't any! Somehow, I got through the meal and hardly said a word.

After dinner, I excused myself and went back to our room to indulge in a mini-meltdown, but this time, I struggled not to excoriate myself and feel inadequate intellectually. While I reminded myself that a conference like this was not a natural environment for me, the feeling I didn't fit in—which is something I have always struggled with—was an old tape that continued to proclaim: You are stupid.

About an hour later, I was still lying on the bed in our room when Stuart came in. He flopped down on the arm chair next to the window.

"Is anything the matter? You didn't come back." I tried to explain why I had left and how I was feeling. I was in control of my feelings.

"I am going back out," he said. "Are you coming?"

"No thanks, I'm going to stay and read."

I had a good book to read and had no problem with him going back out. This conference was important to him and not to me. Now that was a step forward in my self-concept.

A good thing happened this night when I was about to fall

asleep. I had a vision of an elderly Asian man with white hair. There were no words; I knew it was Wei Chi. I thought this was his way of saying he was with me and perhaps even thanking me for spreading the word about his ancient healing practice.

In the fall of 2009, Ruby's daughter-in-law called to say Ruby had taken a turn for the worse and was hospitalized. Evidently, her son had found her gasping for breath and cyanotic — bluish around the lips due to a low oxygen saturation — and he had called the ambulance. By the time I could visit Ruby, she was out of intensive care and in a regular room. Before I went in to see her, I spoke with her other daughter-in-law who told me Ruby —now seventy-six — had said she was exhausted from life and ready to go. In fact, she had said her goodbyes to all her family.

When I entered Ruby's room, she did not appear to be close to death, but when we talked, I got the sense she was saying goodbye to me as well, talking as if she would never see me again. I did not believe she was going to die at this time. I am not sure why I believed this — maybe intuition coming into play? Ruby rallied once more and went to rehab for a month where she flourished and acquired a new-found energy. When I visited her there, her mood was upbeat. She participated in activities and enjoyed roaming the halls in her wheelchair. On one visit on a warm late fall afternoon, we even went outside.

Two messages from Wei Chi came during this time at moments when I was doing a self-treatment: "He is in the darkness. You are in the light" and "You are loved even though Stuart might not be. We understand you."

Around the time of the marriage counseling in September I wrote about, I was doing the next requirement of the Wei Chi practitioner training. During the summer we had each completed

Shadows and Light

a seven-session treatment on a volunteer client in front of Kevin. Now, we were to give another volunteer client the seven-session treatment series by ourselves. I was nervous going solo, but this was softened by knowing Kevin was available for help via telephone calls. The most important thing I learned from this client — a young man — was I needed to improve how to guide others in a visualization. I had a long way to go, but I was starting to see myself as a healer.

While this was going on, Kevin stunned Katie, Kim, Linette, and me when he told us he would be moving to Arizona. He assured us he would be back to see clients and continue to teach Wei Chi. There was no clear reason for his going. In fact, what he told us seemed rather vague, but I had to believe he would not abandon us; still, as I look back, I realize there was certainly "writing on the wall."

As early December 2009 came, Stuart and I were still not doing well, and I was unhappier than ever. His emotional detachment was at an even higher level, so much so that I clearly no longer felt emotionally or physically close to him. In fact, it was now I who didn't want to hug him. I was involved with the Wei Chi work and had little time for Stuart. It seemed easier just not to try anymore. I am sure, in my own way, I pushed him further in the opposite direction. The gulf between us was widening.

Something about his physical appearance put me off. He was starting to look and act old — his balance, for instance, was not as good. He had also become a person who was no longer invested in his appearance. For instance, he was not shaving regularly. The last two or three years we were together, he lacked enthusiasm for life.

One late Sunday afternoon with the gas log in the fireplace providing some ambience and warmth on a chilly day, Stuart and I talked while sipping a glass of wine. I didn't like what I was doing to Stuart so I initiated a relationship talk by asking him his thoughts about us as a couple. He answered, "I don't think we are getting anything from our sessions with Kevin that would change our relationship."

"What do you suggest?"

"A shift is needed."

"And how would we make that happen?"

His idea was for one of us to talk for a set period of time while the other one listened. Then, the process would be reversed.

"I think the issue is far deeper than listening to each other," I replied.

It was good that Stuart had put some thought into our marriage, but I had a hard time with his solution. I felt it would turn out to be an intellectual exercise — one Stuart was comfortable with — and would not be a heart-felt talk about our relationship. In retrospect, maybe I should have listened to him and followed through with his suggestion about listening to each other, but I couldn't. We were stuck and needed outside help, professional help. Stuart's idea seemed to be a simplistic approach to a wound that had festered to degree that would require several major reconstructive surgeries over a period of time to heal it. From my years of therapy with a variety of counselors, I had learned a lot about myself and the process. I had no way of knowing what Stuart felt, but to me, it was apparent that he did not want to face his own issues. If we kept seeing Kevin on a regular basis, these issues would come up and have to be dealt with. After this Sunday afternoon discussion, the prognosis for our marriage looked even grimmer.

Two weeks later, in mid-December, we had our last counseling session with Kevin. It started off badly because Stuart overslept, and I had to wake him up so we would not be late. I don't recall the details, but I knew Stuart was giving up. He no longer wanted to see Kevin as a couple, but he felt — when he saw Kevin individually — that he had gotten some good stuff from him but could no longer afford him. I could not recall him bringing up the subject of our marriage and what we needed to work on since our last session with Kevin. If Stuart was unwilling to pay his share for further sessions with Kevin, I doubt that finding a new marriage counselor would have been a solution. Besides, I don't think I could have started from scratch with a new marriage counselor, even if it meant saving our marriage.

The holidays were coming soon, and I decided to put things on hold with Stuart because I simply did not have the energy to face all the negative feelings I was having until after the New Year. The thirty-first was our fourth anniversary and that was not comforting since neither of us were in a celebratory mood. After our fiasco in St. Martin the previous January, we held back from talking about any sort of commemoration of the date. In January, I would be going to Arizona to Kevin's house with Linette, Katie, and Kim to complete the next part of the Wei Chi practitioner training, the intensive week known as the "Pressure Cooker." The following days in Sedona with Linette would be my time to relax in a warmer climate. For now, I had to concentrate on getting through the holidays. A couple of parties and family get-togethers would provide some distraction.

I wanted to do something special for Ruby this Christmas once I realized her family wasn't going to do any decorating for her, so I bought a four-foot artificial tree. At first, she protested that she didn't need a tree, but when we decorated it, she soon got into the spirit. I put it right next to her chair so she was able to lean over and put some decorations on. How she enjoyed the tree and Christmas that year! We exchanged presents. Recently, I found the card she gave me that year.

> Peace and Remembrance. Love, joy……complete
> closure in my head.
> Gift of Susan's exuberance!
> Love,
> Ruby

I was touched by Ruby's words. I had no idea I was having such a positive effect on her. Our relationship had deepened. It was unique in that there were no conditions or expectations attached. She had opened up to me and was processing what she needed to. I was learning about dying and gaining confidence in doing energy work. It appeared that our lives had a parallel theme of letting go. She was letting go of her life; I was letting go of Stuart. I couldn't help but think, How much longer was she going to live and how much longer am I going to be with Stuart?

Chapter 22
The Pressure Cooker

In January of 2010, my Wei Chi group — Kim, Katie, Linette, and I — went to Phoenix for seven days to complete the next part of the practitioner training. We had each already given a seven-session Wei Chi treatment to two clients. Up to that point, providing treatment involved focusing on clients. This focus permitted us to remain somewhat aloof from our feelings, but we were not entirely exempt from feelings. Our clients had a way of bringing our issues to the surface. Then there was the feedback we received after being observed — always "room for improvement," which evoked feelings. Soon, that was about to change: we were going to be the client in Phoenix, an experience that would not allow any of us to escape feeling whatever we needed to feel. Kevin's workshop term alone, the Pressure Cooker, was enough to evoke anxiety.

We were about to find out how intense the Pressure Cooker could be!

On the plane flying to Phoenix with my friends, I had time to think about Stuart and about the experience I was facing in the coming week of training. Stuart had told me, "I will be fine for two weeks. This experience will be good for you." I was pleased he reassured me that all would be fine, but when we said our goodbyes, I wanted him to give me some indication that, beyond being fine as he stayed alone, he would miss me. But he didn't say anything of the sort.

Flying across the country to an experience that was reputed to stir deep feelings, I wished he had said something nurturing. Was he just sending me another indication of how far apart we had wandered? The next week at the workshop, my marriage would certainly be a topic for discussion. What insights — I much wanted some—would I get?

As I made my way to Arizona, I knew I needed to make peace with my past. Even though I had been working on letting go in my individual sessions with Kevin, I had had a recent message from Wei Chi that I hadn't let go entirely. Might this be the reason I still felt tired, lacked energy, and continually had my typical head and neck aches and pains. The pains were less frequent, but because of them, I found it hard to muster up the energy to exercise which would have helped me to be healthier and more positive.

I wanted to get rid of the black, depressed moods that appeared out of nowhere for no apparent reason. They were less frequent and did not last as long, but the moods still cropped up on occasion to drag my day down. I am sure these emotional upsets might have played a part in our marital issues. While I explained to Stuart that they would not last, he must have felt the weight of the depressive nature of my reactions and must have wanted to be out from under them. How could my moods not seem to him to be everlasting even though I claimed the opposite? Here again the residue of childhood neglect, of sexual abuse, and of the effects of past life traumas were interfering with my everyday life. If this was difficult for me, imagine how it was for Stuart!

I felt better about my spirituality, about connecting to Spirit and the afterlife and to where I was headed, but I sensed I needed to open up to Spirit even more than I had. Because my intuitive skills were were still underdeveloped, I knew this might affect

Shadows and Light

my Wei Chi work. I hoped the week would help me develop and feel more confident about my intuition.

Besides wanting to open up to Spirit more, I also wanted to gain self-confidence and stop feeling that I never measured up to others. My goals for my life generally and for the Pressure Cooker in particular were ambitious, but I had hope. I wanted to believe that my perseverance would help me get through the week.

Once landed in Phoenix, we headed for Kevin's house where we would stay and do our Wei Chi work. This would consist of administering and receiving Wei Chi sessions. Eating, sleeping, and workshopping under the same roof in close quarters with the same people for seven days made it easy to grasp why the experience was called the Pressure Cooker.

What is the worst that could happen? I asked myself by way of reassurance. While I was apprehensive, I was reasonably sure I could handle whatever might occur. I kept thinking the workshop would be a safe place to get to know myself better and to give my confidence a boost.

Linette and I planned to stay after the workshop to have a few days of vacation. As Kevin had foreseen, we had become close over the past year since we found out we had a lot in common. At times, it was uncanny how alike we were in the little things. We often split meals at a restaurant because we found the single servings too large. We had similar food preferences so sharing was easy. We would be sitting across from each other and notice we were mirroring each other's position. We had a lot of laughs about this.

We had gotten into the habit of saying, "Why did I even ask if you wanted to? I knew you would like this."

We got along fabulously. Why did she even ask if I wanted to stay a few extra days!

Shadows and Light

It is difficult to describe the intensity of the Pressure Cooker experience. The four of us were isolated in Kevin's house for seven days working morning, afternoon, and evening. We all had a seven-session treatment series done to us. We were either receiving the session, giving the session, recording the session, or in our free time, doing homework and preparing meals. In addition, Kevin would often use meals as a teaching time.

Kim was my practitioner. At the first session, we agreed on a goal for what I wanted to accomplish for the week. My goal was: "To be safe and secure enough to be Susan." This made a lot of sense. I never really did feel safe in my relationships — always thinking I would be left or rejected. I feared that I would be impoverished and alone in my old age. Lastly, I was waiting for the next bad thing to come around the corner and hit me head-on or knock me over. I felt, if I were safe and secure, I would be able to be my true self.

In order to reach my goal — according to the treatment-series format — I had to release something in the third session. I had a long list of things I would be thrilled to give up! However, in order to encompass everything and be meaningful, I settled on the release of the belief that I was not good enough, that I felt I never measured up. Even though, since I had started my spiritual work, I had more self-confidence than I had had, I often felt I could be doing better in whatever I did.

In the third session, Kim was to lead me through a visualization. I was sitting in a chair across from Kim. She had me sit back, relax, and close my eyes. Then she asked, "What symbol or thing comes to you when you think you are not good enough?"

A black hole popped into my head.

Next, I got up and lay down on the table, and Kim led me through the visualization. In it, I was walking in a forest on a warm, cloudy day with no humidity. As I looked down, I saw I was wearing a simple dress, similar to Snow White's in the Disney movies. I was smiling with happiness. A variety of animals and birds greeted me, and I heard joyful tunes in the background. Along the way, I found three flowers, and each one had a message on the back of a petal. On the daisy, the message read, "We love you." On the lily was written, "You are strong." Lastly, on the lady slipper was, "You have self-confidence."

Soon, I came to a clearing with a big drop-off to a moat. On the other side of the moat, I saw a castle with a cave next to it. An old biddy witch, who looked like my mother, was standing by the cave. A deer helped me lower the drawbridge so I could walk over. I entered the cave and found my mother — in a witch's outfit — standing in back. I told her, "I am angry at you. I hate you. I am sick of all the crap you put on me. Why did you do it?" I found a hand mirror that absorbed the old Susan energy from me. I faced it toward my mother for her to absorb it. She said, "I am sorry." I found a poison apple in a basket on the floor and fed it to her. Slowly, she evaporated, and I saw no trace of her. Then, I walked out of the cave. The sun was shining. I sat down on a bench, and a rabbit brought me a book. It was a book of all the spells that had been cast on me and, for everyone, there was a counter spell. Now I held the power to both cast spells onto people and to cast them away from myself.

At this point, Kim left me on the table for a few minutes to see what, if anything, would continue to come up.

In no time, as I was lying there, a feeling of being stupid came up, and I found a counter spell, but I could not release the feeling. When Kim came back, she continued the visualization.

I saw a black hole in front of me and looked for a spell to close it. I conjured an earthquake to do the job. Next, I found a spell to create an earthquake that would swallow the castle and the cave, both of which, I now understood, represented an illusion of who I was supposed to be.

I went back across the drawbridge to the first side. I was

Shadows and Light

scared as, facing the castle, I raised my left hand to start the spell. At that moment, Mattie, my great-great-grandmother, who had given me guidance recently, spoke to me: "You can do it." That gave me the confidence I needed to cast the spell again. With a deafening rumble, the quake started, the castle crumbled, the black hole disappeared, and there was nothing left. The animals and Mattie were with me as I walked around, listening to Diana Ross's "I'm coming out."

As Kim helped me sit up, I exclaimed, "Wow! What a powerful experience that was!" I was feeling light-headed and relieved when Kim gave me a glass of water. Although I could not "see" the witch, the castle, or the cave, I knew I had been there crossing the bridge, feeding the apple to my mother, and sensing the power of the earthquake.

Since coming to Phoenix, there had been times when I wanted to withdraw from the group in order to feel sorry for myself. There were moments when I did not believe I could do this work. It seemed too hard. But now I had a new tool: my book of spells. If an emotion arose that I could not identify, I resolved not to quit trying until I had identified the emotion and what issue had given rise to it. For example, I would ask: "Was this feeling related to sexual abuse, to parental abandonment, to marriage failures, or to something else?" Next, I used my spell book to "find" a counterspell to cast. Implausible as it seems, the process of identifying a negative emotion and countering it actually worked.

Once I did the release — to continue the format of the treatment series — I had to transform/transmute something in the next session, which happened to be the fourth. After much discussion and energy work, Kim and I agreed that I needed to transform my bitter, angry energies/experiences into healing, teaching tools. Again, I had to sit back, close my eyes and wait for cues.

"What object or symbol comes to mind when you think of your bitter angry energies and experiences?" Kim asked me.

"A knife", I replied.

"What comes to mind when you think of healing, teaching tools?"

"A shining star."

Kim led me through another visualization, and this is what happened:

I was a hobo sitting on a pile of hay in the corner of a coal car of a moving train. It was warm and smelly. I wore tattered jeans and a plaid shirt; my shoes were black and scruffy. I was tired, dejected, and hungry, and I wanted to give up. There was a wrinkled paper bag next to me with a knife and ball of string in it. The train slowed down, and I picked up the bag and got off at the station, which was called Meridian and was in the Midwest. I waited for someone to pick me up. Soon, a Cadillac pulled up, and I was driven in it to an old, white farmhouse with green shutters. I got out and entered the house. On the left was the parlor with old, Victorian furniture. I found a magic marker on the desk and wrote on an ugly pink chair, all my angry, bitter energies/experiences that I had ever had.

I wrote so much on the chair that no pink could be seen. Then, I took the knife from my bag and slit and shredded the upholstery into little pieces. Then I kicked the frame until it broke. I gathered all the pieces that I then put into a garbage bag. I had to destroy the bag so I put it in the fireplace, but I could not light the match to burn it. My fear was of the actual fire itself and of burning the house down. I started to cry and, knowing I couldn't burn the bag, I took it outside to the backyard where I saw a blue blanket hanging on the clothesline. I covered the bag with the blanket and beamed love and energy from my hands into it, saying, "I can do it." The blanket slowly shrank and eventually disappeared. I was confused; nothing was left. I looked up at the

Shadows and Light

sky and saw energy swirling around and dancing. After a bright flash, a new star appeared. It winked at me and shined down on me and my new healing space.

This was another powerful visualization! My angry, bitter feelings were hard to give up. I had needed a second visualization — after all, my negative feelings had been part of my life for sixty-plus years. Since I started the Wei Chi work, I have been getting messages about doing healing work in my automatic writing and when receiving sessions. Maybe I am meant to do healing work, but committing to doing so would need more thought.

In order to keep the energies flowing forward, one of my homework assignments that night was to do automatic writing on this visualization. These are the words that came to me:

> As I look at my shining star,
> I see hope and faith
> Transformed from a pile of rubbish
> Collected over many years.
> The star will become my beacon
> To connect me to those in need.
> Tonight, the star shines even brighter
> Since it knows my secrets.

Now that I had given up the belief I was not good enough, and transformed my bitter angry energies and experiences into healing, teaching tools, it was time to embrace something that was the next part of the process format. The empty space that had been left by my letting go needed to be filled. For the fifth session, Kim had me close my eyes while she read the following, which she had found on the internet:

> A symbol of inherent wisdom comes from experience. You have lived through love, sorrow, hope, and

fear. You have come out of it all a wise and confident spirit. Through these experiences, you have learned the secrets of life and death and the mysteries beyond this world. You have been touched by death itself and watched those you loved make the journey before you. It is through your mourning that you face death, grow to understand it, and become the gatekeeper between both worlds.

I started to cry as Kim continued to read. My great well of sadness was overflowing. I wanted to be acknowledged and supported, and this reading was doing it for me.

The crone is full of power. Her body is no longer fertile, but her mind is sharp and able. She is often seen as the healer, working in tune with nature, and she guides those ready to leave or enter the world. She is the grandmother whose words are few yet priceless in their wisdom.
Next Kim said, "You are to embrace cronehood."

While I was moved to weep by the words, I was not moved to accept being called a "crone." I felt uncomfortable with the word's negative connotations. It made me think of an old hag or a witch who is attached to evil. I liked the concept of "crone" but I needed a different word for the concept.
At this point, Kevin, who was observing my session, came in with a lengthy explanation about the positive meaning of cronehood. I surmised that this positive side to cronehood was the reason my mother had appeared as a witch rather than as a crone in the visualization I had recently done. Separate from the label, I intuited I needed to break the line of negative energy coming from my mother and my grandmother. Also, I needed to claim the powerful woman in me who had suffered many times

in this lifetime from abuse. Finally, I agreed to embrace cronehood if it meant I was to love from a more transcendent level, was loved for my age, had the ability to think outside myself, and was a wise old sage.

I had one more visualization while at the Pressure Cooker. This was also during the fifth session.

I was at the base of a cold, snowy mountain and had a long trek up to the summit. On the way up, I stopped and found two rings and a blue crystal. I saw a cliff ahead of me, and I took the rings and crystal out of my backpack and laid them at the edge of the drop. I put on my power outfit, stood back, and watched lightning strike these three objects and turn them into something meaningful. I had to decide what I needed to take with me to the top of the mountain and what to leave behind. The first ring represented my first marriage to Michael. I absorbed the wisdom I learned from it into my body and left behind the sorrow and pain. The second ring represented my second marriage to Stuart. I absorbed all the good, healing parts into my body and tossed the rest. I picked up the third object, the crystal, and felt it pulsating as I absorbed it into me. It gave me the power to continue up the mountain.

I continued up the mountain and met a different old witch — not my mother this time — who gave me a book of wisdom, which I placed on my book of spells. As I watched them grow smaller and smaller in my hands, they turned into a necklace with a charm. The witch placed the necklace around my neck and said I could use it at any time I needed. She added, "This is a gift. You will see me as I truly am, radiant, and stunningly beautiful." She walked off the edge of the mountain and disappeared into the clouds. I continued to walk up the mountain and looked at my walking stick — a tree branch that I had picked up — which had changed into a staff embedded with crystals and etched with ancient symbols. My grandfather, the Bishop, appeared in front of me. He said, "I am here to give you wisdom. I have faith in you." Then, my great-great-grandmother, Mattie, made her appearance for added support. The three of us walked along, talking and laughing for a while. I felt the energies of Maggie, Tim, Peter, and my grandchildren inside of me. Finally, we reached the top of the mountain. My grandfather handed me his Bishop's staff, and I held it in the same hand as my staff. Mattie handed me hers. My staff became one with the other staffs and their energies were joined. I raised the staff I now held high above my head. I had the power to do anything I wanted.

Doing this visualization, although I was lying on the table, I felt myself on top of the mountain. I was wearing a long, white dress with my hair blowing. I was in total command of everything, the powerful woman I was supposed to be. It was an amazing feeling that would take a while to get used to. For a homework assignment that evening, I drew a picture of my staff. It was carved and embedded with crystals. One day, I knew that I would find the right walking stick to be my staff and, several years later, I did, but I have not yet put the crystals in it. It may take a few more years to do that.

The sixth session included checking in to see how I was doing and experiencing more energy work. By this session, I noticed that I was changing. I found myself sleeping with my legs out straight. This was new since I usually slept in the fetal position — a self-protective position. I interpreted this as feeling safe. I also found that, if I started to cry for an unknown reason, I would identify the emotion and then use the spell book to get rid of it. Generally, I was calmer and my aches and pains had become negligible. I stopped withdrawing from uncomfortable situations. I knew these changes might have a positive effect on my marriage but would not assure its success. Perhaps the most surprising revelation I had was how my accent had changed. At one point, Kevin said, "Are you aware you speak with a slightly clipped British accent when you get upset?"

"Oh, my goodness, no!" I said. "That's my mother's voice; she always retained her accent." I had always tried so hard not to be like her and, obviously, I had not totally succeeded. In certain instances when I was upset or angry, I had not let go of her persona.

I had a plethora of emotional issues to think about but I also realized I had some practical ones. Was I really going to start a healing practice once I finished the Wei Chi practitioner training? Was I going to quit my part-time job and officially retire from career work? It was becoming a possibility. If I did retire on more limited funds, a healing practice would provide additional income.

The seventh and last session would be held six weeks after we had returned home. The lapse of time was needed to integrate our experiences and come up with an action plan to help us keep moving forward.

The intensity of the Pressure Cooker came from different sources. Each of the four of us faced her own demons while watching the other three face hers. We were all evaluated in many ways, including how we gave a session. We learned so much; the pressure was unrelenting, causing tears but also laughter to release the tension.

When the Pressure Cooker was finally over, I was feeling empowered and ready for the next chapter of my life! Staying in Arizona and going to Sedona was the best thing Linette and I could have done since it provided time to unwind from the intensity of the previous week. I loved the beauty and energy of Sedona and immediately felt at home. I can't remember ever feeling so good about myself as I did that week. I think it was because my body was totally relaxed, once I had gotten rid of all that negative energy I was holding on to. I slept soundly every night. The weather was cool and sunny — perfect for walking. We walked every day and meditated on the red rocks absorbing energy from the vortexes. Linette and I got along so well we had no problems deciding how to spend the day or where to eat.

On one walk along the path by Oak Creek in Sedona, Linette and I came across stacks of stones — cairns — formed by previous visitors. "Let's each build one," I said as I looked around and found "my" spot. Linette chose hers, and we each started our stack. I took my time picking up individual rocks — examining each one for size and shape — before I selected the perfect one. As I was working, I wondered about all the other people who had come here and left their mark with the stones. I found connecting to nature to be a very spiritual and uplifting activity. When I finished my stack of stones, I found a large rock to sit on and rest for a bit. The sound of the flowing water of Oak Creek was soothing, and the sun warmed my back. As I looked up, I saw the magnificent red rocks — known as Cathedral Rock — framed by the deep blue sky. I thought this was Mother Nature at her finest. As for

Susan and Linette in Sedona

me, a poor soul trying to navigate life, I was in awe and felt ready to continue on my healing path. After sitting for a while and writing in our journals, Linette and I continued to walk along the river before heading back to our hotel.

One day, we went to a New Age Center to have our auras read, which was something I had wanted to have done. The owner of the shop gave us the results. The first thing she said to me was, "Would you like a job?"

I was stunned. "What on earth are you talking about?"

"I want to hire you because you came into this life with higher vibrations to do healing. I would like you to work here."

Susan meditating in Sedona

I explained I lived in New Hampshire so working in Sedona was not realistic and thanked her for both the offer and the information about my vibrational level. Here was another sign that I should do healing work. It was flattering to hear. This was something I never knew about myself. I was beginning to think of what else I was going to discover. At any rate, it sure gave my confidence a boost, but I had to remember that my aura showed blocks in my chakras that would require work at one point.

On our last day in Sedona, Linette and I went for another hike. I was sitting surrounded by the glorious red rocks facing the Kachina Woman, one of the famed vortexes in Sedona to be found in Boynton Canyon. I had scrambled higher up than Linette and could see her sitting below me. The clouds predom-

Shadows and Light

inated that day, but the sun peeked out on occasion. As I looked at the incredible beauty in front of me, I felt at peace with the earth, grounded, and rooted like the trees. I had no aches or pains. Nourished and soothed as I was by the beauty, I was also in harmony with myself. In the past week, a psychic integration had taken place within me and now I needed to move forward. I took time to thank Master — Wei Chi's higher power — and Wei Chi for their help. I knew they would be available to me when I needed them. My past bitter, angry feelings have been transformed, and I was ready for the next step. These are the words I heard from Wei Chi:

You are in a beautiful spot.
You are a beautiful spark of nature.
We will help you along the way.
Speak from the heart and you will be heard.
See from the soul and you will be given third-eye vision.
Listen to your inner voice and cancel out the clutter.
Know that you are right and will walk in the path of light.
You have come far and will be listened to and gain respect
   and honor for your path.

As I finished writing these words in my journal, I heard Linette calling, "Look at the sky." I saw storm clouds forming. We gathered up our jackets and bags and left before the rain came.

Linette and I had different flights home so I had time to myself as I crossed the country again. I was excited to be going home to see Stuart. I had genuinely missed him, and being a homebody at heart, I had missed our home. I know I had changed but did not know what effect it would have on our marriage. I had my spell book to help me cast a spell on any unwanted emotions that arose. The support I received from Wei Chi, Kevin,

Katie, Linette, Kim, the afterlife, and Spirit — whomever that might be — was evident and steadfast. I had never had support like this before.

I felt ready to tackle anything, but the big question remained: had Stuart shifted in any way while I was gone? Had he even missed me?

Chapter 23
Stuart Fails to Rise to the Occasion

Of course, as I flew back from Sedona, I fantasized a bit about my relationship with Stuart and made it over into the relationship I wanted. As I walked briskly along the Manchester-Boston Regional Airport concourse, anxious to see Stuart, my fantasy faded a bit and I wondered if he would be happy to see me.

I recalled how, several years earlier, I had picked up Johnnie at the airport, and when he saw me, his whole face had lit up with a smile. His obvious pleasure at seeing me warmed my heart. But along with the joyous memory, a negative energy immediately chilled me. I remembered another airport where I had picked up my parents. They were landing in Brussels, and upon seeing me after more than a year, they showed no emotion for me — nor for their baby grandson, Tim, whom they were seeing for the first time.

That arrival so many years ago had left me feeling confused and disappointed, but now I was meeting neither Johnnie nor my parents. I wanted to focus on the present. What would I find when Stuart and I met again?

When I got to the top of the escalator, I saw Stuart standing at the bottom, waiting for me, not seeing me yet. I wanted so much to be scooped up into Stuart's arms and be welcomed home with animation and a kiss. I rushed down the moving escalator, shouting, "Here I am." I wonder now whom I thought I might be meeting at the bottom of the escalator. Surely, I knew Stuart enough to know he was not that person.

He looked up at me, but he didn't smile. My heart stopped. Is it the same old thing? I wondered as I stepped off the escalator and walked over to give him my own hug. His face was quizzical as if he was wondering what I was doing.

Where was the husband who would scoop me up into his arms as he welcomed me home with gusto and affection?

Instead, when we came together, I got a perfunctory hug.

This was not a good sign.

On arriving back at our house, I tried to remain hopeful that Stuart and I would reconnect on some deeper level than that at which we had been before I went to Sedona. The two weeks I had been gone were the longest we had ever been apart. Hadn't he missed our conversation, our walks together, our casual touching? If he did, he gave me no indication.

That evening, we decided to go out to dinner. As we sat in the living room having a glass of wine before leaving, I said, "Even though I was so busy with the Wei Chi work, I did miss you and our home. Did you miss me?"

"Well, it did seem lonely at times because it was so quiet," he replied, but did not say more as I was hoping he would.

I concluded it would be more conducive to a serious conversation to explore our relationship away from the house — there could be no running out of the room (me!) and no avoiding (him). I would wait until later when we were out to dinner. Meanwhile I gave him two gifts I had bought him in Sedona. Two days later, I realized that he had not thanked me for the gifts.

The restaurant was not a better venue. Was choosing to talk there how I was slipping into my usual denial? The dining room was particularly noisy so once there, I knew better than to initiate a relationship conversation. At least, I knew that much. It was as if I wanted to let myself off the hook — why else would I have put off a conversation until we were in public?

The next morning, when Stuart was making our bed. I walked over in front of him, placed a hand on each side of his head as I pulled him toward me, looked him directly in the eye. Before I had left, Kevin had suggested that I reassure Stuart at some point, so I did.

"No matter what happens, I still love you," I said. It was true that I did not love him in the true sense, but after almost seven years of being together, I still had some feelings for him and felt some love. I was OK saying it as I was feeling very upbeat when I came back. Then, I kissed him on the lips. Doing so, I felt maybe a slight twinge of emotion coming from him, but he turned his head away and did not hold the kiss. What could the touch of emotion I had felt from him be?

He turned back to me and muttered, "Thank you."

I went on to share what I had learned recently about myself, and added that I did not know the effect it would have on our marriage — hopefully, I had brought back some "tools" that would be useful.

"You had time to think while I was gone. What do you think our marriage needs?"

"We need to have more fun together," he replied. We talked about going out for a walk, which was something we both enjoyed; but something happened and we ended up in Best Buy to purchase a printer for me — not exactly an amusing excursion. While I did need a new printer, it was not an outing that promised to strengthen a relationship by adding any spark to it. Again, as with planning a conversation at the restaurant, I allowed the set-up of a situation that did not meet my needs.

At dinner that evening, however, he said with some emotion

Shadows and Light

— at last, a vestige of emotion! — "I am glad that you had such a good time."

While I had known for a while that Stuart and I had some big issues to address and though I had been aware we might not be able to resolve them, I had always hoped we could. When I came back from Sedona and saw how we interacted, I could no longer pretend to myself that we could get through this. The manner in which he greeted me was not that of a man who was trying to get closer to his wife, who was attempting to bridge a torrent of neglect. It was the reaction of a man who was investing in distancing himself.

I deserved better in a partner than a man who did not want to be with me, who seemed to feel I was imposing on his life. When I thought of how, when I said I loved him, he had turned away and did not hold my kiss, I felt it as the final straw. I had gone into this marriage of my own accord thinking that I had changed, but I guess I hadn't changed enough, since I now found myself stuck with an unloving husband who appeared to be unwilling to work with me to change our marriage. I thought I had broken the cycle of the sham marriage that my parents had had.

Yes, Stuart was an improvement over Michael and Johnnie, but evidently, I still had more to learn in this school of intimacy — or perhaps I should call it the school of hard knocks.

Feeling rejected and needing to be solaced and still not ready to take decisive action, I soon found myself back to my old responses. My shoulder pain returned and I slept badly, waking up numerous times during the night. But worse than the physical pain, there seemed to be that continuous battle within me — my mind was fighting my spirit. I had lost my feeling of empowerment that I had struggled so mightily to create in Arizona and I felt such irritation with Stuart —and I could feel his with me.

Why could I not muster the energy to make decisions about my marriage, to go on my own? Wasn't it like why I could not

Shadows and Light

muster the energy to arrive at some decision about how to be with my parents? Why had I put up with their neglect and abuse for so long? Therein, of course, was my answer. My character, which did not like conflict, was willing to endure much abuse if only there were no overt conflict. The irony, of course, was that my life was overtaken with internal conflict, and I knew no peace.

After my return, so many little things became the occasion of conflict. When I forgot which way to turn our gas fireplace on, Stuart snapped, "It is so simple! How can you forget?"

Instead of simply lighting the fireplace for me, doing a little thing such as I had done on many occasions for him, he used the occasion to belittle me.

It always had taken me a moment to get it right about manipulating buttons and levers and switches. The only way for me to remember which way to turn something was to repeat, "Lefty loosey, righty tighty." A contractor had taught me that years ago, and it had worked well for me, but Stuart thought it was really stupid of me not to know what to do without a little jingle — as if something was wrong with my brain. He was sure I should remember immediately without having to think.

Another occasion of conflict happened regularly in our shared office space where we both did our online work. Fortunately, we worked at the same time for only two hours in the morning, but during that period, Stuart, would do downloads for his job. These downloads would slow up the internet, which caused me to be very inefficient with the data entry I needed to send in. Each keystroke took so long I ended up frustrated beyond belief. We had had numerous discussions about downloading a few months earlier. Stuart had not thought my slow-down problem was one he should have to deal with and so he would continue to do these downloads. Eventually, through my persistent requests, he learned to ask me if it was a good time to down-

Shadows and Light

load. If it were not, he would wait until I was done, but with time — as I did with lighting the gas fireplace — he would forget. I would find myself again slowed down beyond belief by a download of his.

One morning soon after I had come back from Sedona, we were both in our office working. I asked, "The internet is slowing down. Are you downloading?"

I was pleased to notice I did not react angrily as I usually had. I felt it was a sign of growth.

"I forgot," he replied. "I am not used to having you home." Stuart did stop his downloading until later.

I refused to get caught up in his issues and continued to expect him to do his downloads when I wasn't working. If I had asked him why he continued to do these downloads during the two hours our time overlapped in the office, I am sure he would have had no idea why — he was so out of touch with his feelings. His downloading seemed to reflect his need to control. It also seemed a passive-aggressive way of expressing his anger at me.

I had felt positive about handling the downloading so well. After my return from Sedona, we had about two weeks of silence. I was irritated that we were not speaking about our marriage, and so I initiated a conversation with Stuart. I kept trying because I wanted to feel happier than I was, but the conversation went nowhere, and I ended up in a foul mood. Dealing with Stuart sucked the energy right out of me.

It was time for a clearing. I pictured the murky marriage junk in my life going down a drain, eventually to be recycled by Mother Earth. The clearing didn't work, and I could not overcome feeling tired and depressed, not wanting to do anything except curl up in bed and sleep. I had not been able to release the belief that our marriage and keeping Stuart happy was something I wanted to do or had to do. Realistically, I knew it was not my responsibility, but somehow, I had always accepted that savior role and I no longer wanted to do that.

In March, six weeks after the Pressure Cooker, Katie, Kim, Linette, and I had our last and seventh Wei Chi session, to complete the training.

Little by little, after the freedom of the Sedona experience, I had fallen back into my old ways — it was a constant challenge not to — of putting myself down and feeling overwhelmed. Fortunately, I was now at least more aware of the emotions that would waylay me. One day, for instance, I was glancing through my Boston College alumni magazine when I was struck by the accomplishments of some of my classmates. Immediately a feeling of sadness that I had not measured up spread though me. I felt inadequate. Remembering that I had used my spell book successfully to cast counterspells, I decided to cast a counterspell to my feelings of sadness and failure. That day, I was able to get rid of the feeling of not being good enough.

When Linette and I had been in Sedona, I had bought myself a star-shaped ring. I wore it to remind me of the star visualization which I could do whenever I needed to. While I still sometimes fell short, I do believe a significant transformation had taken place in me as the following words in my automatic writing indicated:

> I am a healer with a lot of potential at this stage in my life. The moon shines down, and I see my star, shining brightly with my secrets. The energy is now transformed to heal others. I was separated at birth. Now, I am at peace. If I forge ahead on my own, I will understand and know that I was right all along.

I had learned over the past four years to pay attention to my "inner voice" more and, as a result, had taken Reiki and trained as a hospice volunteer. The words *Tai Chi* had been coming to the forefront of my mind for a while, so when I read the continuing-education flyer from the local high school that an evening class was being offered in the spring, I thought, This is perfect — the right time and place.

When Stuart and I were eating dinner that evening, I said, "I saw a Tai Chi class is being offered at the high school on Tuesday evenings. It's a beginner class so I think I will sign up for it."

"I am interested in Tai Chi, too," Stuart said.

"Let's take it together," I replied with enthusiasm, thinking this was something we could do together as a couple. I wasn't expecting a miracle, but it would give us something to talk about and alleviate long silences at mealtimes.

When the time came to sign up, Stuart said he didn't want to take the class. Nothing I said changed his mind and so I went alone as I had originally planned. It turned out to be a good beginner class, which I really enjoyed.

As I remained perplexed about the next step to take with Stuart and how to summon the energy to do it, I still struggled with thinking that I needed to help him with his emotional work and even do it for him. Fortunately, I was able to understand that this compulsion was my old stuff and I now had no interest in taking on his burden. I even understood that he had no interest in my taking up his stuff. What a relief!

I pondered my big questions about the future. Where was I going in my life from here? If I was going to separate from Stuart how was I going to support myself? More than anything, I wanted to stay in my power. How best to do that? Was my part-time, home-based job a good safety net for me to keep for when Stuart and I were separated? Or, could I earn enough in a Wei Chi healing practice to warrant quitting my part-time job to do something I now preferred? When I looked into Social Security

— I was coming up to the age at which I could claim my full retirement benefits — I discovered I would receive enough income to make it financially feasible to retire. Retirement would free me up to start a healing practice, which was what I really wanted. The prospect of retirement was reinforced by my automatic writing. I was getting a lot of messages from Spirit that I was a healer.

I resolved to push my marriage to the side for the time. Saving it did not seem hopeful, especially as I grew more interested in creating a new life for myself. I was dealing with Stuart only on the side, participating at this point only in what might be called "damage control." I was tired of investing emotionally in a marriage that wasn't showing any signs of becoming successful. At that point, if he had wanted to give the marriage some energy, I was ready to respond, but I would not be the initiator. In essence, this was my farewell to an active involvement with Stuart.

My real interest at this point was pursuing Wei Chi for itself and for the possibility of establishing a healing practice. It seems incredible to me now that I was not ready emotionally to strike out on my own, which ending the marriage would require. I had the finances set up, and from what Stuart was letting drop in our perfunctory conversations, he was not attached to the house so I could likely manage to stay put while he would eventually go away.

But, perhaps the reluctance was not in my finances or in my housing. It had to do with my still maintaining an illusion of being in a working marriage. Ending it would be admitting to the world that I had not been in a functioning relationship and that my marriage was a failure. It was a failure, of course, but I could not yet publicly admit it. For now, I would bide my time and see what unfolded, but I was growing aware that I was hoping Stuart would do the work of moving out. Being abandoned was a passive role that I was familiar with and so I did not create a more active role for myself in ending this marriage.

My experience of Wei Chi generally was satisfying, but try as I would to change the connotation of cronehood that Kevin was suggesting, I found calling myself a crone to be unappealing. That changed when a time in the eighties came back to me as I struggled with accepting being a crone. I was holding a temporary job at the ophthalmologist's office where a young woman, Connie, was the technician. She was going through a difficult period in her life. When we had our lunch together, she and I spoke about her options. A couple of years later, after we had both left the office, she wrote me a letter to share how meaningful our talks had been to her and how they had helped her to sort out her life. At the time, I had no idea I had even helped her in any way and so her appreciative words had touched me. By the time I was doing the Wei Chi work, I had forgotten Connie's letter; but as I questioned how I could possibly think of myself as a crone, her words came back. I had to accept that, even when I was in my early forties, I had garnered a bit of wisdom which had had a positive effect on some people. How much more might I give people now that I was more mature and had followed the Wei Chi program! Perhaps I was a crone even if I still did not like the name. Certainly, I needed to accept the concept.

Having finished the Pressure Cooker portion of the Wei Chi practitioner training in March, we had to complete the last part of the training by finding seven volunteers to practice on and then write up case studies. Four or five of these case studies had to be in the seven-series format but the rest could be shorter—a series of three or five sessions. I set a goal for myself to complete my seven case studies by the fall. This was possible since, even though Kevin was still living in Phoenix, Arizona, he would be back about every two to three months for us to confer with about our case studies and be available by phone when we needed guidance.

The next few months were a whirlwind of activity. Somehow, the case studies came to me through Katie, Kim, or Linette — we helped find case studies for each other. The more Wei Chi healing I did, the more evident it became how powerful the ideas and the processes were and how Wei Chi actually worked. It was evident why we had to go through the seven-session treatment series to become better practitioners. I understood that now.

Wei Chi healing brings clients forward so they are able — maybe for the first time or in a new light — to face themselves and have a simple or even a profound breakthrough. Wei Chi is more than relaxing on the table and letting the energy flow. As the questions start to form — Who am I? Where am I stuck? How can I move ahead? — healing occurs. My own experience of making a breakthrough in feeling accepted and secure in a group healed a portion of what I needed to heal. That is why I wanted to share this healing modality with others. When I thought about sharing an article on Wei Chi for a magazine, these words came as I did my automatic writing.

> The light shines down and picks a spot to radiate and fill with love to warm the soul in a time of disillusionment and despair. The glow permeates through my being; each vessel vibrates with hope, thereby letting me live.

By the end of April, I was approaching the time when I could retire. Spirit was insisting, "Get on with your healing work. That is where your talents and gifts lie." But, I was still filled with fear of the unknown, and I asked Spirit how to get rid of that fear. Spirit answered, "You will always have love and abundance. You will never be alone. You do not need to fear because we are with you and love you, so leave that job and follow your path. You have our support, and we will cheer you on."

But, as I contemplated launching We Chi work with some excitement, I had to deal with the sorry state of my relationship. It would take a lot of stamina to get through a breakup with Stuart, and I was not sure I had enough. I was afraid of a lot of things. Among them was dealing with the legal issues. Would I need to get an attorney or could we file for a no-fault divorce? Then there was the logistical work. Could I afford to buy out Stuart and remain in the condo? How would we split up objects we had acquired? Following on this were emotional issues. I would be on my own again to handle everything alone. Worrying about being alone was ironic as I was not receiving any emotional help at the time from Stuart. Still, we did share expenses and I was anxious about not having enough money to support myself.

I was also embarrassed to tell people that another marriage of mine had ended in failure.

Then one evening when I did my automatic writing, Mattie added her advice: "Open up to the new experiences you are having. You know deep down you can do it. It is the fear that is keeping you back. Fear of being all alone and having no one to help and support you if you are in need. Age has nothing to do with it because you are going to live for many more years now that you have found what you need to do."

I still had a hard time believing all the support I was getting from the afterlife was so relevant to my current situation. I was grateful and made it a point to thank them periodically. The messages were effective however, as shortly after receiving these messages, I quit my part-time job with its benefits and officially retired. At the end of June, I began collecting both Social Security and a pension from Brigham and Women's.

One day, Stuart and I went for a walk on Plum Island near Newburyport, Massachusetts. The beach was a favorite place of mine to walk. The warm sun felt good, and the salt air was refreshing. It would have been a good time to have a serious talk, but I was resolved not to bring up the subject of our marriage any more. It seemed to be working since, in the last weeks, I was not reacting to Stuart. I felt less stressed.

As we were walking along the lapping water, he asked me, "How are you feeling about quitting your job?"

Surprised that he was inquiring about my welfare, I replied, "On one hand, I'm overjoyed about not having to do the actual work and about receiving Social Security, but on the other hand, I am petrified about facing the unknown. I'm thinking of starting a healing practice — both because I like the work and because I might be able to produce some supplemental income from it."

"I am overjoyed you retired as well!"

Finally, I thought, he was about to express words of encouragement and perhaps offer to help me segue into retirement in some way. I waited for him to continue.

"Now, I can do downloads anytime I want."

As usual, Stuart's reaction was all about him. It was, for me, another example of why our marriage had to come to an end. I refused to get sucked back into relating to him in my customary angry way, which Wei Chi had helped me to understand was not viable. I would have to continue to work on my own exit to our declining marriage. That was the only work on my marriage I could undertake. I understood that. This realization was very liberating.

Working part-time from home eased me into retirement, but it had not prepared me for not working at all. If I had had a job I loved, I probably would have worked much longer, but medical coding didn't satisfy me and that had prompted me to retire. That summer I learned to live with retirement. I focused on my Wei Chi case studies to finish up by the fall, and I saw Rosemary every week. This would give me some scheduled things to do but it was hardly enough.

Shadows and Light

I tried hard to create some structure in my life — I liked to have some type of schedule for weekdays. Being a bit footloose after retirement, I was feeling sad and the muscle aches and pains were appearing more frequently. Then in July, I got an intestinal virus that kept me home for a few days. What was going on with me? Where might I turn for help?

After I finished the beginner Tai Chi class, I felt there was a lot more to learn. Since the teacher did not offer classes on a regular basis, I looked around for other teachers. Soon I found classes about a half hour drive away in Amesbury, Massachusetts. I signed up for two evening classes and one morning class every week. For some reason — maybe at an intuitive level, Tai Chi resonated with me, and I wanted to experience where it took me. My body responded well to doing it, and I felt my tense muscles welcoming the movement. Taking care of myself had always been a priority, and over the years, I had done some form of exercise, off and on, as time allowed, but now that I was free from work, there was no excuse not to be more seriously involved. In the past, I had jogged, swum, done Yoga and Pilates, and had worked with exercise videos. Now that I had found Tai Chi, I hoped I could continue to do it for a long time.

In my automatic writing, I asked Spirit, "Why do I need to have this physical and emotional pain? What purpose does it serve?" This is what I wrote: "It serves as a reminder of where we found you. Black and shrouded in guilt. Guilty that you do not love your husband anymore. You look at him and see how far you have come and where he is — left behind and unwilling to change."

This message made a lot of sense to me as I did feel guilty about not loving him enough. After I got back from Sedona and told Stuart I will always love him, I meant it on some level, but at the time, I had not really thought about it. It is true, I will love him for believing in me and in the spiritual work I was doing and for showing up at the time when I needed to do it. I just had not identified feeling guilty for not loving him enough for our relationship to work. There may have been other underlying issues going on that I was not aware of. After all, I had a lot of negativity in my childhood and early adult life. Had I gotten over it all? I was also a bit apprehensive that, because some of the clients I had for case studies had serious mental health issues, they could be triggers for me.

I thought I should be feeling great after leaving my job and all the paperwork of retirement was taken care of, but I wasn't feeling great. I didn't have a lot of money coming in, but it was plenty to live on. That was not really the problem although, if I started a healing practice with paying clients, the extra money would help when Stuart and I split up.

The insecurity I felt that summer after retirement had the all marks of a vacuum. I did not realize that this was a time when I could easily be inveigled into a new venture before I was aware of what was happening.

That is exactly what ensued — and it began to overwhelm me.

Chapter 24
Shop Plans and Ruby's Decline

During that summer of 2010, our Wei Chi group, which had long but abstractly considered opening a healing center, started to plan how to launch one. We had almost completed the training and were ready to be practitioners, but we lacked a venue. Why not create one?

Although Kim worked full-time as a school administrator, she wanted to do healing work on a part-time basis, and now that I was retired, I thought I wanted to as well. Linette and Katie lived out of the area so it was not feasible for them to be fully implicated, but they assured us they would be available for an occasional weekend event.

In addition, when Kevin was back in New England from Arizona to teach classes and see clients, he was renting a space from a local massage center. If we started a business, our healing center could provide him with a permanent venue and his work and ours would complement each other's. Kevin came up with a plan in which he would be the owner of the business — the umbrella organization had transmuted from "our" business to "his" business without our quite being aware of it — and a younger man who worked for him, Edgar, would do the business-management portion. Since business management was not in our field of interest, Kim and I just wanted a room to see our clients, for which we would pay a portion of the rent. By the end of the summer,

Shadows and Light

Kim and I were looking at available spaces to rent. Taking on this task seemed to make sense as Kevin was in Arizona and we were in New England.

Ruby and I continued our journey that summer. We were connected on a soul level, and both of us were struggling with where we were in our lives. I visited her every week and gave her energy work. She had had a recent anxiety attack, which had led to an increase in her antidepressant medication. Although she continued to talk and tell me things, I sensed there was something else going on with her that I could not identify. Ruby was facing an inevitable death, and I was facing a major breakup. Our souls were often in the dark, suffering, and then in a flash, change would cause more anxiety and fear. It was as if the two of us were walking in the light supporting each other. One afternoon when I was visiting Ruby, we were sitting in her living room since it was too hot to go outside and Ruby needed the air conditioner to breathe on humid days. We were having our usual chat to catch up on the week when Ruby said to me, "You do so much for me. I want to do something for you."

"It is really not necessary," I replied and told her all that she gave me, the confidence in my healing work, her friendship, and the testimonial for my brochure she had provided recently. She had written: "As a hospice volunteer, Susan immediately sensed my anxiety and vulnerability. Her loyalty and compassion, her intelligent approach in recognizing the sources of pain and her strong dedication to the study and practice of Reiki have aided me in finding and exploring untapped mental and physical strength."

Wow! I had no idea the effect I had had on her, I thought. Then, I realized I needed another case study for my certification. "Would you be willing to do a different kind of energy work with me?" I asked her. "It is more involved than what I am doing with

Shadows and Light

you now. You would have to participate in your own healing." I went on to explain how I needed two more case studies and what it would consist of.

"Sure," Ruby said. "Anything to help you out."

Soon after this conversation, Ruby's breathing worsened and she was readmitted in the ICU for a couple of days. When I saw her next, she was home again and wanted to start the Wei Chi sessions with me. I decided to give her the three-session treatment series as I felt a longer one would have been too much for her.

Ruby proved to be my most challenging case study. Even though she was familiar with the hands-on energy work, she needed lots of explanation and extra time to compensate for her physical limitations. She tried very hard — wanting to please me — and even answered her homework questions. In the midst of a visualization, she sat up suddenly and said, "This is the craziest thing I have ever done." Keeping my cool, I responded, "Yes, this does get a bit strange at times. You have a choice. We can continue or we can stop if that is what you want."

She decided to continue, and I finished the visualization with her. I couldn't really blame her for thinking it was crazy because, in her visualization, an alligator had approached Ruby and handed her a paintbrush. In a visualization, everything has a symbolic function, so the paintbrush was for Ruby to paint a picture for her transformation. In spite of her doubt, Ruby painted the picture. This was an important step for integrating the inner work with her daily life.

At one point, when, as part of the format, I went into my intuitive to get a message for Ruby from Spirit/Wei Chi, I got the following, which I shared with her: "You are a child of light and the others gone before you live on through you. May the rest of your journey on earth be filled with peace and love. You are loved." When I got this message, I saw white doves and flowers.

Shadows and Light

Tears formed in Ruby's eyes. She was visibly moved, so this message resonated with her. I thought about how Spirit/Wei Chi knew exactly what a client needed. All this cannot be explained scientifically, but the more I did the work, the stronger my belief in the afterlife became.

During this time of Wei Chi work with Ruby, the relationship between Ruby's two sons grew worse. They and their wives had never gotten along well, often barely tolerating each other. The family business was struggling financially, and the son who shared the family house and ran the business wanted to start collecting against Ruby's death benefits. This understandably caused her undue angst because she thought this son did not care for her and wanted her dead. I think she knew now that she would never see her sons get along in her lifetime. I hoped the Wei Chi healing might offer her solace and support to get through this difficult time.

In mid-September, I got a call from the second of Ruby's daughters-in-law. The situation in the first son's house had become intolerable, and Ruby had asked to move out to be with her second son and his family and he had come to take her away. When I visited her in her new surroundings, her mood had changed from what I remembered. She was visibly depressed and stated that she did not want to live any longer. As she put it, "It would be easier for everyone if I were dead." She had taken over a smallish master bedroom with an attached bath on the first floor of the house; her son and daughter-in-law had moved to an upstairs bedroom. Ruby had her privacy and help was close by if she needed assistance. This second family was supportive, caring, and upbeat. Having her two young granddaughters around gave Ruby some joy, which she so needed. She wanted to complete the last Wei Chi session, but we agreed to postpone it for a couple of weeks until she had time to adjust to her new surroundings. I left that afternoon feeling concerned for Ruby. A huge shift had taken place — her mental and physical status had deteriorated. I couldn't help but wonder how much longer she was going to live.

The following week when I saw Ruby, she had just returned from an appointment with her doctor. He had told her, "I am surprised you are still living because all your organs are failing." Essentially, her health was horrendous, and her doctor wanted her to go into a nursing home. She refused. Her son and his wife wanted her to stay with them and that is what Ruby wanted as well. She went back on hospice services.

For Ruby's last Wei Chi session, I knew there was a limit to what I could do for her since she had essentially given up. Even though Ruby stated, "I feel dead in my head" and she could not remember the two previous sessions, this last session turned out to be meaningful. She was visibly moved — and I had tears in my eyes — when I read her new goal that I had devised with Wei Chi's help. It was, "Recognize and utilize the love and support I have to live the rest of my life in peace." When I gave her the hands-on energy that day, she said that on many occasions when I had given her a session, she had felt something had been healed. She also shared that she was handling everything as positively as she could only because of what I had given her. Her words confirmed the power of the Wei Chi work and that I was good at doing it. It was an emotional time for both of us, not knowing how much longer she would live. I hoped to continue to provide some comfort and peace in her remaining days. I resolved to continue to visit her every week and give her energy as long as she wanted me to.

My time spent with Ruby helped solidify my decision about having a healing practice. I enjoyed doing the healing work and had found it rewarding to witness her come to terms with her past. While she understood she was not going to see her sons get along, I think she made some inroads and resolved issues that

Shadows and Light

she had never spoken about to anyone.

Because of all the messages I got from the spirit world, I realized that I did have a gift and a healing practice might be a good choice for me to pursue. But there were other factors I had to think about beside skill and gift if I were to create a practice. A full practice would require a lot of promoting and talking to people. This was not one of the strengths of my introverted nature.

Did I really want to do all the work involved, I was asking myself repeatedly, of setting up a practice and getting clients to fill that practice?

As I have done in the past, I let other people's energy carry me along. In this instance, Kevin was the prime motivator. He had rented a space in a recycled factory building to teach and see clients in. While there, he had learned about a suite of rooms on the lower level of the building that he believed would meet our needs. It was to become available at the end of September. Although not ideal, the space met most of our requirements: three small individual offices, a large space for teaching — big enough to create a larger office for Kevin at one end — a reception area that could be a multipurpose room, and a small kitchen area with room for a table and chairs. The downside was that accessing the space was a bit confusing. Clients would have to go up some steep stairs to enter the building, then walk down a flight of stairs or take the elevator to the lower floor. Once there, the client would have to walk down a corridor to enter our reception area. All rooms but one were lit with ceiling-height windows that looked out on the sidewalk.

In spite of these limitations, we felt we could make the space work. The rent would be discounted if we signed a three-year lease. The savings part made sense, but three years seemed like a long commitment. We had only sketchy plans in place, and nothing like a business plan. Would a long lease come back to

Shadows and Light

haunt us? Kim was also reluctant with the three-year lease. I myself felt some pressure from Kevin and Edgar, his assistant, to make a decision about signing the lease with Kevin.

In the end, Kim and I joined Kevin and signed the lease, hoping for the best — which was not a good business plan! We were lucky to have a benefactor pay the first year's rent for us, and after that, Kim and I would be responsible for a quarter of the rent each month. Kevin, as the owner of the business through which we would be practicing, would pay the other half.

Originally, the plan for the healing center was for Kevin, Kim, and me to have a private office and one large space that could be used for classes. Around the time the lease was signed, Kevin announced — without discussion — that we would have a retail section to sell crystals, jewelry, books, and so on. Friends of his had just closed a metaphysical shop where they had sold crystals, did healing and psychic readings and had a lot of inventory, shelving, and other items for sale. What better time, Kevin told us, to open our own shop! Did Kevin take into account who would staff a retail section and whether a retail store could be profitable in the community? We were launching, after all, with the materials of a failed venture!

None of us had any experience in retail. A shop seemed a bit much to add to our tentative plan of a healing center, but I had faith Kevin would help us and have the knowledge to make it happen. Without investigating the level of Kevin's ability to run and sustain a shop and having no idea how this all was going to work, I brushed any fears aside and got busy making the shop idea happen. A lot of fixing, painting, and organizing the space had to happen before our opening, which we decided would be on Halloween weekend, just a month away. The Wei Chi Healing Center and Shop was now underway — for better or for worse!

When I look back at this decision I made, I must have had blinders on. I don't know what I was thinking at the time! I have an investigative personality and always like to check things out before making a decision, especially a major one like this. I ought to have known better than to jump into a big venture like this without exploring its possibilities more!

I got caught up in the emotion and the excitement of the launch and considered this an opportunity that had appeared out of nowhere for me to have a part-time job just when I needed it. Everything seemed to be falling into place. My case studies were done and I had one more thing to do — give a single modified treatment — before I became a certified Wei Chi practitioner and could charge for healing sessions.

The Wei Chi Center seemed a way to structure living without Stuart. What I couldn't know was that this project would end unhappily.

Chapter 25
Misunderstanding with Maggie, and Ruby Dies

While preparing for the opening of the Wei Chi Healing Center and Shop, I still had to deliver a single, intense, two-hour treatment. This modified treatment was to include all the elements of the Wei Chi healing rolled into one. Although my seven case studies were completed, to finish the requirements to be a Wei Chi practitioner, I had to complete this one last treatment, which called for the most response from the practitioner in the least amount of time. Since, without passing it successfully, I could not be certified — and without certification, I could not practice Wei Chi — I could not afford to fail. For clients, the two-hour treatment made clear which areas of their lives — physical, emotional, career, and so on — they needed to work on rather than provide a big immediate result.

My client for this single, modified treatment was going to be Kevin, and that made me all the more nervous. To combat my anxiety, I did a lot to prepare. Since there was much to accomplish in a short amount of time, I created a timeline and a cheat sheet I could refer to. I visualized myself doing the treatment and being relaxed, including everything I had to do, and giving Kevin a meaningful experience. The evening before, when I did my automatic writing, I asked Spirit if there was anything else I needed to know. This is the answering message I wrote: "No, you know

Shadows and Light

everything. Go in with a clear head and open heart and you will be fine. There is no need to fear as he is an easy client."

I knew there was no need to fear the session with Kevin because he was known to lead the visualizations required in this session. For me, leading visualizations was the most difficult part of my work.

The next day, the session went well, and I kept to the time constraints. Then, Kevin told me the good news: I had passed! I was relieved and happy since I was now an official Wei Chi practitioner and could charge for my sessions. It had been a long haul with many hours of hard work. Of course, I learned a lot about myself. It felt great to have met the challenge, but I still kept putting myself down. Even after having the validation of certification, I was still asking, "Was I good enough to do this work?"

What would it take for me to ever get over my lack of self-confidence?

The other question I had, "How was I going to get clients?" was less subjective and amenable to pep talk! I had to develop some strategies.

That fall, Stuart and I were living like roommates. I continued not to discuss our relationship issues, as they were energy and time sinks, and I just let things go. This seemed to be the best way for us to live together. We were both so busy. Stuart was writing his second book, and my focus was the Wei Chi Healing Center and Shop and not our relationship.

I concentrated on setting up my office at the Healing Center. Although the space was small — just enough room for a massage table, a desk, and two chairs — I wanted to create a warm, welcoming space for my clients where they could relax and unburden their souls. I found the perfect chair in Home Goods, an upholstered semi-recliner for the client and a large, soft swivel office chair for myself. I decided on a color scheme of teal with

Shadows and Light

black accents. I was thrilled to have a window even though it was at street level because the light — even as little of it as there was — meant I could have a plant. At home, I had a philodendron, several feet in length, which was perfect for this window. Accessing it for watering would be a little tricky as I would have to stand on the desk. The *pièce de resistance* was the quilt I had my daughter-in-law, Amanda, make for me. I selected the material — assorted batik prints in a variety of blue and green shades — and then she worked her magic and created a fabulous quilt. I used it to cover the massage table on which clients lay for the energy work and/or visualizations. My office was attractively decorated and ready for clients before the shop opened at the end of October, and I was pleased with the results. I felt at home in my space, and I hoped my clients would as well.

Susan in her office at the shop

In the common areas, Katie and I put up a wallpaper mural in the large, multipurpose room that we would use for classes, and we painted the bathrooms. Katie, Kim, and I all contributed in various ways — bringing things from home or buying new items — to add to the ambience of retail, classroom, and kitchen spaces. Linette brought in some jewelry she had made to sell. Kevin, when he was in town, and Edgar worked on the business details, fixing their offices and the retail space where they set up the shelving and cases for the crystals, jewelry, books, and other items.

Somehow — that is, with a lot of attention and work — the Wei Chi Healing Center and Shop came together, and we were ready for our grand opening on Sunday, October 31, 2010.

Maggie and I had continued to write letters to each other. When she asked to meet again and spend more time together, I felt we were on the right track. I wrote back how happy I was that she wanted to be with me again — I had been thinking about it as well and was waiting for her to bring it up. I suggested that we meet somewhere on Cape Cod, which would be closer to Martha's Vineyard where she lived. We could spend part of the day together, and I could then spend the night with my Wei Chi friend, Linette, who lived close by, or I/we could stay at a B&B. Maggie responded by email immediately saying that she needed time to consider my proposal and would write in the next two weeks.

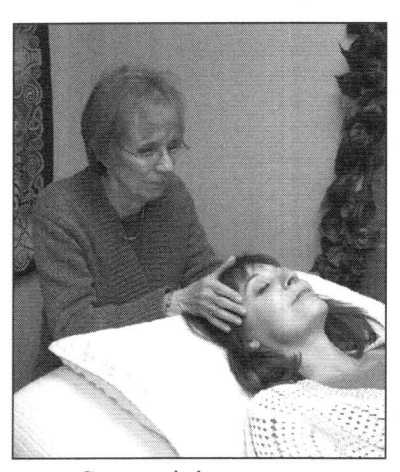

Susan giving energy to Linette

When I received a reply from Maggie in early November, I was devastated. She wrote:

> ...I was surprised you were waiting for me to bring up the idea of getting together again. Why is that? You said you had no idea what to do, and that made me feel like you were not that interested in getting together, or that it was not important to you. I may have misinterpreted what you were saying, but there are times when it

seems like you have not been forthcoming with information. If I don't ask you things, then you won't tell me ... I have to tell you that, in general, I have a hard time with wishy-washy behavior. Are you hesitant to share information with me, or to just put the truth out there?

Sometimes I wonder why you contacted me. What did you hope for in meeting me and getting to know me? Did you think I would be receptive to the idea of getting to know you? I have kept an open mind and have reserved judgment where you are concerned. I have tried to imagine where you are coming from and to really look inside myself to see how I can make sense of getting to know you. I hope you can appreciate how difficult this situation has been for me — I think you do because in your last letter you mentioned wondering how I was doing, because you thought your contacting me must have thrown me for a loop. Yes, hearing from you was a shock of a lifetime, and I know I would not have looked for you. That is the dilemma for me ... there is a part of me that is very angry that you contacted me because I feel pressure to communicate with you. It would have been easier for me not to know who you are. I don't mean to sound harsh, but I didn't need to know. I have had a wonderful life and had no questions that I needed to be answered. The problem then becomes that I do know who you are, and it doesn't feel right to ignore you or shut you out of my life. I have been open to the idea of getting to know you because I think it is the right thing to do, not necessarily the easy thing, but the right thing.

You made a decision that changed the course of my life by giving me up and then you chose to turn it upside down by contacting me. I wish you could be straight with me, to tell me what your intentions really are. Will it ever be right for me to meet your husband and/or your family? Is that something you are comfortable with? Do you really want to get to know me and hear all that I have been saying in this letter? Your questions challenge me sometimes to look deeper into myself to figure out what I think or how to respond to you and that is really difficult at times.

I really have come to a point in the process of getting to know you that I really don't know what I think about the future, and if I want to be in contact with you, or not. I still feel like continuing to get to know you is the right decision, but in order to really know you, I think we need to spend more time together.

Maggie went on to say that she would like to meet in the Boston area so she could stay with her brother. She was starting a new job so our meeting would have to be on the weekend.

I was so upset by Maggie's letter that I cried on and off all that afternoon and evening. Once again, I felt like I had screwed up the possibility of having a relationship with her. When I thought about it, I realized there was a misunderstanding and I probably should have taken an active role in suggesting we meet. As for being wishy-washy — it was clear that she did not know me at all. How could she? I emailed her that evening saying I would write in a couple of weeks as she had given me a lot to think about, but I did appreciate her honesty. When I reread Maggie's letter several times, I realized it was not as painful as I had first thought. Yes, she was angry at me — for abandoning her at birth — and coming into her life. I hoped that, with time, her anger would fade and she would grow to accept me for who I was. I knew it was in her best interest to know me, her birthmother, as we shared genes.

Besides my coming into her life, Maggie had been going

through some rough times recently. She had had some health issues, a job change, and had broken up with a boyfriend. Were we running parallel lives at this time? I was going through a lot of change as well — newly retired, starting a healing practice, facing a potential breakup and living through the ongoing quest of finding my identity. Was this change, happening in our lives simultaneously, indicative of our paths crossing? Did we have to stumble on the rocky terrain for a while before finding smooth ground to walk together in harmony? The pressing question still remained: what could I do to fix my own part/contribution, to repair our fragile relationship?

In my letter two weeks later, I reassured Maggie that I had always wanted to know her and have some kind of relationship with her. I told her that my approach with her in the last year — not being pushy and demanding things but rather acknowledging where she was at, knowing how difficult it was for her — had not worked. I had told her in an earlier letter that I was going to wait for her to bring up when or if we were going to meet again. I had not suggested meeting close to Boston with her staying at her brother's house because she had told me before she didn't want to stay with him. I stated firmly, "I am not holding any information from you! I never have and never will." I reiterated that I thought my intentions were clear about meeting her from the beginning and went on to tell her about the time I went to her house on Martha's Vineyard with the two adopted women I knew. As much as I had wanted to come into her life at the time, I thought it in her best interest not to. I did not apologize for asking challenging questions and explained, "I am the type of person who is always looking to delve deeper into life. Instead of being so angry at the fact that I contacted you, maybe look at it as a learning experience. I came into your life for a reason — and that was to help you grow and look at your life from a different perspective. In fact, I know I have a lot to teach you."

I gave her several ideas about when and where to meet, even suggesting that if she was at her brother's house in Wellesley, Massachusetts, for Thanksgiving, I could arrange for her to meet my son, Peter, and his family close by in Dedham. Maggie had never given me any indication in the past that she had wanted to meet my family. The last thing I said was, "I need to know what you are really feeling about me. You said you feel pressure to communicate with me. Why do you feel it is the right thing to get to know me and not ignore me? If all you are feeling is pressure and it is the 'right' thing, maybe it is best that we do not stay in contact for a while to let the dust settle. At times, I feel that you really do not want to get to know me as a person and that I am an inconvenience that showed up in your life."

I was relieved to get Maggie's email reply in which she said she understood what I had written and had no more questions for me. Maybe she had just needed reassurance from me? Thanksgiving would not work, but she offered to let me know her plans for Christmas soon — when she was coming to the Boston area — then we could set up a definite time. I felt a big burden had been lifted off my shoulders, one less thing to fret about. I was thinking Maggie and I were back on track, and now I would have to plan something fun for us to do including meeting my family. I realized that it would be good for her to see me with them and perhaps, then, she could see me as a tangible person, not an imaginary one from a letter. The two times we had already met had been brief.

Thanksgiving 2010 came and went in a flash — I'm not even sure if I cooked for everyone at my house that year or if we went to Peter's. I had a cold and was feeling lousy. When I get a cold, it is accompanied by a throbbing, frontal headache for three or four days which adds to my discomfort. On one of those mornings, I was lying in bed, feeling very angry. In fact, I wanted to wake up Stuart who was sleeping peacefully next to me and yell at him. I knew yelling at him to demand he comfort me would be nonproductive and would probably make things between us worse than they already were. I wanted to be comforted but I knew our relationship had gone way beyond where that was possible to ask from him. I yearned for a husband to hear my frustrations about this headache pain which I believed to be emotional as well as physical. The two dimensions seemed to go hand in hand, and I wondered if I could ever understand what was keeping them together. Since I knew I wouldn't get any comfort from Stuart, I decided to seek solace by writing in my journal and hoped that exercise would provide some relief.

I wrote that my current headaches were most likely physical due to my sensitive head. More importantly, I wrote about endurance and how much longer I could live with Stuart. I had put off making a decision, but I knew I could not move ahead until I had done so. My marriage was a farce, and tolerating it was taking its toll. At times, I could be myself, but then, in a moment, I got those black feelings of hopelessness and despair with physical pain thrown in. I was confused. I was moving ahead in understanding myself and my past, but I seemed stuck in my marriage. I was aware that I would have to make a decision about my marriage eventually; but, I felt it more important to concentrate on myself and tie up the loose ends of my past before dealing with Stuart — intuitively I sensed I would be in a stronger place if I resolved my personal issues.

I pulled myself out of the funk, and as soon as my cold was gone, I visited Ruby again. Since Christmas was coming, I took the tree and the decorations I had bought her the previous year. Her spirits were better overall, but she rarely got out of bed. She wasn't reading anymore, which had been a favorite pastime of hers. From her bed, she could watch me set up and decorate the tree. She was not in the same house as the previous year so this made the experience different. I involved her by asking her where to hang a particular ornament. As I was decorating the tree, I thought that this would be her last Christmas, and I wondered how her death would come. I felt it would be peaceful since she was with her second son's family who obviously cared for her — unlike her other son's family — and she wasn't in any pain. Hospice would make sure she did not suffer in any way.

My immune system must have been low because I got another cold at Christmas. Stuart and I got through the holidays on an even keel since I did not attempt to rock the boat by challenging him in any way; but I was starting to question whether my marriage to him was actually making me sick.

Soon after Christmas, Maggie came for our luncheon date with her new friend, Keith, whom she had just started to date. We met with my son Peter and daughter-in-law Erin and their two daughters, Keira and Ailish, who were around six and three years old. Erin and Peter were easy going and sociable so lunch was relaxed and conversation flowed. The two girls were their usual cute selves and behaved well in spite of the long lunch on restaurant chairs. It was gratifying to me for Maggie to see me with family, especially when my granddaughters fought over who was going to sit next to me. After lunch, the men went their way — Keith had to leave to go home to Connecticut and Peter had to go back

Peter, Erin & daughters
2009

Shadows and Light

to work. Erin, Maggie, the two girls, and I drove up to a dollhouse store in New Hampshire. This was part of my Christmas gift to them, and I thought it would be enjoyable for Maggie to come with us. The store was overflowing with every imaginable type of dollhouse furniture and accessories, and it was fun exploring and picking out what the girls wanted for their dollhouse. Maggie seemed to appreciate our outing as well. I thought my plan was working as I had intended — Maggie got to see me in assorted roles as a grandmother, mother, and mother-in-law.

I had invited Stuart to come to lunch to meet Maggie (and offered him an out about coming to the doll house store) but he had declined to accompany me. He seemed rather vague about his excuse. In fact, he had no real reason. In retrospect, it was probably for the best since I was more relaxed without him there. I took it to be another indication, on his part, that he was pulling away from me and my family and no longer investing in us.

After seeing Maggie on the weekend following Christmas, it was time to visit Ruby again and take down the Christmas tree. I hadn't seen her since before Christmas, and on seeing her, I noticed a significant change in her status. She looked as if she had shrunk in her bed, appearing smaller and frailer. She was barely conscious and her voice had diminished to a whisper. When I dismantled the tree, I thought, "The lights on the tree are now out, and the light in Ruby is rapidly fading. Death is creeping in." She wanted me to give her a short Reiki treatment, and I did. There were few words spoken that day. Before I left, I walked over to the head of Ruby's bed and took her hand as I said goodbye.

"This is the end," she whispered.

"I know," I said as I bent down so we could give each other a kiss. Words at this point were not even needed. We both knew what was happening, and she appeared to be at peace.

A week later, Ruby was unconscious but still alive, so I went again for a visit. When I got to the house in the early afternoon, her daughter-in-law was obviously stressed. Ruby was propped up in bed, and her breathing indicated she was near the end. I took the daughter-in-law aside to calm her down and suggested she take a break; I would stay with Ruby for a while. There was a CD playing which I changed to the one I had brought with me. I told Ruby, in case she could hear me, "I think you will like this music more." Actually, it was one meant for people in their last stage of life and had appropriate, soothing music on it. I proceeded to pull a chair next to Ruby's bed, getting comfortable since I was going to be there for a while. I took her hand in mine and could sense that she knew I was there. Her breathing was noisy and stopped for a few seconds, then started up and stopped, started again.

In this way, I waited out Ruby's last moments. Then, as I was listening to her breaths, there was a time when she did not breathe again, and I realized she had taken her last breath. Her life on this earth was over. I felt sure her husband and her third son were on the other side to help her cross over and welcome her into the afterlife. I stayed with her a few seconds and went to find her daughter-in-law.

What a privilege that she let me be with her when she took her last breath. I believe she waited for me. I had told her I would be with her to the end and I was, but I had never thought it was going to be two and a half years to the end. I had always been a bit afraid of how I would feel when Ruby did eventually die. I need not have been. It was so natural and peaceful — at home with her family — and I felt I had done all that I possibly could for her. I was strangely calm and not emotional, which I thought I might have been.

It was only after Ruby had written the testimonial for my brochure that I had realized what a profound effect I had had on her. Maybe I really was a healer; the energy work had been helpful to her, as she said, "in finding and exploring untapped mental and physical strength."

As I reflected on Ruby after she died, I thought about the words, "To give is to receive." Certainly, I was familiar with the expression but had never thought about its meaning until now. I had given Ruby my time, my understanding, and my best efforts at creating periods of relaxation for her with the Reiki sessions. I had given of myself as much as I was able. Perhaps because of all of this she had come to closure in her life and to peace about the inevitable.

I learned much from spending time with Ruby. She gave me confidence in my role as a healer and helped me to believe that I was on the right path. As a result, I gained confidence I could succeed in my Wei Chi practice. I also acquired firsthand knowledge of death and dying as something not to be afraid of. She challenged me intellectually by asking a lot of questions. She also helped me to experience joy in the simple things of life: a touch, a gentle summer breeze, a vibrant flower in bloom. We both gave each other love and lots of laughter.

I believe Ruby came into my life for a reason. Our relationship was a unique one. We were two souls connected on an unconscious level and could intuitively understand what the other one needed. Since I could never reconcile or talk with either of my parents before they died, Ruby gave me the opportunity to relive what might have been with my parents. My mother had Alzheimer's so — no matter what our relationship had been — it would have been impossible to make any reconciliation with her at the time of her death. I am sure, in some ways, Ruby represented a mother figure of the kind I never had, when she poured her heart out to me and understood me. I felt I really knew Ruby in the short period I visited her but I never knew my mother after fifty-plus years. Ruby and I both had difficult relationships with our mothers, another way in which we resonated with each other.

It would have been possible under different circumstances to reconcile with my father since he took months to die and there were multiple opportunities for us to talk, but he was unable to. I did give him an opportunity to be personal with me when I asked, "Do you believe in the afterlife?" He had nodded yes but had said nothing to extend the conversation. After that, we had sat in silence until one of us changed the subject. There was another day when my father was apneic and everyone thought his time had come, but he rallied and lived for a couple more months. Diana had said that my father crossed over once but came back to live longer since he had more work to do. I think he must have crossed over temporarily the time he was apneic. I so wanted him to make some amends with me. How I wished he had! It would have meant much to me and hastened me down my healing path.

By the way, I still have the Christmas tree I bought for Ruby, and each year when I decorate it, I take time to think of her and our time together.

Chapter 26
Some Dark Days

Sometime in February 2011— that is, a little less than four months into the experience — the excitement of having a shop and starting a healing practice started to wane. Reality struck like a swift punch to the ego. The winter was dragging on. No matter what Kim and I did to get paying clients — and we were not professional marketers — they were few and far between. We did the usual: put up flyers, distributed brochures in local business, and advertised in the local newspaper. In a free monthly clinic, we offered hour-long Wei Chi healing sessions. It was our hope people might sign up for a longer series. Some did, but the effort did not produce the numbers we needed. I took a workshop on marketing with social media — we utilized Facebook — so I could understand the process better. While I knew we had to have a website and I was going to look into creating one, I realized I did not want to do this. Web design was something totally out of my comfort zone.

That winter, I became painfully aware that, while I had wanted to be a healer and not a marketer, I had somehow allowed myself to be signed up as a marketer! I was now stunned to realize that my relationship with Kevin and the retail shop was not my ticket to a full practice.

The shop was a bottomless pit for consuming time and energy. I staffed the shop every Tuesday through Friday from 11 to 5, and Kim did the weekends. The days were long, and as a result of not having many clients, they afforded me plenty of time to think or accomplish any work I had to do. Some of it was personal, such as writing to Maggie, but work also included cleaning and arranging the display cabinets. This work was neither bringing in a salary to me as a sales clerk nor business to me as a practitioner.

Because of our location in the basement of the old factory at the end of a long hallway, we did not get much foot traffic. An occasional interested person would come in to check out our space to see what we did or to buy crystals — our biggest sellers.

We had no budget for outreach. I felt a website would help spread the word and get Kim and me more clients. Since I was not the owner of the business, however, I did not feel I should have to pay for a website. It was clear that Kevin was not going to invest anything more to help us pull through. I swallowed the bullet and left my comfort zone to take it upon myself to have a website created.

Fortunately, Kim had a friend who designed websites so I had him do ours. He was pleasant to work with and took care of everything technical. With Katie's help on the design and color scheme and a logo created by Linette's son, we had our website up and running in a few weeks. The web designer taught me how to post events, news, and other things, and I took on responsibility for maintaining it.

I thought Kevin would be really pleased with the website as it would also bring clients to the shop, but he did not have much to offer other than a lukewarm response. It felt familiar because this was very similar to how my parents would have reacted. No matter whether I had worked really hard on a project and had done a good job, their response would have been minimal and it would contain no real praise. In this instance, unlike years ago

Shadows and Light

when my parents had been under-reactive, I did not let Kevin's response get me down. The website was an attractive, well-designed one, logical and easy to navigate. Besides, Kim and I needed it to generate clients for our practices.

One day at the end of February, after a day at the shop just across the border in Haverhill, Massachusetts, I drove the twenty minutes home in the New England early evening darkness. When I pulled up to our house, it was in darkness as well. There was not a light to be seen. It was as if no one lived there. Is this where Stuart and I live? I asked myself. It did not seem like a home to me anymore. It was a house occupied by two strangers.

Stuart should have been in the house, but I wasn't sure he was or was not. When I opened the garage door, I could see Stuart's car. This made me think he was inside, but there were no lights. Had he fallen asleep?

When I entered the house, I flicked the light in the hallway and shouted, "I'm home."

I thought I heard a murmur from upstairs in the office, but Stuart did not come down to greet me. When I had lived in Newton, upon returning home, I recalled being warmly greeted by our dog Muffy. There was no greeting whatsoever that evening.

I hung my coat and went into the kitchen. There was no aroma of a meal waiting. I turned on lights, and the room was brightly lit — if not yet welcoming. I went over to the phone and, as I was checking my messages, I heard Stuart descend the stairs into the hallway and then come into the kitchen.

At that moment I was overcome with anger at having entered a dark house. He knew I was coming home at this time. Why had he not, at least, turned on the outside lights and the kitchen light to welcome me home? A bonus would have been to see the table set and the leftovers from yesterday ready to heat up. Was I asking too much?

And wouldn't it have been lovely for Stuart to come down to greet me when I called to him. That's what I still wanted even if our relationship seemed well beyond that stage. We were now each one for herself and himself.

What I still wanted was for Stuart to say, "You look exhausted. Go sit down while I find us something to eat. Let me pour you a glass of wine."

I wanted to be cared for. At that moment I spoke harshly to him. I didn't want a roommate who hardly acknowledged me.

When I finished venting my anger with him standing silently, I realized it was time to start dinner if I was going to eat any time soon. I had leftovers from last night's dinner, and I was thinking of those and a frozen vegetable. When I looked into the refrigerator, tired and wanting an easy solution for the dinner, I could not find what I had planned to put together.

"Stuart," I said calmly, "where are the leftovers?"

Stuart said he had eaten them for lunch. He said it matter-of-factly and made neither an apology nor offered to help make a meal. He said just that he had gotten caught up in his work all day. He had eaten what was most handy for lunch and he had lost track of time in the afternoon.

It was as if he lived alone — or with his mother. This scenario was happening in one version or another all too often. Had I had a sense of receiving regularly from this relationship, I might have easily overlooked what had happened that evening and together we might have prepared a meal. But, his lack of attention to our marriage was occurring too often, and I was not in any mood to be indulgent.

I found something for us to have for dinner — I usually have an "emergency" meal backup in the freezer. After a hasty preparation and a meal spent avoiding each other and being minimally polite, somehow the atmosphere cleared enough for us to talk. I was surprised that Stuart wanted to talk after I had been so angry with him. I have to admit I hoped that he might have felt guilty because I thought he should after he had been caught being inconsiderate, but he did not seem to be feeling any guilt at all.

"Separation is an option," he said, "but I do not want to go through the hassle of finding someone new."

He reiterated that he was loving and affectionate and that he did all that he could.

I almost wanted to say, "Is this the Stuart that I know whom you are talking about?"

He said, "I like myself the way I am and see no reason to change. You don't know how much I really care about you even though I think I show it."

He talked about how, although Kevin was a great person, he had no handle on what was going on with us as a couple and what to do about it.

Although I found his comment that his biggest hassle in a separation would be having to find someone new for a relationship rather odd, I felt our conversation had cleared the air, and I now knew Stuart was thinking about separation but did not appear ready to act on it.

While he had opened up a bit, he seemed defensive and did not mention how sad he would be to separate or how he might miss me. I still wanted to be important to him just as I had wanted to be important to my parents. It did not make sense that I should be asking this of him. I now needed to be able to ask this of someone else — that is, get out of this relationship and prepare myself for another.

That, I knew, would be painful. I understood exactly what Stuart meant by not wanting the hassle of finding someone else, but I did not mention this to him and I wished he had not mentioned it to me. I assumed he had spent the last few months trying to rationalize his feelings — his way of buttoning up his emotions to keep in control — and had come to these conclusions.

Hearing him say that he did not need to change since he was fine as he was, I knew there was no hope for us as a couple. The fact was both of us had to change in order to move ahead together, and I could not see Stuart changing since his mind was made up. To me, it was another step toward the end but I did not know yet how it was going to play out in the drama of the actual separating.

In the spring of 2011, my automatic writing was full of messages about writing. I had never thought of myself as a writer nor had I ever had a desire to be a writer. Automatic writing had not struck me as the work of a "writer" but as therapy of some sort. In automatic writing, the words flowed and I did not have to think about what I was writing or how I was writing it. Up to the time of my undertaking automatic writing, I had struggled to write anything; the words were stilted or lacked passion. I had associated being a "writer" with something difficult.

In the mid-1960s, in the beginning of my psych rotation in nursing school, one of my professors had told me, "Susan, you have to learn how to share in your writing." I had no idea what she meant. When I pushed her to explain, she said I needed to express my personality, my preferences, my fears, and so forth, but I was so shut down that I had no idea who I was. My identity had been shattered by family abandonment and sexual abuse. There was a big question mark at my core as to who I was. I just didn't know this about myself so how could I share what I didn't know?

Two decades later, in the early nineties, I had taken a weekend writing workshop called "Writing on Both Sides of Your Brain." As workshoppers introduced themselves, I realized some were published writers. I was quickly intimidated. But, I needn't have been. The instructor created an environment in which I was able to concentrate on myself and do the assigned writing. I left

Sunday afternoon with new ideas and concrete ways that I could put to use when I wrote employee evaluations — but I still had not accessed writing more personally, as employee evaluations did not call for personal writing.

Now in 2011, the messages I got from my automatic writing were that I needed to write an article, a blog, or poetry using my "words of wisdom." While I had thought about writing an article about the Wei Chi healing system and/or my experience as a hospice volunteer with Ruby, I could not — in spite of the urgings of my automatic writing sessions — get motivated to do so; but the notion of writing "words of wisdom" kept popping up in my automatic writing. I was not sure what this automatic writing was about nor how I could make use of the idea of producing "words of wisdom." Was I supposed to write about myself and my experiences for these articles I had been thinking of writing?

Mattie came to give me her advice. "My dear, the time has come; no more excuses. You are a lot like me — yet not like me. Why don't you write? It would be so freeing. Just do it. You are a far better writer than your husband, Stuart. His writing is flat and has no emotion or passion, and you have so much of that. And now to sleep. May your life continue to be rich. Think of me often; I am with you."

I felt so lucky to have Mattie in my life. She knew me well and what my weaknesses were that she had to work against.

In April, we scheduled another weekend open house at the Wei Chi Healing Center and Shop. Kevin who had come back from Arizona to participate in the event had already asked some other psychics he knew to come to do readings. Katie, Kim, Linette, and I were all scheduled to give talks or offer Wei Chi healing sessions during that weekend. Rita, a friend of Linette's for many years, had now joined our Wei Chi circle. She had her own hair salon and did mediumship on the side. Rita had taken the first part of the Wei Chi training and — being a natural at it — she fit right into our original group of four.

I was scheduled to talk on my journey past pain. Although I had taken a public-speaking course several years earlier in one of my many adult education classes and actually had some practice speaking before a group, I hated standing up and talking before people and had always avoided it. When I thought about giving this talk, however, I sensed I could do it — I just had to calm myself. I prepared an informative and emotional presentation about my past physical and emotional pain and how I dealt with it.

The Saturday morning of the open house, I woke up with a really bad cough and felt wiped out even though I had slept well. I had had a mild cold that week but was not coughing. When I got to the shop, I told Kevin, "I can't seem to stop coughing. I won't be able to give my talk." With his characteristic understanding, he rearranged the schedule so I didn't have to speak.

I was glad not to deliver my talk, but not doing so felt like a cop-out. I had let everybody down including myself. It was not a big leap to wonder if I had "manufactured" this cough. A cough is located in the throat, which is the *chakra* — the energy center — of the neck area associated with communication. Was I avoiding confronting my fear of speaking or had I developed this cough because I was not ready to communicate some of this information about myself? This reserve about divulging my inner life was different from fear of public speaking and the distinction made sense. Once I accepted that I was not ready to share certain information about myself, the cough lessened and was gone by the next day.

For the rest of the weekend, I helped out wherever I could — whether it was talking up Wei Chi to anyone who came in or working the register. One of the psychics whom Kevin had asked to give readings was Jen. When I first met her that Saturday, the energetic connection I felt impelled me to ask her for a reading. When I sat across from her for that reading, she took a moment to collect her thoughts and started right in.

"You have been sexually abused."

I nodded yes.

"There were several times. First you were molested as a child. Next there was the group of boys when you were twelve. Your brother was present and watched it all."

I was astounded that she "knew" about these incidents and therefore impressed by her psychic skills.

"It destroyed your foundation," she continued, "and your sacral chakras."

In my energy field, Jen "saw" a dagger in each of my shoulders and she seemed surprised. "I have never seen daggers go so far up. I see that one is related to the sexual abuse and the other is related to your ex-husband."

"What about my ex-husband?"

"Did he rape you?" Jen said.

"No, absolutely not," I replied, knowing Michael never would have raped me.

At the end of the session with Jen, she told me she was trained to do soul retrievals and suggested that I might benefit from one. A soul retrieval is a classic shamanic method to search for a person's lost piece of soul and restore it. I took her card and said I needed time to think about doing a soul retrieval. This session with Jen really shook me up, and I thought about it for the rest of the day as I continued to help out at the open house — whether I was at the cash register or answering questions for people.

That evening, still absorbed in what Jen had said, I made the connection to a party Michael and I had attended while living in Paris. Michael was intoxicated, but I knew I had not had too much to drink since I would have kept to my policy of no more

Shadows and Light

than two drinks at a social event. I never was much of a drinker, and being married to a man who liked his drink, I always had to remain sober in order to be ready to drive home. I had talked to an attractive man — even flirted a bit — but I could not recall what had happened after that time or anything about leaving the party or how we got home. That limited memory of talking to the man and flirting with him had recurred over the years, and although I could feel no emotion attached to it, I couldn't help but wonder about what had really happened, if anything.

Jen's reading made me realize that, whatever had happened, it must have been horrific if I had blocked it out from memory. Perhaps some of my present pain issues were due to abuse I might have experienced that night. There had to be a connection, and I was determined to find out what it was. I also wanted to find out why these memories were resurfacing now? Perhaps a soul retrieval would provide some answers?

I had been zapped fifteen times at age twenty-four, as part of electroconvulsive therapy (ECT) as it is called now, to alleviate depression. These shocks had affected my brain. Now, as I contemplated a soul retrieval, I wondered how the shocks had also affected my emotions, my soul, my spiritual being. As a way of answering these questions, a soul retrieval offered me possible information I had not had before. Having decided to have a soul retrieval, in preparation for working with Jen, I bought a couple of books to learn more about the experience. One of the books was *Shamanic Journeying / A Beginner's Guide* by Sandra Ingerman.

Weeks before we were to have Easter dinner with Tim and Amanda, I had told Stuart that they had invited us for a family get-together with them. A couple of days before Easter, however, Stuart announced that his family had invited us for Easter dinner.

"But, Tim and Amanda invited us a while ago, and I told

them we were coming. I asked you weeks ago if that was all right with you. They are expecting us."

Because things were so miserable between Stuart and me right then, I did not want to spend the whole day with his family — especially because the gathering was at his ex-wife's house. While I had anticipated the pleasure being with my family all day, I was, however, willing to compromise and split the time between the two families. Since I did not really want to go to his family's house at all, I don't know why I was willing to compromise, except that I was characteristically trying to be the peacemaker regardless of what I needed. Stuart, however, was adamant about going to his family and only to his family. We went back and forth and could not come up with a compromise wherein we would go to both houses. I suppose I was still trying to keep up a public façade of a relationship, but Stuart was not. He simply refused to include Tim and Amanda in any part of his day. It was as if he had written my family off and could not be bothered being polite with them.

Tim, Amanda & sons
2009

Sticking to my sense of a compromise being the best solution to maintain some illusion that I was a viably married woman, I decided to go to Tim and Amanda's by myself, stay for a while and then drive the half hour over to Stuart's family later in the afternoon. When it was time to leave Tim and Amanda's, I was reluctant to go, but I felt some loyalty to my marriage — if it could still be called that — so I left my family too soon for my taste and headed for Stuart's family party.

When I got to his ex-wife's house, everyone was in the back yard, observing the children in an egg hunt. Easter was on April 24 that year and so the snow was gone and the ground on which the children were egg hunting was again firm after a lengthy mud season. I spied Stuart standing on the sidelines, and I started toward him. Since I had passed up extra time being with my family to join his, I felt he owed me something and so I was ready for him to show some appreciation. When he saw me, he obviously didn't think he owed me anything, since he did not walk over to greet me. In fact, he barely acknowledged my presence. My sense of reciprocity was clearly not his — but didn't I already know this?

His cold response activated my abandonment issues, which brought up feeling like an outcast in his family as I had once felt in my birth family. When I attempted to have conversations with his daughters and the other adults present, I read their energy as guarded and not connecting with me. I didn't know what it was, but since I am so sensitive to other people's energies, I know I was not imagining this. That Easter was the first time Stuart and I had gone separately to his family get-togethers so how could anyone — even though they didn't say anything — not have noticed? Maybe Stuart had even told his family that we weren't getting along and that was the reason for their lack of interest in me.

I supposed I was an outcast, and it was time, seeing as how my marriage was on the rocks, to accept that. In his family, I had become just one of many women who had been in and out of Stuart's life. We were around for a few years and then we were gone. I felt that was how I was perceived — one of a string of women whom they needn't invest in.

Shadows and Light

Such a realization was both liberating, as it signaled that I could leave this family of his more easily than I might have had they been attached to me, but it was also unsettling. I was on my way to being single again and I was not ready for that. Additionally, was I caught in the feeling of "Susan failed again"?

We left at the same time, each in our own car. In the quiet of the trip, I was able to do some more thinking. Why had I left my family where I was the welcomed mother and grandmother to go the Stuart's where I was the woman on the way out? I guess I was still trying to hang on and not ready to cut the cord just yet, but it was apparent our relationship had deteriorated significantly. I probably would not make the effort to be with Stuart's family again, I told myself as I made my way back to Atkinson. That was a sad realization. I was withdrawing more from my marriage, and while that is what I wanted to do, it did not feel good. It was as if our marriage were headed toward a cliff, and sooner or later unless something intervened, our marriage would fall over the edge and be permanently shattered.

But the marriage would hold on for yet a while.

Chapter 27
More Healing and Integration

In May 2011, there was a psychic/metaphysical expo in southern Maine — just across the New Hampshire border — and attending and exhibiting was something we felt had to be done to promote the shop and attract clients. Kevin, Edgar, Kim, and I went and set up a table with informational handouts to introduce Wei Chi to people and promote visits to our shop. We sold crystals and other paraphernalia. The weekend involved a lot of set-up, much conversation, being "on" most of the time and then taking everything down. The experience proved tiring, and I did not find it fulfilling in any way. I had wanted to be a Wei Chi practitioner, and I had become a shop manager. I was getting discouraged about how my time was being used up with supporting the marketing and the maintenance of the business and not with being a practitioner. This discouragement was made worse because I was starting to observe Kevin and Edgar losing their commitment to the shop. Their withdrawal meant other people had to step up if the shop was to survive. I was willing to contribute to keeping the shop open, but I was unwilling be the leader. Something had to give.

The day following the exhibition, Edgar came into my office at the shop. As soon as I looked up to acknowledge him, he began to rant loudly about how I was not meeting his and Kevin's expectations of how I was to support the shop and about how little business Kim and I were bringing in.

"I am supposed to be responsible for getting myself clients and helping out in the shop," I replied, as I kept my cool. "I have been doing that. I never expected to be in charge of marketing."

His viewpoint differed markedly from mine as to what my commitment was to the shop, and there was no agreement to be reached. Later, he and Kevin had a meeting, after which Edgar came back and apologized. The apology was appreciated but it did not include a clear sense of how he and Kevin were going to salvage the shop. The retail part had been Kevin's idea after all, an idea he had sprung on Kim and me.

I have always liked a well-run, orderly workplace with clear communication, most likely because my astrological sign is Virgo. Our shop was none of these, and I was dismayed that I had allowed myself to be involved with the business side in the first place. It seemed to parallel so many other times when I had allowed myself to be involved beyond what I had wanted. I decided to continue to do what I had been doing — but not take on more — and proposed we have meetings to clarify each of our expectations and to articulate our responsibilities. It was like being in my marriage all over again. Was I doomed to an endless cycle of repetition? I knew I had done things to create the little success the shop had realized to date, but it would take a lot more patience and hard work to make the shop a big success. In view of my barely functioning marriage and the need to think of how I would live a future as a single person, I needed to shift my focus back to myself instead of allowing myself to be distracted by the needs of the shop.

It was easy for me to be distracted. I had allowed the shop to take up a lot of my energy. I had to admit that that had been a relief since it distracted me from life at home. I needed now to stop allowing myself to be distracted. I had to come to a decision that Stuart and I could not continue as we were, but I was at a loss

Shadows and Light

about moving that decision along.

One evening, as I was doing my automatic writing, I sensed Mattie hovering over me.

"Is that you, Mattie?"

"Yes, it is, my dear. You are in a pickle deciding what to do. Kick him out or be miserable — not much of a choice — but you know what to do in order to keep your sanity and mine. I don't want to see you making another big mistake. Staying with Stuart would keep you from moving ahead. Watch the flowers come up and think of me often; I am here for you. Find your deep roots — go down deep and go up high searching everywhere to see what you can find. Goodnight, my dear, and pleasant dreams. Oh yes, keep writing. Do you see what I see? Carved in stone. No not in stone, but malleable and supple. Not tense and tired but loose and free to go where you want. The pain of it all will fade until it is hardly discernible on the screen of life, not to return except when you need a reminder. Keep working and keep writing."

Leave it to Mattie to come in at the right time with advice. At some part of myself, I knew it had been a long time since I wanted to work things out with Stuart. What I wanted was my single life back. This was a change from the Easter party at his ex-wife's when I had not felt myself ready to be single again and now being single was what I yearned for. I thought about what Mattie had said and how the mature — and effective — response to my dilemma would be to give myself and Stuart a deadline to be single again!

The first thing I needed to check was whether it would be feasible to buy Stuart out — or did we have to sell? If I deduced I could afford to buy him out, I had to be frank and tell him, "I want to stay in the condo alone." If he agreed to being bought out as I believed he would — he had told me he would not want to stay in the house — I needed to add, "You can have three months to pack up and move out. I think this will give us enough time to tie up the loose ends."

This financial homework followed by a deadline idea sounded good to my rational self, but my courage was not up to demanding what I needed. If the circumstances had been different and he were abusive and I were afraid for my safety, I would have moved out myself until he quit the premises. Because none of these things were true, I waited on taking a firm decision. I knew I was deciding to be miserable for a while — anticipating the endless time of living with a man who had become a roommate I did not like — but I was a hanger-on, unable to make right decisions. If Stuart made a move, the decision would not be mine. That's what I had done with Michael. I had waited until I could hardly stand it any longer, until the bitter end when I made the decision. Maybe the break with Stuart would play out differently, but I wasn't doing my part any differently than with Michael. I supposed I needed another "bitter end." If I wasn't doing anything differently, what else might I expect?

Why did I think it was all right to let myself in for a hard time like that?

My soul retrieval with Jen was scheduled for the end of May 2011. Since I was not sure what to expect, I decided to go in with an open mind and let my senses be on high alert. As I was lying on the table in Jen's healing space, surrounded by her sparkling crystals and spiritual ornaments, I had different sensations as she worked on me. She burned sage at my feet and blew energy into my pelvic area where she had seen a band of red. I felt the energy come in and was aware of it moving around my body. Then I noticed a pain in my left side which moved up to my left shoulder. When Jen was finished and I tried to sit up, my body felt fine but my head was spinning. It took a while to ground myself before I could get up off the table. We talked for a bit, and Jen told me that her spirit guide, from whom she got information for her clients, said that I had had nine different traumatic, abusive attacks. This was a lot for one person. I didn't want to think about it — nine traumas were a little too much for my mind to handle. I just wanted to get home to rest. When I did get home, Stuart was out playing tennis so I lay down for two hours in the master bedroom trying to make sense of what had just happened. What were those nine incidents? I was exhausted, physically and mentally, just thinking about it all.

The next two weeks after the session with Jen were quiet ones. I had a couple of times when my spirits were low, but overall, I had more energy and very little pain in my shoulders. Because what little pain I had was fleeting if anything, I thought the soul retrieval had helped. The evening before I was to see Jen for a follow-up session, I asked Wei Chi for a message.

"Your body is still fighting for survival. You will open up soon," I heard.

That made a lot of sense because I felt I was still struggling and fighting myself. Wondering what had really happened to me those nine times, I wrote a list of nine events, but I was not sure they would all even be considered traumatic. For instance, there was the summer of 1962 when I started working at the Howard Johnson's in West Roxbury, close to where my family had moved. When I was out back in the storeroom, the manager — he was older than I and already had a wife and kids — would grab my shoulders, pull me toward him, and proceed to kiss me. He was very strong so it was impossible to pull away. Needless to say, I learned how to avoid the storeroom when he was around. It felt repulsive, but I would not consider it traumatic. For me, it was minor compared to other abuses. I doubt that I told anyone. In the early 1960s, the words "sexual harassment" were not in one's vocabulary. Did that mean there were other events that I could not remember that were actually the traumatic ones Jen had been told?

Shadows and Light

At the next session, Jen did more energy work on me. Afterwards, for homework, she had me take each incident on the list and do a specific visualization in which I cut the cord — the energetic connection. At home, I completed the assignments and cut the energetic cords nine times, but I had no new insights while doing these visualizations. I was especially aware that, with two of the events — the 1971 party in Paris and the 1964 summer on Cape Cod — I needed more insight into what had happened. After the visualization exercises, I still felt bound up with the pain of these two events. It was as if my mind was never going to be free of whatever I needed to let go of concerning what happened in Paris and on Cape Cod. I longed for the day when my shoulders and neck would stop hurting, and I knew that I would have to do some letting go to have no pain.

At the end of June, I met with Jen again and she pulled out black, icky junk that she "saw" in my shoulders and chest. A part of my soul was still hanging out there, so she restored it in me. My brother, Mark, had a message for me from the afterlife. He apologized for not standing up and protecting me from the group of boys when I was twelve. I had always wondered if he had been there in the basement. Now I knew for sure. He said his life had essentially been a mess and he asked for my forgiveness. Of course, I forgave him, as he was as screwed up as I during his childhood. In adulthood, I sought help to get my life together, whereas he didn't. I wished he were alive so I could have talked to him. Maybe he would have known what had really happened to me and why or be in a place he could talk about it. Some years earlier, when I asked him in a letter, he had had nothing to say about the incident when I was twelve.

In my heart, I wanted to believe that he loved me, but his actions, his silence, made it hard to believe he did — at least, in the way I needed to be loved.

And why had Mark called me "Susie Slut" on occasion when

Shadows and Light

I was home from Saint Mary's? I always recalled his nickname for me but I never knew what he was referring to. Now I assume it was the incident when I was twelve and he was present — or was it and was he?

A few years before this session with Jen, when I was up at my cabin on Maidstone Lake, I was talking to Zack, who married Linda a few years after my brother left her. He told me something I never knew. My brother and Zack became friends while attending Hoosac School, the Episcopal boarding school where my father had taught after he was suddenly booted out of Haiti by the dictator, François Duvalier. I assume my father was offered a job there before Christmas of 1958. When I was not at St. Mary's or away working for the summer, I spent time at the Hoosac School.

"It was a school for boys with emotional problems," Zack told me.

Zack & Mark
circa 1959

I had not known that.

Zack went on to tell me that he had been expelled from his previous high school for bad behavior. And why was Mark sent there? I have no idea why my parents chose for him to go to Hoosac, instead of another boarding school, while the rest of our family was in Haiti. Mark had attended Shattuck Military School when my father had taught there, but something untoward had happened. He was taken out and attended the local high school until we moved. Zack did not know why Mark had been pulled out either, but he told me another interesting thing that day we talked. He said I was known at Hoosac as the "Ice Queen."

After this June session with Jen, remembering the conversation with Zack, I thought about Mark a lot and understood that there would always be blanks that would remain unfilled. One evening as I was doing my automatic writing, these words came to me.

> They called her the "Ice Queen."
> She was frozen in fear,
> Afraid they would come back and kill her.
> Her heart was cold, and her blood ran thin.
> Her smile was just a crack of the mouth.
> She had forgotten how to laugh.
> They stayed away; she was irreproachable.
> And so, she remained for many years
> Until she realized,
> All that had happened to her and she gradually thawed.

That summer, Stuart and I did not make any plans for a vacation or even a short getaway. As our relationship was so strained, I knew I didn't want to go away with him for very long, but then I came up with an idea. I thought we were due for a relationship conversation since it had been a while. When I had spoken to Stuart earlier about separating, he had said he needed "more time before making any decisions." I had no idea if this decision involved a separation and I wanted to know, so I took action. I found a quiet inn overlooking a lake in New Hampshire where we could spend two nights on the Fourth of July weekend. One day, we found a woodsy trail in a nearby nature preserve and went for a walk. This helped calm me; I am not sure if it helped Stuart; in any case, the walk did not produce a conversation. I looked for another venue. The inn had a private library, which was also used as a healing space — a very appropriate serene place to talk. When we were settled in comfy chairs facing each other, I asked Stuart, "What are we going to do? Neither one of us is happy, and it is time to come up with a plan. Are we going to split up and sell our condo?"

Characteristically — we were well matched in this regard — he again said that he needed more time before making any decisions. We discussed the condo, and I said, "If we split up, I would like to stay there." I can't recall his exact response about the condo, but I learned clearly it would not be an issue if I wanted to stay — as long as I could reimburse him for his share. I did bring up sprucing up two of the bathrooms in the event that we had to sell our condo. I was surprised that he agreed since he didn't like to spend money when it wasn't absolutely necessary. This project wouldn't cost much, however, because any expenditure would be for new countertops for the vanities and accessories. Perhaps it was a way on his part to appease me. I don't know, but he was amenable.

Redoing the bathrooms would take a lot of labor, and I knew I would be doing the majority of stripping wallpaper and painting since it was not only my idea but I was the one who was most likely to benefit from the results. I didn't expect Stuart would pitch in to help except for installing light fixtures or towel rails, which he could handle easily.

When we left the inn to go back home, I felt the weekend had been successful in that we had talked and I had stayed focused and in control of my reactions. Maybe the change of scenery even helped us to communicate. Once again, I accepted that Stuart needed more time — this was the second time he had said so — but I wondered if he was ever going to come to a decision? I didn't feel angry at Stuart, but I did feel sad for myself that he was unable to do the work he needed to in order for us to

Shadows and Light

continue as a couple. I would have much preferred that, but he appeared metaphorically as dead as a doornail: no expression, no emotion, and very few words. At least, I knew he would not be precipitating a separation soon, nor would I since I had consciously made the decision to wait him out. I was in the midst of dealing with the shop business — or the lack thereof — as well as continuing to deal with my past, but I knew, at some point, this relationship issue would come to a head and I would need to take action.

I needed to review my options now so that I would have clarity then.

In mid-July, I had an individual session with Kevin. He wanted me to embrace life fully and all that it has to offer. My question was, "How can I embrace life when, some of the time, I am in pain and closed down?" I told him how I would make a change and then more old junk would resurface that I had to deal with. It was obvious that I was still holding onto negative stuff. In my desire to move on, I asked myself if it was really necessary to know exactly what happened to me. I knew I didn't need the details, but there were still those couple of incidents that I would have liked filled in. I had a choice to make. Do I lie fallow in the field until a plow runs over me or do I bloom as a flower — albeit an odd one — in a field of wheat? In order to bloom, I would have to open up my heart more, feel more confidence, and continue to learn and grow. To bloom, I would breathe in life, letting the air flow. My muscles would be relaxed and my mind uncluttered.

Kevin gave me an assignment that would take a month to fulfill. For twenty-one days, I had to write about one thing I wanted to let go of and one thing I was ready to allow to become fertilizer in my growth garden. It was an interesting assignment as it gave me a lot to think about. The release could be anything —

something from my past or something current. For example, one of the days was Stuart's seventy-first birthday. I had bought him a present, a bag to carry his laptop in. When he opened it, he seemed pleased as he gave a partial smile but said nothing — not even to thank me. I decided to let it go because it would have been counterproductive to reproach him since our relationship was already strained enough. When I wrote that evening, I released both any anger toward Stuart for not thanking me for his present and the belief that I still needed him in my life. I fertilized my growth garden with appreciation for what others do for me.

Another evening when I was writing about what to release, I started to feel my shoulders tense up so I decided to release the pain and tension in my shoulders because I didn't need them anymore. Also, they hurt, wasted time, and did not allow me to be my true self. I decided that whenever I felt the pain or tension, I would try to identify who was sitting on my shoulders. As I kept writing my way through my twenty-one-day assignment, I wondered why I had not gone through with the suicide attempt when I was twenty-four and sought help, but as I was doing assignment after assignment, I realized I probably did not need to know any more, other than the fact I needed to learn from the experience. I fertilized my growth garden with love. I would try to love myself and others more. I still shortchanged myself — even though I was more accepting — by putting myself down. I knew I did not show my love for others enough by verbally telling them so; I would work on that as well.

That summer, not wanting to pick up Stuart's negative vibes, I put up an energetic shield between Stuart and me when we were in bed together. Even so, I was sleeping poorly — waking up and being unable to go back to sleep. I stayed over on my side of our king bed as close to the edge as I could get. I felt twinges of guilt because I didn't want to be near him anymore. As I lay awake one night, my mind wandered to a picture I had cut out of a magazine — a bathroom with a color scheme and beachy vibe that would be perfect for the guest bath. Maybe I would sleep better expending more energy — physical and mental — if I started redecorating the bathrooms. I had always liked doing projects around the house and especially enjoyed the results. In the morning, I told Stuart I was ready to start redecorating the bathrooms as we had agreed to do it a few weeks earlier. We picked out countertops for the vanities together, and while waiting for them to be installed, I started stripping the wallpaper.

    I spent one entire weekend stripping wallpaper. The walls of the guest bath and the powder room on the first floor both had outdated wallpaper. I planned to remove it and paint the walls. The wallpaper did not come off easily so I had to rent a wallpaper steamer. Standing on the ladder, feeling hot and steamy, I recalled the time I stripped wallpaper for my parents when they had moved into a new house in West Roxbury. My sons were in summer camp and I was at home not working, so I had offered to strip wallpaper and paint three upstairs bedrooms. The summer heat was assaultive. When it was done, however, I thought the rooms looked good. My parents hadn't seemed to appreciate all I had done, judging from their minimal praise for the job. Now, in my own home, I was hoping that Stuart would praise me — a bonus would be an offer to help. Why did I still need that sort of response? It was like I was a girl who needed affirmation from her parents?

    While up on the ladder, I did more thinking and fantasized how good the bathroom was going to look and how I would like to use it now that it would be decorated to my taste. Then an idea popped into my head. What if I moved out of the master bedroom and into the guest room? Then I could use the redecorated guest bath. It would be so freeing to be away from Stuart, have my own space. I would likely sleep better, too. What would Stuart think if I announced I was moving out of the master bedroom?

He might suspect something like that when he saw me putting all this energy into the bathrooms. I decided to wait and tell him after all the work was completed. I definitely wanted to stay in the condo, and now the bathrooms would look better and to my liking.

Thus, at last, began my active restructuring process of leaving Stuart.

By late that Sunday afternoon, when I had just finished getting the wallpaper off and was exhausted — Stuart walked by and stuck his head in and asked how I was doing.

"I'm beat and have some cleaning up to do before starting supper," I said. "I would appreciate it if you could take the steamer back to the hardware store."

"Okay, I have time now."

I hadn't minded the hard work, which after all would accrue to me, and appreciated that Stuart returned the steamer for me.

By the end of August, I had finished writing all twenty-one of my releases. Since there were a few consecutive days I had missed releasing, my last release was of the belief that I did not do a good job. I fertilized my growth garden with my intuitive because the majority of the releases came from it and I had received a lot of messages. I knew now that I did need to know more about the two "fuzzy" incidents. I could not remember the complete stories, just the facts leading up to them.

After I completed the twenty-one releases assignment, I had my two recurring dreams and remembered fragments the next day. The "bathroom" dream in which I could not find a clean bathroom stall had vastly improved. This time there was only a drop of urine on the toilet seat — not an uncommon occurrence — so I felt hopeful, that maybe all my excrement, my negative experiences, had been cleaned up. My other dream, "teeth falling out," had improved as well. I had connected this dream with the incidents I could not remember. The previous time I had had the dream, I had dreamed I had two loose teeth but neither had fallen out. These dreams confirmed that I still needed to know about the two "fuzzy" incidents. This was my interpretation of the dreams. I felt I had a growth spurt in my progress to understand myself and what had happened to me. There were times when I was feeling more confident and in control of my emotions, but my interactions with Stuart left me always on the alert as to how to respond. I'm afraid I fell into reaction more times than I wanted to.

By the middle of September, I had finished painting and Stuart had installed new light fixtures and towel rails. At last, the bathrooms were done, and I was pleased with the results. All this while, I had kept in mind that this work would lead to moving out of the master bedroom and I had looked forward to this change. Now I would have to tell Stuart.

Chapter 28
The End of My Second Marriage

"I am having trouble sleeping and so I have decided to move into the guest room," I told Stuart after the finishing touches were done on the bathrooms. It was the middle of September and it had become time to tell him that I was moving into the guest room. I don't recall my exact words but I know I said it simply.

"You can have the master bath to yourself, and I will use the guest bath."

Stuart gave me a strange look which I was unable to interpret — was he feeling the relief I was feeling or was he confused? Maybe he had already figured out why I had put all the energy into fixing up the bathrooms! I waited to see if my statement of moving into the guest room was going to precipitate his own response? He remained silent, seemingly accepting my decision. I was left with no clear idea of what he was thinking other than he did not want to talk and so I did not encourage him. If Stuart had wanted to discuss what was happening, I would have spoken with him.

As I look back, I realize that I was in a process of shutting Stuart out of my life. I had taken this step of isolating myself from Stuart and it was obvious to me that he had no desire to undo it. Was Stuart relieved that I had made a move? I had to conclude that he was perhaps and he, too, wanted to isolate himself from me.

What was important to me was to stick to my plan to separate from this man whom I didn't know anymore. I had lost the witty, intelligent, interesting man that I had fallen for eight years earlier. Was he still there? I didn't know.

Once relocated in the guestroom, which was much smaller than the bedroom I had known, I chose to sleep on a different side of the bed than I was accustomed to. At first, I felt disoriented, but from where I lay, I could look out to tall pine trees silhouetted in the moonlight and that was comforting. It was also comforting to know that, in the middle of the night, if I couldn't sleep or felt like writing, I could turn on the light and do what I wanted. I was soon looking forward to these night periods. I also felt a certain sense of freedom simply from being in a different bedroom from Stuart.

Our mutual office was in the loft area above the master bedroom. Stuart liked to work later than I, and so he had been going up to the loft to write on his new book at a time when I was ready for sleep. As a result, the light had been on while he was working on his computer long after I had gone to bed. I was often fuming that his light late at night was disturbing me. In my new bedroom, I could turn the light off when I wanted. My sleep patterns improved, and I began to awaken feeling refreshed.

I had not made a total separation from him, however, as I still had clothes and belongings in the master bedroom. Leaving them there felt like a compromise that would not last long since I was sure Stuart was on his way out and I was thinking that I would be moving back into the bedroom soon. I was starting to imagine what it would be like to live in the condo by myself and not have to deal with Stuart or with patching our marriage. I sensed lightness of body and spirit in addition to a renewed hope that I would be better off alone in every way. I had been fine living by myself before, and there were many advantages to the single life. I would be fine again.

I had no desire to have another man in my life. If such a time ever came, I would consciously keep in mind the type of men I was attracted to and what I had learned in my marriage to Stuart.

Now that I had made my move, I hoped Stuart would make his, too! Since Stuart had said during our July get-away that he did not want to remain in the condo, it was definite I could buy Stuart out and stay in the house. I was fortunate to have good neighbors and their presence helped me feel safe living in my present condo community. I would not be the only single woman as there were several.

What was keeping him in the condo? It would be a relief if he left, but knowing Stuart, I doubted if he would rush into anything since, all along, he had said that he needed much time to make a decision. I had a lot of passivity also, which is a form of patience, so I knew I would continue to wait him out but, in the meantime, I had to prepare myself for any eventuality.

Besides buying Stuart out, I needed to consider whether it was financially feasible for me, however, to pay my expenses alone in the condo? Just to be safe, I started a search online for less expensive places.

On a Saturday morning about two weeks after I had moved out of the master bedroom, Stuart and I had an argument. It started over his very large dream catcher which he wanted to hang from a beam in the master bedroom. Since we shared the office in the loft above the bedroom, I felt I still had some stake in the esthetics of the master bedroom. I didn't like the look of the dream catcher hanging where he wanted it to hang. Instead of letting him have his way, which I probably should have since I now had my own bedroom, I reacted and couldn't seem to maintain the calm demeanor that had served me well in more recent times when dealing with Stuart.

After our argument, I had needed to get out of the house and do something for myself, so I drove to a crystal store that was a forty-minute drive away. By the time I got there, I was feeling calmer about the confrontation with Stuart. When I walked into the store, the crystals welcomed me, and I soon felt energized by them. Having worked in the Wei Chi Healing Center and Shop for almost a year by then, I had become very attached to crystals. I enjoyed looking at them, rearranging them in the display cases, and reading about them. At the crystal store, I could feel energy coming from some, and from others, I felt nothing. I wondered why that was. After a few minutes of browsing, I spotted a sodalite sphere. Its medium-to-dark shades of blue were interspersed with light tan swirls. When it fit perfectly in the palm of my hand, I knew I had to have it but decided to look some more to see if I might find one I liked better. I didn't and I bought the sodalite sphere.

That evening, I did a meditation with it, and when I got my mind in a quiet space, I felt a connection going from my heart up to my third eye. This was the message I got: "Honor yourself; honor your journey. You are on the right path. Take care of me, and I will take care of you." Wow! It was amazing because, when I went to read about sodalite in Naisha Ahsian's book, *The Crystal Ally Cards*, I learned this crystal is about the journey and activates the third eye. Naisha's book reminded me that the journey is more important than the destination, and her text made sense because I wanted to have a session with Kevin to work on opening up my intuitive and finally deal with the two "fuzzies"— the summer on Cape Cod and the party in Paris.

Although I had been psychic as a child, this ability had been shut down for the majority of my life. Would I get it back fully? That is, would I not only have visions and receive messages but also be able to interpret them?

Shadows and Light

In my next session with Kevin, he did energy work on me and then led me in a visualization. In it, I was on a barge going down a river, lounging on a deck chair wearing a long dress and — since it was an earlier era — holding a parasol for shade. A handsome young man came up and spoke to me. We chatted for a while, and then he left. A duck flew up and landed on the railing next to me. As I sipped my tea, I was so relaxed that I was in a dreamlike state. Suddenly, I was rudely shaken when the barge slammed into something. Bits of the boat were flying around in front of me. It was then I thought of the message I had received earlier: "You were meant to die and didn't." Next, I found myself in a crystal healing space surrounded by every imaginable crystal. I felt the energy flow through me, and my feet were tingling.

When the session was over, I realized that we had never talked about the two "fuzzies." I must have needed the visualization more. It is said that Spirit works in mysterious ways. That evening when I did my automatic writing, I asked the question, "Why did I choose not to die — my attempted suicide at age twenty-four — when I wanted to go so badly?" This is what I wrote in automatic fashion: "You needed to figure it out. Death is a willing friend, so easy, when life is so hard. This time you chose not to let it go. You had done it before in another time and place and you did die. In this life, you have suffered just as much as before, but this time, you needed to learn about the experience of having to go forth and live despite the circumstances. There was no one to help you. There was no one to guide you. You made your own decision to experience the mending of your life: to go from darkness into light, to go from wounded to healed, and to go from unloved to loved. You had so many lessons and so many truths to master."

I had learned a tremendous amount in my life so far and finally the pieces were coming together. It is my belief that I came into this lifetime with an agenda of lessons I needed to learn. The suicide attempt was one. It would have been easier to die, but instead it was my choice not to: I did need to go through the experience of putting my life back together. This particular message from Spirit confirmed my question — why did I choose not to die? — and finally, I could put it to rest.

In mid-October, I saw Kevin again to work on the two "fuzzies." I started to talk about the memories I had of the party in Paris and how I could not recall going home: "I have a clear vision of the room and sitting on the floor talking to an attractive man who was across from me at a coffee table. We were flirting a bit. I had a drink and was smoking a cigarette that he had offered me. At some point, I turned around and saw Michael in the front hallway with a couple of people beside him. He had had too much to drink and was clearly in trouble. I put out my cigarette and walked over to him. What happened after that remains a blank.

The whole time I was talking, I could see Kevin's mind going as if he was getting intuitive information and then he spoke: "The man whom you were talking to drove you and Michael back to your apartment, came in with you to make sure you were okay and that is when he raped you."

"Oh my God," I muttered, "That makes sense why I couldn't remember. It was so traumatic that I must have blocked it out." Kevin left me alone for a few minutes, and when he came back into the room, we continued the session. This is what I learned: when I was sexually abused at age twelve by a group of boys, my brother was present but did not protect me. The time of the Paris party was thirteen years later and my husband — most likely passed out or too drunk — was unable to protect me. Over the years, I never had any more clues as to what had happened. Periodically, I would ask myself, Why couldn't I remember any more? It made no sense since this incident came several years after the shock treatments.

Shadows and Light

Several years later, when I was having an individual follow-up session with Kevin, he asked me, "Have you been thinking about the Paris party?" Of course, I had been but was not planning to bring it up. It never ceased to amaze me how he knew what was going on in my mind. As I went over the scene again, I could sense Kevin's mind working. He said, "That man slipped a date-rape drug into your drink." An expletive came out of my mouth. I said, "That makes so much sense. It explains why the rest of the evening was blank." Kevin said these drugs were available in the early 1970s and went on to say how this predator picked up on my vulnerability and Michael's intoxication. A perfect opportunity to give us a ride (or offer to drive our car) home. At last, another loose end was tied up!

I told Kevin about the vision I had had two days earlier of the word "HELP" written on a screen, and while speaking to him, I made the connection to the summer of 1964 — between my sophomore and junior years at Boston College — when I was house-sitting by myself for people my mother knew and waitressing at Howard Johnson's on Cape Cod. I have no recollection of the house or of living there, but I do have a vague memory of meeting some guys, possibly three or four, near this house. I knew I did something with them, and one came back the next day to check on me. The details are blank so I always worried that something so bad had happened that I had to block it from memory, or the memory loss was a result of the shock treatments. Again, Kevin used his psychic abilities to get a sense of this to "see" what had happened to me.

"Yes, you did ask those men into the house," he told me. "You all did some drug, probably LSD (after all it was 1964). Your trip was a bad one as it brought up all the sexual abuse and bad things in your past, one scene flashed after another like a horror movie. It terrified you to such an extent that you entered into a catatonic-like state. These men had no idea what to do with you and so they left you alone to sleep it off. One did come back the next day to check to see if you were all right."

It finally made sense because I could never figure out why someone came back to check on me. I was relieved that it was drugs because I had imagined it was another incident of sexual abuse.

With this first experiment with drugs, I think the dutiful Susan was beginning to crack a speck by showing some risky behavior. The effect of the past abuse was starting to peek out as well.

When I look back at this incident, I know I needed help and did not want to be left alone in that drug-induced state. What had become of me to take such a risk as to take drugs? I was so fragile that I am surprised I did not break down mentally. I was being held together, barely, by a weak thread that could break with a quick tug. The ramifications of this summer manifested later when I went back for the fall semester. Soon after I started my pediatric rotation, I was out sick with a throat infection for a week. The throat is the communication chakra so I must have needed to talk about that LSD trip and what I had seen — but had no opportunity to communicate it. I realize now that a "normal" person would have told someone, but I had gone beyond the point of normalcy and was heading toward mental illness — rooted in depression — if I wasn't there already.

At the end of this second October session, Kevin did a chakra healing on me, and in a visualization, one of my past lives gave me three things: a smooth flat round stone, a gold cross, and a pewter cup with a stem. That evening when I did my automatic writing, I got the meaning of the gifts. The stone was a gift from my soul to keep as a reminder for what I needed to do — live the basic truth of who I am. I needed to connect to my psychic and healer abilities and to take the risk of going forth to spread the word. The gold cross was from my grandfather, the Bishop, to remind me of my connection to God. I had shunned organized religion since high school but had always thought I would return one day. So far, it hasn't happened but I know I still need to figure it out — how to bring God back into my life — and it doesn't have to be religion *per se*. Last was the pewter cup, which I understood to be a symbol of forgiveness. I had to let go of any resentment and anger and forgive those who harmed me, turned against me, or misunderstood me. I needed to forgive my family because only then could I rise up. In order to do this, I needed a solid foundation chakra, a solid base, and this was what Kevin was helping me with.

By this time, the Wei Chi Healing Center and Shop had been open for almost a year. After the incident with Edgar in which he insisted that Kim and I be responsible for far more than we had agreed to, not much had changed. I realized I had fallen back into my predictable pattern of taking on too much responsibility in a work situation or a relationship. I was aware that my marriage was running in parallel to the shop and both were causing me grief and that, in the future, I would have to make sure not to let this sort of thing happen again in any area in my life. At the shop, I recognized fairly soon what I had done and that was an improvement.

Then a huge frustration happened at the shop. The computer used for sales and shop business crashed. When I called Edgar in Arizona for help, he said, "You can keep track of any sales and do the credit card purchases manually. I can take a look at it when I come next month."

After we hung up, I felt something in me had crashed a bit as well: I hoped that we would have a computer system up and running soon. Having the owner and businessperson for the shop approximately 2,600 miles away was not working out.

It took more than a month, perhaps two or three, to get another computer up and running. Kim and I asked for meetings to discuss shop issues, but I don't think they really helped except to let us voice our concerns. Kevin did hire a young man to help staff the shop so I was able to have time to run errands or see a client.

I had two paying clients around that time. This was not enough to provide an income that would supplement my retirement funds, and I was hoping to get more work. Perhaps having help at the shop would allow me time to attract new clients.

Help was an improvement, but the new hire was not comfortable talking to customers and he did not relate well to their needs. As a result, while he took care of some administrative tasks, he did not improve sales of either products or Wei Chi services. The young man lasted for a few months before he had to go back to graduate school.

It was around this time that I woke up one morning feeling very angry and had pain in my shoulders. As I thought about the anger, I realized I was angry at many things — the status of the shop, Stuart for shutting me out and not being the husband I was longing for, and myself for slipping back into old, negative, self-destructive patterns. Since these feelings were overwhelming, I knew I had to deal with them rather than ignore them. Had I forgotten the symbolic cup of forgiveness so soon? I was to let go of my anger and resentment instead of wallowing in it.

The first thing I did was have a long talk with Kim to understand whether she and I held similar feelings regarding the shop. When she came in the following day in the late afternoon, she was just as frustrated. "No one is in charge!" she complained. "We get no validation for what we do."

We agreed that we would have to wait it out, but in the meantime we would keep the energy in the shop clear and maintain a freshness hoping it would help. By the time we had finished talk-

Shadows and Light

ing, my anger had dissipated. As for Stuart, I had to understand my anger as it arose and I had to continue to talk to Kevin about it when I had sessions with him. I had faith that I could eventually let go of my anger once we had parted ways. I am sure Stuart was angry at me as well. After all, our marriage would be the third one for him that had not worked out. How I wished Stuart and I could talk about what was happening with us. I had to think it would have made things easier but I knew that it was not possible — the gulf between us was too wide and the bridge too difficult to cross.

I still wondered what he felt about my moving out of the bedroom? Would he himself make a move soon — I supposed I meant move out of the house and leave me to continue my life alone? I knew in my heart that it would be the best for me to have Stuart leave, but I must have been somewhat reluctant since I had not taken stronger action with him than to wait him out. I chose to heed Kevin's advice and not confront Stuart in any way, which seemed the best way to deal with him.

By the end of October, I sensed that Stuart and I would be parting in the near future. I wanted him to go, but I didn't know how to make it happen sooner. Would I get so frustrated that I would give him an ultimatum? Stuart was still not talking, but he did not exhibit any unusual behavior. I was gone most of the day so if he was up to something — spending long periods of the day away — I would not have known.

How was he dealing with our impending separation?

I was sitting tight ready to wobble or fall off at a moment's notice if Stuart decided to stay. I didn't like this passive manner of mine — not talking about anything serious with Stuart — but that was what Kevin had suggested that I do. Looking back, maybe I should have confronted Stuart but, knowing him at the time, I thought it was best to continue like I was.

Since I knew a separation was inevitable, the practical side of me took action to prepare myself financially and legally. Kim gave me the name of a woman she had met at a business group who was a financial planner — I no longer wanted to travel to see my old one in Newton, MA — so I made an appointment. I discussed many things with my new financial planner, but my main goal was to figure how I could buy Stuart out of our condo and how I could increase my monthly income so I could afford to live there on my own. It encouraged me to discover I was far better off financially than I had thought, and so I would be able to accomplish my goals. Living carefully for years, selling the lake property at a profit, and having sound financial advice had paid off.

Having reassured myself that my finances were sound, my next step was to see a divorce attorney. I didn't think Stuart would contest a divorce, which was definitely in the future, but I thought I should be ready for the possibility. He had always been reasonable about finances, but under the recent veneer of his coldness, he might have a well of anger about finances that could gush up if he were provoked. I saw an attorney, and we discussed possibilities, but I didn't think I would need a lawyer. This premonition became a resolve after finding out how much an attorney would cost. Stuart would not want to spend all that money when it would be easier and far less expensive to file a no-fault divorce on our own. A simple divorce would be feasible since we had kept our finances separate and our children were grown. I couldn't believe that I was going through divorce again after almost thirty years. In many ways it would be easier, but I was sure the pain and emotion would catch up to me at some point.

November was a pivotal month. I was still seeing Kevin for an occasional session when he was in Massachusetts. He still advised me to stay calm with Stuart, not to provoke him in any way, and to keep waiting him out. Now that the work on my foundation chakra was completed — I was feeling more secure and safe — we were working on opening my intuitive, third-eye chakra, which had been shut down in my early childhood. It was coming active again slowly. I was meditating with crystals, and having a lot of visions, but I was still unable to interpret them. I was wrapping up loose ends in my individual work with Kevin. His skill as a spiritual counselor continued to amaze me, and I knew I had progressed in coming to terms with my childhood. I only wished that Kevin's skills could have included running a business.

I went to a big holiday craft fair before Thanksgiving. I was walking around looking at the booths to see if I could find some Christmas gifts, when I spotted it — the walking staff that I recognized was the one I had been looking for. The walking stick was perfect. It was from a special type of willow from the American South, with several indentations to put crystals in. I had always known that someday I would find the right staff. When I did, I felt it to be a positive sign as the staff represented my empowerment. In the coming months, I would have to dive deep into my well of strength to lift myself up and feel empowered.

How long I would continue to live in the emotional limbo that Stuart and I were maintaining became clear just before Thanksgiving. Stuart and I were together — the scene and circumstances have escaped me — but his words remained clear. "I bought a house and will be moving out in about three weeks. The movers are scheduled to come on the 19th of December."

I was expecting some action from Stuart, but this floored me. I would have liked to have had some warning that he was planning on buying a house but I should have known better. He must have been looking at houses when I was at the shop during the day. It was sad that I didn't know him anymore. He might have been afraid of how I would react — he hated emotion — and that might have been a reason for waiting until the last minute to tell me or perhaps he simply didn't care what I thought.

Once I got used to the idea of his moving out so soon, I concluded maybe it was for the best he was doing it so quickly. I didn't have any time to think about my emotions because the practical Susan went into high gear. But first I had to tell my family and decide what to do for Thanksgiving.

I was grateful I had Peter and Erin and their girls to go to for Thanksgiving that year. I would go by myself and be myself. I was blessed to have such a welcoming, warm family. If I felt weepy, I wouldn't have to hide my emotions. I certainly felt very shaky emotionally that Thanksgiving and recall very little other than just being there. I was still in a state of shock with Stuart announcing he was moving out so fast.

After Thanksgiving, I threw myself into buying presents for my family, shopping for a few pieces of furniture and other items I would need to replace what Stuart would take. Stuart and I had very few jointly owned possessions, and we managed to divide them without confrontation. Stuart was reasonable throughout, which helped me not to react and to stay calm. We talked more than we had in a while about practical issues — finances and filing for a no-fault divorce in the coming weeks.

Despite the looming circumstances weighing heavily on my mind and watching Stuart packing up his things, I decided to decorate the house as I usually did for Christmas, but I would buy an artificial tree — it would be far easier to manage a fake one. I found a seven-and-a-half-foot tree to fit in the corner of the living room. As I was sorting through and separating out any of Stuart's decorations to put aside for him, I started to think about past Christmases and how things had changed. The first one after Michael and I had divorced was a memorable one. I had been dealing with the loss of my first marriage and learning to be a

Shadows and Light

single parent. I wanted the support of my parents but they and my sister hadn't come for Christmas dinner at my house, as they had wanted to have a "quiet" day with no children. Now I was going through another divorce and realized how much change had taken place. I was wiser because I was now in touch with my emotions and had a better sense of who I was.

As I looked out the living room window and watched the moving van come into the driveway on the morning of December 19, my heart was so heavy it felt like it had sunk into my abdomen and my hands were shaking. Reality hit! Stuart was moving out, and I was no longer married. Realizing I needed to let my mind take over to focus on what I needed the movers to help me with — I would have plenty of time to think and cry later — I decided to ask the men to help me with placing a couple of big furniture pieces in a new spot once Stuart got his things loaded on the van.

"You can't have them do that; it will add to their time." Stuart said.

"They are here and available, besides, how can I possibly move that big bookcase and a queen bed by myself?"

Begrudgingly, Stuart agreed.

Finally, all his things were in the van, and the bookcase, the bed, and a few other pieces were in their new places. It was time to say goodbye. We stood in the front hallway looking at each other not knowing what to say. There was no hug or emotion. I finally said, "Just go." I wanted him out of my life. When I closed the door and watched Stuart drive away, I didn't know whether to laugh or cry. I was happy to see him go so I could get on with my life like I was meant to live it, but distraught because my second marriage had just ended. A few minutes later, the dam burst and a river of tears flowed. How was I ever going to pick up the detritus and move on?

Then I remembered a message I had gotten from Mattie earlier in the month. "We will be dancing in the heavens for you. Just wait and see how much better off you will be. You have done it before and you can do it again. It is much easier this time, but not less sad and painful. Go forth with joy — take your staff and decorate it. Use it as a reminder of who you are, all the work you have done, and who you can now be."

Mattie was right. I had faith that I could get through it, but I knew one thing for sure and that was I was never going to find myself in this relationship pattern again. It had to end, but even so, I doubted that I would ever get married again.

Chapter 29
Moving On

Three months! That's what I allotted to feel sorry for myself and then I was determined to move on. I had done most of my grieving while the marriage had been slowly unraveling over the past couple of years. Being alone again, without the tensions that had characterized my last years with Stuart, I was amazed at how I began to relax. Every day seemed a better day. While I had thought, when with Stuart, that I would not look for another relationship, alone now, I realized there was a lot I enjoyed in sharing my life with a partner. Although I was just then releasing the emotional impact of Stuart in my life and was not ready to find someone new, I sensed, however, that I might do so when the time was right. Meanwhile having done online dating in the past and curious to see who was out there, I was now willing to try it again to look for — if not "find"— a special someone. I signed on to a couple of websites.

"Just browsing," I told myself. Finding someone for companionship for doing activities with and not for a permanent relationship was a good start. Still healing from Stuart, I was not ready for more than just doing things with someone. Little did I realize how soon my life was about to change.

One day in February 2012, as I was reading the Boston Globe, I happened to scan the obituaries, which is something I don't usually do, when a woman's picture and name caught my eye. I realized I knew the deceased person as she had been a condo neighbor of mine. While I hardly knew her or her husband, Don, I had known she had been battling cancer for a long time. Her obituary was not a surprise. On occasion, I had run into Don at the condo mailboxes, and the last time we had been there together, he had said she was off chemo because it was not helping her anymore.

That February day, after a trip to the store for a sympathy card, I wrote:

Dear Don,

I was very sad to read about Suzanne in the Globe. Although I did not know her well, I do remember her great smile and friendliness. My heart goes out to you and your family.

Just know you have an empathetic neighbor who is a good listener if you need to talk or anything during this difficult time.

With sympathy,
Susan

This note would have a large impact on my life.

During my self-pity phase, although I continued to work at the shop four days a week, I was putting minimal effort into finding clients and promoting my healing work. At this point, I was not even sure whether I wanted to keep a healing practice going. After my marriage was over, any interest in the shop dwindled. It is possible that I needed to go through this experience in order to heal myself. Did I have to see myself as a potential healer before I could move on?

The shop now seemed to be left over from another time, and

it had long since stopped reflecting my priorities. Maybe I knew at this point that the shop was not going to succeed. I did know, for sure, that marketing was not something I wanted to pursue, nor was it even interesting to me. If I were going to have my own healing practice, I would have to continue to do marketing. With that in mind, I decided to wait and see how my life without Stuart played out. Except for my Tai Chi classes I had put everything else — including any spiritual work — on hold. While I continued Tai Chi because I knew it would help me keep calmer and it was good for my muscles, I really had to drag myself to classes.

One day when I was at the shop, sometime in the early spring of 2012, a high-school classmate surprised me with a call. It was fun to catch up with Peggy until she told me our classmates were planning for our fiftieth high-school reunion in September and she hoped I would attend. Because I considered my time at St. Mary's to have been mostly unhappy, I told her that I would have to think about showing up. However, I doubted I would go since I had never been to any reunions, either for high school or college. In fact, I had seen no one nor corresponded with anyone from St. Mary's since we had graduated in 1962.

Susan's graduation
St. Mary's, 1962

There was a pattern to how I left things — not only schools but also houses. When I had left a place I had lived in for a while, I shut the book on those chapters of my life and never picked it up again. The physical leave-taking always led to an emotional letting go.

Was this abandonment of my connection to the past an adaptation to shut out some of the unhappy memories from my early years in British Columbia, Virginia, Minnesota, Haiti, and St. Mary's?

Even though reminiscing with Peggy had kindled a slight curiosity about how my classmates had turned out, I decided not to attend. Fortunately for me, emails started to appear in my inbox. I wanted to ignore them, but because of the numbers, it was very hard to. My former classmates were saying how much fun it would be to get together again, and some said how they were looking forward to seeing me specifically.

St. Mary's School, Peekskill NY

After talking it over with my Wei Chi friends, who thought I should go, I began to look at the reunion differently. Instead of reliving trauma, they suggested, maybe the reunion would help me see my high-school years in a softer, gentler light. Maybe the reunion would be an opportunity for me to heal wounds that were half a century old. Once I began thinking that way, it took only two weeks for me to change my mind. Just maybe, attending was something that would have rewards beyond the nostalgic connection with the women.

One morning during this time, I walked into the shop and noticed immediately that some of the large crystals we were selling on consignment for Kevin's friend were gone. "This will be a huge loss to the ambience of the shop," I said to Kevin and Edgar who were again in New England. "These were the best-selling crystals we had. What are you going to replace them with to produce revenue?"

Shadows and Light

One of them replied, "We will pick up some new stuff to sell."

Then Kim and I were asked to pack up all the jewelry that we were selling on consignment for two local women, since it had to be returned as well. I don't recall getting a satisfactory answer why these consignment items were being terminated. My only consolation was that I bought myself a consignment labradorite necklace and matching earrings that I had admired.

Returning the merchandise irritated me. It was done without consulting Kim and me. Had we been asked, we would have protested that these items were the largest and most attractive, although the most expensive, merchandise in the shop. We would have complained that this reduction in inventory would also have an impact on the look of the store. Customers would walk in to see an empty space. How could that be encouraging to them? I saw this return of consignment merchandise as a sign of the beginning of the end. It was the first time I had thought that the shop might not survive.

After this, I realized I had to figure out how much more was I willing to put up with at the shop? I knew getting clients was my responsibility and I had to continue to do so if I wanted income from Wei Chi healing sessions. The shop, however, was not my interest, and it was proving to be a volunteer activity. Had I been compensated in some way for all I did, I would have felt better about the experience.

With these conclusions in mind, I realized I needed to ask to be compensated for my hours. Asking couldn't hurt. If Kevin's answer was a "no," then I would have to decide whether I would stay at the shop or not.

Much to my surprise, Kevin agreed to pay me $100 per week. It wasn't the amount of money that mattered to me, although it was reassuring to get off volunteering my services for something I did not believe in. What most mattered was being recognized for the work I was doing. I was proud of myself for asking for what I wanted. In the past, I had often accepted being ignored and taken for granted. Perhaps things were really changing for Susan.

This experience seemed another emotional step away from Stuart, and it marked the end of my three-month allowance for feeling sorry for myself.

I did not have any contact with my neighbor Don until later, in April, as I was doing my weekly grocery shopping at the local Market Basket and chanced to come across him. It was like seeing a long-lost friend even though I hardly knew him or knew anything about him. We both had big smiles on our faces, and the energy between us was sparkling, to say the least. We spoke for several minutes, exchanging pleasantries and taking up space in the aisle. He thanked me for the sympathy card, saying it had meant a lot to him.

"I read it over and over, not really knowing why."

Later, I thought to myself, Why was I so pleased to see this man? I barely know him.

At the end of April, we had a crystal show at the shop. Kevin did not attend as he was away giving a talk, but Edgar was there. In addition, Kevin had asked a friend to join us to give readings and sell his crystals. Despite all the advertising Kim and I had generated, few people showed up.

The day ended a disaster as I had a confrontation with Edgar over a minor issue. Fortunately, there were no customers left in the shop. Edgar's behavior, which included swearing at me, was rude to say the least. In all the years I had worked, I had never had anyone be so disrespectful of me. I asked Kevin for a one-on-one meeting with him to share my viewpoint about what happened with Edgar.

However, when we scheduled a meeting, Kevin said he also

Shadows and Light

wanted Edgar there since he had been involved. I did not feel entirely safe with Edgar, so if Edgar was to be there, I felt I needed to have someone on my side to witness the scene. If Edgar were again verbally abusive, I wanted someone to witness his behavior and come to my defense, and so I asked Kim to accompany me. I was beginning to feel out of trust with Kevin. He had proven himself to be a great spiritual counselor but he had also willingly dragged me into the energy-sink of a shop — possibly to meet his own needs.

At the meeting, I spoke my thoughts and asked to be respected in the workplace. Edgar was not confrontational. He stated that his anger was a result of all the frustration he was having with the shop. Now that his anger and frustration had been released, he admitted he felt better.

Fine to release, I thought, but not on me!

When I left Kevin and Edgar, I was not convinced my relationship with Edgar or the business would get better, but at least I had stood up for myself. The question remained: do I stay at the shop and try to work things out or do I leave and do healing work on my own?

It was becoming clear at this point, however, that there was not much left to keep me at the shop, in spite of my $100 victory, so it didn't take long to make up my mind to leave. In the middle of May 2012, I wrote to Kevin. "After much thought and with regret, I have come to a decision. As of June 8, I will no longer be helping out at the shop on the regular basis as I have. I will help out at events and do the energy work clinics but will not maintain the website, prepare a newsletter, post on Facebook, etc." I offered to pay rent on my room through the summer, which would give them enough time to find someone to rent it. I went on to thank Kevin: "I will continue to admire you as a teacher and will be forever grateful to you as a spiritual coach and counselor. I thank you for all that you have done for me over the past few years. Wei Chi will always have a special place in my heart."

In a few days, I heard back from Kevin. He thanked me for what I had done in the shop and said it had been a learning experience for all of us. He reminded me that he could no longer make any decisions but had to bring my request — to be released from the lease — to the next meeting of the board. I had forgotten that Kevin could not make this decision by himself. A few months earlier, a board had been formed — Kim and I had not been included — to oversee all Kevin's business ventures, which included the shop. I did not understand why the board had happened, but apparently, I was subject to the board's decision making.

Waiting for a response, I packed up my little office, which I had decorated with loving care. Doing so, I felt sad. This was a sort of divorce, and I felt the loss of hopes and dreams. I hoped that a new tenant would be found for my room or for the entire space, but I soon learned my request to get out of the lease was not granted. I would have to continue to pay rent on my empty room until a new tenant was found, or failing that, until the lease was up in a year and a half. As it turned out, neither Kevin nor the board could find a practitioner who wanted my space and so my getting out of the lease didn't happen. Not very long after I resigned and departed, the Wei Chi Healing Center and Shop met its demise. Nothing special was done to keep it afloat and eventually Kevin, Edgar, and Kim packed up their things and the space remained empty until the lease expired.

In the time after leaving the shop, I felt a burden lift from me — I let the responsibility I felt for it float away in the breeze. Any attached worries floated away with it. How freeing to be rid first of my marriage to Stuart and now the shop!

While I was still paying rent, I took it in stride because I had

Shadows and Light

willingly signed the lease and meeting its terms was my responsibility. (Later in the year, my rebellious streak kicked in and I did not pay rent for a few months. When I received a threatening note from a lawyer the board had contacted, I paid and continued until the lease expired.)

Maybe it was the wrong time and place for this kind of healing work or maybe we were the wrong group to get it done. One thing was sure: I had opened up to let new experiences come into my life.

Now, what was I going to do?

Sometime in June, around two months after we had seen each other at the Market Basket, Don and I crossed each other again as our condos were only five units apart. He was backing out of his driveway, and I was driving by. He signaled me to stop, and when I did so, he rolled down his window. We chatted for fifteen or twenty minutes. I found out he was a retired physician who had gone to Boston College.

"I went to B.C. also," I said, "but I probably graduated before you." He looked younger than I.

"I don't think so," he smiled back. It turned out he was eight years older than I.

My face must have fallen!

Changing the subject, I asked how he was holding up.

"Not so good! I have no hope."

"There is always hope; you can never give up," I responded. "My offer still holds, if you want to talk."

Soon, we terminated the conversation, and I started the car again and headed for my house.

Hmm, I thought. That was an interesting conversation. It appears we have quite a lot in common. It was more than our commonalities, however, that I was struck with. As when we had met at the market, I had a sense that I was talking to an old friend.

Shadows and Light

What was that about? Had we shared a past life? Or, was it simply chemistry, chemistry that might fascinate me but for which I was not ready. The trauma of my experience with Stuart was still too much with me.

On a gorgeous warm day in the beginning of July, I saw Don again. I was cleaning out my garage, something I had never done before as Stuart would do that. I was going through some of the junk that he had left and separating what was still useful from what could be thrown away. While I was picking through his boxes, I decided the garage also needed a general cleaning. I was doing just that when, facing out toward the front as I was washing a window, I saw Don walking by with a child. I was so happy to see him that I ran out to say "Hi." I had never seen him walking by before, and I had just seen him when we met in our cars.

After greeting Don, I turned to the boy and asked him who he was. As I suspected, he was Don's grandson. His name was Ian, and he was six years old.

"What a coincidence," I said. "I have a grandson named Ian and guess how old he is? Six years old."

Don and I chatted some more before Ian began to squirm. Don said, "I better move on." As he was turning away, I thought I heard him say, "I'll call you."

I returned to my garage cleanup, thinking, This is really weird. There are so many coincidences bringing Don and me together!

The next day, my Wei Chi friend, Linette, who had gone to Arizona for the Pressure Cooker with me, was visiting, and I told her about meeting Don.

"Maybe I should call him and see how he is since he had sounded depressed last month," I wondered out loud.

"Don't call him," she said. "Trust me. He will call."

Shadows and Light

As Linette had predicted, Don did call me a week later. He told me afterwards, "I needed a week to get my courage up. I called you earlier on Monday evening knowing that you had Tai Chi class and wouldn't be home." We chatted for a good forty minutes before he asked, "Would you like to go out to dinner sometime?"

I felt a thrill of pleasure. Why was I so pleased? We settled on the following Thursday for dinner at the country club in town.

"You don't have to pick me up," I said. "I will walk down to your house."

This felt like a date. All the following week, like a schoolgirl, I was unsettled. Opting to walk to his house, however, made going out to dinner with Don seem a little less like a date. I told myself, "We were just getting together for dinner and a friendly chat. This is not about romance. Neither one of us is ready."

In spite of the downgrading talk about what was about to happen, I took care to plan what I would wear for dinner. I found myself thinking of this or that pair of pants and which jewelry would look best with what blouse. This was a lot of planning, I found myself realizing, for someone who was "just getting together for dinner and a friendly chat" with her neighbor.

On Thursday evening, which was a warm summer evening, I settled on light tan pants and a silky purple print blouse. For jewelry, I wore the labradorite necklace and earrings that I had purchased when the decision was made not to sell jewelry on consignment in the shop anymore. It had been a favorite of mine; a consolation then was making me feel great now. After spritzing myself with a light summer fragrance, it was time to summon my courage and walk down the street.

Fortunately, I did not run into any of our neighbors who would have asked, "Why is Susan all dressed up as she is walking toward Don's house?"

The only way I know how to describe the dinner and the time that surrounded it is to say it was a most unusual evening. The energy between us was so high; it was like we were long-lost friends who were catching up after too much time apart. After sitting down at our table, we both proceeded to talk nonstop, often interrupting one another. We both had so much to share — it was a weird thing that two people who did not really know each other should have so much to share! We were slow to order — we must have been there a good hour before we decided what we wanted. I am surprised our server did not give up on us. When we got our meal, we barely ate, still talking as fast as we could.

After dinner, Don asked me back to his house, and I agreed. However, I said I could stay only for a short time. The high energy continued as we both could not even sit down and were standing in his kitchen walking around and talking. At one point, he took me by the shoulders, looked me in the eye and said, "I want to see you again and again and again."

This is getting too intense for me, I thought to myself. It is time to leave.

Don walked me home. Soon afterwards, my head began aching. What was this all about? I could guess it had to do with the evening with Don. The whole encounter was so profound, and both of us had been flying off the walls, totally ungrounded. I can only think that it was like the two of us had known each other and were catching up after having been apart for a long time. Was the universe trying to get us together for some reason?

Although I wanted to call Don to see if he was all right after our evening out, I decided to wait at least a week. He did call, and the first thing he said was, "I am so sorry. I made a complete fool of myself."

"No, you didn't," I replied. "For whatever reason, we were both off energetically that evening, talking up a storm and interrupting each other. We were in it together." We both agreed the whole outing was rather strange, to say the least, and that we should make plans to go out again. A few days later, we went to Ogunquit, Maine, during the day. We had New England clam chowder for lunch at a waterfront restaurant and then walked along Marginal Way, a scenic, cliff-side walkway overlooking the ocean. This time our energy together was balanced and not crazy like the last time. Being outside and walking certainly helped ground us, but we still talked the whole time, nonstop, for at least six hours until we got back home.

Don had spent a total of seven years caring for his wife through chemotherapy, surgery, and other treatments. Her initial diagnosis was incurable lung cancer, and by the time of diagnosis, the cancer had already metastasized into her bones. He had been through so much and had never talked to anyone about it. It was like a floodgate had opened. This was his second time around. His first wife and the mother of his four children had died of a chronic illness when he was in his early forties.

From the very beginning, I made it clear to him that, since I was recently divorced and he was recently widowed, I thought it best that we just be friends. Neither one of us was ready for a relationship.

Around this time, someone whose profile I had seen online whom I was interested in had contacted me. Earlier, I had wanted to respond, not really knowing why. While I presumed my intuition was speaking to me, I didn't contact him, however, since he was several years younger than I. I thought, What sort of man would want to go out with an older woman? Most men, I said to myself, gravitated to younger ones. It turned out that I was wrong about his interest, at least, in younger women as he contacted me. In my profile, I had said that I was intuitive and did energy work and that had interested him. After a short correspondence,

I learned that we had a lot in common from a metaphysical, spiritual viewpoint and I decided to meet him. When we got together for breakfast, we hit it off.

That summer, free of Stuart and free of the Wei Chi shop, I was happy and life was going in the right direction again. Now I had two men interested in me; it was almost too much for me to comprehend.

I told the second man, Brian, that I was only interested in a platonic relationship at this time and that I needed some time since I was newly divorced. He was amenable to it.

How was this dual dating going to turn out?

In June, it hadn't taken me long to know I needed something to keep me busy, so I had signed up for the six-month online class, "Becoming the Human Crystal," taught by Naisha Ahsian. It entailed working with actual crystals and becoming attuned to them and how they affected us as humans. The class required daily meditation and writing. It happened to be a very interesting time for me to be taking this class as it was opening me up psychically. While doing a meditation one day, I heard, "Give Don the Lepidolite crystal you have."

I recognized the crystal immediately as one on my bureau; it was a lavender-colored stone with white flecks and silver sparkles in it. I knew I had to take this information to the next level. I soon did another meditation while holding this crystal in my hand and asked the question, "Why does Don need this?"

This is the message I got: "Since he is going through the grief process, this stone will help him to handle unexpressed emotions and to do a realignment and help bring him into reality. You will give him the opportunity to grow and heal just by being with him. He has a big heart and soul worthy of you."

Since the class required an "awakening" type of meditation

— which clears the energy of the stone and allows the stone to resonate with your energy — with various crystals we were given, I decided to do this with the Lepidolite I was to give Don. Again, I held this particular Lepidolite stone in my hand while I did an "awakening" meditation to see what energies it was connected with. The color surrounding the stone was many shades of green with pink running through it. I felt a tremendous amount of love for myself and my friend, Don. I heard, "The stone is for love and healing. He is to keep it with him. You are meant to help him heal." I was very emotional at this point with tears running down my face.

The next time Don and I got together, as we were sitting in my living room chatting, I remembered what I was to do. I jumped up, exclaiming, "I have something for you." I ran upstairs to get the stone, and upon returning, gave it to him.

"I am here to help you heal," I said. "This is the reason we are meant to be together."

He was visibly moved by my words and he took the stone from me. Once again, I felt the universe was trying to get us together.

During this time, I had had a couple of dates with Brian, and we were getting to know each other. During a daily meditation, I asked about Brian. Was he someone worthy of me? Here was the response: "Yes, you need to go slowly. He has a lot of old wounds that are still being healed. He would be a refreshing spirit for you, and you could create something together with him. Look beneath the exterior deep within, and there is someone like you. Time heals all wounds."

At some point I "knew" that I had to give Brian a crystal. It was a Lapis Lazuli which is a brilliant royal blue crystal with flecks of gold. I chose one at a store for him since I didn't have one at the time. For Brian, the meaning of the stone was love:

love of self, love of divinity, and love for others. He was to use it for clarification, hope, and patience. When I gave him the Lapis Lazuli with its meanings, he was visibly moved. He said, "You nailed it; those are the things I need to work on."

The mid-September 2012 date for my high school reunion was rapidly approaching and was only about two weeks away. Earlier in August, we had each been asked to write about ourselves and what had happened in our lives for a reunion book. I tried to write something meaningful, but I felt I couldn't say what I really wanted to because it would sound too sad. I went into my negative space and felt embarrassed not to have gone to grad school nor to have had an interesting career. I was filled with the fear of not measuring up to others who, I was sure, had had stellar careers. Even though I knew these thoughts about myself and about others weren't true, I still believed them to be true enough, especially about myself, on certain occasions. Rather than write a heartfelt statement, I wrote these safe thoughts for our reunion book:

Reunion Thoughts

Connecting after such a long pause

To share our stories and dreams

Is indeed a blessing for us all.

Much has passed to form us

Into who we are today.

The pain, the scars we have endured

Were tempered by joy and the gifts of life.

Our coming together will be healing,

Releasing any leftover hurt, shame, anger,

And the ghosts of the past, real or imagined,

Forgiving those whose words or actions harmed us.
This new energy and love will help us on our journey forward
To know our true selves and be closer to the Divine.
The bonds over time do not diminish
And with these friendships from the past,
Anything is possible.

Rereading this now, I realize I was outlining my hopes for the reunion, creating an agenda for what I vaguely wanted perhaps to happen. As many times in the past, I did not set out to create what I definitely wanted. I was used to hinting to myself what I hoped for in life, as I did for the reunion in this piece of writing.

Because the reunion was to be held in Rehoboth Beach, Delaware, which was about a six-hour drive south for me, I could have met classmates in Connecticut to share the travel; but I decided to drive the whole way down by myself. If I had my own car in the parking lot of the Episcopal retreat house where the reunion was happening, I could leave anytime I wanted. If things became overwhelming or uncomfortable, I could drive myself away.

On Friday afternoon, I pulled up in front of the retreat house. It was a huge, unpretentious white building nestled in tall pine trees. It had been the du Pont family summer home, which the family had gifted to the Episcopal Diocese in the 1950s. The retreat house was in a tranquil spot that backed up to a lake, yet it was only two blocks from the ocean. After parking, I walked up to the front door with some trepidation and let myself in. I was immediately greeted by a woman who clearly thought I would know who she was. Only when I heard her name did I recognize her. By then, I was feeling more comfortable and my anxiety

Shadows and Light

about coming started to dissipate.

Incredibly, sixteen out of the twenty-one women in our graduating class had come from all over the country. A few of us had been together for the whole four years. While I was nervous about sharing a room with someone I had not been particularly friendly with fifty years earlier, and about whom I could not recall a thing, it turned out we had a lot in common and were able to connect on our spiritual journeys. That was a definite bonus. The group spent the whole weekend reminiscing and sharing stories. At times, we broke into smaller groups. I went on a couple of walks on the boardwalk and beach with three other women I had known better than others. We had some great philosophical and heart-to-heart talks.

I was impressed by the intelligence of my classmates. They were well read and had traveled a lot; some were accomplished in their careers. Everyone had her unique perspective and insight on life. At some point, I realized how lucky I had been to have these women in my life so long ago. As we shared our stories, I learned a lot about them. Many had had to go to our boarding school for a variety of sad reasons: their parents were separated or divorced, one had a mentally ill mother, another had been abused and needed to get away from her former school. After hearing all of this, we realized that we had been family to each other while at St. Mary's, supporting each other the best we knew how. I was surprised at how little I recalled about our lives together. I had been living in my bubble of pain and shame — keeping a safe barrier up, not letting anyone in. I wondered how that need to protect myself might have affected my adult relationships — with Michael, Johnnie, Stuart.

How healing this reunion was for me! Driving back up the New Jersey Turnpike across New York City and up through New England, I had plenty of time to think. I realized that we had, in fact, had many good times at St. Mary's and I now could recall

Shadows and Light

that I did have some friends. The school provided a sanctuary for us, albeit sheltered and structured; it was a place to learn and grow. I regretted that I had not written about myself for our reunion book. It was selfish on my part not to take the time to overcome my negativity. I could have done a brief overview that left out a lot of the bad. Once again, I had done what I had done for so much of my early life and well into adulthood: I went through the motions of living and not really participating.

When I came home to Atkinson from the reunion, I was in a good space — glad that I had attended and buoyed by the insights I had had. Could I make use of the experience to affect a better decision about which of the two interesting men in my life I should choose? I didn't want to go on seeing both Brian and Don simultaneously, and I was increasingly aware there was a complication in my relationship with Don: I had started to have some romantic feelings for him.

Now what was I going to do? I needed to think about the two men and choose which one would be best for me.

Although the shop with Kevin as the owner had not worked out, I still respected him as a spiritual counselor. I made an appointment to see Kevin when he was next in New England. In the session, he said, "Think about the two stones you gave them. The Lapis Lazuli is connected with the mind; the Lepidolite is connected to the heart. Do you want a relationship based on the heart or the mind? Do you want an emotional connection or an intellectual one?"

I had wanted an emotional connection with both Michael and Stuart. I still yearned for an emotional connection and so my choice landed easily on Don. I felt a deep soul connection to him.

The universe, it seemed, had been trying to get us together, and now I would see how much of a connection we really had.

Shadows and Light

Chapter 30
Making a Choice — A Right Choice

After I decided not to continue seeing Brian, Don and I settled into a regular routine of seeing each other rather more frequently. Many times a week, we walked from one house to the other — for meals, for a chat, for companionship. Noticing this, sometimes more than once a day, our neighbors must have wondered what was happening! How could they not have begun to piece together what was going on between us? Surely the visits were for more than a neighborly cup of sugar!

Sadly, a daughter of one of our neighbors died. When we discussed attending the funeral mass, it was a given between Don and me that we would attend together. Not only did we travel together and sit with one another at mass, but when it came time to offer the sign of peace to each other, instead of extending our hands, Don and I instinctively kissed each other on the cheek — that's how comfortable we had

Don, 2013

become as a couple by then. When we turned to extend the sign of peace to people in the pew immediately behind us, we saw they were four of our neighbors.

We had outed ourselves as a couple! Oh well, I smiled to myself, shrugging my shoulders. If they didn't know, they do now.

Don and I had a good chuckle about it later. It was a relief to be public about our relationship, and at the end of October, we went to a neighborhood Halloween party, which we called our official "coming out." We got a few surprised looks as more neighbors asked, "You're together now?" Going public felt right. I was content to be part of a couple again and was proud to be with Don. I had no fear that he would say something to embarrass me or drink too much.

In November, while I was preparing dinner for us at my house, Don walked up to the refrigerator with something in his hand. Soon, he was placing a newspaper clipping beneath a refrigerator magnet.

"Come over and read this 'Dear Abby' clipping," he said.

I put my utensils down, and wiping my hands, I walked over to the refrigerator. What was up? I wondered as I began to read. The "Dear Abby" clipping was about the meaning of a committed relationship. When I finished reading, I looked at him. This seemed like a message he was trying to give me. Part of me wondered what he was trying to tell me while the other part knew, of course, what he was communicating.

"Are we committed?" he asked.

"Yes!" I had already told him I had taken my name off the dating websites and was no longer seeing Brian. "Yes, I am committed to you and will be faithful."

"That's what I wanted to hear," he grinned. "I am committed to you as well."

He threw his arms around me, and we hugged. That evening was the beginning of a new phase of our relationship. It had only

Shadows and Light

been some three or four months that we had been "seeing" each other, but I felt comfortable with Don. Being together felt good to both of us. Of all the men I had known, Don was the least into games and hidden agendas. I felt safe with him. Given my history, however, I was a bit apprehensive about my ability to judge the viability of a romance and perhaps to handle the challenges of a relationship. A lot of time had passed, it was true, since I had married Michael in spite of my misgivings that my wanting to be a wife was not enough for a relationship to endure and since I had married Stuart who turned out to be such a stranger. And then there had been Johnnie who had been a playmate that I had not demanded much from and who had left me without warning. In fact, both Johnnie and Stuart had left that way. I was still a bit stunned that I had chosen men who would do this.

What was different with Don and me, however, was a feeling of security from early on and of not needing to protect myself from the relationship. I sensed that I was free of the unhealthy element of willing a relationship into existence, which had been with me earlier in my life. I felt that this loving relationship with Don was coming into my life naturally. The intense and mutual dependence that had characterized my parents' relationship had also plagued all of my relationships to date and now that dynamism seemed to have dissolved — or, at least, to be dissolving.

I was also solaced to realize that, however much I enjoyed being with him, I was fine without Don. I did not feel dependent on him for security or happiness, but I understood that I was so much better and happier with him.

How had this feeling free from the past that had so limited me come about? How had I become so much freer? Well, for starters, there was all the counseling I had invested in over the years and more recently all the spiritual, psychic, and energy work I had done — including messages from Wei Chi, Mattie, my grandfather, my parents, and spirit guides. Somehow, little by little, these had brought my essence up out of the muck of antecedents. In the light of what I was living, my individuation work seemed to have grown and matured, and I was now experiencing its ripeness. The human spirit has a desire for wholeness, and I was now feeling more whole than I had ever felt before.

Don and I enjoyed being together. If we had no specific plans, we would alternate going to each other's house for a cup of tea in the afternoon. That's how, in November 2012 — just a week or so after we had declared our commitment to each other — we found ourselves in my living room, sipping tea. The heat emanating from the fireplace warmed the chilly, gray afternoon. It felt good to be together, and as a somewhat new or at least unexpected feeling, it was good to be Susan.

"I am dreading Thanksgiving this year," Don told me. "It was Suzanne's favorite holiday, and we always had it at our house."

I had guessed the upcoming holidays would be really tough for Don — his first without Suzanne. While I did not doubt his commitment to our relationship, I also knew that he was still going through a grieving process.

He continued by sharing that neither Kathleen nor Alison (the two of his three daughters who lived nearby) nor he were into cooking a big meal, so he was thinking of going out for Thanksgiving that year.

Wanted to support Don's grieving, I said, "You can all come here. I haven't made final plans yet, but I think Peter, Erin, and the girls will be able to come. What do you think?"

It just felt right to offer this to Don and his family. It was not that I was trying to replace Suzanne in his family's holiday traditions, but I knew that going to a restaurant would not add up to a Thanksgiving that would be healing for any of them. The feeling of love that was growing in me for Don urged me to be compassionate and be a support for Don in his continuing grief.

Shadows and Light

Suzanne and I were different women who had been with Don in different ways at different times. He would perhaps always love her, but I knew — or at least I was sensing more and more — that he could also love me. One love did not subtract from the other. Suzanne and I were not in competition.

I also remembered how difficult the previous Thanksgiving had been when Stuart and I had gone our own ways. Going to Peter and Erin's alone, I had felt grateful to have family to include me but I had also struggled with the anxiety of an imminent break. (Had I known how good I would be feeling in a year's time, I would have celebrated going our own ways!)

"That sounds great." Don replied quickly, sounding relieved and grateful not to have to take up the restaurant option. "But, won't that be too much for you?"

"Not at all. I always say the more the merrier, especially at Thanksgiving."

I wasn't nervous about having Don's daughters and grandson for Thanksgiving. As for Peter and Erin, they were sociable and easy-going so I knew they would be gracious. I did, however, wonder whether Peter was thinking, Another man in Mom's life! I think my sons were used to new men by now and accepted that. I believe they just wanted to see me happy — I had been depressed on and off so much of their lives. And now I was happy and more confident than I had ever been.

Thanksgiving couldn't have gone better. While I did the majority of the cooking, everyone else helped out by bringing a side dish or pie. Erin brought supplies for the kids to make place cards, which gave them the opportunity to get to know each other. I wanted the day to be memorable for Don and his family since it was the first one without Suzanne — and the first one with me. I asked his family if there were any specific, "must have" dishes that they wanted me to prepare, but there weren't.

Although there was not a special food I could prepare, I did think that I might bring Suzanne's memory into the meal in a special way. I prepared a grace with a slight religious component for the meal. Creating and saying grace was something I had never done before.

"Let us take a moment to remember those who have gone before us," I said.

As we ate around the table, we talked and laughed with our kids and grandkids. Don told me later that Kathleen, his eldest daughter had said, "Susan is a doll." There was not even a hint of tension like there had been in the last couple of years when Stuart and I were together at his family's gatherings.

Becoming the Human Crystal class came to an end in late November 2012. During the last four weeks, we had had to do "past" life meditations. As I explained when I wrote earlier about how I visualize, I don't actually "see" the scenario, but I "know" what it is. In this visualization, I knew it was during the French Revolution in the 1790s. It felt familiar, as the scene had come up repeatedly in sessions with various psychics. In this particular past life, I am a redheaded barmaid wearing an apron over a long cotton dress and am working for an opposition faction running information. Eventually, I get caught. My punishment for taking a stand in what I believed in was to be guillotined. My brother in that life is somehow involved perhaps in my capture and certainly in not protecting me.

I have often wondered if there was any carry-over to my current life. I have often chosen not to speak out until late after the events have happened. In my early years especially, I kept all my emotions bottled up inside. To my knowledge, I had never told anyone of the abuse I had undergone — much less how it had felt. This is an assumption, since because of the electroshock treatments I am only able to remember fragments or pieces that have come through psychic channels. Most likely, I was threatened at the time of the abuse that, if I told anyone, something bad would happen to me. In my family, furthermore, displaying emotions —whether positive or negative — was not viewed favorably. As a result, expressing emotion was simply not done. It wasn't until I was thirty years old and at Liberty House, the residential therapy facility I had sought help from, that I realized how angry I was and I started to express it by speaking up for myself.

This execution in a past life in France both explains my difficulty in speaking out — after all, who wants her head cut off! — and confirms why I had such difficulty speaking French when I lived in Paris. Oddly, I knew the words for things but couldn't formulate them into phrases or sentences. It was as if my mouth went slack. Perhaps I did not want to speak the language that I had used to bring so much pain onto myself?

That month of November, other past life experiences had also brought other painful memories to the fore. I was particularly pained about being aware that my brother had been unable — or was unwilling — to protect me from the group of boarding-school boys when I was twelve. Where was the brother I could turn to for help, and, for that matter, where were the parents I could depend on to listen to me speak my pain and to demand justice for me?

This abandonment, this not being protected, was repeated again in Paris when Michael had been too drunk or passed out to save me from being raped by a predator I met at the party.

These past life experiences validated what I already knew and, coming from my meditation, must have meant it was significant for me to hear again and understand. In these memories, I was looking for protection and defense; but at the time, I was forming a relationship with Don, I was moving beyond this passivity and learning that I could protect and defend myself. It was not only all right to do so but it was downright wonderful!

Another past life meditation was also relevant to understanding more about myself and how I was taking better care of myself. Again, I was a woman — most likely, a Native American — in a cave wearing skins. I was squatting by a fire near something cooking in a pot. I felt lonely and isolated. My being a Native American in a past life had also come up in a few psychic sessions or readings. Therefore, it must be important for me to know. It would explain my interest in exploring shamanism and journeying as well as these lines below that had come to me a few years earlier:

Woman by fire

A woman sat by the fire, stirring the soup

As an owl flew down, sat beside her and said,

"You salted the soup with your tears.

You sweetened the soup with your love.

You peppered the soup with your anger,

And you will live long like me.

You simmered the soup a long time, a broth so fine

That it will feed many souls for life."

As I read this poem now, I interpret these words as indicating I have tried hard over the years to understand myself and make sense of my childhood — and perhaps even more than make sense, to heal the insecurity created by my childhood. I "salted the soup" with my tears, and for a long while, turned my rage inward yet was able to love — in the only way I knew how to — the men I was married to or had a relationship with. Because of this work, I and perhaps others will be better off in this lifetime and those to come. I was growing beyond my past.

Having finished the Becoming the Human Crystal course

successfully, I had the option to take all that I had learned to the next level and get a certificate as a Crystal Resonance Therapist. Crystals fascinated me. I would have been thrilled to learn more about them, but I made a conscious decision not to study crystals any further. I had already done enough healing work on myself and, if I wanted to do deep work, I had already learned the Wei Chi healing system for which I was certified as a practitioner. I wasn't assured that placing my confidence in another modality and doing all the work certification required would really add up to a financial support for me. It hadn't in setting up a Wei Chi practice.

I decided to put off pursuing more training. Maybe I would come back to it and maybe I wouldn't. For now, I felt happy with my life as it was opening up to Don. My best investment of time and energy was to concentrate on my relationship with him and enjoy the life I was now having. Just the previous year, I had been all pins and needles living with Stuart and I had been so unhappy. Now because of a blossoming relationship with Don, my life was so much more enjoyable. I did not want to complicate life with a time-consuming certification program. It felt like a diversion rather than a centralizing impulse.

After the pleasant Thanksgiving came my first Christmas with Don. It, too, was a happy day so unlike the previous year when Stuart had just left and I had felt so raw, so publicly a failure at a marriage. A few days before Christmas, Don asked me to celebrate with his daughters and grandson down the street at his house. Then, on Christmas morning, we were just the two of us. I should have anticipated that it was consistent with his generous character to present me with many lovely presents. I was totally not expecting Don to shower me with gifts that he had put a lot of thought into. My two favorites were a Lapis Lazuli necklace with matching earrings and a Swarovski crystal snowflake ornament.

I myself had not showered him with gifts, and for that I was a bit embarrassed. I had, however, bought him some thoughtful gifts, and one had a special meaning. As Don opened this gift, he saw three ornaments. Each was labeled with a single word: Hope, Joy, and Noel.

I told him, "Do you remember how, last summer, when we crossed each other on the condo road and we stopped to talk in our cars, you said you had no hope? The first ball is to remind you that there is always hope, always something to look forward to. The second ball is for the bit of joy I hope you have found in our relationship. The third is to underline that, during this Noel season, we are all capable of rebirth."

His eyes glistened with emotion as he thanked me. I loved that about Don that he showed his emotions. I no longer was with an inscrutable man.

That Christmas afternoon, Don and I went to Tim and Amanda's for dinner. Amanda's family had come, as had Michael and Carol who were there again. Don fit in easily with everyone.

Don and I ushered in 2013 with a champagne toast to our relationship: "May it continue to grow!" And grow it did, for at the end of January, for our first overnight away, we went to a romantic Vermont inn. The weekend couldn't have been better. In fact, it was a special weekend that neither of us will forget. As we were checking out in the morning, we must have been beaming, and the innkeeper said to us, "Looks like you two had a good time."

Did she think we were a couple who had been together for decades instead of a newly minted one? It's not that I wanted to pretend we had been together a long time; it's just that I felt as if we had.

Shadows and Light

Don assured her, "We had a lovely time, and I am sure we will be back." On our way home from the inn, we even discussed where we would go next.

Don started a travel journal of what we did, of the nature of our accommodations, of dining venues and what we ate there, and so on. It proved to be an excellent resource for our future trips.

Don would say, "Do you remember those scrumptious lobster rolls we had? We sat outside overlooking the water. Where was it?"

"It was somewhere in Maine, but I have also forgotten the town. Let's look it up in your travel journal," I'd suggest.

Don was nostalgic and he liked to reminisce about different things we had done. Even little things were grist for nostalgia. "Last summer, if you drove past my house and saw me sitting on my breezeway," he said, "you would stop and talk. Sometimes you would bring me tomatoes from the farm stand. And… remember when I said I had feelings for you and you patted your heart?"

"Yes, it was my way of saying that your words got to me emotionally, and you had no idea of what I meant until I explained it later," I replied with a smile.

With wonderment, Don would often say and still does, "How did I find you?" My usual light-hearted answer is, "I was right down the street the whole time." I knew what he meant and often responded, "I am so fortunate to have met you also."

Don explained to me that, after Suzanne died, he thought he would be alone for the rest of his life, so it was a surprise to find me so close by. At times, I was still in awe of how we met — I was sure the Universe played a role in it — and delighted that Don would bring it up so often and freely. I believe it helped solidify our relationship. I myself had thought that I might not find another partner and that would have been acceptable, at least for the time being.

Don had a pessimistic streak. For a man who had achieved professional success in his working life, his lack of belief in himself was amazing to me to witness. There was no reason for it. Having been married twice and been in one long-term relationship and having all three end badly, I was the one who should have doubted her chances of success; instead it was Don who had had two successful marriages—each of which had ended only due to death — who doubted his ability to find another mate.

His pessimistic attitude would declare itself in any number of little ways, and I would feel a bit less enthusiastic in face of it. Could I live with his negativity over the long run? Would it wear me down? Was I asking for too much? I was afraid of another relationship failure even though I had learned so much about myself. After all, failure was also something I had learned. For the time being, I was okay with letting this doubt ride.

By the end of February, we had gone from saying we had "feelings for each other" to expressing "I love you." I can't recall if Don had already expressed his love for me, but one evening I told him, "I love you." For me, it was a big deal because I took saying "I love you" very seriously. I had already told Don that I had to feel the love first and only then could I express it. I told him that it was not something I said often but I knew some people did. Being more expressive was something I needed to work on in the future. I don't remember my parents ever telling me that they loved me, so I had not told them I loved them. I had not developed the habit of saying words of love. Even more important, I had been a person who, because she did not experience love early in life, had a problem with the concept of love. How do you know what something is if you've never had it?

Now with Don, I was feeling something that I knew instinctively was this thing called love.

During the next couple of months, we were seeing each other almost every day. In April 2013, we decided to spend several complete days together by taking a trip. We spent two nights at an inn in Ogunquit, Maine. When we walked along the Marginal Way again — it was a lot colder than the previous summer when we had been there together — we reminisced about that time.

"It was the second time we had gone out," I said. "Do you remember holding my hand when we crossed the street?"

"I do and I still like to," Don replied as he took my hand and kissed it. I felt my heart skip a beat with joy, and we continued to hold hands as we walked along Marginal Way. I was so far removed emotionally from the day I had landed in Manchester after being away in Sedona for two weeks. I had hoped that Stuart would take me in his arms and kiss me. No such thing had happened, and here was Don spontaneously taking my hand and kissing it! As much as I felt unloved then, I now felt loved. This time with Don was perhaps the first time in my life that I had felt loved for who I was.

We both enjoyed travel, and having done the Ogunquit overnights successfully, we felt we could handle more. At the end of May, we planned a trip lasting nine days. We drove up the Maine coast, stopping to sightsee in Boothbay Harbor, Camden, and Rockport, and ended up in Bar Harbor for two nights. From Mt. Desert Island, we turned around to head home. Despite Don's observation that "it's going to rain the whole time," the weather, for the most part, was sunny but still a bit cool. I was learning not to be stopped by Don saying negative things like this before we went somewhere. I myself might say, "I hope we have good weather," whereas he might have said, "I hope we don't have bad weather." When I asked him why he framed many of his statements in the negative, he would always reply, "I am a realist." Seeing that he was comfortable with his reaction, I accepted that his glass-half-empty response was something I would have to get used to. It seemed little to adjust to compared to all I was receiving. That sense of reciprocity in a relationship was another first for me. I had always felt that I was giving too much for what I was receiving.

After this trip, I knew we travelled well together, free of issues that arose when we decided where to eat and what to do. Fortunately, money also was not a problem. It had not always been this way with me. When I had traveled with Michael, he always wanted to spend more than we could afford, and at times, he would not agree to the more economical places I suggested we go to. For instance, when he selected restaurants and hotels, he did not pay much attention to the cost or whether there were less expensive alternatives that would be just as acceptable. Stuart had been more appreciative of my need to be more aware of costs, partly because he had less money to spend than I.

I had never had a high income, but I had been prudent in placing discretionary funds in investments. I had also had a small inheritance from my Aunt Clare which I had spent on house repairs but later recouped and then some when I sold the house. I had had a much larger inheritance from my godmother. In addition, I had done well when I sold my Newton condo and later my cabin on Maidstone Lake. The result of being fiscally conservative and of the inheritances and profits of sales of property had generated a financial ease greater than Stuart's. Now Don, because he had practiced medicine all his life, was also in a secure financial position. Between us, money was simply not a matter of concern.

Maggie and I still kept in touch via email, but I had not seen her for well over two years. At the time, she had just met Keith who had joined us for lunch with Peter, Erin and the girls. By 2013, her life had changed. She was getting married to Keith. When she wrote to me with the news, I was delighted for her.

Shadows and Light

From what she had told me, Keith was a marvelous choice and would make a loving husband and father if they were to have children. While I was pleased for her, I never expected to be invited to her wedding. I understood and was not upset when I did not receive an invitation. Later, Maggie told me that she regretted not being comfortable inviting me. I assured her that I understood and all I wanted was to see some pictures of her and Keith, and she did send me some.

Summer was flying by as it often seems to in our short New England season. Before I knew it, July 19, the day Don and I were celebrating as our first anniversary together, came up. Knowing Don's love of nostalgia, I had thought that we would probably go to the Atkinson Country Club for dinner as our first date had been there. Sure enough, we went, and of course, we talked about our first time in the restaurant. (We have made going a tradition every year since.)

One late August evening, we were sitting on my deck when Don said, "For your birthday, I want to buy you a ring."

"As long as it is not an engagement ring", I quipped. "Neither of us is ready to think about getting married."

"No, this ring will not be an engagement ring," Don smiled. "But, it will be a symbol of our committed relationship."

"That's better! I would love a ring. Marriage is just a piece of paper to me. The only benefit — according to my financial advisor — is if you were going to leave me a huge inheritance, and I know that's not going to happen."

To me, marriage was about loving, supporting, and nurturing your spouse. If one does that already in a relationship, what is the point of marriage later in life when no children are involved? Besides, our track record wasn't favorable. Don had had two wives die — and I wasn't ready to be dead! — and I had been divorced twice.

The bottom line was I felt comfortable being in a committed

relationship with Don and a ring would serve as a reminder of that for us. When we talked further about marriage, he said he didn't want to get married but wanted assurance that I was committed.

We went to the jewelry store, and I picked out what I wanted for a ring. Don was at ease in the store since he had had experience buying jewelry for Suzanne there. I was anxious because I can have trouble making up my mind if I am given too many choices. After I had a ballpark figure on how much Don was willing to spend — I was not used to such generosity as he was displaying. My anxiety eased up and I decided on a gorgeous sapphire, my favorite and my birthstone. Having selected the stone, I then chose a simple — not too big — setting with diamond chips. It would be so sparkly, and I couldn't wait to wear the ring, but it would take a week or so to set the stone.

Knowing that Don was financially comfortable and that money would never be an issue between us made me feel secure about our relationship continuing to the next level. Was that next level moving in together? Would we be able to create a real home where we could nurture and love each other? I was beginning to think it possible. A real home was what I needed at this point in my life so I could put my unhappy childhood, where I felt abandoned, behind me and savor Don's generosity and love.

Chapter 31
Final Healing

In November of 2013, a few months after I picked my sapphire ring, Katie, Kim, Rita, Linette — my Wei Chi friends — and I went to a workshop given by two mediums.

One of the exercises called for everyone in the audience to contact someone from the afterlife. On hearing this, I immediately started to doubt whether I could be successful. My inner critic was putting me down again, and for a moment, as I had done so many times in the past, I believed her. Quickly, I realized I had fallen into my old ways! This was not the Susan I wished to be. I hate it when that happens, but that day, I reversed my old pattern of negativity.

Of course, you can do it. Just relax and let it come, I admonished myself, so pleased to have redirected my energy so as not to spoil my opportunity.

The medium led the group in a visualization to get us into a deep, relaxed state. We were brought to a door and asked to open it to see who was on the other side waiting to speak with us. I saw figures I was familiar with — my grandfather, the Bishop, and my great-great grandmother, Mattie. Encountering these two when I opened the door was not a surprise. There was also someone else whose presence I sensed right away. It was Don's late wife, Suzanne. I didn't have a vision of her but knew she was there.

"Tell Don I am sorry I went before him." These are the words I heard from her. Then she graciously thanked me for helping him during his difficult time of grief. I responded with a simple, "You're welcome."

"Tell him to sell the jewelry," she advised me. What a meaningful message that was! The jewelry message was significant because Don was not sure what to do with most of what was left. Some pieces he had already given away, but there remained much.

We were to ask the spirit who had come to us for some gift. In this visualization, Suzanne produced a single red rose for me. It was a rose without thorns.

The red rose could be interpreted in two ways. First, a red rose with no thorns indicated I had healed myself. Years earlier, these words had come to me: "A rose of great beauty succumbed to her thorns: she withered and died. Only a gradual picking out of these thorns will restore her wounded self."

I always thought I was the rose and each thorn represented a negative incident or belief in my life. In order to heal myself, I would have to know what each thorn meant and understand how it affected me. Subsequently I would have to forgive and move on. Only then would I be whole.

My second interpretation was this: Suzanne and I were the only ones Don had given a red rose to. In being given the rose — Don's token — by Suzanne, I seemed to be told she saw me as important. Evidently, she wanted to say something about being special, about her seeing me as special. Since we had not had much of a relationship when she was alive, her giving me Don's symbol seemed to say she saw me as an important person in Don's life.

In giving the rose, Suzanne's spirit offered, "It will be smooth sailing for Don and you."

Subsequently, after we had contacted the spirit and had received something, the medium had assigned us a second task and that was to give the spirit something.

"What can I do for you?" I asked her.

"Remember me at this Thanksgiving," she replied.

Now I had to tell Don about the messages I had gotten from Suzanne — but when? He did not believe in the afterlife, so I was not sure what his response would be. I was nervous about telling him and decided not to say anything until after the holidays when everything quieted down.

For our second Thanksgiving, we had the same group as a year earlier with the addition of Erin's parents who were up from New Jersey. It was another pleasurable family time, and I did acknowledge Suzanne's wish to be remembered at Thanksgiving. I suggested that Don and I toast her, and for grace before dinner, I included — as I had the year before — "Let's take a moment to remember all those who have gone before us."

In 2014, anxious to get a break from the cold and snowy winter in New Hampshire, Don and I made plans to drive to Florida for the month of February 2014. I understood spending all this time together would give me the opportunity to get to know Don better. How would we relate to each other away from the supports of home — and the opportunity to get away from each other — and out of our daily comfortable routines? While we planned a tentative itinerary and booked rooms in St. Augustine and Key West, we were winging it and many decisions — where to eat, what to do, where to spend the night — would have to be made on the spot. In our earlier, shorter getaways, our traveling personalities meshed and we were compatible, so I hoped this would prove to be true on a much longer trip.

Since Don liked to drive, he did almost all the driving, and I did the navigating. This system worked well for us. Don would listen to my ideas of things to do. For example, when we stayed

Shadows and Light

in Fort Myers, close to Sanibel Island, he was willing to walk on the beach with me, something that Johnnie had refused to do. Don appreciated that I could not go a long time without food — I would get grumpy and headachy — so we kept a bag of snacks in the car to stave off my hunger until we found a place to eat. Our month in Florida had proven to be great, and Don and I had again proven ourselves to be compatible travel companions. We had left a couple of swing days so we had time to stop in Savannah for two nights on the way home.

The day we arrived in Savannah, we took a trolley tour of the city, and the next day, we walked around some of the historic squares. I kept imagining how beautiful it would be later in the spring with all the shrubs and magnolias in bloom. Even though it was a gray, cool day, I could still appreciate Savannah's charm — the live oaks were a favorite of mine. We were walking around the Colonial Park cemetery reading some of the headstones.

"I've had enough. Let's get going," Don insisted and he proceeded to walk over the graves to get to the nearest exit.

"You can't walk over the graves," I replied with dismay. "It's disrespectful."

"You do what you want. I am leaving now," Don said as he distanced himself from me in a huff.

I was irritated. I am not sure why his action pushed my button, but it did. Maybe it wasn't reasonable on my part. Perhaps I was projecting some hurt from one of my former husbands when he was critical of me or distanced himself. Johnnie was not critical of me but he turned out to be emotionally distant.

Angry at seeing Don rush away, I stood by a gravestone, thinking, I can find our hotel by myself so to heck with Don. I'll walk by myself. I turned away from him and began looking for an exit path that would not have me walking over graves.

When I found it, I started toward the exit. I could still see

Don, but he was walking quickly and I would soon lose sight of him. I started to think that this disagreement was not a good development. What if something happened to Don on the way back? He might fall and hurt himself, and I surmised he did not have his cell with him. I always carried mine, and he usually didn't. Since I was worried about leaving him on his own, I decided to accompany him. But, it was more than a worry about his safety.

I had made his actions an issue by placing far too much emphasis about walking on the gravestones. At that moment, Don and I were on our way home after a very successful jaunt around Florida, and it would be a shame to have a huge fight about walking over graves detract from our lovely trip. Since the disagreement happened in a graveyard, was it possible Spirit was playing a part in this scene? Was I being tested to see how I would react? A compromise was in order, and I knew Don and I could work it out. Once I came to this conclusion, I could feel my anger float away and my shoulders relaxing. This was a big step forward for me in understanding how to negotiate in a relationship and not turn my anger into bodily symptoms. So often, in the past, it was easier to give in rather than face the consequences — insecurity and loneliness — of being shut out.

I hurried toward him as he retreated and was approaching the cemetery gate. Seeing that he was keeping his distance, I realized I would not catch up with him.

I shouted for him to stop.

He did stop and waited for me to catch up. When we stood facing each other, I said, "I would like to talk about what just happened. I don't want to be angry with you." As we continued to walk, I asked Don, "What do you think happened? Were you angry at me?

"Not at all. This is our last day in Savannah, and I want to get more walking in. I have seen enough of the cemetery."

"I really misunderstood you," I smiled, with relief. "I thought you were mad at me. Are you still going to walk over graves?"

"Yes, I don't think it makes a difference. It is not like someone will feel me walking over them."

We agreed to disagree about walking on graves. Because Don was respectful of me and because we resolved this disagreement with a truce, I was hopeful that we could continue to do so in arguments to come. In the future, when Don "pushed my buttons," I was determined to figure out why I might have reacted negatively to him. I realized that there was a strong possibility that my reactions might not be warranted and have to do with something that was totally about me. If we were both "in the right," a compromise was needed. There were no repercussions from our discussion, other than a return to our compatibility, and I could detect no changes in Don's behavior towards me. I had no further pain — often a signal of conflict — and we continued on as we usually were, delighted to be together.

From Savannah, we drove north through Virginia, around Washington, D.C. and up the New Jersey turnpike. In Connecticut, we stopped to visit with Maggie whom I was eager to see. It had been about three years since we had visited and her life had changed dramatically. She had married Keith the previous year and had just given birth — three weeks previously — to a baby boy they named Finley. I was so happy for her since she had believed, based on being advised by a physician, that she would never get pregnant. We had a short but delightful visit with her and Finley — we did not see Keith, as he was working — and I got to hold Finley, which was very special. He was my grandson, and, at the same time, not my grandson. I was in an undefined zone, and I was okay with the nebulous nature of my relationship.

In the previous two years, there had been so many changes in my life and in Maggie's. She was married now, and I had Don in my life. I wondered if there was any significance to it. Had we finally settled down in our lives? I sure hoped that was the case for us both.

Back in New Hampshire, as we drove into our condo association, it felt gratifying to be home. But, after Don dropped me off with my luggage and he left to go to his condo, it felt strange to be separated, alone in our individual homes after having spent the whole month together.

After this trip, which we both judged a huge success, our

Maggie, Keith, and Finley, 2018

relationship reached a higher level. We broached living together, but I insisted, "I am not ready yet. I still think it would be too soon." We did agree, however, that if we did move in together, Don would come live with me. Although our condos had a similar floor plan, there were significant differences. Mine had a two-car garage while Don's had a one-car. I also had more square footage that included a family room in the basement and a private, larger deck. It just made sense for us to have him move in with me.

When Stuart and I moved in together all those years ago, we had the challenge of filling a large blank wall in the living room. Fortunately, he had a folding wooden screen which held a collage of family pictures. He took half of his pictures out to make room for some of mine. We placed this screen at one end of this blank wall which helped to distract from the wall's emptiness, but it was never enough. I had always thought this wall needed bookcases or cabinetry.

One cold afternoon in early March 2014 when I was at Don's house and he was heating water for our tea, I walked around his living room. My eyes fell on a set of bookcases which I had seen many times but, that day, I realized how well they would look in my living room along the blank wall. If we were to live together, his bookcases would look great in my living room. When I found myself thinking this, I realized that the idea of living together was ripening, and I was trying different parts of it out for size.

Don interrupted my thoughts as he came in with the tea, and we sat down on the sofa.

"How are you coming along sorting through and giving away Suzanne's things?"

"I'm getting there, but there is still a lot to do."

"I can help you if you want," I offered. "Have you thought about the rest of her jewelry?" He had earlier told me to take what jewelry I wanted, but I had declined to take any. To me, jewelry was very personal and I would have felt funny wearing any of it, especially since Don had given these pieces to her. Although he had given some away to his daughters, a lot of the jewelry remained untouched.

I turned so we were facing each other. "Speaking of jewelry, there is something I need to tell you!" I proceeded to tell him about the November workshop when we had to contact someone from the afterlife. I explained how I had sensed Suzanne's presence and told him about the messages I had received from her. He appeared to listen to my words, but I was not sure how much sank in. I didn't know if he was uncomfortable with the concept of the afterlife or with what I was saying. He didn't ask any questions, however, nor did he want to talk about Suzanne's jewelry and the significance of the red rose, which he had only given twice — once to Suzanne and once to me.

When something psychic comes up in a conversation we are

having, he has responded at times by referring to me or my Wei Chi friends humorously as "witches." I now understand that to be a way of saying he is uncomfortable with the subject — it is easier to joke about it so as to diffuse something he does not want to deal with. I was not unaware that in the past I might have reacted had he said something of that nature. Now I could think of being called a witch as something that was about him and not about me. Always as a girl and a younger woman, I had owned comments that were really about others, and taking them on had made me miserable. I had been completely unable to see them as saying something about someone else.

After this conversation, Don did take the most expensive piece of Suzanne's jewelry — a diamond pendant — to a shop to be sold.

Beginning the previous fall, I had undertaken a flurry of house activities. I had replaced worn carpeting in the living room with a new hardwood floor. Don had been characteristically generous and had helped me with the cost of the floor — was he thinking that he would be living in the house in years to come? His was a totally unexpected gesture which I was grateful for, not only for the financial help but for what it represented of his investment in me and in our relationship. I too seemed to be thinking that he would be living there.

That spring of 2014, after Don and I returned from our trip to Florida, I began thinking of repainting the downstairs: kitchen, dining room, living room, and hallway. This would complete the work I had commenced in the fall. I had never liked the color I had chosen for the dining room, and the living room color, which was the original one, did not compliment the stone fireplace. With the help of a designer, I had put a lot of attention into selecting better paint colors that I was going to apply myself. I was bursting with energy and had the time since I was not working

Shadows and Light

nor doing much except spending time with Don.

On the week following our conversation about Suzanne's jewelry, on a brisk, but sunny morning, Don and I went for a walk in a nearby town where the sidewalks were clear of ice. Don dropped me off at home around lunchtime and took off, as he had an afternoon appointment. After a quick lunch, and buoyed by the energy from the walk, I decided to make use of a long afternoon by myself to start painting the living room walls. As I look back on all the activity I engaged in that year to freshen the house up, I believe I was unconsciously in the nesting mode, getting ready for Don to move in with me.

I was sitting on a stool, cutting in at the baseboards when I thought with some contentment, Don could be in the house with me all the time. I pictured a scene of cooking dinner for him and watching TV together in the evening. The domestic visual was tempting, but was I ready — and able — to make a wise decision?

I remained unsure about trusting my skill at making a right choice for my future, and at the same time, I wanted to resolve my hesitation about taking a next step. The hesitation itself seemed to be a step, but one I no longer was willing to take without questioning it. I had trusted my judgment before in choosing men, and my judgment had proven to be untrustworthy. Was that happening now, too? Of one thing I was sure, I would no longer force what I wanted to be true to fit into the "true" slot. I had become cautious and, in my better moments, I believed wiser.

I had seen how hesitation had led me to justify taking so long with Stuart to terminate our relationship. The hesitation then had produced months of unhappiness, months when I might have lived a better, happier life. I had hesitated so long that it was he who had precipitated the end. This time, I wanted to be a more active player in the decision to move in or not with Don.

One evening as I was doing my automatic writing, I turned

to Mattie for advice, asking her, "What do I need to do?"

"You know what to do," she answered. "Don is still fragile. Be patient and stay grounded, compassionate, non-judgmental and you will find out what you need to know about Don. You think too much, and it can get you into trouble. Spend more time enjoying life and think less. Fix up your nest to your liking, do some gardening, and maybe write a poem or two."

This was an interesting communication. Mattie was telling me about what Don needed. Being sensitive, I knew that he still had some grieving to do and my hesitation to have him move in was in part due to my intuition that it would not be good for him — just yet. So, my hesitation in this instance was not just about something needing to be worked on in me; it was also some wisdom about Don. I had to allow both of these insights to co-exist in me: needing to work on being more active at the same time as needing to respect a slow pace, which fed into my default hesitation. I took this insight to reflect another instance of my growth as I was now not seeing everything being about me. My intuition was telling me this hesitation was about giving Don time and that was good. Moving in together was simply not a best next step right now for him — it would probably be great at some point but just not right now.

At the same time as I had this insight into Don's deeper needs, I also could see he seemed needy or out of sorts at times, but as long as I gave him my attention and affection, he was fine. Was this part of the grief process or did it mark a character trait that would never change?

Since I had seen Maggie on our return through Connecticut, I had been thinking a lot about her and her baby. I wondered if she would see me in a different light now that she was a mother. While I hoped we would become closer, I knew that Maggie's mother had moved to an assisted living place to be close to her. Her mother was well into her eighties and was having some memory issues. She needed Maggie's help at this juncture of her life and that was as it should be. I thought that, perhaps after Maggie's mother passed away, then a shift between us that would bring us closer would be more likely to occur.

I knew the connection between Mattie, my great-great grandmother, and me since we shared many biographical elements. I believed we shared a soul — and if we did not, at least, we seemed to share a fate. The question remained, "How did Maggie fit into the larger scheme of our lives?" (I loved the similarity of these two names, Mattie and Maggie! Surely that could not be an accident and perhaps pointed to a connection?) Maggie and Emma, Mattie's daughter, also shared biographical similarities that were more than coincidental. The logical conclusion was that Maggie was the soul of her daughter Emma.

"You guessed correctly. It took you awhile," Mattie answered when I addressed her through automatic writing.

It all made sense when I thought about it. My father's genealogical research (which was about his line also) had found Emma's birth certificate, which listed "unknown" for her father — Maggie's was also "unknown." Emma was born in August of 1855 and Mattie did not get married until November of 1856 and had five more children with her husband. If I am the soul of Mattie, then I would have come into this lifetime to have the experience — in order to develop my soul and grow — of getting pregnant when unmarried and not keeping the baby, the opposite of Mattie's experience at a time when keeping her baby would

My great grandmother Emma (Vertue) Yerburgh circa 1880

have been even more difficult than it would have been for me. What might this difference mean for me now in this life?

How had the pattern continued into the next generation? Mattie had raised Emma, while I had sent Maggie to be adopted. The concept is complicated, but I do believe in the afterlife and that I was born with an agenda of things I needed to experience in my lifetime in order to heal from them. I could never figure out why I allowed myself to get pregnant before I was married. Was it only the result of the sexual abuse in my earlier years or did my soul life play a part? I will never know for sure, but having contact with the afterlife has helped me sort it out a bit. As I was growing up and into adulthood, I felt disconnected from my family and my ancestors — I was the black sheep that never fit into the fold. But now, knowing Mattie and believing in the afterlife, my attitude had changed. I wanted to know more about my ancestors, to have insight about where I fit into my family and why I had had to experience the childhood I had.

The afterlife has also provided me with guidance and support. I am still amazed that Spirit and the departed know me so well and tell me what I need to know at any time. Of course, there have been many factors that helped me heal my life: counseling was important, hearing apologies from my parents, mothering my sons. One thing is certain, however: I will be forever grateful for how emissaries from the afterlife have helped me put my life together. They have been with me on this healing journey.

Even by the end of April and into May, I was still in a holding pattern, still not sure if Don and I should live together. We had been a couple for almost two years. The financial positives were tempting, but something was continuing to hold me back. When I did my automatic writing, I asked Spirit, "What is holding me back?"

"Your fear," Spirit replied. "Fear of losing your independence. Fear that Don will get needier than he already is. Fear he will turn into an old man even more set in his ways."

These fears seemed both legitimate and unwarranted. I asked Spirit one more question.

"Is there a legitimate reason why I should not make the move when he is ready?"

Spirit replied, "No, it will be another learning experience for you with a man who is totally different from the others. He will demand to be loved by you. You already do. That will continue. He will frustrate you, which he now does at times."

Because this message confirmed my fears about what I had seen of Don's neediness, it rang true. I did get frustrated with Don's pessimism and his lack of belief in himself because there was no reason for it. Having been married twice and been in one long-term relationship and having all three end badly, I was afraid of another failure even though I had learned so much about myself. I knew I could not change Don and had to accept him for who he was. Don had no idea why he was negative at times and had no interest in exploring it.

Among the negative responses he held on to was his refusal to embrace technology. (He has always said that he would be happier living in the Middle Ages.) Since I was asking Don to accept me for who I was, of course, I had to reciprocate. I had to accept that he would not become adept at computer use and that he would turn companionably to me for help. So, our tasks came down to accepting each other for who we were. It was not only fair but also the only way our lives together would flourish. This was a big jump from my earlier thinking.

"Let go of your past insecurities," Spirit continued, "and of your fear of repeating failure in a relationship. Don is good for you, and you know that. You do need more affection and connection in your life than you can possibly get by being alone, so stop thinking about what you could do and do it. Expand, grow and learn, keep writing."

I was so much more willing to make the compromises in regards to issues that arose between Don and me, but I was also much less willing to compromise who I was as a person than I had been in the past. For me, this was a huge development.

A week later, in mid-May when I was again doing more automatic writing, Mattie returned with more advice: "Stay in the present. You have to let go of the past. It is over, kaput, gone. It will float up in your mind from time to time. Let it go away gently without dwelling on anything. Stay in the present. How many times do I have to tell you that? Why are you so scared? You have nothing to lose — he is a good man and he loves you. You are scared because you have not experienced love and acceptance before to such a degree — he gets you and appreciates you."

Mattie was right when she said I was scared. I was not used to love and affection such as Don was able to shower me with. So much attention was new to me. He let me express an opinion without interrupting me. He complimented me freely, thanked me for every meal I cooked for him, and if I repeated myself — which I tend to do if I am processing something — he would not put me down for it. This was so different from being with Stuart because, after being married to him a while, I was not sure I could trust him enough to overcome my fear of rejection. It is hard to be affectionate with someone and to accept affection from someone if you are afraid of being rejected. I never knew how Johnnie felt since we never had counseling together and he took off without telling me how he felt about our relationship.

My relationship with Don was not all Mattie and I explored. I had been thinking about planting a moon garden — all white flowers — and she went on to ask me how I was doing with that project. She also told me she would help me pick out a crystal at the crystal show I had planned to attend the following weekend with Kim, Katie, Linette, and Rita. I thanked Mattie for all her help to date.

I was — and am — so grateful to have Mattie in my life. It always amazes me how well she knows me and my idiosyncrasies.

Chapter 32
Making the Commitment

In spite of my recurring hesitations, my relationship with Don seemed to be going in the right direction and I felt affirmed by his love and attention.

"Do you feel that I love you?" I asked Don, not once but on many occasions.

His answer was always something like: "Of course, I do. You may not tell me as much as I would like, but you show it to me in so many different ways — in the little things you do for me."

I felt reassured when he'd said this. Had I had this response and reassurance in my previous relationships and had I felt that my opinion would ever be valued, it might have calmed me sufficiently to be more present to the men I was with. Who knows but that one of those relationships might have survived?

In spite of Mattie's words, I was still in a quandary, uncertain about Don. Doubt was my *modus operandi*, and it would not easily go away. I knew I needed to get out of this holding pattern, make a decision, and get on with my life in one way or the other. Then one day, just when I thought Don and I could move forward, he chastised me for reading a text message on my phone while we were together. This is something I hardly ever do when I am with him. At the time of this misunderstanding, his ears were plugged up and he was having difficulty hearing, so he cupped his ears to hear me responding to his rebuff of my reading a text. His gesture struck me as a reminder of old age — and how he was ahead of me going there. I knew my own old age was coming around the corner but my reaction was stronger than that reminder would have warranted. What bothered me was deeper than that: I realized that Don's gesture reminded me of my father, who would also cup his ears hoping to hear better. I could feel my father's silence and his locking me out of his life, as though I were utterly unimportant to him.

Susan, I said sternly to myself in my best adult voice. You can't dump how you feel about your father onto Don!

At the time, I had already suggested on several occasions he get an appointment with his ear, nose, and throat doctor as soon as possible to get his ears irrigated. Since I had been wearing hearing aids myself for about eight years by then, I could not conjure up a lot of sympathy for Don's resistance.

To my reminder that he needed an appointment, he replied, as if he were dismissing my suggestion, "Suzanne always irrigated my ears when I needed it done."

This comparison to Suzanne irritated me, and I replied, "I'm sorry but I am not Suzanne and I have never irrigated ears."

My rather brusque response could have triggered Don's continuing grief because he then rejected any help or my ideas of what he could do about his hearing. We were back in Savannah! This is one of my fears: my partner's negativity will get me down and wear away at me and then I will start to pull away. At times, Don does say things which I let push one of my buttons. Even though I know what he says is usually his issue, I can't let it go to the degree I want.

After that unpleasant incident, however, Don did make a doctor's appointment and apologized to me. In turn, I apologized for my negative reaction. I was comforted by this adult behavior, which, once again, presaged being able to communicate at a functional level.

Shadows and Light

As a result, I knew he cared about me and that we were — and would be — able to work things out. This was comforting, but I was still not able to decide where I wanted to go with this relationship. Do we live together or separately? After all, many relationships endure for years in separate households. Do we grow closer — whether we live together or not — or do we stay at the level of intimacy we were at?

In late May, we booked a three-night stay in the Berkshires at the Red Lion Inn in Stockbridge. After we checked in and got to our room, I realized there had been a mistake in room assignment. "Don't unpack anything yet," I said. "I booked a room with a Jacuzzi and this one has a shower only — there is not even a bathtub. We have to go back to the front desk and change the room."

"We don't need to; this room is fine," Don said, trying to appease me and make good of the situation, but I was not about to forfeit what I wanted. After more discussion, Don saw that having the room I had reserved was important to me and we went down to get the room changed. Because of this mix-up in rooms and how respectfully we resolved it, I felt once again that Don had listened to me and that was so important. Stuart would have told me not to get so emotional about a room — it was not worth the energy. That would have left me frustrated; however, Don's response made me happy to be out of the relationship with Stuart and into a very good one with Don. So many interactions between us were now calming, soothing and — yes — healing. We had fun just being together, away from home. Things like wrong room assignments did not get in our way.

In that trip to Western Massachusetts, we visited some historical sights. We enjoyed entering The Mount — Edith Wharton's summer home — and strolling around the mansion's splendid gardens. Nearby in Stockbridge where we were staying, we also checked out the Norman Rockwell Museum and then headed north to the Hancock Shaker Village.

On our last afternoon in the Berkshires, we were on the veranda of the Red Lion Inn, sitting in rocking chairs having a glass of wine before dinner. There was a chill in the May air, and as I adjusted my sweater to cover my arms, I said, "Isn't this the life?"

"It sure is. We could be together all the time now," Don commented.

"I know. I am closer to making a decision to live together but I am still not ready. Are you?" I asked.

"I could be persuaded. We are spending so much time together that we might as well be living together. Besides," Don added with a smile, "I wouldn't have to cook for myself anymore."

Over that weekend in the Berkshires, there had been a deepening in our relationship and perhaps it was time to make the move and live together. Neither of us was getting younger and who knew how much time we would have left together! We had both been through a lot, but we could continue to enjoy life. By living together, we would enhance our relationship and love for each other.

Sometime before July 4, I made up my mind that I was ready to commit to living with Don. It was time to move forward. As usual, I had given it more thought than was necessary. Any emotional ties I had had with Stuart had been severed. I hardly thought about him. His name would come up in conversation from time to time, and it did not appear to affect Don. I felt Don was ready to move on as well. I had seen him going through his grieving period. He hardly talked about Suzanne any more, and if he did, it was in reference to something we were talking about. There were a couple of times when he seemed down, and I asked him if something was bothering him. He might tell me it was Suzanne's birthday or their wedding anniversary. I knew this was part of the grief process, and it didn't bother me in the least. I knew she had died in the beginning of February so I tried to keep that date in mind when it came around so I could be more sensitive to Don's needs. Don had sorted through and given away most of Suzanne's belongings, but the jewelry remained untouched even two years later. This did not bother me as I knew he would dispose of it when he was ready.

Over the Fourth of July, Don and I went to a resort on a Vermont lake for three nights. The location was idyllic as our room had an expansive view of the lake. I had made up my mind about Don and decided to talk to him sometime that weekend about my realization that I could now live with him.

We spent the first two days exploring the grounds and surrounding towns. On our last night at the resort, we were in the dining room — sitting again by the window overlooking the lake — and had just finished sharing a slice of cheesecake when I decided now was the right time. The previous evening, the power had gone out during a storm. If it did again while I was making my declaration, that would indeed be an ominous sign. After a deep breath, I proceeded, "Don, I think I am ready, and the time has come. Would you like to move in with me?"

He beamed, "Absolutely! I thought you would never ask. I've been waiting since our trip to the Berkshires in May and I think we are both ready for the merger."

"The merger? That's cute," I smiled. "We are not a business, but a household is an organization of sorts with a financial component, so I guess 'merger' works."

I knew it would take a lot of time and energy to learn to live together every day, but I had come to accept that the rewards would outweigh the negatives. I was looking forward to feeling settled, and having made up my mind, to continue with life and get out of the holding pattern. A week later as I was doing my automatic writing, I heard confirmation from Spirit, "You are doing the right thing for yourself. Get settled first and then you can move on and help others."

Don was concerned about getting his condo sold and about packing up. I think he was overwhelmed by the enormity of the effort it would take on his part. I assured him that I would help, and together we could get it done. Being both retired, we had the time and there were no deadlines to meet.

One afternoon, we were down in Don's unfinished basement. As I looked around, I saw it was full of furniture, boxes of Christmas decorations, tools, garden furniture, and so on. "What are we going to do with all this stuff?" I said, feeling anxiety creep up into my throat.

"I have no idea," Don said, as he shrugged his shoulders.

I thought and said out loud, "We will break it down in small pieces and tackle it one by one. It has always been said that dealing with smaller units is what you should do if you are overwhelmed. Don't worry. We will work on creating little piles that can be disposed of daily."

When we told our families of our plans to move in together, none of our children seemed surprised. They had seen us together at holidays for two years by then.

Over the rest of the summer, we sorted, packed up, and gave away lots of furniture to both sides of the family. (Yes, we now thought of our kids as part of each other's family.) We made numerous car trips to my place with Don's books — he had hundreds, or so it seemed — and

Don with his grandson Ian
2014

with glass, china, and kitchenware.

I had been a board member of our condo association for a year at that point so at our August meeting, I told everyone, "Don and I are merging households. His unit will go on the market soon." My announcement was well received. If there were any negative reactions, I was not aware of any. Besides, I was beyond the point of worrying about what other people thought. (I would not apprise my immediate neighbors until just before the movers were scheduled to come.)

While I helped Don sort and pack and give away, I also found him a realtor I had met briefly when Stuart and I had moved to Atkinson. I could not recall how I met this woman but I remembered she lived locally and had years of experience. She proved to be an excellent choice as she was able to get Don's condo sold quickly.

Susan with her five grandchildren, 2014

Early in October, the movers packed up Don's heavy things and drove down the street to unpack at "our" condo. All the furniture was placed where we wanted it — including the bookcases that filled the bare wall in the living room — and everything else that we did not want, or know what to do with, was stored in the two bays of our garage. It would be dealt with in time.

What a happier experience with movers than when Stuart had moved out!

That evening, tired from the move, we sank onto the sofa in the living room to have a glass of wine. We faced the fireplace

— away from all the boxes stacked behind us — and, as I looked around, I thought how homey the room was going to look. The blank wall was now filled where it had been half empty for so long. More important than the wall, however, was that my life was finally full — of love and peace. I turned to face Don and said, "I want our living room to be warm and welcoming. I hope in time you will feel at home here."

"I'm sure I will. Let's call it the gathering room," he said.

"That's a perfect name. It's our home now, and everyone is welcome to visit. We were so lucky to find each other so much later in our lives," I said as I held up my glass of wine. "I propose a toast. To us."

"To us and our new life together in this house."

We clinked glasses and kissed. I felt a warmth course through my body. It dawned on me that, although I had lived in the house for years, I now had a home; a place where I would be loved — even with my quirks — for who I was.

The pain of the past was finally behind me, and I looked forward to the new chapter of my life.

My life with Don.

Afterword

Seven years have passed since Don and I met, and as I write this, we have lived together for almost five. Our relationship is solid, and for the first time in my life, I feel secure, loved and safe. All the personal work I have done has paid off. Of course, any relationship has its issues, but fortunately, we are able to resolve any conflicts that arise. When these arise, I stop to say to myself, "Remember, you wanted someone that showed his emotions." I chuckle to myself and proceed to listen to what is going on with Don. On the anniversary of our first date, we still celebrate by going to the country club for dinner.

Don has been supportive of my writing. I am able to talk to him freely. He listened when I retold my stories or vented my frustrations. Now that I will not be disappearing in the loft to write, I look forward to doing more with Don — he was shortchanged a bit while I have been writing. We will be able, once again, to do more together, I am sure Don will be happy about this.

My two sons, Tim and Peter, and their wives, Amanda and Erin, lead busy lives working, caring for their homes, and raising their children. All four are excellent parents — loving and actively involved in their children's upbringing. I am so proud of them! My five grandchildren — now twelve to fifteen — are thriving and growing rapidly, and I cherish the time I spend with them. I look forward to watching them grow into adulthood and seeing where life takes them.

Don and I get together with my sister, Clare, and her husband who live about a half hour from us. We especially enjoy Christmas with them and our annual summer cookout. Clare and I keep in touch via mail throughout the year.

Linda is busy in her retirement, teaching two online courses, participating actively in her community, and traveling. In January 2019, Linda and I had a "trip of a lifetime" when we went to Thailand for her son's wedding. The experience was amazing — from the wedding to the sightseeing. In fact, all of it was!

I have seen Maggie, her husband Keith, and their young son, Finley, a number of times in the last couple of years. Don and I have enjoyed receiving them in our home when they have come to New Hampshire to stay a night with us. Linda and I had gone to visit Maggie and her family when they lived in Connecticut. Linda was one of the few people who saw Maggie at birth and had always wanted to meet her as an adult. After this visit of ours, Keith landed a job in St Louis, Missouri, and he, Maggie and Finley moved there. Fortunately, they have made it a point to come back to visit family in New England. Maggie and I also keep in contact by having a long phone conversation every now and then. I am so lucky to have her in my life!

At least every year and sometimes twice a year, my Wei Chi colleagues and friends — Linette, Katie, Kim, and Rita — and I get together for an overnight. It is a time to catch up, reminisce, and do readings or energy work on each other.

Now, I would like to catch you up with the previous men in my life. Michael married his partner, Carol, about four years ago. On occasion, I see them at family holiday gatherings or at events our grandchildren are involved in. I have not laid eyes on Johnnie since he fetched his belongings at my condo in Newton. Linda sees him once in awhile and says he is still living with the same woman that he moved in with after he left me. I also have had no contact with Stuart.

Shadows and Light

Tai Chi has become part of my life. I have been doing it for eight years now. I continue to take classes two times a week and practice at home at least three days every week. I realize now that Tai Chi is a lifelong learning process. Over the years my body has gradually become less tense and more flexible. Recently, I was playing a game with my granddaughters in which they had to come up with an answer to "What would Grammy be doing in twenty years? (I would be ninety-five.) They answered that I would be in a nursing home and doing Tai Chi! I hope I will not be in a nursing home but I will be doing Tai Chi.

In addition to Tai Chi, I have done strength training at a gym for the past six years.

I will continue to learn and do volunteer work of some kind.

I still startle easily — jump when the telephone rings. I have always thought that this reaction was due to abuse or the shock treatments and that it will never go away. I rarely get a headache these days. If I wake up with one in the morning — not knowing the reason for it — I take care of myself with Ibuprofen, a hot shower, and a cup of coffee. Usually, my now-infrequent headache will ease up and go away.

My shoulder and neck muscles still tense up at times, Again, I don't think I will ever get rid of this tension entirely. Sometimes the reason for the discomfort is positional, and at other times, the reason completely escapes me. I still think it is the past that haunts me and that this, too, might never go away. When I am really feeling headachy and tense, I take what I call a "spiritual nap." I lie down with my heating pad under my shoulders, breathe deeply, and let any thoughts arise and drift away. Usually, relaxing this way helps to ease any pain.

Parts of writing this book were difficult to face. Beside the inherent difficulty of some of the material, I struggled with trying to remember things I thought I should know as opposed to those memories obliterated by the shock therapy. I did get clarification why I can't remember periods of my past. It was depression that clouded those times and that makes sense.

Now that my story has been told, I can finally put my past behind me. I embrace the next phase of my life and whatever the future brings. I feel ready to savor the joys and deal with loss. My past has prepared me well.

Dear Readers,

I would like to leave you with a few parting words:
- Never give up; there is always hope even if it takes a while to find.
- Seek nontraditional methods of healing.
- Listen to your inner voice — open up to spirit and the afterlife.
- Keep learning and growing.
- It is never too late to find love in your life or to tell your story

In light,
Susan

If you enjoyed my book, please take a moment to write a review on Amazon for me. Many thanks.

For questions or comments: syerburgh@gmail.com

Shadows and Light